Esotericism in Western Culture

Esotericism in Western Culture

Counter-Normativity and Rejected Knowledge

Wouter J. Hanegraaff

BLOOMSBURY ACADEMIC
LONDON • NEW YORK • OXFORD • NEW DELHI • SYDNEY

BLOOMSBURY ACADEMIC
Bloomsbury Publishing Plc, 50 Bedford Square, London, WC1B 3DP, UK
Bloomsbury Publishing Inc, 1359 Broadway, New York, NY 10018, USA
Bloomsbury Publishing Ireland, 29 Earlsfort Terrace, Dublin 2, D02 AY28, Ireland

BLOOMSBURY, BLOOMSBURY ACADEMIC and the Diana logo
are trademarks of Bloomsbury Publishing Plc

First published in Great Britain 2025
Reprinted 2025, 2026 (twice)

Parts of this work were published previously as *Western Esotericism: A Guide for the Perplexed*

Cover design: Elena Durey
Cover image © Large Owl on a Screen, 1913 by Jan Mankes (from MuseumMore)

A catalogue record for this book is available from the British Library.

Library of Congress Cataloging-in-Publication Data

Names: Hanegraaff, Wouter J., author.
Title: Esotericism in western culture : counter-normativity & rejected knowledge / Wouter J. Hanegraaff. Other titles: Western esotericism
Description: London ; New York : Bloomsbury Academic, 2025. | "Parts of this work were published previously as Western Esotercism: A Guide for the Perplexed." | Includes bibliographical references and indexes. | Summary: "This expanded new edition of Western Esotericism: A Guide for the Perplexed (2013) brings a foundational text in the field up to date. Hanegraaff surveys key topics for which "esotericism" has become the preferred label: gnosticism and hermetism in antiquity, "occult sciences" (astrology, alchemy, magic), Renaissance hermeticism, Rosicrucianism, Christian theosophy, occultism, spiritualism, and related currents up to and including the New Age. New sections include Jewish and Islamic Esotericism, global perspectives and politics, and a final chapter on The Future of Esotericism. The book has been updated throughout to reflect current scholarship and increased accessibility for non-specialists"– Provided by publisher.
Identifiers: LCCN 2024051016 (print) | LCCN 2024051017 (ebook) | ISBN 9781350459687 (hardback) | ISBN 9781350459694 (paperback) | ISBN 9781350459717 (epub) | ISBN 9781350459700 (ebook) Subjects: LCSH: Occultism.
Classification: LCC BF1411.H364 2025 (print) | LCC BF1411 (ebook) | DDC 130–dc23/eng/20250106
LC record available at https://lccn.loc.gov/2024051016
LC ebook record available at https://lccn.loc.gov/2024051017

ISBN: HB: 978-1-3504-5968-7
PB: 978-1-3504-5969-4
ePDF: 978-1-3504-5970-0
eBook: 978-1-3504-5971-7

Typeset by Deanta Global Publishing Services, Chennai, India
Printed and bound in Great Britain

For product safety related questions contact productsafety@bloomsbury.com.

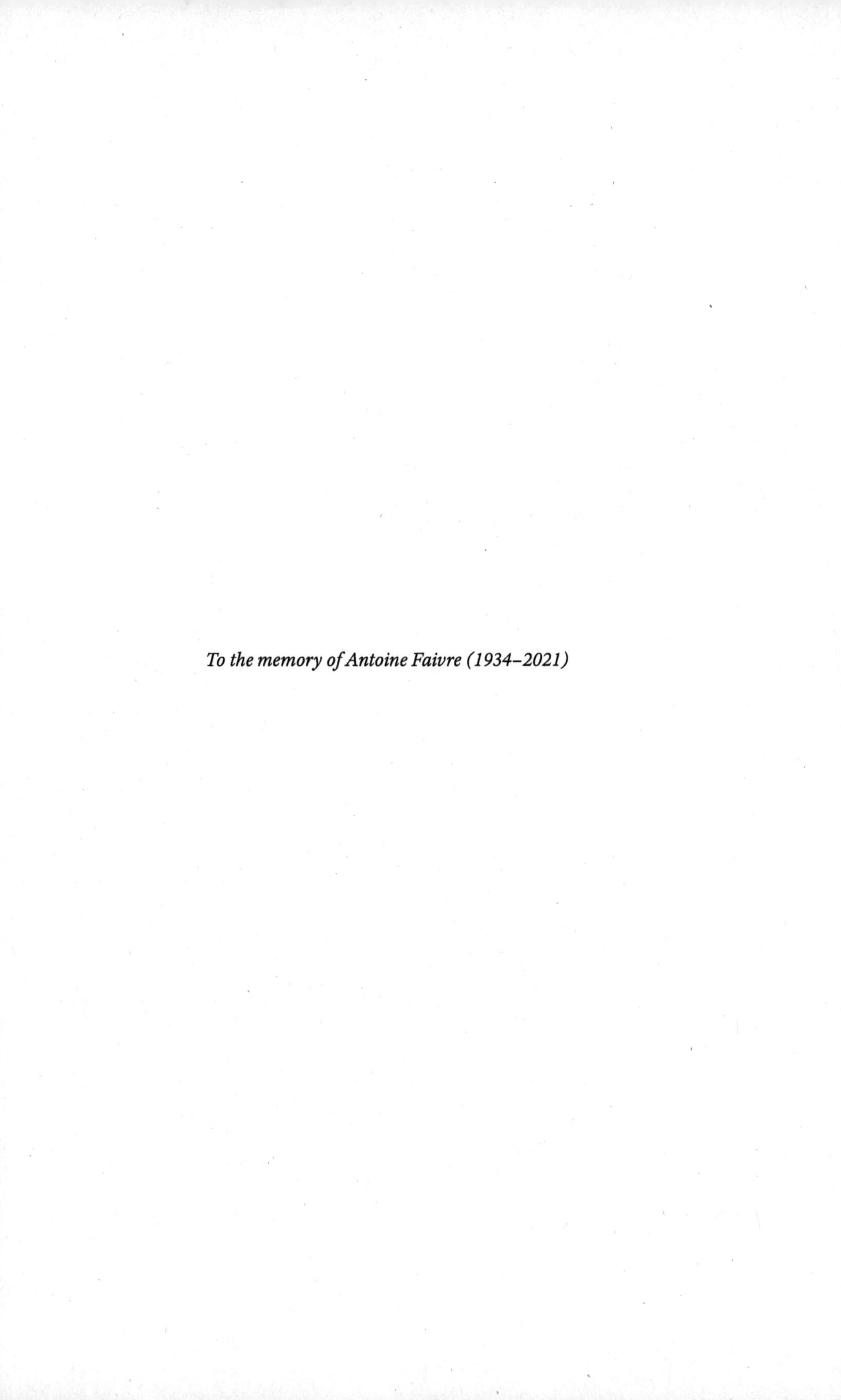

To the memory of Antoine Faivre (1934–2021)

Contents

Introduction

A young man has rented a cheap single room, five storeys high in the center of Paris, right next to the Sorbonne and not far from the *Jardin du Luxembourg*. Every day, while walking the streets of the city, he has weird experiences and disturbing encounters. He is afraid. Everything feels alien, the world seems very strange. Yet other people just appear to be going about their business without noticing anything out of the ordinary. The young man writes in his journal that for some reason, he doesn't understand why, he is learning *to see*. Everything affects him more deeply than it used to do and leaves lasting impressions that he cannot ignore. Something is changing his life. But to what purpose? At the age of twenty-eight, he is forced to admit that he's been wasting his life on pointless pursuits. And then, one gray afternoon, five storeys high, he has the following thoughts:

> Is it possible that nothing true and important has been seen, recognized or said?
> Is it possible to have had thousands of years' time to look, to think and note down,
> and to have allowed these thousands of years to pass by
> like a school break in which you eat your sandwich and an apple?
> Yes, it is possible.
> Is it possible, in spite of inventions and progress, in spite of culture,
> religion and worldly wisdom, to have remained on the surface?
> Is it possible to have covered this surface, which was still something at least,
> with some incredibly boring fabric, so that it looks like the room furniture after the holidays?
> Yes, it is possible.
> Is it possible that the whole of world history has been misunderstood?
> Is it possible that the past is wrong?
> Yes, it is possible.
> Is it possible that all those people have incredibly precise knowledge
> of a past that never existed?
> Is it possible that all realities are meaningless for them,
> that their life is passing without connection to anything,
> like a clock in an empty room?
> Yes it is possible.[1]

I was a young man myself when I first read these lines, and they have kept haunting me ever since. They were written by the great Austrian poet Rainer Maria Rilke (1875–1926) and express more clearly than I could ever do myself why I believe it is critically important to pay attention to *rejected knowledge*. Could it possibly be true that, in the academic study of human culture and history on a global scale, we have not yet been asking the right questions, because we have not yet been paying attention to what was actually most important? Could it be true that, in some essential respects, we still need to begin? Is it possible that the normative stories we've been told about the world, about what is real and what is true, leave out precisely that to which we should have been paying attention?

Take Rilke himself. He is among the most famous of all modern poets, and his work has been studied for about a century by countless literary scholars. There is something like an academic Rilke industry going on. So you might think that, by now, we know more or less everything there is to know about the poet and his writings. And yet, that is not true. As demonstrated in meticulous detail by a contemporary Icelandic scholar, Gísli Magnússon,[2] specialists of Rilke have been neglecting a major dimension of his oeuvre that goes to the heart of his poetry and is impossible to miss, once you see it. And yet it has not been seen. Why? Perhaps you'll understand the problem if I just mention the *words* that we're obliged to use if we try to speak about these things: *esotericism*, *occultism*, or somewhat related words such as *spiritualism*, *spirituality*. For very precise historical reasons that I will explain in this book, these words have come to signify more or less everything that academics learn to see as weird, embarrassing, disreputable, and definitely to be avoided if you want to be taken seriously by your colleagues.

To ignore the social and intellectual taboo on these topics means engaging in a critical project that I have baptized *counter-normativity*, because it refuses to accept our normative standards of what is supposed to be taken seriously and what may safely be dismissed out of hand. Its concern is with things that are there but are not supposed to be there (such as Rilke's deep interest in esotericism and the occult), with stuff that is real but isn't supposed to be real (such as Rilke's experiences with spiritual presences). In short, it is concerned with the truly enormous domain of *counter-normality*, colloquially known as "the weird stuff" that usually stays below the radar of official scholarship and science.

This book has been written from a deep conviction that historians and scholars in the humanities have a responsibility to do better. Our work is not about making careers in the academy by devoting our energies to the conservative enterprise of confirming what most of us already take for granted about the world anyway. I see scholars as explorers, charged with a mission to boldly go where no one has gone before. Our task is to venture out on a limb and explore the unknown. In Rilke's precise terms (just check the quotation), our ambition should be to try and find out what is "true and important." Therefore our calling is not to just remain "on the surface," we're not supposed to cover up reality with some conventional fabric but to uncover what lies beneath. The work of historians, more specifically, consists in trying to "understand," to the best of our human abilities, ultimately nothing less than the history of the world in which we are living. Whatever "knowledge" we claim to possess should refer to something that is actually there—it should consist of more than just "meaningless" discourse disconnected from anything real, "like a clock in an empty room." This is my ideal vision of the humanities. I hope to convince you of my thesis, unlikely as it might seem at first sight, that the study of esotericism goes to the very heart of what the humanities are all about.

But do not expect that you'll be reading an "esoteric" or "occult" book, full of weird and wondrous insights into secret knowledge and hidden mysteries. This is a scholarly introduction, meant as a *portal* (a doorway or gate, like Alice's looking glass) through which you may find access to esotericism as a modern field of research.[3] It is up to you, gentle reader, whether or not you wish to step through that portal and explore whatever secrets may be waiting on the other side. You'll not encounter any mysteries on *this* side of the glass, for the peculiarity of this field (as of the study of religion, more generally) lies in its focus on the strictly historical and empirical study of ideas, traditions, and practices that claim precisely to venture *beyond* the academic domains of history and normal sense experience. This inherent tension is of critical importance.[4] I will be making no claims of any kind about the *truth* of esoteric beliefs that bear on what might lie beyond, because I do not believe that scholars can make such claims while still remaining credible as scholars. Very much in the spirit of Rilke, I embrace a position of open-minded agnosticism about ultimate questions of reality and truth, "not because I believed in nothing, but because I consider everything possible."[5]

This book is the completely rewritten and greatly expanded new incarnation of a modest introductory textbook published in 2013, under the title *Western Esotericism: A Guide for the Perplexed*, which I hereby declare obsolete. I have done what I could to write this new volume in an accessible style, because I see my primary audience as consisting of general readers who may simply be interested in an introduction to esotericism in/and Western culture. Yet I also address more technical questions, partly in the notes, that will be of interest to scholars who are already active in the field. In the intervening period of just twelve years, the study of esotericism has been developing very rapidly and has started moving into entirely new directions. A new academic generation has begun experimenting with new theoretical perspectives and has been asking new questions that were scarcely yet on the horizon just a decade and a half ago. Grappling with these new approaches has been an intense educational experience for me. I have learned many new things that have led me to broaden my perspectives and change my mind about quite a number of important issues, while also confirming some of my most basic convictions and intuitions. I have found that certain key aspects of my earlier work have been misunderstood by some of my colleagues, so I have tried to explain my true opinions even more precisely than I did before. I hardly expect to convince or satisfy all my critics, but I'll attempt to do so anyway. In any case, I hope at least to make my position on key issues as clear as possible so that future discussions can be conducted on a fair basis of correct understanding.

The study of esotericism is not an academic discipline. It is a highly pluralistic *field* of scholarly research in which there is and should always be room for many disciplines, methodologies, and theoretical approaches. My ideal is that of an ongoing academic dialogue between a multitude of different voices, conducted in an open spirit of charity and generosity, a constructive conversation based on the tacit understanding that "No One Captures the Flag."[6] To place extra emphasis on this point, I have changed the plural "we" that I used in the first edition to the more intimate first person singular. Although I try to do justice to the plurality of approaches that currently exist in the study of esotericism, I have no desire to speak on behalf of anyone else than myself, let alone on behalf of the field as a whole. What you will find on the following pages is my personal contribution, based on my personal thirty-plus years of experience(s) in the field, and my mature convictions about what the study of esotericism could ideally be like.

The book consists roughly of three parts, each one made up of three chapters. The first triad is meant as a basic introduction to the field. The first chapter does *not* try to answer the question "what is esotericism?," as such a formulation carries the crypto-essentialist suggestion that there *is* such a thing out there, waiting for us to discover its presence or identity. I see "esotericism" as just *a label of convenience*, but it is important to make clear what the label is supposed to refer to. I have added a new section about the "discursive turn" in the study of esotericism, where I also discuss the key difference between two popular ways of understanding the word (*esotericism*$_1$ and *esotericism*$_2$). Importantly, I have added a substantial new section on the crucial question of "the West" and the adjective "Western." In contrast to the first edition, I speak not of "Western Esotericism" but of "Esotericism in Western Culture," and you will see that this difference is by no means trivial. The second and longest chapter is devoted to a broad *historical overview* of what the term "esotericism" (*esotericism*$_1$) is meant to refer to. In line with my basic understanding of the Greater West, I have not just rewritten and expanded the original chapter very considerably but have also added substantial new sections about Jewish and Islamic Esotericism. For these parts of the book, I am profoundly indebted to the invaluable corrections, additions, and advice of my friends and colleagues Boaz Huss, John MacMurphy, and Matthew Melvin-Koushki. The third chapter discusses the history of how esotericism has come to be constructed, in the imagination of elite intellectuals, as a separate field of "rejected knowledge." Here the concern is not with history but with *mnemohistory*, the history of how we come to remember and imagine the past. This chapter carries a new title, "Internal Eurocentrism." It captures an intention and an entire program that has been implicit in my work since about fifteen years. I now make it explicit, as part of my broader agenda of dismantling narrow Eurocentric understandings, not just of esotericism but of Western culture as a whole.

The second triad consists of three somewhat shorter chapters that should add more flesh to the skeleton of names and dates. Here the focus changes from theoretical conceptualizations, history, and mnemohistory to the actual *contents* of the field. Again, I think of this book as a portal for helping my readers find access to an enormous wealth of human creativity that still tends to be neglected. It could be useful to point out here that I see academic theories as pragmatic tools, that is, as means to an end, subservient to the work of studying primary sources in all their depth and complexity. Therefore our scholarly work is ultimately not about theorizing "esotericism" (interesting as this may be) but about studying the materials that are covered and referred to by this word. In these three chapters, I look at structural communalities and differences between *worldviews*, key approaches to *knowledge*, and *practices* that we encounter in the field.

The third and final triad consists of three chapters devoted to further dimensions that were not covered in previous parts. First of all, I look at the crucial topic of *historicity* in the study of esotericism. I exemplify it by discussing what I see as the five most crucial dimensions of *modernization* (concerned with causality, globalization, evolutionism, psychology, and marketization). Next, I show that the relevance of esotericism is by no means limited to the domain of religion or spirituality but covers *all dimensions of the humanities*, including the visual arts, literature, and music, but also such important domains as social dynamics and politics. Finally, I have written an entirely new chapter on the global *importance* of esotericism. Here I explain why I consider this field to be not just interesting for specialists but extremely relevant to wider issues of general concern. I return to the key topic of dismantling deep patterns of Eurocentric prejudice *without*, for that reason, dismantling the idea of Western culture itself. Rather than just deconstructing "the West," I believe we need to *re*construct it on new and better foundations. Against the background of the book as a whole, I then make a new argument that (again) has been implicit in much of my previous work in the study of esotericism but was never theorized explicitly. As already mentioned above, I refer to it as *counter-normativity*, in close connection to a focus on *counter-normality*. As I hope to make clear, this ultimately brings us full circle, back to the basic questions about *im/possibility* formulated by Rilke in the opening quotation.

I am grateful to many of my colleagues for precious pieces of advice during earlier phases of this project and for many publications and conversations that have given me new ideas. While three of them were already mentioned above, I owe a special intellectual debt to four scholars whom I am happy to count among my best friends in the world of academia. Matthew Melvin-Koushki's expert advice has not just been crucial for my section on Islamic Esotericism, but his work has been a decisive influence on my conceptualization of the Greater West. As regards my final chapter, even though the terminology of counter-normativity and counter-normality is my own, the argument is indebted on a deep level of inspiration and theoretical reflection to Jeffrey J. Kripal's work on *the impossible*, Erik Davis's on *weirdness*, and Gísli Magnússon's on Rilke's *metaphysics of experience* (*Erfahrungsmetaphysik*). I discovered that these three perspectives converge and mutually confirm one another in very interesting ways. Together, in combination with my own agendas of *historical empiricism* and *radical agnosticism*, they provided the basic inspiration for my attempt in this book to explain the emancipatory potential of esotericism as a field of research. I would also like to mention the help I received, at various stages and in different ways, from J. Christian Greer, Massimo Introvigne, Avery Morrow, Mriganka Mukhopadhyay, Dimitry Okropiridze, Marco Pasi, Francesco Piraino, Liana Saif, and Mark Sedgwick. If I have omitted anyone, I hereby express my sincere apologies! As always, of course, I take sole responsibility for all the opinions expressed in this book and for any mistakes that I might have committed. I also want to thank the editorial staff at Bloomsbury for inviting me to rewrite my earlier book and for the friendly and constructive collaboration; specifically, a big thank you to Lalle Pursglove, Stuart Hay, Seb Claas, Emily Wootton, and Clara Ferreyra.

This book is dedicated to the memory of Antoine Faivre (1934–2021), the original pioneer of esotericism as an academic field of research. Antoine and I first met at a conference in 1992 and were friends ever since, until his death in December 2021.[7] Antoine was an impressive scholar with a broad vision and an enormous depth of knowledge, a true model of the modern *homo universalis*. He was also a mercurial personality in every sense of the word, always willing to offer his help and act as a mediator to bring people together. But most of all, he embodied the humanistic spirit of openness, tolerance, and deep curiosity that I believe must always lie at the heart of esotericism as a field of research. His work is done, but he will not be forgotten.

Last but not least, I want to thank my daily companions at home, who were always there to remind me of the existence of an exoteric world. First of all Pillows the cat, who embodies the true spirit of feline sovereignty. Secondly, his two furry and funny sidekicks from Ukraine, Levke, and Bobke. But more than anyone else, I want to thank my beloved Margôt, for her spirit and her wisdom and quite simply for her presence in my life. Is it possible to find the love of your life? Yes, it is possible.

1 What Do We Mean by Esotericism?

"Ah, esoteric." Agliè smiled, and Belbo blushed.
"Should we say . . . hermetic?"
"Ah, hermetic." Agliè smiled.
"Well," Belbo said, "perhaps I am using the wrong word, but surely you know the genre."

(Umberto Eco, *Foucault's Pendulum*)[1]

"Esotericism" is an elusive concept that refers to an even more elusive collection of traditions and ideas, beliefs and organizations, spiritual practices and experiential pursuits. The term evokes strong associations in almost everybody's mind, and yet nobody finds it easy to explain exactly what it means—or why we should bother to pay attention to its history or contents. Nevertheless, "esotericism" (often with the adjective "Western" added to it) has been on the agenda of the academic study of religion for several decades now and is attracting more and more attention in other disciplines of the humanities as well. Behind this development lies a growing recognition that something is wrong with our conventional ways of thinking about "Western culture." Most people take it for granted that modern European and American societies come out of a long tradition of Christian monotheism (with deep roots in Judaism but entirely distinct from Islam), combined with rational philosophies that go back to the ancient Greeks, from which modern science and technology developed over the past few centuries. Studying esotericism and its history means challenging those assumptions on a very basic level. The argument of this book is that we have been overlooking extremely important dimensions of Western culture that in fact are quasi-omnipresent not just in all the three major monotheistic religions but throughout the long history of philosophy, modern science, and the arts as well. Because they were mostly at odds with the normative ideologies of intellectual elites and dominant powers, these ideas and traditions have been marginalized in standard textbooks, are often dismissed as delusional or even dangerous, and tend to be discussed under questionable labels that make them look not entirely serious. The first example of such a pejorative label is "esotericism" itself.

To illustrate this phenomenon, let's begin with a simple observation. Regardless of what you think "esotericism" is all about or what it might mean, clearly "it" doesn't seem to fit all that comfortably in any established scholarly discipline or any of the well-known fields of academic study. Somehow, "esotericism" seems different from "religion," as commonly understood, but it doesn't look like "philosophy" either, nor would it be accepted as "science" today.[2] So what is it? "Esotericism" is present in all these different fields, and in the arts as well, but it cannot be reduced to any of them and has been seriously neglected by all. It is important to consider this fact from a historical perspective. Prior to the watershed of the eighteenth century, when the academic disciplines began to be established in their present form, the ideas and traditions that are nowadays labeled as "esotericism" were still widely recognized as important albeit controversial topics of intellectual and scholarly inquiry. We will see that theologians, philosophers, and practitioners of the natural sciences were seriously debating such ideas and their implications. Only in the wake of the Enlightenment did these traditions vanish almost completely from accepted intellectual discourse and standard textbook narratives. The field became academically homeless during the nineteenth century, and so the level of general and expert knowledge about it declined dramatically. This situation has begun to improve somewhat in the decades after the Second World War, since the 1960s and increasingly since the 1990s, but we still have a very long way to go. It is fair to say that, for the moment, popular perceptions of "esotericism" are still largely dominated by the products of possibly well-intentioned but factually unreliable amateur scholarship and the commercial media.

So here we have the basic fact that lies at the heart of this field of research. A vast and fascinating domain of religious, spiritual, and intellectual activity that has been a pervasive presence in Western culture, from late antiquity to the present, has been virtually ignored by the modern academy as if it did not exist—or treated as if it *should* not exist. This phenomenon has no parallel in intellectual history, and the reasons why it happened will be explored in Chapter 3. At this point we just need to note that the history of academic exclusion and neglect has problematic effects even when it comes to basic scholarly terminology. Without a single exception, all the available terms or labels in this field have their origins in heavily polemical contexts, which means that they are loaded with pejorative connotations in general and academic discourse. Although "esotericism" has become the label of preference among specialists since the 1990s, most people still think that it has to do primarily with contemporary phenomena such as New Age. The same is true for such terms as "the occult," "occultism," or "the occult sciences," which have specific meanings in contemporary scholarship but carry doubtful associations in wider society. The sober truth is that all the available labels are bound up with misleading perceptions of what the field is all about. We simply do not have a terminology that is both neutral and generally accepted—and if we were to invent a new label from scratch, that wouldn't help, because nobody would recognize it as pertaining to the field in question! The emerging consensus among contemporary specialists is to be somewhat pragmatic about this situation. I will be using "esotericism" as an umbrella term in spite of its disadvantages, while hoping that, as serious scholarship becomes more widely available, it will eventually start losing its questionable connotations.

From Definitions to Prototypes

What, then, do I mean by "esotericism"? The adjective "esoteric" (Greek *esōterikos*, "inner" or "reserved for initiates") first appeared in the second century CE, but the noun "esotericism" is of much more recent date. It seems to have been coined in German (*Esoterik*) in 1792, migrated to French scholarship (*l'ésotérisme*) by 1828, and appeared in English in 1883.[3] Therefore the noun "esotericism" is not a conventional term with a well-established traditional meaning in European languages. It is a modern coinage invented by intellectuals and practitioners who applied it retroactively to a wide range of currents, practices, or ideas that were known by many *different* names prior to the end of the eighteenth century. Those various currents, practices, or ideas were not strictly defined by a focus on secrecy or concealment, as the term might seem to suggest, nor were they necessarily seen as belonging together. Only as recently as the later seventeenth century do we encounter the first attempts to present them as one single "field" based on a common worldview or spiritual perspective.[4] In sum: "esotericism" is a modern scholarly construct, not an ancient and autonomous tradition that already existed out there and merely needed to be discovered by historians.

Experience has taught me that many readers may be initially disappointed or even annoyed by such statements. While pondering the previous paragraph, perhaps you think that I want to tell you there's nothing "real" about the field or its historical traditions. It may feel as though I'm beginning an entire book about "esotericism" by denying categorically that it even exists! But that's a misunderstanding—the true intention is different and quite a bit more subtle than that.[5] We will see that the category of "esotericism" emerged in early modern Europe because intellectuals and historians became attentive to structural similarities that actually *did* exist between the ideas and worldviews of a wide variety of thinkers and movements. In this sense, it is the outcome of a new comparativist enterprise that began to perceive patterns and continuities in history to which earlier scholars had been oblivious. We will look more closely at these commonalities in Chapters 4 and 5.

Several modern scholars have attempted to define the nature of esotericism by proposing *sets of criteria* that could be used to decide whether something does or does not belong to the field. The most famous and influential example comes from the French pioneer in this domain, Antoine Faivre (1934–2021), who in 1992 came up with a list of four "intrinsic" characteristics of esotericism (correspondences; living nature; imagination/mediations; transmutation) next to two nonintrinsic ones (transmission; concordance).[6] Other scholars have criticized Faivre's criteria and proposed alternative approaches, resulting in a wide spectrum of theories and definitions that differ considerably in how they demarcate the historical and conceptual boundaries of the field as a whole.[7]

To understand what is really at stake in these technical debates, it could be helpful to make a brief excursion to modern theories of cognition. As pointed out by the anthropologist Tanya Luhrmann, in everyday practice we do not usually categorize things by using formal lists of criteria but by comparing them to "prototypes." A prototype is a cluster of characteristics that is seen as constituting a "good example" of a class:

> When you use prototypes in your thinking, you ask whether the item in question resembles the best example of that class, not whether it meets specified rules or criteria of that category. Is an ostrich a bird or a grazing animal? A prototype user asks himself whether the ostrich is more like a sparrow or more like a cow, relying

> both on what he can see and on an array of background theory and assumptions. . . . When you look at a piece of furniture to decide whether it is a table or a chair, you do not list the rules of membership in the "table" and "chair" categories in your mind. That takes time. It also often does not work, since many category members do not have all the apparent criteria of the class (A bird that cannot fly, like the penguin, is still a bird). . . . You do not ask yourself whether this chair meets the criteria for chairship. You look at it, and you know it's a chair.[8]

Scholars have come up with various sets of formal criteria to define what should or should not fall under the category of "esotericism," but the truth is that, in fact, they are almost always reasoning by prototype. That is to say, they *already* have some "best examples" in mind of the class that they see as "esotericism," after which they proceed by comparing specific historical phenomena to that dominant model ("this reminds me of x, so it must be x"). Depending on the prototypical models they have in mind, specific historical currents may be included by some scholars but excluded by others, and this accounts for much of the confusion about the field and its boundaries.

The three most common models underlying current concepts of esotericism appear to be the following. Firstly, esotericism has often been seen as an "enchanted" pre-Enlightenment worldview with ancient roots that flourished particularly during the European Renaissance. Secondly, many influential authors have seen esotericism primarily as the social phenomenon of "the occult" *after* the Enlightenment. Finally, we have the very popular view of esotericism as a universal, "inner" spiritual dimension of religion as such. I am not convinced by any of these three approaches, but they are so influential that we must begin by taking a closer look at them.

Prototype 1: Enchantment Before Modernity

If you look more closely at the famous set of criteria proposed by Antoine Faivre (already mentioned above), you will notice that they actually read like a definition of "enchantment" set against the "disenchanted" worldviews that are associated with modern post-Cartesian, post-Newtonian, and positivist science. Faivre's concept of "correspondences" has its ultimate origin in the Stoic notion of universal cosmic sympathy as explained for instance by the great Neoplatonic philosopher Plotinus:[9] it means that all parts of the universe are seen as deeply interconnected but *without* a need for intermediary links or causal chains. This is clearly intended as an alternative to the kind of linear or instrumental causality (material causes and effects) that is associated with modern materialist science. "Living nature" stands against mechanistic worldviews as well, for it means thinking of the world as a living organism that is permeated by an invisible life force, not a dead mechanism that functions like a clockwork. As for the notion of "imagination/mediations," this one is rather complicated, because it consists of two components. It suggests a multileveled Platonic cosmology, as opposed to a cosmos that can be reduced to nothing but matter in motion; and it also states that, intermediary between the poles of pure spirit and pure matter, there are "subtle" levels of reality to which we can gain access through our faculty of imagination (which is therefore seen as an organ of knowledge and not just a fabricator of illusions, as Enlightenment rationalists would have it). Finally, "transmutation" refers to a process through which human beings, or the whole of nature, may move into a higher spiritual state or even attain a divine condition.

Esotericism according to Faivre's definition is depicted as a radical alternative to the disenchanted worldviews that came to dominate Western culture in the wake of the scientific revolution, the Enlightenment, and positivist science. For Faivre himself, the prototypes par excellence of Western esotericism could be found in an early modern intellectual movement (roughly from Paracelsus in the sixteenth century to the Romantic era) that is known as Christian Theosophy and *Naturphilosophie*. As a result, in terms of prototype theory, whether any other religious or intellectual currents should be seen as "esotericism" now depends on how closely they resemble these "best examples" of the class. In practice, this means that the early modern period looms largest in Faivre's work, as the golden age when Western esotericism flourished like never before or after. Ancient and medieval sources are acknowledged as a necessary historical background but not as manifestations of esotericism in their own right.[10] Most importantly, it remains somewhat questionable whether the many esoteric or occultist currents that developed through the nineteenth and twentieth centuries up to the very present are still close enough to Faivre's Theosophical/*Naturphilosophical* prototype to qualify as "esotericism" at all.[11] In terms of Luhrmann's analogy, we could say that if "esotericism" is an enchanted sparrow that clearly differs from a disenchanted cow, then these post-Enlightenment forms of esotericism seem rather like hybrid animals that could easily be dismissed as "pseudo" esotericisms.

Faivre was certainly the most prominent scholar who presented esotericism as a prototypical worldview of enchantment, opposed to the disenchanted worldviews of modern and contemporary society, while highlighting the early modern period as its golden age. But he was not the only one. From a very different perspective, and with different arguments, the English historian Frances A. Yates (1899–1981) promoted a similar vision with her extremely influential grand narrative about the "Hermetic Tradition" of the Renaissance.[12] According to her, this tradition emerged from the rediscovery and translation of a collection of texts from late antiquity, the *Corpus Hermeticum*, by the Florentine philosopher Marsilio Ficino. In the wake of this seminal translation, which was first published in 1471, Renaissance Hermeticism flourished from the fifteenth until the seventeenth century as a worldview dominated by magic, spiritual experience, and the powers of the imagination. It promoted a world-affirming mysticism consonant with an "enchanted" and holistic science that looked at nature as a living, organic whole permeated by invisible forces and energies. Moreover—still according to Yates—it was the reflection of a confident, optimistic, forward-looking mindset that emphasized humanity's great potential to operate on the world by using the new sciences, so as to create a better, more harmonious, more beautiful society.

Just like Faivre's Western esotericism, Frances Yates's Hermetic Tradition was focused on the early modern period, and she described it as a magically "enchanted" alternative to the establishment dogmas of religion and rationalistic science. Its literary sources hailed back all the way to late antiquity, but Yates drew a sharp line of division between the "dark" Middle Ages and the new phenomenon of a beautiful and elegant Hermetic magic that flourished in Italian Renaissance culture. More sharply and decisively than in Faivre's narrative, she claimed that the "Hermetic Tradition" had come to an end by the early seventeenth century, due to the rise of modern philology and the natural sciences. But many of her enthusiastic readers during the 1960s and 1970s went a step further. They concluded from her work that, at the very dawn of modernity, this magical and enchanted worldview of the Renaissance had tragically lost its battle against the Christian-theological and rational-scientific establishment. As a result of this defeat, "the Hermetic Tradition" had fallen into oblivion and the world had descended into cycles of ever-deepening disenchantment and spiritual alienation. But now this ancient wisdom tradition had been rediscovered, thanks to the profoundly heretical scholarship of an academic outsider who even happened to be a woman as well! Perhaps the tide was finally turning. Perhaps the time had come to take the Hermetic project up again, by "re-enchanting the world" and "bringing the imagination back to power." In short, for the countercultural generation of the postwar period, it was almost unavoidable to perceive Frances Yates's Hermetic philosophers of the Renaissance as their own historical predecessors.

Yates and Faivre are the most prominent examples of an approach that imagines esotericism as a profoundly enchanted worldview flourishing from the Renaissance until the Enlightenment. This has an important implication: it means that, by definition, esotericism must be fundamentally at odds with the secular world and can never be seen as an integral dimension of *modern* culture and society. Even if it manages to survive under post-Enlightenment conditions, it can do so only as an anti-modern "counterculture" engaged in an ultimately hopeless "flight from reason."[13] At least, that is how many sociologists during the 1960s and 1970s were looking at the unexpected boom of new esoteric movements and occultist currents that became so prominent during that period. The dominant "secularization thesis" took it for granted that religion or magic were things of the past that could have no real future in an age of science and rationality. This "occult revival" (along with the deeply interconnected "Oriental Renaissance" that was also taking place)[14] therefore had to be dismissed as a manifestation of irrational drives and futile longings for a romanticized past.

Prototype 2: The Modern Occult

Nobody doubts that modern and contemporary forms of esotericism, from the eighteenth century to the present, are grounded in ideas and traditions that can be traced very far back in time. We will encounter many examples on the pages that follow. Yet it has often been assumed that these traditional worldviews must have made their way into modernity simply as "survivals" from the past, moving forward in their original form without being affected or transformed all that seriously by the impact of new trends and developments.

That assumption is mistaken. The positivist cliché that magical, esoteric, or occultist concepts are inherently static and "resistant to change" has been proven wrong again and again.[15] On the contrary, as will be seen in Chapter 7, ideas and worldviews inherited from pre- and early modern periods were thoroughly *transformed* in their very substance by the impact of new social, cultural, and intellectual developments in secular society since the eighteenth century.[16] The result was a flurry of *new*, surprising, historically unprecedented esoteric phenomena.

The "Enchantment before Modernity" model discussed in the previous section tends to neglect this fact or play down its significance. It rests on the implicit assumption that post-Enlightenment forms of esotericism can never be more than second-hand, derivative, or defective deformations of "the real thing." Whenever esoteric traditions are forced to compromise with modern secular thought and its materialist background assumptions, the argument goes, this can only go at the expense of their original integrity and authenticity. Therefore modern and contemporary esotericism will always, and necessarily, fall short of the ideal "enchanted" model and its historical prototypes, such as Renaissance Hermeticism or Christian Theosophy. It then becomes hard to avoid the conclusion that modern and contemporary esotericism is some kind of "pseudo" esotericism.

But the argument can easily be turned around, resulting in a second influential model. Only during and after the eighteenth century do esoteric or occultist traditions actually begin to emerge prominently into public view, as social phenomena in their own right. One might argue that in earlier periods, esotericism had been largely just a matter of intellectual speculations restricted to the learned *writings* of an educated elite—whereas now, for the first time, it emerged in the form of actual *organizations* and *social networks* of practitioners that started competing with the established churches on a pluralistic "market" of religion. For social scientists, *this* new phenomenon would have to be placed at the center of attention, rather than the intellectual history (interesting as it might be) of where these new movements had taken their ideas. From such a perspective, it makes sense that the "best examples" or prototypes of what esotericism is all about will be taken from the occult milieus of the nineteenth or twentieth centuries. Any formal criteria for defining and demarcating the field must thus be based on its *post*-Enlightenment manifestations. Programmatic statements of this position are somewhat more difficult to find than in the case of the first model, precisely because social scientists tend to be less interested in historical contextualizations and long-term comparisons with pre- or early modern traditions.

In research that reflects this second model, "esotericism" or "the occult" does not function so much as an object of nostalgia for a lost or forgotten worldview of magical enchantment but rather appears as a vital dimension of the here and now—with implications for the future.[17] During the "occult boom" of the 1960s and 1970s, most sociologists perceived it as an unexpected and somehow worrying phenomenon of social "deviance" concerned with "anomalous" claims of knowledge and as a symptom of youthful rebellion against science and established religion.[18] Most of these academics had trouble seeing more in the occult than a heartfelt but ultimately futile reaction against rationalization and the forward march of modernity. This attitude has changed in more recent years, as optimism about modernization as social progress has declined, while sociologists and historians of religion have learned to think of the occult as a significant dimension *of* modernity.[19] Predictions about the imminent demise of religion turn out to have been premature, to say the least. It is now widely accepted that esoteric or occultist spiritualities are a permanent feature of society under conditions of modernity and postmodernity.

Most scholars today no longer perceive the occult as a marginal and irritating anomaly, as something that "should not be there," but as illustrating a basic fact that had not yet been so clear to previous generations. We have learned to see that traditional concepts of "religion" or "spirituality" (like those of "esotericism" or "the occult") do *not* refer to something stable and permanent that can be clearly defined once and for all but rather to flexible historical formations that are continually being transformed and reinvented under the impact of changing social conditions. For instance, the rapid expansion of new information and communication technologies since the 1990s and the spectacular development of new media during the same period (not to mention the explosion of social media since the 2010s) now appear to result in post- or metamodern occult milieus that deliberately blur the boundaries between fiction and reality.[20] This is clearly something new. To give another example, scholars of religion are now pointing to the fascination with "superpowers" in popular comics or role-playing games as a significant example of how occultist traditions appear in contemporary popular culture.[21] In the scholarly literature that is currently emerging about such topics, the terminology of "esotericism" or "the occult" tends to be used as a convenient shorthand reference for anything touching on "the psychic or paranormal," "mysteries of the unexplained," or simply "the weird stuff."[22]

So what is the conclusion? The chief weakness of our first prototypical model of "esotericism" is that it can never take these new and contemporary phenomena entirely seriously on their own terms, because in some sense they are seen as inauthentic deformations or distortions of the "real thing." The idea is that modern mass society flattens or cheapens the profound worldviews of the past. By contrast, the weakness of the second prototypical model lies in a lack of historical depth. Its adherents tend to forget that the roots and origins of *any* phenomenon are always an inextricable part of that very phenomenon itself. Studying "the occult" without placing it in a broader historical perspective is a bit like reducing the events of 9/11 to "a terrorist act," period, while dismissing the history of Islamic radicalism or Western colonialist politics as irrelevant to understanding what it was and why it happened. Against the anti-historical drift of this second model, then, I firmly believe that to understand "the occult," we need to integrate its study in a wider historical context concerned with the *longue durée*.[23] But against the anti-modern drift of the first model, modern and contemporary esotericism should be approached with exactly the same seriousness as its pre-Enlightenment ancestors.

Prototype 3: Inner Traditions

According to a third influential model of esotericism, the term stands for "inner" traditions. Its central assumption is that behind the surface phenomena of our material world lies a universal spiritual dimension that may be accessible to initiates but remains hidden from the general population. This model stays closest to the original meaning of the adjective *esōterikos* ("esoteric") in late antiquity, where it referred to secret teachings reserved for a spiritual elite, such as the Pythagorean brotherhoods or some mystery cults. In Jewish esotericism, we find such terms as *Torat ha-Sod* ("doctrine of the secret"), *Torat ha-Nistar* ("doctrine of the hidden"), or *Sitrei Torah* ("hidden secrets of the Torah"). And in Islamic esotericism, we often encounter the key distinction between an external (*ẓāhir*) meaning of the Quran, intended for the masses, and its "inner" (*bāṭin*) meanings that are revealed only to an elite of initiated insiders.

These backgrounds explain why the study of "esotericism" is so often understood in terms of a dialectics of secrecy and revelation, concealment and disclosure, or the internal and external dimension of sacred scriptures or the whole of reality.[24] We will turn to that approach in the following section. In our present discussion, it is of crucial importance to see that the "inner traditions" model is *not* defined by just a focus on secrecy and revelation as such but by an additional and much more radical claim about *the ontological truth and reality* of "the esoteric." For instance, in an influential historical survey of "the Western esoteric traditions," we read the following lines (emphasis added):

> My own perspective . . . is that definitions of "the esoteric" in terms of discourse, social constructions, and legitimacy lack a hermeneutic interpretation of *spirit and spirituality as an independent ontological reality*. By seeking to define the esoteric in terms of human behavior and culture, it becomes a reflective cultural category rather than *a philosophical or spiritual insight*, which remains the essential component of any claims to real or absolute knowledge. . . . Moreover, these perennial characteristics of the esoteric worldview [as defined by Faivre] suggest to me that this is an enduring tradition which, though subject to some degree of social legitimacy and cultural coloration, actually reflects *an autonomous and essential aspect of the relationship between the mind and the cosmos*.[25]

According to this well-known specialist, Nicholas Goodrick-Clarke (1953–2012), esotericism is not just defined by human *claims* about an inner, hidden, concealed, or secret dimension of reality. Rather, he insists that it gives us direct *philosophical or spiritual insight* into an autonomous or independent ontological reality, an ultimate spiritual realm or dimension of truth that actually exists beyond the external surface of social and historical events.

This specific approach to the study of religion, with its ontological claim about an esoteric reality beyond the screen of historical phenomena, is technically known as *religionism*.[26] Please note that precisely its desire to "move beyond history" defines what this perspective is all about—merely believing in an "inner" dimension of reality does not yet make you into a religionist. Religionism in a technical sense rests precisely on the claim that belief in the ontological presence and autonomy of a spiritual reality sui generis (i.e., a reality "all of its own") is indispensable in order for historians of religion (or esotericism) to understand the very nature of what they are studying and thus to properly do their work. At the heart of this scholarly approach, therefore, we find a profound paradox: questioning or ultimately denying the very relevance of historicity and historical criticism is an essential requirement for practicing history of religions (or esotericism) the way it should be practiced![27] The true "esoteric" referent of religion or spirituality is not considered to lie *within* the sphere of social events and cultural productions that are accessible to normal historians, but only in a direct unmediated experience of the spiritual as such, often referred to as "the sacred."[28] To put it bluntly, this means that historians of esotericism must in some sense be esoteric initiates themselves. Many of the most influential scholars in the field, from Henry Corbin and Antoine Faivre in his earlier work to more contemporary authors such as Nicholas Goodrick-Clarke and Arthur Versluis, have been explicit in their embrace of a religionist perspective.

A very important implication of the religionist insistence on "inner traditions" is that "esotericism" in Western culture cannot be specific to the West. If "esotericism" is all about a universal spiritual reality that is not crucially conditioned by history or culture, this means that it will have to be accessible in *all* cultures and societies across the globe and from archaic times up to the very present. The "true" esoteric teachings of Western and non-Western religions or spiritual traditions (for instance in Hinduism, Buddhism, Shamanism, etc.) must ultimately converge in one and the same perennial esotericism, sometimes referred to as "the transcendent unity of religions."[29] The most radical expressions of this doctrine (i.e., of religionism taken to the ultimate degree of denying historicity altogether) have often been labeled "perennialism," although today they are more commonly referred to as Traditionalism.

Religionist scholarship was extremely important in the study of esotericism during its earlier phases (roughly from the 1960s through the 1980s, dominated by the so-called Eranos school in religious studies, to which we will return) but has now been widely discarded in the academy. This is because the "inner traditions" model has some deeply problematic implications. Most obviously and most importantly, it rests upon the conviction that a universal, hidden, esoteric dimension of reality really does exist. But disappointing as this might seem to some readers, such a statement of esoteric belief can neither be verified nor falsified by any independent scholarly methods that we have at our disposal. Please note (for the point is often misunderstood) that this is *not* a metaphysical claim or a dismissive statement on my part. It is a simple observation about the limitations of academic research. Perhaps a sacred or divine presence *is* really active in or behind the world—but if so, still it will not be among the possible objects of scholarly investigation.[30]

The point I am making here is not theoretical but methodological. Scholarly methods are very sharp tools, but they are designed for specific ends and may be useless for other purposes, such as spiritual consolation or gaining insight into the ultimate truth about reality. The metaphor of "tools" is actually helpful to make this clear. Would you think of hammering nails into your wall with a spoon or eating your soup with a knife? Of course not. Well, the knives of scholarship are perfectly suited for cutting the meat of historical data, but you will be disappointed if you try using a knife to hammer holes into the wall of material reality to get through to the other side. You won't succeed because that's not what knives are made for. Conversely, to continue the metaphor, perhaps the hammer of deep meditational or entheogenic practice will get you through that wall into a spiritual reality on the other side, but that hammer still remains useless to slice even a tiny piece of social or historical butter in *this* world. That's not what hammers are made for either. The point is simple. Scholarly tools have their uses and their limits. Spiritual tools have their uses and their limits too.

A further problem with the "inner traditions" model results from its emphasis on eternal Being at the expense of temporal-historical Becoming. Religionist scholars tend to be most interested in discovering universal archetypes, recurring symbols, or mythical structures. By contrast, historians focus precisely on everything that is *not* universal and stable or predictable—think of unique events, historical contingencies, the infinite variety of factual details in literally everything that exists, or the creative inventions of gifted individuals who may come up with amazing new ideas that had never occurred to anyone before. The insistence that "in the end it (esotericism) all comes down to always the same thing" is frankly a bit boring and may easily turn into a self-fulfilling prophecy. If you don't expect to ever be surprised by anything new and unexpected, you will probably not even notice when it actually does occur.

In contrast to the characteristic religionist focus on a universal wisdom tradition concerned with eternal "inner" truths, my focus will be on the enormous historical variety and sometimes stunning creative complexity of "esotericism" as a field of study. If you zoom in a bit more closely on these "universal wisdom traditions," you discover that, in actual fact, Hermetic texts from antiquity, Jewish kabbalists, Islamic Sufis, alchemical practitioners, Theosophical visionaries such as Jacob Böhme or Emanuel Swedenborg, occultist magicians such as Aleister Crowley, contemporary New Agers, Chaos magicians, teenage witches, or QAnon believers in the *Illuminati* all have extremely different worldviews and spiritual agendas. In the end, their beliefs and activities tell us more about themselves and their specific sociohistorical contexts than about the abstract truths of a universal spiritual wisdom. These contextual factors should not be dismissed as just "external" and ultimately irrelevant in regard to the all-important "inner" dimension. On the contrary, they are precisely what makes the field so endlessly fascinating.

The Discursive Turn

In addition to these three dominant models of what "esotericism" is all about, we need to discuss an academic perspective (not a model) that has become extremely popular in the humanities over the past few decades. Deeply indebted to poststructuralist and deconstructionist theory, it claims that "the study of esotericism" must be reduced to a study of "esoteric discourse" or "discourse about the esoteric." Interestingly, key representatives of this approach adopt the same understanding of "esoteric" as the religionists or perennialists who adhere to the "inner traditions model"—for them, too, it is all about the distinction between "exoteric" teachings intended for the masses and "esoteric" teachings passed on secretly to an initiated elite. But in sharp contrast with the religionists and perennialists, discursive scholars emphasize the *adjective* ("esoteric") while avoiding the *noun* ("esotericism"), because they insist that "esotericism" has essentialist implications and cannot be a proper object of historical study. As formulated by the original pioneer of this approach, Kocku von Stuckrad,

> The noun "esotericism" tends to suggest that there is an objectively identifiable "tradition" or coherent "system of thought and doctrine" that can be studied as a separate topic. Talking of "esoteric discourse" avoids this suggestion and puts the emphasis on the discursive operations that are at work in Western culture, including its academic study.[31]

Taking his cue from the "esoteric/exoteric distinction," von Stuckrad described esoteric discourse as "a secretive dialectic of concealment and revelation which is concerned with perfect knowledge."[32]

What does this mean exactly, and what are the implications? The "discursive turn" has much stronger ambitions than just adding another interesting approach to the study of esotericism or calling attention to esoteric discourse as an important topic of scholarly research. Of key importance is that it ultimately does not look at "esoteric discourse" (let alone "esotericism") as a possible object of study at all but turns it into an instrument for analyzing *another* object, described by von Stuckrad as "European History of Religion."[33] More recently, but following a very similar argumentative logic, Julian Strube has called for expanding the scope of research even further, toward a "Global History of Religion" based on the "esoteric/exoteric distinction."[34] In other words, we are no longer dealing strictly with "the study of esotericism." Its place is taken by a more general project of historical and comparative research in the study of religion and culture.

By all means, such a program may lead to important new insights. By studying the dynamics of "secrecy and revelation" on a European or even a global scale, the comparative study of religion can be approached from an angle that allows us to see patterns that would otherwise remain invisible. As helpfully explained by Hugh Urban, such a research program takes for granted that "esotericism" refers to *secrecy* and should be understood *not* in terms of its contents or substance

> but rather in terms of its *forms* or *strategies*—the tactics by which social agents conceal or reveal, hoard or exchange, certain valued information. In this sense, secrecy is a discursive strategy that transforms a given piece of knowledge into a scarce and precious resource, a valuable commodity, the possession of which in turn bestows status, prestige, or symbolic capital on its owner.[35]

But does such a research program have any necessary or inherent connection to the study of "esotericism" understood as a label for a specific collection of historical traditions, ideas, practices, or social formations? Clearly the answer must be "no." These are two different projects, based on different premises and research agendas and concerned with entirely different questions. If they tend to get confused in current discussions, this happens simply because they are using the same "esoteric(ism)" terminology. I find it unfortunate that those who promote discursive approaches so often insist, quite incorrectly, that the two types of project are in radical competition, implying that scholars should feel compelled to make an either/or choice. Such a rhetoric of fierce competition and mutually exclusive agendas is entirely unnecessary.[36] It could easily be avoided by agreeing on a simple distinction along the following lines.

> ESOTERICISM$_1$: a collection of historical traditions, ideas, practices, or social formations that are grouped together because they are considered to have certain things in common.
>
> ESOTERICISM$_2$: the dialectics of secrecy concerned with the social regulation or negotiation of access to specific forms of knowledge.

The book that you are reading is concerned with *esotericism$_1$*. Therefore the relevant question it will have to answer (and to which I will turn shortly) is *how, on what basis, for which reasons, in terms of which commonalities* certain historical traditions, ideas, practices, or social formations should be grouped together under the "esotericism" rubric. Other fields of academic research, for instance in such contexts as European or Global History of Religion, are concerned with *esotericism$_2$* and focus their attention on how the dialectics of secrecy functions in an enormous variety of social settings—many of which have no connection whatsoever with *esotericism$_1$*. To give just one clear example, Hugh Urban has written a fascinating book about the workings of secrecy in the political administration of George W. Bush,[37] but surely it would be absurd to conclude that the former US president is therefore an "esotericist" whose practices and ideas should be grouped together with those of Mme Blavatsky or Aleister Crowley.

A far more serious obstacle to fruitful collaboration and peaceful coexistence between historical and discursive approaches has to do with fundamental philosophical differences about language and reality. Here we encounter a crucial "fork in the road"[38] where radical constructivists part company with historians and other "critical realists."[39] The point of contention is whether discourse is merely self-referential and strictly contained within itself or whether it allows us to speak about things and events that have some kind of reality *beyond* discourse. In this regard, the discursive turn is deeply indebted to the core poststructuralist and deconstructivist thesis that language cannot *communicate* meaning or knowledge but can only *construct* it. The argument is that written texts consist of signifiers that never refer to an external reality but only to one another, and therefore historical scholarship cannot possibly refer to an actual historical past.[40] As a necessary result, the study of esotericism must then be conceived strictly as *an academic discourse about discourse(s)*. It cannot be about the historical and social "realities" that are the topics of discourse.[41]

Are we compelled to take that road, because there is no reasonable alternative, as discursive scholars tend to claim or tacitly assume? To answer that question, we must discuss two separate theoretical issues that often get confused: (1) the constructivists' argument for rejecting *essentialism* and (2) the deeply controversial question of what is meant by *reality*. As regards the former, it is easy to agree that the linguistic signifier "esotericism" does *not* refer to some entity or essence that is present "out there" in the world and could therefore be "discovered" by scholars. If we think that such is the case, we have fallen prey to an extremely common fallacy, known as "psychological essentialism," by which we imagine that concepts have essences.[42] Most certainly there *is* no such thing as "esotericism," nor can anything ever *be* intrinsically, inherently, or essentially "esoteric." I cannot insist strongly enough on that simple but crucial point, because it keeps being misunderstood.[43] A word such as "esotericism" can never *be* anything else than precisely that—a word in the English language. This is why the title of the present chapter does not ask what esotericism *is*[44] but what we *mean* by it.

So what, then, do we mean by "esotericism"? Here I need to get technical, so please bear with me (while checking my notes). Words are rendered "meaningful" (i.e., they come to carry some fullness of meaning) by the *discourses* in which they function, and I hold that they do this in combination with *the reified imaginal formations* that language conjures in our minds. Let me begin by unpacking that statement before discussing its implications.[45] First of all, it is human discourse that renders words "meaningful," by allowing them to function as *mediators* between what is said or written and what is meant. [46] If they lose that mediating function, as in radical deconstruction, they become strictly meaningless (this is not a cheap stab at Derrida but an attempt to capture the exact meaning [*sic!*] of his argument about *la dissémination*).[47] Secondly, it is our human consciousness that makes such mediation possible in the first place, by converting words such as "esotericism" into inherently ambiguous *imaginal formations*[48] that "re-present" reality in our minds and thereby allow us "to see in a thing what it is not, to see it other than it is."[49] This weird and wondrous imaginal capacity of human consciousness is of enormous general importance—in fact, it has been described as the evolutionary key to the very phenomenon of human civilization.[50] Be that as it may, the all-important point I wish to make here is that *mediation* is the key function of both language and imagination and the actual foundation of what "meaning" means.[51] As such, it is central to all endeavors in the humanities that are concerned with such indispensable hermeneutical tasks as *understanding, interpretation, communication*, and *translation*.[52] Of course, the very concept of "mediation" implies a distinction, in this case between language and nondiscursive reality, between what is said or written and what is meant, between what appears in our imagination and what appears to be happening "out there." It does *not* imply that language is unreal—rather, language may be defined with great precision as "reality that can be understood," as opposed to reality that can only be experienced directly but cannot be understood.[53]

The conclusion is that there *is* such a thing as reality beyond discourse, and discourse itself is part of that reality. What, then, is reality? We actually know the answer to that question, for we are all familiar with reality from our daily experience! It is literally all we have. We know about people and objects, plants and animals, planets and spaces, visions and sensations, smells and tastes, fantasies and ideas, stories and images, insights and delusions, books and manuscripts, music and poems, sounds and symbols, tastes and smells, hopes and dreams, even energies or other kinds of unspeakable stuff—and yes, of course, we also know about language and discourse. All of it, and much more, is part of our human reality. The Norwegian writer Karl Ove Knausgård has explained the point much better than I could ever do myself. Reflecting on his academic education in literary studies, he writes the following:

> I had been trained, like so many of my generation, to think abstractly . . . such that thinking was in the end wholly an activity played out among secondary phenomena, the world as it appeared in philosophy, literature, social science, politics, whereas the world in which I lived, slept, ate, spoke, made love and ran, the one that had a smell, a taste, a sound, where it rained and the wind blew, the world that you could feel on your skin, was excluded, was not deemed a topic for thought. Actually I did think there too, but in a different way, a more practical, phenomenon-by-phenomenon-orientated way, and for other reasons: while I thought in abstract reality in order to understand it, I thought in concrete reality in order to deal with it. In abstract reality I could create an identity, an identity made from opinions; in concrete reality I was who I was, a body, a gaze, a voice. That is where all independence is rooted. Including independent thought.[54]

None of those realities that we know from experience (including our experience of language itself) can be put into words *directly*, because that is not how language works.[55] But we can talk about them *indirectly*, by the mediation of language, and we are actually doing so all the time. We keep trying as hard as we can *to say what we mean* (i.e., what we mediate) or write down what we mean (again: what we mediate). I certainly do![56]

And so we return to our question: What do we mean (mediate) by "esotericism"? Using this term is just another indirect way of speaking or writing about certain events or phenomena that occur in the total reality of our human experience, past or present. It is really no more than that. Against the extreme obsession with words that results from an extreme doctrine of discursive exclusivism, the *only* good reason I have ever seen for making "esotericism" into a scholarly rubric is purely pragmatic and strictly provisional.[57] The word is useful for the purpose of calling attention to certain historical traditions, ideas, practices, or social formations that used to be neglected by scholars but deserve our serious attention. For easy reference, such a collection of "stuff set apart for special study" requires a label. My simple suggestion is, and has always been, that "esotericism" can serve that purpose.[58]

This Book's Perspective: Rejected Knowledge

It is now time to be explicit about *how, on what basis, for which reasons, in terms of which commonalities* I propose to group certain historical traditions, ideas, practices, or social formations together under this "esotericism" rubric (or, more precisely, under what I referred to as *esotericism*$_1$). We will be exploring esotericism as a radically pluralistic field of historical currents, ideas and practices that have developed from late antiquity to the present day; and no historical period or particular worldview will be given a privileged status as "more truly esoteric" (i.e., as closer to some preferred prototypical model) than any other. Once again: esotericism in this book is literally just a label, nothing more.[59] Compared to the contents to which the label refers, the label itself is of little importance. The field does not have some core "essence" that defines "its" intrinsic nature and would allow us to determine "what esotericism *really* is." Hence there is no such thing as a "best example" of esotericism either, and we have no prototypical "esotericists" that could serve as ideal models for comparison with others.

If so, what *do* we have? If this book is about "esotericism" in Western culture, then what do I mean when I use that word? For a complete answer you will have to read the next two chapters, but a brief version goes as follows. The field of study that we refer to as "esotericism" could be described as the chief casualty of academic specialization after the eighteenth century. What initially sets it apart is its *modern* status as "rejected knowledge" (or, if you prefer, knowledge that has been "dismissed," "discredited," "delegitimated," or "marginalized"). More precisely, it contains precisely everything that was consigned to the dustbin of history by European Enlightenment ideologues and their intellectual heirs from that period to the present, because it was (and is) perceived by them as incompatible with their own normative concepts of religion, rationality, and science. Imagined as the radical counterpart of everything that serious, educated people should take seriously, the consensus among intellectual elites was that this domain should better be avoided and ignored in academic discourse—instead of being dignified and somehow given legitimacy by serious study and close analysis of its ideas and their development. This process of exclusion, marginalization, and neglect did not just happen overnight. It was the final outcome of a very long history of apologetic and polemical battles and negotiations, beginning in late antiquity, about the question of which worldviews and types of knowledge or practice should be considered acceptable and which ones should be rejected. This is a topic of enormous importance, not just for esotericism but for the study of Western culture as a whole, because it is precisely by means of *these* debates that the emerging religious and intellectual elites came to define their own identity while creating the normative foundations of secular modernity.

That esotericism in Western culture is the academy's dustbin of rejected knowledge (the imaginal domain of "otherness" against which it came to define its own identity) does not imply that it is just a random collection of discarded materials without any deeper connection at all. On the contrary, a broad consensus emerged around the eighteenth century about the chief characteristics of the rejected domain. Although we should never take polemical narratives at face value (almost by definition, they exaggerate and simplify for maximum effect), those characteristics do in fact correspond to recognizable worldviews, traditions, and approaches to knowledge that have played an important although always controversial role in the history of Western culture.[60]

In the rest of this book we will, therefore, be studying a large and complicated field of research that has two basic characteristics. The first is that it has been set apart as the negative or problematic "other" against which the dominant religious and intellectual elites defined, and still define, their very identity. The second is that it strongly emphasizes specific worldviews and epistemologies (as well as associated practices) that are at odds with normative post-Enlightenment culture in the modern West. This is the closest we will get to a formal definition of esotericism.[61] The first of these two aspects of "esotericism" is discussed in Chapter 3, the second in Chapters 4 to 6; but to prepare the ground for those discussions, in Chapter 2 I will begin by sketching an overview of the chief historical currents, traditions, and influential personalities that may be studied under the "esotericism" rubric. However, before moving on to that chapter, there is one more critical issue of key importance that we need to discuss.

Esotericism and Western Culture

When the study of esotericism began to emerge as a new academic field during the 1990s and into the 2000s, it was very much dominated by the perspective of the leading scholar at that time, Antoine Faivre, who referred to the field as *l'ésotérisme occidental* (Western esotericism). This terminological choice reflected a very specific understanding of what the field was all about. In the wake of Corbin, Faivre argued that a worldview of spiritual transmutation grounded in correspondences and analogical thinking mediated by the imagination (as summarized in his famous definition discussed above) used to be extremely common and widespread in all ancient and premodern cultural traditions. But it began losing its credit in the Latin West under the impact of intellectual revolutions (from Averroism through Cartesianism) that became dominant during the later middle ages and the early modern period. As a result, all those ancient traditions and their literatures found themselves pushed toward the margins of acceptable intellectual discourse and finally ended up being perceived as a quasi-autonomous domain or reservoir of rather dubious "rejected knowledge."[62] It was only toward the end of the fifteenth century, with the translation of the *Corpus Hermeticum* published in 1471, that these perspectives began making their comeback in the wider context of the European Renaissance. These background assumptions explain why Faivre always insisted on "Western esotericism" as an essentially *modern* phenomenon that had emerged in a specifically *Christian* context. As a logical implication, Jewish and Islamic traditions had to be seen mostly as "influences on" or "backgrounds to" rather than as integral "parts of" what Western esotericism was all about. It is important to keep in mind that, at least from Faivre's perspective, the fields of Jewish and Islamic esotericism were themselves already "covered," anyway, by the influential work of his close colleagues and friends—notably the great kabbalah scholar Gershom Scholem and the specialist of Shiʿi esotericism Henry Corbin.

Faivre's theoretical assumptions were not necessarily shared by all his colleagues, as illustrated by the landmark 1,200-page *Dictionary of Gnosis and Western Esotericism* (*DGWE*), which was conceptualized during the later 1990s and got published in 2005. Its very title was the reflection of a compromise, for this dictionary covered not just Faivre's modern and contemporary "Western esotericism" but extended its reach all the way back to late antiquity, with special attention to the pursuit of *gnōsis* that had been central to the "gnostic" and Hermetic traditions. While the resulting overview was much more comprehensive than anything available at that time, still the editors were forced to impose limits on what to include and exclude. Most notably, they lacked the competence and resources to cover the enormous fields of Jewish and Islamic esotericism, not to mention practical restrictions imposed by the publisher on an already massive project. Still, these choices were sensitive and far from easy to make, as acknowledged in the introduction to the *DGWE*:

> From both a historical and a theoretical perspective, excellent arguments could be adduced for including the entire domain of "Jewish gnosis and esotericism." . . ., and along similar lines one might argue in favour of including the domain of Islamic gnosis and esotericism . . . The editors are aware of the cogency of the arguments that can be adduced in favour of a concept of "Gnosis and Western esotericism" that fully and systematically includes the three great Religions of the Book; and they are acutely conscious of the fact that doing otherwise might be perceived by some readers are reflecting a Christianity-centered bias that incorrectly seeks to exclude Judaism and Islam from the domain of "European history of religions" or from "Western culture" as such. No such exclusion or marginalization is intended here.[63]

As could be expected, many scholars over the past two decades have been working hard to fill these and other gaps that were left by the *DGWE*, resulting in increasingly comprehensive, complex, and inclusive understandings of what the field of "esotericism" is all about.[64] In the context of the most important scholarly organization in this field, the European Society for the Study of Western Esotericism (ESSWE), Jewish and Islamic esotericism have long ceased to be perceived as mere "influences on" and have become integral "parts of" the field as a whole.[65]

As part of these developments, the adjective "Western" itself has come under critical scrutiny in recent years.[66] In the current academic climate, these debates are often conducted in rather aggressive terms so that those who are perceived (correctly or not) as defending the adjective risk finding themselves accused of "Eurocentrism," "essentialism," "exceptionalist assumptions about 'Western civilization'," complicity in a "whiteness discourse," or even an agenda of erasing the agency of non-Western peoples.[67] The unfortunate effect of such polemics is that they obstruct a constructive dialogue about topics, such as "the West," that are of great importance and deserve serious discussion. The previous edition of this book was published in 2013, before these critical debates got underway, and was titled *Western Esotericism: A Guide for the Perplexed*. The new title of this rewritten edition is programmatic and intends to make two points. First, while the terminology of "Western esotericism" gained considerable traction under Faivre's influence, it is correct that the adjective does no significant theoretical work in this specific context and might therefore as well be dropped.[68] Second, I will be insisting that "esotericism$_1$" cannot be understood unless we contextualize it as part and parcel of Western *culture* and its complex historical development.

So what then do I mean by "Western culture" in the title of this book? As already stated, and explained at greater length in Chapter 3, the fact that "esotericism" came to be perceived and set apart as a semi-autonomous domain of "rejected knowledge" must be seen as the result of a pervasive polemical discourse (or series of interrelated discourses) that developed in Christian culture and became dominant specifically in the Latin West during the European Renaissance and the early modern period. It is very important to see what this means and why it matters. As the newly Christianized Roman Empire was divided into an Eastern and a Western part in 395 CE, Rome became the center of Latin Christianity and Constantinople of its Greek counterpart in the Byzantine Empire. Much later, this split was consolidated and deepened further in the "Great Schism" of 1054 between the Eastern Orthodox churches and Roman Catholicism in Western Europe. Four centuries later, with the Fall of Constantinople in 1453, Christian Byzantium lost many of its territories to Islam; and in the wake of Luther's Reformation in 1517, the Roman Catholic Church lost its dominance over large parts of Western Europe. We will see that precisely Protestant theologians since the sixteenth century, who were profiting from this latter development, played a decisive role in radicalizing the long-standing tradition of Christian polemics against "paganism," "idolatry," "superstition," and "heresy," resulting in widespread patterns of demonization and radical rejection of everything that could be associated with "magic" or irrational "enthusiasm." This Protestant polemical discourse was adopted by the Enlightenment, which ended up defining its very identity against a waste-basket category of "rejected knowledge" known by such labels as "superstition," "irrationality," or "the occult." Once this entire field had been clearly set apart as the polemical "other" of Christian orthodoxy and Enlightenment rationality/science, it obviously became attractive for those who disliked the reigning orthodoxies of Church and Reason. This is how the literature of *rejected* knowledge became an attractive reservoir of *alternative* knowledge often referred to as "esotericism."[69]

All of this means that our modern understanding of "esotericism" as rejected knowledge is the historical product of quite specific *Christian* polemical traditions that developed initially in the *Latin West* and were taken up by *Protestant* and *Enlightenment* authors in Western European countries such as Germany and France. In other words, this modern discourse about "esotericism" as a separate field does not originally come from Judaism, Islam, Byzantine Christianity, or any of the various types of "pagan" religion.[70] But if so, then what about the presence of "esotericism" in all those cultural and religious contexts? This question brings us face to face with a formidable problem that I believe lies at the heart of current debates about "the West." I am referring to the enormous cultural and intellectual influence, even up to the present day, of narrow hegemonic and Eurocentric views of "Western culture" that (1) systematically privilege the Western over the Eastern half of Europe, (2) generally privilege Christianity over all other religions north, south, and east of the Mediterranean, notably Judaism, Islam, and everything perceived as "pagan," (3) either privilege Roman Catholicism over Eastern Orthodoxy or privilege Protestantism over all other types of Christianity, and (4) finally ended up privileging Enlightenment "science and rationality" over "religion" as a matter of principle. Taken as a whole, we are dealing here with the cumulative logic of an *Internal Eurocentrism*[71] that systematically marginalizes, suppresses, excludes, or discredits anything that does not fit a narrow ideological vision of what (according to its adherents) Western culture is or should be "really" all about.

The modern study of esotericism, as I see it, seeks precisely to correct the countless distortions that resulted from these long-standing discursive patterns of internal

Eurocentrism. It does so by restoring all those marginalized, forgotten, excluded, and discredited beliefs or practices back to their legitimate place in the complex history of Western culture. As hinted in the Introduction to this book, the implications of such an agenda reach very far indeed, both for the project of a global history of religion and the study of Western culture more specifically. It exposes and undermines the ideological operations not just of *internal* Eurocentrism but also of its well-known *external* manifestations that are basic to colonialist, imperialist, as well as racist politics and typically operate by means of projecting Western heresiological stereotypes such as "primitive superstition," "sinister magic," or "the horrors of pagan idolatry" upon non-Western cultures and peoples in Africa, Asia, or Latin America.

Post- or decolonial critics are right to reject this Eurocentric discourse and its far-reaching political implications. But the deep irony is that, in doing so, they usually take that very same discourse for granted as though it were an adequate description of what "the West" is all about—instead of deconstructing it as a narrow ideological fiction that distorts our view of Western culture and its deep historical complexities. My argument proceeds by an entirely different logic and goes as follows. Rather than rejecting "Western culture" altogether as a meaningful concept, our agenda should be to *reconstruct it* by taking a radically different, much broader, much more inclusive, and consistently nonideological perspective that is free from hidden implications of Western superiority (or, for that matter, inferiority) but is grounded in solid historical and empirical knowledge—not just of what used to be considered "acceptable" in terms of standard Eurocentric prejudice but of *all* its "rejected" dimensions as well. In a nutshell, this is the optimally ambitious agenda of esotericism research as I see it.[72] According to such an understanding, I suggest that "Western culture" can be delineated as follows.

- *Geographically*, its initial scope, for a period of circa two thousand years (i.e., before the age of global colonialism; see below), covered the entire area around the Mediterranean—that is, not just Europe but also Northern Africa above the Sahara and what we nowadays think of as the Middle East. Why refer to these parts of the world as "the West"? Because it just so happened that all major cultural and commercial connections in the ancient world ran along an East-West axis that coincided broadly with the path of the sun: the famous silk roads extended from countries like China or Japan in the Orient, all the way to the Mediterranean basin in the Occident (from *occidentem*, the part of the sky where the sun sets).[73] This part of the Eurasian landmass *lay obviously in the West*: it was known that, from here, you could travel all the way Eastward, but you could not move into the opposite direction—beyond the strait of Gibraltar there was nothing but open sea.
- *Culturally*, I understand Western culture as grounded in the profound dialectical patterns of interaction between two basic components that were in conflict from the very beginning, nevertheless influenced one another profoundly, but could never be truly reconciled: firstly the cultures of "pagan" Hellenism that emerged in the wake of Alexander's conquests and secondly the radical or exclusive monotheisms of Judaism, Christianity, and Islam. In the sharpest possible contrast with traditional

Eurocentric or "philhellenist" narratives of a civilization that derives its sense of superiority from combining "Greek rational science and philosophy" with "Judeo-Christian religious morality," this implies that Islam must be fully recognized as an integral part of Western culture, just as it must fully include Judaism (not as some kind of preparation for Christianity but on its own terms) next to a great variety of "pagan" traditions.[74]

- *Historically*, on these foundations, we can think of Western culture as a dynamic formation that develops from the fifth century BCE to the present and is defined by continually developing cultural patterns based on foundational stories and ideas that have their origin in Greek-Hellenistic culture and the three great monotheistic religions. Along with the rise, expansion, and fall of empires from one century to the next, the ever-flexible boundaries of Western culture are best seen as coinciding with how far in geographical space these foundational stories and ideas were reaching at any given moment in time. The decisive historical shift comes in 1492, when Columbus reaches the Americas and "Western" culture begins its colonial expansion beyond the traditional Eurasian West. No longer defined geographically as a space on the Eurasian map, we might say that it now becomes a space in the mind, still defined by its continually evolving pattern of foundational stories and ideas that have kept developing into new directions, by responding to those of their predecessors *and* to those that come from other, non-Western cultures.[75]

Since writing the first edition of this book, published in 2013, I have become convinced that the modern study of esotericism requires a broad and inclusive understanding of Western culture more or less along these lines. Yet it must be admitted that, at least for the moment, the innovative potential of such a program must still largely be realized. We do not yet have an authoritative, synthetic, non-Eurocentric history of Western culture based upon these or similar premises, let alone an integral perspective on all its "esoteric" dimensions. In fact, the considerable conceptual problems of gathering Jewish, Christian, Islamic, pagan, and modern secular forms of esotericism under one comprehensive conceptual umbrella (not to mention their possible relation to equivalent phenomena in non-Western cultures) have not even been approached yet, much less resolved. To begin with Jewish kabbalah, this has become a perfectly normal topic at academic conferences in the field of esotericism, but we have not yet seen systematic attempts to achieve a conceptual or historical comparison between Jewish esotericism (still often referred to as "mysticism"[76]) and its parallels in other cultural and religious contexts.

Likewise, "Islamic esotericism" is becoming more prominent at academic esotericism conferences in recent years, but basic questions of definition and demarcation are still very much a matter of debate. Similar to what we see in current "global religion" approaches to esotericism, many scholars seem to be focused far too exclusively on just the search for equivalents in Arabic or Persian to the term "esoteric" understood as "secret," "inward," or "nonmanifest" (with *bāṭiniyya* for "esotericism")—as if the *word* esoteric(ism) is all that counts to establish a field.[77] By contrast, many recent projects that prioritize history of ideas in the *longue durée*, emphasize critical philology and editions/translations of neglected sources, or pursue a structural comparativism of religious or spiritual practices in Islamicate contexts (in short, what I refer to as *esotericism*$_1$) have tended to prefer such terms as "the occult sciences" or "occultism"[78]—with the unfortunate risk of creating confusion with established terminology in the study of European esotericism, where the latter term refers to ideas and traditions that emerged specifically in the nineteenth century.[79] In the following chapter and in this book as a whole, I adopt the second type of scholarship but refer to it as "Islamic Esotericism." In other words, my concern is not with a possible *Islamic Esotericism*$_2$ but with *Islamic Esotericism*$_1$. Finally, concerning the neglected question of esotericism in Byzantine culture, it seems that no systematic or comparative approaches have been attempted as yet.[80]

The present state of research imposes important restrictions on what can be done in this volume. Its most central focus is on a specific number of historical traditions, beliefs, and practices (*esotericism*$_1$) that gained a more or less dubious or controversial reputation in Western Europe over long stretches of time until they finally ended up in a conceptual waste-basket of "rejected knowledge" under the impact of Protestant and Enlightenment polemics and their hegemonic claims of cultural or religious superiority. Again, this history of internal-Eurocentric rejection and marginalization (the topic of Chapter 3) occurred specifically in Latin Christian contexts from late antiquity up to the period of the Enlightenment, after which it continued its career in the context of modern and postmodern secular societies. But while this story is central to the very emergence of "esotericism" as a field of academic study, I will try to do justice to the much wider context of Western culture as outlined above, by discussing not just the trajectory that leads from pagan through Christian to modern and secular forms of esotericism but fully including the Jewish and Islamic dimensions as well.

As regards Judaism, there is no doubt that the European Enlightenment's narrative of rejected knowledge affected influential Jewish intellectuals associated with the nineteenth-century *Wissenschaft des Judentums*, such as the great historian Heinrich Graetz, who imagined the kabbalah as a poisonous fungous layer that had come to surround the "noble core" of true Judaism.[81] It was against such perspectives that Gershom Scholem was responding in his pioneering efforts to establish kabbalah as a legitimate field of academic research. But to what extent the dynamics of "internal Eurocentrism" might be parallelled by similar processes in the Byzantine or Islamic contexts, not to mention other parts of the world, remains as yet unclear. It would be crucial to study the prior histories of how apologetics on behalf of "orthodoxies" have been conducted by means of negative polemics against the equivalents in non-Christian contexts (by whatever terms may have been in vogue!)[82] of what modern scholars have come to refer to as "esotericism." It has indeed been suggested that, next to "European processes of 'rejecting knowledge'," similar processes should now be investigated also

> in Antiquity, or in Arabic and/or Jewish discourses . . . or even in non-European contexts . . . thereby possibly contributing to advanced scholarly taxonomies for processes of postulating, rejecting, or rehabilitating differents forms of knowledge.[83]

This is exactly the agenda that I believe should be pursued. Our view of esotericism in Western culture will necessarily remain incomplete, as long as such historical analyses remain unavailable—but they can only be written by specialized scholars with deep linguistic expertise who have access to the primary sources in all the relevant languages. Such research will take a lot of time, for the sad reality is that enormous quantities of vital manuscripts are still lying in archives waiting for scholars to read them, prepare editions, and make translations so that academic audiences and the wider public can gain access to them.[84] It will certainly take several decades, at the very least, before a truly comprehensive perspective on "esotericism in Western culture" can even begin to appear at the horizon! Meanwhile I will do what I can to give at least an impression of the field *and* of its enormous potential for a future, inclusive, non-Eurocentric history of what we may still refer to as the West.

2 A Short History of Rejected Knowledge

. . . the development of humanity is a series of interpretations.
(Michael Foucault, "Nietzsche")[1]

In this chapter I will provide a short overview of those historical currents, traditions, and historical personalities that seem particularly important to the field of esotericism as a whole. The intention is to provide a preliminary "map" of the territory, as a means of orientation, while taking into account that countless further names and data could always be added. Think of a map on Google Earth. At a certain level of resolution, you will get a broad overview with rivers, mountain, seas, and cities. If you zoom in further on a particular city, you will see a grid of streets and squares. Zooming in even further on one particular street, you will see separate houses or gardens. If you zoom really far enough, you might be able to discern individual people. But each one of them is again like a separate world—they all have their unique lives and memories and ideas and emotions, all of which will have to be explored in infinite detail if we *really* wish to understand deeply what is going on in that street. Because human history has infinite levels of depth and complexity, any historical overview must be limited and selective, and the present chapter is obviously no exception. This map is not the territory.

Nor do I seek to establish some kind of esoteric "canon." The intention is not to draw boundaries around a field, so as to demarcate "the esoteric" from the presumably "non-esoteric" or stipulate what is "in" and what is "out." On the contrary, the idea is precisely to break free from the restrictions of traditional canons, to dissolve the artificial boundaries by which large parts of Western culture used to be excluded and pushed toward the margins of what was supposed to be "central." As will be seen in Chapter 3 and the rest of the book, precisely such a noncanonical agenda goes to the heart of what I believe this field is all about.

Gnōsis and Spiritual Practice in Late Hellenistic culture

For the origins of the field to which I refer as "esotericism" (or *esotericism*$_1$) we must explore the Hellenistic culture of late antiquity that emerged in the wake of Alexander's conquests between 335 and 323 BCE. As Greek became the lingua franca for commercial and intellectual exchange over very large areas, Hellenic philosophical and religious concepts spread widely and began to interact with the intellectual or spiritual traditions of ancient cultures, for instance, in Egypt, Persia, Mesopotamia, and even India. In the writings of many authors during the late Hellenistic period (roughly the first centuries of the Common Era), PLATONISM developed not just as a tradition of strictly rational philosophical inquiry but also as a *paideia*, a path or way of life[2] that could take the form of religious or spiritual worldviews, mythological systems, and ritual practices. The central focus in these broadly Platonic milieus was on the attainment of a salvational *gnōsis* (Greek for "knowledge") by which the human soul could be liberated from its material entanglement and regain its lost awareness of the divine reality of pure spiritual beauty and light. Among thinkers and practitioners who pursued such paths, it was widely taken for granted that the philosophy of Plato himself had not been an original product of Greek rational thinking but was grounded in the much more ancient spiritual wisdom traditions of "barbarian" peoples of the Orient, notably the Persians, the Egyptians, and the Hebrews. This popular understanding of Platonism as "spiritual wisdom from the East" will be referred to as PLATONIC ORIENTALISM,[3] to distinguish it from Platonism understood as a tradition of Greek philosophical rationalism grounded in Socratic dialogue.

The search for a salvational *gnōsis* in a broadly Platonic framework was widespread among thinkers who would be classified today as "Middle Platonists." In view of the later history of esotericism, among the most important traditions informed by Middle Platonist philosophy is the Egyptian Hellenistic tradition known as HERMETISM.[4] The name refers to a legendary, semi-divine wisdom teacher, HERMES TRISMEGISTUS (originally a syncretic mixture of the Greek god Hermes and the Egyptian deity Thoth), who was widely believed to have flourished in Egypt in very ancient times. The surviving texts that are attributed to Hermes, or in which he plays a central role, can actually be dated to the second and third centuries CE. As far as the spiritual teachings of Hermetism are concerned, the most important of these texts are the so-called *Corpus Hermeticum* (seventeen separate treatises that would be collated together in medieval Byzantium); a larger work that was known as *Logos Teleios* ("Perfect Discourse") and, except for some shorter fragments in Coptic and Greek, only survives intact as a Latin version, the *Asclepius*; a visionary-initiatic text in Coptic that is known as *The Ogdoad and the Ennead* ("The Eighth and the Ninth") and was discovered in 1945 as part of the famous Egyptian Nag Hammadi library; a collection of short statements that survive only in Armenian translation and were discovered even more recently; and finally a long series of fragments that were collated by a certain Johannes of Stobi (Macedonia) in the early fifth century CE.[5] These texts contain technical discussions about the true nature of God, humanity, and the cosmos, but they make clear that philosophical discussion is strictly subservient to the quest for spiritual salvation. While scholars long dismissed them as just "literary fictions," in fact they must have been used in small communities devoted to a spiritual and ceremonial praxis.

Hermetic devotees embarked on a meditational path of spiritual exercises to cultivate the latent potential of their *nous*—an important key term that is often mistranslated (at least in Hermetic contexts) as "intellect" or "mind" but actually doesn't mean what we understand by those words today. In Hermetic circles it meant the supreme spiritual

Light of Divinity, as well as our human capacity to apprehend and experience the presence of that Light in ourselves and in the world. Therefore the activity of *nous*, known as *noēsis*, did not mean "thinking" (as suggested by most modern translations) but referred to an unmediated direct perception of the divine Light. Only by using this faculty of *noēsis* could human beings come to see through the delusions of normal sense perception and gain salvational knowledge, *gnōsis*, of *ta onta* ("the things that really are," or "reality as it really is").

By means of transcending mere sensory experience and strictly "rational" understanding, Hermetic practitioners could find liberation from worldly attachments and attain salvation. Such an ultimate spiritual release was held to be possible not just after death but even during their lifetimes on earth, by being reborn (not metaphorically but quite literally) in a new spiritual body of immaterial noetic Light. The entire process of transformation through liberation and rebirth could culminate in a supreme experience of spiritual ascent and blissful unity with the divine powers of Light and Life that were seen as emanating eternally from the mysterious *pēgē*, the divine Source of all that is. Hermetic practitioners believed that the human passions keep us addicted to bodily sensations and worldly desires. These were administered by dark daimonic entities linked to the zodiac, whose power over body and mind must be broken in order to gain salvational *gnōsis* through spiritual rebirth. Once Hermetic practitioners had been reborn and their "spiritual eyes were opened," they would discover that the divine is universally present throughout the whole of creation—or even, more radically, that nothing was truly real except universal spiritual Light.

Hermetism was a product of pagan Egyptian Hellenism, but the search for *gnōsis* was widespread among Christians as well. The term was used in a positive sense by a few of the Church fathers, notably Clement of Alexandria, but is mostly associated with GNOSTICISM. Under the influence of polemical campaigns launched by church fathers such as Irenaeus, Hippolytus, or Epiphanius, who presented it to their readers as the heresy of all heresies, gnosticism has been perceived as a dualistic religion, which taught that sparks of the divine light had become imprisoned in the world of matter and therefore sought to escape from it again to find the way back to their divine source. According to basic gnostic mythology, human beings who carried the spark in themselves and woke up to its presence would seek liberation from the tyranny of the "demiurge," an ignorant or evil deity (often associated with the God of the Old Testament) who had created our material world of darkness and ignorance as a prison for the soul and therefore sought to prevent human beings from waking up to their inner divinity. By attaining *gnōsis* (knowledge) of their true identity and their situation of imprisonment, gnostics were set on their way to escape from the world of the demiurge and his demonic helpers, the archons, who would try to prevent them from rising up through the heavenly spheres after death and return to their divine home of Light.

After the sensational discovery in 1945 of the so-called Nag Hammadi library, which contained a whole range of previously unknown manuscripts,[6] our picture of these "gnostic" currents and their relation to Christianity has become infinitely more complex than before. In contrast to the simple polemical antithesis of an orthodox Christian theology faced with the dualistic heresy of the gnostics ("the gnostic religion" against the religion of the Christian church), most scholars now emphasize that during the first centuries, Christianity itself was by no means homogeneous but existed in many different shades and varieties—including more or less "gnostic" ones. This great variety is evident from the Nag Hammadi texts. While many of them hardly fit the heresiological model of a gnostic-dualistic "counter-church," it appears that the concept of an evil or ignorant demiurge who tries to imprison the spiritual sparks of light belongs to a specific Christian tradition referred to as SETHIANISM. Because of these new discoveries and insights, most specialists today would argue that the monolithic concept of "gnosticism" is misleading and must be replaced by much more complex views of Christian diversity as it existed during the first centuries CE.[7]

A third important trend during the late Hellenistic period is a ritual practice known as THEURGY. Its earliest testimonies are the so-called *Chaldaean Oracles* attributed to a certain Julian the Theurgist (second century CE).[8] Theurgy flourished not just in the spiritual and social milieus of Hermetism in Egypt but also in a new philosophical-contemplative tradition commonly known as NEOPLATONISM (a term invented by modern scholars). Its founder PLOTINUS (c. 204/5–270) was born and educated in Egypt but became famous as a teacher of Platonic philosophy in Rome. The most important source for Neoplatonic theurgy is a long treatise addressed by IAMBLICHUS (c. 240/50–325/6), an original thinker and spiritual teacher from Syria, to Plotinus's pupil PORPHYRY (c. 234–305 CE). Although traditionally known as *De mysteriis* ("On the Mysteries," a title invented in the late fifteenth century by Marsilio Ficino), it is better referred to simply as Iamblichus's "Response to Porphyry."[9]

Presented by Iamblichus as "the Way of Hermes" grounded in ancient Egyptian wisdom, theurgy was a ceremonial practice involving alterations of consciousness by means of which the gods appeared to practitioners as luminous entities that could beneficially take possession of their bodies and assist in healing their souls. Platonists like Plotinus or Porphyry believed that philosophy could lead to spiritual states of ecstasy in which the soul escaped from the body and reunited with the divine—but Iamblichus had a sharply different perspective. He argued that theurgy was not about leaving the body through philosophical contemplation but about *embodying* divine energies into the world, by means of a ceremonial practice that went beyond philosophical understanding and could simply not be captured by words. Through the works of later authors such as PROCLUS (412–485 CE) and an anonymous author referred to as PSEUDO-DIONYSIUS THE AREOPAGITE (because he was identified, incorrectly, as the Athenian convert of Paul at the Areopagus, mentioned in Acts 17:34), Neoplatonism had a deep impact on the development of Western culture through the middle ages and into the Renaissance.

From Egypt during the Roman period and up to the twelfth century, we also have a large collection of writings in Greek, Demotic, and Coptic that are known conventionally as "MAGICAL" PAPYRI[10] – a problematic title, because magic (*heka*) in Egyptian culture did not have the dubious connotations that it acquired as *magia* under the Roman Empire and successive periods of history even up to the present. Many of these texts contain precious information about private spiritual practices designed for coping with the realities of daily life, in a culture that was going through profound transformations as traditional Egyptian religion gave way first to Christianity and then to Islam. They also contain frequent descriptions of rituals that were designed to make a deity appear to the practitioner,[11] and of impressive visionary experiences. A particularly famous example is the so-called *Mithras Liturgy*.[12] It describes an ecstatic ascent, induced by psychoactive substances combined with ritual incantations, in which the anonymous female practitioner encounters awe-inspiring spiritual entities and finally comes face to face with the supreme solar deity Helios Mithras. This text, with its spectacular content, has been an object of fascination not just for scholars of antiquity but also for influential practitioners and authors in modern esotericism, notably Carl Gustav Jung.[13] More generally, these "magical" papyri became enormously attractive for modern occultists toward the end of the nineteenth century, from the Hermetic Order of the Golden Dawn and Aleister Crowley to the present day.[14]

The Occult Sciences

Magic, Astrology, and Alchemy in the Latin West

Next to the search for spiritual salvation and knowledge of divine realities, esotericism has always been deep involved with the *study of nature* and its hidden laws or dynamics. We usually place these two types of pursuit neatly in two different compartments, "religion" and "science"; but in fact, before the advent of modernity, it is questionable whether those categories can be kept apart. If nature had been created by God or, more radically, had emanated from God's own being (as suggested by Platonic models), then its hidden secrets must somehow participate in the sphere of divinity as well, or at least they would have to mirror the mysteries of the divine economy. Concerning the study of nature in an esotericism context, at least in the Latinate sphere, the three most relevant domains for us are magic, astrology, and alchemy. Since the sixteenth century, it has been very common to discuss them together as the three central OCCULT SCIENCES. I adopt that terminology here with some hesitation, firstly because it suggests that these fields or disciplines are intrinsically connected at some deeper level (presumably as manifestations of one single *philosophia occulta*, "occult philosophy"), an assumption that is questionable to say the least; and secondly because it challenges modern definitions of "science" and begs the very question of whether these practices can be separated from "religion" at all.[15]

Among these three types of practice or fields of study, MAGIC is the most difficult to grasp. Many modern scholars use the term to indicate common everyday techniques or procedures for dealing with challenges, problems, or desires in a person's life (for instance protection against dangers such as sickness and death, acquisition of wealth, gaining power over others, or manipulating their emotions for getting love or sex). Magic in this sense could be seen as a common phenomenon in all human cultures.[16] But as already mentioned above (with reference to the "magical" papyri), the term is deeply problematic not just because of its predominantly pejorative connotations but also because of the central role it has played in the Western discourse of "rejected knowledge."[17] In the wake of post-Enlightenment scholarship, with influential authors such as Edward B. Tylor (1832–1917) and James G. Frazer (1854–1941), it has become intuitive to think of "magic" as a universal category sharply distinct from "religion" and "science." But from a historical point of view, this famous magic-religion-science triad leads to gross simplifications and anachronistic distortions[18] – not to mention the Western imperialist and potentially racist implications of depicting "the evolution of humanity" as a history of civilizational progress that leads from the darkness of magic (practiced by "primitive savages") to the higher stage of religion (epitomized by Christianity, especially its Protestant manifestations) to the highest level of modern science as practiced by white European males. If you look at how the words *mageia* in Greek and *magia* in Latin have in fact been used by practitioners and their opponents, throughout the history of Western culture, you find that they do *not* refer to just one single thing. On the contrary, there are several, very different concepts of what "magic" is supposed to be all about.

One of these, the concept of DEMONIC MAGIC, is a direct legacy of Jewish, Christian, and Islamic polemics against "pagan idolatry" in the wake of the biblical First and Second Commandment. From this point of view, all forms of "magic" are ultimately based on contact with evil demons. The Greek word *daimōn* meant simply a deity or spiritual entity that could affect human beings in either positive or harmful ways; but Christians interpreted such entities as unambiguously evil "demons," arguing that the old pagan deities had always been trying to deceive human beings and seduce them into sin, for example by posing as angels of light and promising them power in return for obedience and worship. The great wave of Witchcraft persecutions in early modern Europe was grounded in such an understanding of "demonic magic."[19] But already during the European Middle Ages, we find many attempts at blurring the boundaries between demonic and angelic entities. Even the dark arts of necromancy ("divination by the dead") or nigromancy ("black divination") could be reinterpreted to turn them into a pious Christian pursuit—for instance by insisting that magicians do God's work by commanding demons in the name of Jesus or that a true and superior magic has been revealed by such holy or divine entities as angels or the Virgin Mary.[20]

An entirely different understanding of magic, known as MAGIA NATURALIS ("natural magic"), began to emerge in Western Europe around the eleventh century. As will be seen below, many ancient texts about natural philosophy had been translated from Greek into Arabic or Persian since the eighth century CE, resulting in a major flourishing of the occult sciences in Baghdad (from this period up to the city's destruction by the Mongols in 1258) and on the Spanish peninsula far in the West. Over a period of many centuries, Christians succeeded in conquering the latter territory from north to south (the so-called *Reconquista*, 722–1492); and notably after the fall of Toledo, in 1085, this gave them access to wealths of learning and scholarship preserved in the superior Muslim libraries. Great numbers of manuscripts devoted to the ancient sciences were now translated from Arabic into Latin, and the result was a medieval "scientific revolution" with enormous consequences for the subsequent development of Christian intellectual culture. Inspired by these new bodies of learning in the domain of natural philosophy, Christian intellectuals now began arguing that many "wondrous and miraculous" phenomena that uneducated people believed to be caused by demonic agents could in fact be explained in perfectly natural terms. The new perspective of *magia naturalis* can therefore be defined as a systematic attempt to withdraw the study of nature from theological control by arguing that it had nothing to do with demonic intervention.

An important part of natural magic was the study of QUALITATES OCCULTAE (hidden qualities). This term referred to mysterious natural forces such as magnetism or the influence of the moon on the tides but also came to include such "invisible forces" as the influences that were radiating from the stars, the (de)formative powers attributed to the human imagination, or the evil eye. The basic project of *magia naturalis* was to explain such phenomena in natural-scientific terms; but of course, it meant that scientists were giving credence to the actual reality of "occult forces" that others were still seeing as supernatural and most likely demonic in nature. From the perspective of such Christian critics, all those Hellenic sciences that had reached Latin Christianity in Arabic translations from the Greek looked very much like a Trojan horse, through which the demonic practices of pagan idolaters were once again given entrance to the Christian world! As this battle between theological and naturalist perspectives would continue right into the Renaissance and early modern culture, it is not hard to see why magic has always remained a deeply ambiguous category, pitched precariously between demonism and natural science.

In sharp contrast to its post-Enlightenment reputation as the epitome of a false "occult science" grounded in superstition, classical ASTROLOGY was actually grounded in a concept of universal, immutable natural law. In Egypt around the second century BCE, it had been developed into a rigorous causal model of cosmology that sought to explain all changes and effects in the sublunar world by relating them to the eternal rotations of the celestial bodies. Classical astrology has therefore been described, quite correctly, as "the most comprehensive scientific theory of antiquity," because it was using mathematical calculations and models to predict all possible changes in the world of cause and effect.[21] On the normative basis of Aristotelian natural philosophy, it assumed that the sublunar world composed of the four elements (earth, water, air, fire) was inert and incapable of moving by itself; the *primae causae* ("first causes") of motion were the stars, which were actually endowed with life and intelligence and were influencing the sublunar world through a subtle invisible medium known as the *quinta essentia* ("fifth element"). Alternatively, in terms of the presumed interrelation between higher and lower parts of the cosmos ("as above, so below"), the sublunar and supralunar worlds could be seen as "corresponding" with one another in terms of a preestablished harmony that was inherent in creation itself.

Astrology was widespread in pagan, Jewish, and Christian milieus before the age of the Emperor Constantine.[22] But as a divinatory practice, it suggested that the heavenly bodies were divine entities, and the idea of a universal astral determinism seemed to threaten the notion of free will. As a result, astrology was dismissed and suppressed by the Christian church as a form of pagan superstition. Only around the eleventh century, with the rediscovery of natural science and philosophy from Arabic sources, did it begin to make its comeback in European Christian culture, as an integral and (in fact) central component of *magia naturalis*. In very sharp contrast with prevailing attitudes in early medieval Christian culture, the science of the stars was not just accepted in Muslim societies but has even been described as the dominant political theory and technology of the great early modern Islamic empires, no less, reaching levels of intellectual sophistication that had no parallel anywhere else.[23] Based on translations from Arabic to Latin, it now also flourished in the European Renaissance and would remain an important dimension of natural science even during the "scientific revolution" of the seventeenth century. Particularly important here is the concept of ASTRAL MAGIC, the belief that powers and virtues from the stars can be "channeled" or drawn down by means of images or ceremonial practices, for purposes of medical or psychological healing but perhaps also to harmful ends. Astrology was part and parcel of the PHILOSOPHIA OCCULTA of the early modern period, with multiple religious connotations and implications (on which more below). As this "occult philosophy" lost the battle with Protestant and Enlightenment opponents during the seventeenth and eighteenth centuries, astrology entered a second period of decline during the nineteenth century and the first half of the twentieth. After the Second World War, it made a remarkable comeback in new and heavily psychologized forms that were largely indebted to Carl Gustav Jung and his concept of "synchronicity."

Western ALCHEMY emerged in Egypt during the late Hellenistic era, as a laboratory practice concerned with the transmutation of material substances.[24] Aristotelian natural philosophy, with its core theory of the four elements grounded in one single *prima materia* ("primary matter"), implied that as a matter of principle, it should be possible to change *any* substance into any other—including gold. Alchemists in their workshops or laboratories were trying to discover the secrets of transmutation by means of practical experimentation. Already at a very early stage, in the writings of ZOSIMOS OF PANOPOLIS, technical descriptions of laboratory procedures were combined with vivid accounts of visions or dreams about initiatory processes of death-and-rebirth that were described in terms of alchemical symbolism. Zosimos, who earned his living by making temple statues and was personally involved in Hermetic experiential practice, believed that human beings could escape from gross materiality by being reborn as spiritual beings.[25]

Like other forms of Hellenistic science and natural philosophy, alchemy was essentially forgotten in the Latin West during the early medieval period but rediscovered there from Arabic sources during the later Middle Ages.[26] Medieval and early modern alchemy is grounded in laboratory procedures that pertain specifically to the domain of science or natural philosophy; but as we already saw in the case of Zosimos, its language of transmutation was a natural fit with religious narratives about "spiritual" transformation and rebirth, suggesting that human beings could move beyond their material and sinful condition to attain a superior state of salvation through *gnōsis*. From such a perspective, Christ himself could be described metaphorically as the "philosophers' stone" (the mysterious key to transmutation) through whose agency human beings were changed in their internal essence and turned from a state of gross materiality into a superior condition of spiritual "gold." Such spiritual interpretations and adaptations grew in popularity after the Renaissance and flourished from the end of the sixteenth through the seventeenth century, whether in close connection with laboratory practice or entirely separate from it.[27] As far as the history of science is concerned, it is practically impossible during this period to separate alchemy from what we would now rather see as chemistry, and hence the contemporary term "chymistry" has been proposed as a general label for covering the entire spectrum (next to "chrysopoeia" for alchemical attempts at making gold).[28] Given this inseparability of "alchemy" from "chemistry," there is nothing surprising about the fact that major figures of the scientific revolution, notably Robert Boyle and Isaac Newton, were deeply involved in alchemical experimentation.[29]

Along with astrology, alchemy was expelled from official science during the eighteenth century and came to be perceived, very misleadingly,[30] as mere pseudoscience or superstition during the nineteenth and much of the twentieth century. After the Second World War, Jungian authors as well as Traditionalists (see below) have sought to rehabilitate alchemy by downplaying its "scientific" nature in favor of its "spiritual" aspects, but such interpretations are usually based on esoteric beliefs rather than scholarly research.[31] From the perspective of the study of esotericism, alchemy is best understood as a multifaceted historical and cultural phenomenon that cannot be contained within any single academic discipline. As such, it is defined by basic procedures of transmutation that may be pursued as science in laboratory settings but can also function as inspiring narratives in religious, spiritual, philosophical, or even psychological discourse. As formulated by Mike Zuber, in a humorous and very apt metaphor, "it seems unlikely that either the 'alchemy is scientific' or the 'alchemy is religious' team will ever succeed in pulling its opponents across the line" because we should "identify alchemy itself as part of the game: it is the rope."[32]

Jewish Esotericism

The Book of Ezekiel in the Hebrew Bible begins with the description of a famous vision that reportedly occurred during the period of the Babylonian captivity in the city of Nippur. Having seen the heavens open, Ezekiel beheld four winged creatures with faces that were partly human and partly in the shape of a lion, a bull, and an eagle. Underneath them were strange "wheels within wheels" covered with eyes, and over the expanse above them was a throne that looked as though made of sapphire, on which a figure was seated that looked like a man and was surrounded by a fiery radiance. Known in later Jewish tradition as *Ma'aseh Merkavah*, "the work of the chariot," this so-called apocalypse ("revelation") became the original model for many later visionary experiences reported from Jewish as well as Christian culture.[33] Visionary accounts influenced by Ezekiel occur in the so-called Books of Enoch (written between the third century BCE and the first century CE), which focus on the antediluvian biblical hero who was said to have "walked with God" for 365 years and did not die even then, but was "taken away" (Gen. 5:21-23). Texts known as "1 and 2 Enoch" and the "Testament of Levi" describe Enoch's awesome adventures, during his ascent through the heavens, in the context of a gripping narrative about the fallen angels (the biblical

"Sons of God," Gen. 6:1-4) who fathered children with the "daughters of men" and were punished by God for their transgressions. This literature is filled with vivid descriptions of heavenly realities and angelic creatures, culminating in the vision of God himself seated on his throne in the highest heaven, and transformations of the visionary himself from a human into an angelic creature who may even catch a glimpse of the divine countenance. Later apocalypses carried this tradition further and attributed impressive visionary experiences to other biblical figures, as in the "Apocalypse of Abraham," the "Ascension of Isaiah," the "Apocalypse of Zephaniah," and the famous Christian "Apocalypse of John." The themes of communion with the angels and ascent of the soul became important also in the community of *Qumran* and the writings of Philo of Alexandria.

In the rabbinical literature that emerged in Palestine and Babylonia after the destruction of the Second Temple in 70 CE, this vision of Ezekiel became an object of exegetical discourse. Whether it also inspired experiential practices of ecstatic ascent is contested among specialists. Rabbinical authorities often warned against the dangers of unqualified exegesis, not just of Ezekiel's vision of the *merkavah* but also of the account of creation in the book of Genesis, presumably because unrestrained curiosity about such mysteries could easily cause the speculative fantasy to run wild.[34] But from another perspective, what makes Jewish esotericism so impressive is precisely the fact that, like Midrashic discourse more generally, it gives free rein to the powers of the exegetical imagination. Notably the Mishnah Hagiga (11a–16a) became the storehouse of later Rabbinical traditions about such topics as the concealed primordial light, the seven heavens, or the four sages that entered the Pardes and was instrumental in defining such topics as "esoteric knowledge."

In the centuries after the destruction of the Second Temple, a body of texts came into existence that are known as the HEKHALOT LITERATURE, full of gripping descriptions of practitioners making a perilous "descent" (rather than an ascent, as one might expect) to the *Merkavah*, that is, to God's throne chariot as first described by Ezekiel. The meaning of *hekhalot* is "palaces" or "halls," for the visionary would typically be depicted as attempting to penetrate a series of heavenly palaces-within-palaces, guarded by terrifying angels who would kill the practitioner if he made any mistake or was seen to fall short of the highest standards of purity. Each palace in succession would present even greater dangers and difficulties than the preceding one, requiring the use of "magical" seals, names, or adjurations;[35] but the successful adept who could master his fears and overcome all obstacles would be admitted at the end of his journey into the innermost palace, where God was seated on his throne surrounded by angels, and he would then be allowed there to partake in the heavenly "liturgical union."[36] Sometimes the person who came this far would himself be transformed into an angel, as seen most famously in a text known as "3 Enoch," where the antediluvian hero turns out to have become a supreme angel, Metatron, who is so close to God himself that he is even described sometimes as "the lesser YHWH."

An important text is the proto-kabbalistic SEFER YETZIRAH ("The Book of Formation," of uncertain date),[37] with its pioneering discussion of an innovative concept that was to become central to Jewish kabbalah—the system of SEFIROT. In its original conception, these were the ten primordial numbers that (together with the twenty-two letters of the Hebrew alphabet) were used by God as his basic tools in creating the world. Under the influence of a seminal text known as SEFER HA-BAHIR ("Book of Illumination," earliest manuscript from the end of the thirteenth century),[38] they would later be interpreted as ten divine essences, lights, emanations, energies, or powers of manifestation that were seen as central to the deep metaphysical structure of divine creation. Visually arranged as *ilanot* ("trees," i.e., arboreal shapes),[39] the sefirotic system became omnipresent and perfectly central to the major tradition of Jewish esoteric speculation known as KABBALAH (literally "reception").[40]

Its most famous expression by far is the SEFER HA-ZOHAR ("Book of Splendour"), traditionally attributed to the second-century Rabbi Simeon ben Yohai (often abbreviated as Rashbi) and his circle of disciples. Among modern scholars, there is general agreement that this enormous work is in fact a compilation of several different literary units, authored by Moses de Léon (1250–1305) and a small group of other Spanish authors from the thirteenth and early fourteenth centuries.[41] Rashbi appears in the Zoharic literature as a supreme master of wisdom, who is frequently on the move, "walking the path" together with his disciples while expounding the awesome mysteries of the Torah.[42] The Zohar is known for its profound mythical-symbolical system of theosophical speculation about the mysteries of God and his creation, often expressed by means of explicit erotic language. For instance, in a famous passage, the Torah is compared with a beautiful lady who hides in a secluded chamber of her palace and is haunted by her lover, who keeps passing her gate. Sometimes she shows him her face for a brief moment, then withdraws it again, and only he is able to get a glimpse of her presence. As he persists in pursuing her, she begins speaking to him from behind a curtain, until insight comes to him (*derashah*); she then moves to speaking allegorical words from behind a light veil (*haggadah*); and finally she reveals herself to him face to face. She then "speaks to him of all her hidden secrets and all her hidden ways, which have been in her heart from the beginning."[43]

Next to the traditions of theosophical-exegetical kabbalah exemplified most impressively by the *Zohar*, a different genre known as PROPHETIC or ECSTATIC KABBALAH is associated with another Spanish kabbalist, ABRAHAM ABULAFIA (1239–after 1291).[44] This school was grounded in the intricacies of *Sefer Yetzirah* and the philosophy of Maimonides (1138–1204). It placed a strong emphasis on spiritual techniques for inducing alterations of consciousness that could result in powerful visionary, paranormal, or ecstatic phenomena. We know this not just from Abulafia's own writings but also from the unique first-person account of an anonymous pupil, written a few years after the master's death (1295).[45] Central to the spiritual techniques of this ecstatic school was the common (not specifically kabbalistic) exegetical technique known as *gematria*, as well as procedures involving letter "permutations" of the Hebrew alphabet according to a flexible system of rules and procedures. Surrounded by burning candles in the middle of the night, the solitary practitioner is described as combining his permutations with the recitation of divine names, specific ritual gestures and bodily postures, rhythmical breathing, inner pronunciation, and imaginal contemplation or inner perception.[46]

Kabbalists were active in southern France during the late twelfth and early thirteenth centuries, after which the tradition moved south, with the Spanish peninsula becoming the center of activity. The expulsion of the Jews from Spain by King Ferdinand and Queen Isabella, in 1492, was therefore bound to be a pivotal event. Many Jews emigrated to Italy, where some kabbalists came into contact with Christian intellectuals, as will be seen. Around the third decade of the sixteenth century, a new center of kabbalah took shape in Safed, Palestine, around the central figures of MOSES CORDOVERO (1522–70), ISAAC LURIA (1534–72), and his pupil HAYIM VITAL (1543–1620). A powerful new tradition of kabbalistic speculation and practice came into existence here, based on Luria's innovative concepts of *tsimtsum* (the idea that God had "contracted" or withdrawn part of himself to create an empty space for creation), *shevirah* (the catastrophic "breaking of the vessels" that could not manage to contain the enormous creative energies of divine Light), and *tikkun* (the difficult process of "rectification," undoing the damage and restoring the lost harmony of being). Luria also introduced a range of new practices and ceremonies, such as *yichudim* (the combination of divine names for such practical purposes as connecting with the souls of deceased saints or attaining prophetic gifts), *tikunim* (the rectification of the human soul and the divine), and concentration on the divine names during prayer, an activity known as *kavanot* ("intentions").[47]

Like most other kabbalistic systems, Lurianic kabbalah was based on a powerful myth of "exile and redemption" that obviously resonated with the traumatic history of the Jewish people, notably the 586 BCE destruction of the First Temple and the Babylonian captivity, the diaspora following the 70 CE destruction of the Second Temple, and now the most recent expulsion from Spain. In this light, it may not be surprising that the Lurianic kabbalah became a major new tradition in Jewish culture. Most notably, it became central to the messianic mass movement of SABBATEANISM that flourished in the Ottoman Empire from the mid-seventeenth century on. It was based on the activities of SABBATAI ZEVI (1626–76), who claimed to be the long-awaited Messiah but then converted to Islam—to the obvious puzzlement and shock of his followers. Many abandoned him, others rationalized his apostasy as a test of faith, while yet others (self-declared *ma'amīnīm*, "believers," called Dönme or "converts" by outsiders) kept faith in his messiahship and converted to Islam. Their beliefs and practices evolved into a mixture of Kabbalah and Sufism.[48] A century later, a charismatic figure from Poland called JACOB FRANK (1726–91) claimed to be the reincarnation of Sabbatai Zevi (and also of the biblical patriarch Jacob), becoming the leader of a large antinomian movement that rejected the Talmud as blasphemous, called for a systematic transgression of traditional moral boundaries, and adopted elements from Roman Catholicism.

During the eighteenth and nineteenth centuries, a new popular movement of pious Jewish revival was founded by the BA'AL SHEM TOV ("Master of the Good Name"; Israel ben Eliezer, 1698–1760). Known as HASIDISM,[49] it absorbed many traditional key elements of kabbalah. In this context, the emphasis moved from theosophical-exegetical speculation to ethics and a life of holiness, as exemplified by the *Zaddik*—the saintly "man of righteousness" who functions as a charismatic channel of divine wisdom for the community. But ecstatic practices remained important in Hasidism, next to the magical use of divine names.[50] Hasidism received strong opposition from the Lithuanian kabbalist

Elijah ben Solomon Zalman (1720–97) known as the VILNA GAON ("the sage from Vilnius") and his followers known as the *Misnagdim* ("opponents"). Yet another school was created in Jerusalem by the Yemenite kabbalist SHALOM SHARABI (1720–77).[51] His system was based on Lurianic theories and meditative techniques and prayers such as the "unifications" (*yichudim*) and "intentions" (*kavanot*). It became the central school of kabbalah in this part of the world and remains active in Israel today. At this point, it may be relevant to mention that kabbalah and Hasidism were sharply rejected during the same period by the influential movement known as Jewish Enlightenment (*Haskalah*), which would have a tremendous impact on the new status of kabbalah as officially rejected knowledge.[52] In this framework, the historical-philological study of kabbalah was initiated by representatives of the so-called *Wissenschaft des Judentums*, who wanted to clean Judaism from backward superstitions. It is against such hostile *maskilic* ("enlightened") perspectives that Gershom Scholem established the modern study of Jewish kabbalah by using similar methods of philological criticism from a positive perspective.

Hasidic types of popular piety and a variety of other kabbalistic movements have continued to flourish throughout the twentieth century and into the twenty-first. But until recently, they were largely neglected by modern historians, most of whom saw traditional kabbalah as "the real thing" and did not have much sympathy for its modern continuations.[53] Only in recent years have scholars of kabbalah begun filling this large hiatus, but there is still a lot of work to be done. During the early twentieth century, several attempts were made to integrate kabbalah with modern ideologies. One notably example is ABRAHAM ISAAC KOOK (1865–1935), an orthodox rabbi with strong nationalist agendas who is considered one of the fathers of modern religious Zionism. Another important rabbi was YEHUDA ASHLAG (1885–1954), whose strong anti-capitalist and anti-imperialist leanings led to a religious form of anarcho-communism explained in kabbalistic terms. The new wave of scholarship focused on modern and contemporary kabbalah is now also calling attention, for instance, to modern kabbalistic circles in Jerusalem (mostly followers of Shalom Sharabi),[54] modern ultra-orthodox Hasidic movements such as MENAHEM MENDEL SCHNEERSON's (1902–94) famous Habad-Lubavitscher community in New York (but now spread all over the globe),[55] the complicated processes of interaction between Jewish kabbalah and modern esoteric or occultist currents of non-Jewish provenance,[56] as well as contemporary forms of "New Age" kabbalah such as Michael Laitman's BNEI BARUCH and the American KABBALAH CENTER created by Philip and Karen Berg, both based on the teachings of Rabbi Ashlag. These organizations seek to promote kabbalah among both Jewish and non-Jewish audiences, famously attracting the attention of media celebrities such as Madonna or Ariana Grande.[57]

Islamic Esotericism

After the victory of Christianity during the fourth century CE, the great pagan traditions of late Hellenistic culture entered a period of steep decline in the Latin West. A symbolic date is 529, when the last Platonic Academy, in Athens, was closed by the Byzantine emperor Justinian I. By now, the Eastern part of the Christian empire reached far into Asia Minor and all along the coast of Syria and Palestine, extending from there to Egypt and the whole of northern Africa. But the map changed dramatically with the meteoric rise of Islam during the seventh century—within just a few decades after Muḥammad's death in 632 CE, the Byzantine Empire had lost many of its territories to the new Arabic empire and then the Islamic Caliphate. This means that intellectuals during the early centuries of Islam (not just Muslims but also Jews, Christians, and Zoroastrians) had easy access to a wealth of Greek as well as Persian or Sanskrit manuscripts that were widely available in these parts of the world. Together, they covered all the overlapping domains of what we would think of today as philosophy, science, and religion or spirituality. Therefore it is no surprise that most of these late Hellenistic traditions (whether Jewish, Christian, Platonic, Pythagorean, Gnostic, or Hermetic, not to mention new religions of the period such as Manichaeism) became factors of enormous importance to the cultural and intellectual development of Islam.[58] While Christian Europe went through its famous "dark" or "middle" ages, between the end of the Roman Empire and the European Renaissance of "classical" Greek culture, Islamicate cultures from West Africa to North India enjoyed several Renaissances of their own in which esotericism and the occult sciences played roles of major importance. It is important to be aware that, during the early modern period, the Islamic part of the Greater West encompassed no less than circa one-third of the global human population.[59]

To begin with, it is not widely known that the Islamic tradition known as TWELVER or IMAMI SHIʿISM (today the largest branch of Shiʿi Islam) began as a thoroughly esoteric type of speculation and practice focused on the attainment of *gnōsis*.[60] The human faculty for spiritual knowledge known as *ʿaql* (strictly equivalent to the faculty of *nous* known from later Platonic and Hermetic spirituality, as explained above)[61] was key to the attainment of supreme divine wisdom, as embodied in exemplary fashion by the twelve acclaimed Imams who succeeded the Prophet through his daughter Fāṭima and son-in-law ʿAlī, the first Imam. It was believed that they were preceded by a long series of pre-Islamic prophets, from Adam through such famous names as Enoch, Noah, Abraham, Moses, Joseph, and Jesus. Of central importance to these and many other forms of esotericism in Islamic contexts was the distinction between two types of exegesis, one that focused on the ẒĀHIR (exterior, apparent, exoteric meaning) of a verse or word and one that was looking for its BĀṬIN (interior, hidden, esoteric meaning).[62] This distinction was applied eventually not just to Quranic exegesis but to the whole of reality in all its dimensions.

Various forms of early Imami esotericism were based on elaborate mythologies of how the primordial divine Light is disseminated to create the cosmos, leading to a fundamental division and strife between spiritual "entities of light and knowledge" and their opponents, "entities of darkness and ignorance." Thanks to the faculty of *ʿaql*, the former can perceive God with "the eye of the heart," thereby emulating the example of the Imam, who appears in these contexts as the Divine Guide, supreme Master, and Thaumaturge who embodies initiatory esoteric Knowledge (*ʿilm*) and possesses enormous wonder-working (*ʿajāʾib*) powers. Like the Jewish "descenders to the chariot," the Imams were said to leave their bodies on a regular basis, as their souls ascended to God's celestial throne; and like later kabbalists, they, too, were seen as masters of the esoteric science of numbers and letters. Around the tenth century CE, these perspectives, aligned to the "Qumm school" of Twelver Shiʿism, were faced with violent opposition by the "rationalizing" perspectives of Muʿtazilism and the "Baghdad school" of theology. As these latter perspectives prevailed, the original esotericism of the *Imami* tradition fell into oblivion and became somewhat marginalized in later Shiʿi historiographies until the early modern period. Rather similar types of esotericism, reminiscent of Syrian Christianity and Sethian "gnosticism," are reported from Shiʿi groups referred to as GHULĀT ("extremists"), who believed in the transmigration of souls and flourished in eighth-century Iraq. Some of them migrated from there to Syria during the tenth century and created a sectarian movement known as the NUṢAYRIYYA (after the name of one of their founders, Muḥammad b. Nuṣayr).[63]

The second largest branch of Shiʿi Islam today is known as the ISMAʿILIS. If anything, they are even more esoteric in their basic orientation (in fact, they were commonly stereotyped and even persecuted by their enemies as *bāṭiniyya* in a pejorative sense, "the esotericists of Islam"[64]). During their own "golden age" (tenth to eleventh century CE), they dominated a vast empire known as the Fatimid caliphate over the whole of North Africa and the eastern Mediterranean. The Ismaʿili worldview was based, again, on a fundamental distinction between the exoteric (*ẓāhir*) and the esoteric (*bāṭin*) dimensions of the Quran and of religious commandments or prohibitions. While everything on the level of *ẓāhir* was subject to historical change and transformation, the hidden spiritual truths of *bāṭin* were considered to be immutable and eternal. They were seen as common to Judaism, Christianity, and Islam but revealed only to an elite of initiates bound to secrecy. The characteristic Ismaʿili type of esoteric hermeneutics was known as *taʾwīl*, or "tracing back to the source," and often relied on the occult properties of letters and numbers. On these foundations, the Ismāʿīlīs developed cosmological systems and views of sacred history that are clearly indebted to Greek-Hellenistic, Jewish, Christian, and "gnostic" models. In a specifically Abrahamic mode, they looked forward to the future age of the messianic savior (the *Mahdī*), during which time there would no longer be a distinction between *ẓāhir* and *bāṭin* because the hidden truth would be manifest to all.

Spiritual contemplatives and ascetics focused on the "inner life" were present in Islam already during the Prophet's lifetime and could be seen as early ancestors of SUFISM. This major tradition is mostly associated with Sunni Islam, although plenty of Shiʿi Sufis exist as well, and is of great importance to esotericism in Islamic contexts.[65] Preceded by eighth-century "proto-Sufis," such as AL-ḤASAN AL-BAṢRĪ, ʿABD AL-WĀḤID B. ZAYD, or the famous female ascetic RĀBIʿA AL-ʿADAWIYYA, among the most important early Sufis to appear in the ninth century CE were the Egyptian of Nubian descent DHŪ L-NŪN (d. 859/60 CE) and his follower SAHL AL-TUSTARĪ (d. 896 CE). DHŪ l-Nūn came from Akhmīm (Panopolis), where Zosimos had been active during the third century CE, and we have good reason to assume that he passed on at least some parts of an original Hermetic tradition that combined alchemy with spiritual pursuits.[66] Suhrawardī, the first Muslim author to develop a theory of *gnōsis* (*ma'rifa*),[67] would later hail him as the essential link in a golden chain that led from Hermes Trismegistus, Empedocles, and Pythagoras by way of Dhū l-Nūn and al-Tustarī to himself.

Meanwhile, Baghdad had become a major center of intellectual and cultural efflorescence, during a long period of time that is popularly (although controversially) known as the "Golden age of Islam." It ran from the mid-eighth century to the brutal end of the Abbasid caliphate with the Mongol sack of the capital in 1258. Among many Sufis who were active here during this period, perhaps the most central figure was Abū 'l-Qāsim al-Junayd, who expounded a "science of God's oneness" (*'ilm al-tawḥīd*, literally "science of One-making") combined with a typology of ritually induced altered states (*aḥwāl*).[68] A particularly interesting aspect of Sufi literature in this period was its strong tradition of erotic speculation focused on divine love. Among the visionaries in this lineage who are known for their extreme expressions of divine frenzy or "intoxication," the most famous are Abū Yazīd al-Bisṭāmī and al-Ḥusayn al-Ḥallāj, the Sufi martyr who was crucified in 922 CE for having declared himself to be God (*anā 'l-ḥaqq*, "I am the Real [i.e. God]"). Some figures who have been somewhat neglected by standard Sufi historiography seem particularly interesting from the perspective of esotericism research. See notably the impressive visionary accounts by Muḥammad b. 'Abd al-Jabbār al-Niffarī (d. after 977 CE), the complicated mythical-theosophical system elaborated by al-Ḥakīm al-Tirmidhī (d. around 932 CE), and the original although obscure cosmology and metaphysics of Ibn Masarra al-Jabalī (d. 931 CE), an early Muslim Pythagorean.[69] Certainly the most famous and influential figure of classical Sufism is the great Sunni theologian Abū Ḥāmid al-Ghazāli (d. 1111), whose strong interest in esoteric topics (and hostility to the Isma'ilis) is evident throughout his oeuvre, including his "Niche for the Lights" (*Mishkāt al-anwār*) and his "Epistle on Divine Knowledge" (*al-Risāla alladuniyya*).[70]

We already saw that Abbasid imperial culture was marked by intense study of the occult sciences, with the "House of Wisdom" in Baghdad as its most important center.[71] Countless Greek manuscripts that were neglected and forgotten during the "middle ages" of the Latin West were preserved and studied in the Islamicate world by Muslims as well as Jews and Christians (especially Nestorians fleeing from persecution) who translated them directly from Greek or via Syriac into Arabic.[72] Particularly important texts in this regard were the so-called *Theology of Aristotle* (actually containing paraphrases of Plotinus's *Enneads*), the Kindī-circle's *Sirr-al-asrār* (later translated as *Secreta secretorum*, "The Secret of Secrets"), and a corpus known as the pseudo-Aristotelian Hermetica[73] – at closer scrutiny, much that was understood to be "Aristotelian" turns out to have been rather (Neo)Platonic or Hermetic.[74] As regards this boom of the occult sciences under the Abbasid imperial aegis, we should mention at least the influential Central Asian astrologer Abu Ma'shar al-Balkhī (797–887 CE, known as Albumasar in the Latin West); the Iraqi philosopher Ya'qūb ibn 'Isḥāq al-Kindī (c. 801–873 CE), whose most famous work on universal radiation, *Risāla fī shu'ā'āt* ("Epistle on Rays," not preserved in Arabic), became known in Latin as *De radiis*; the encyclopedic corpus of natural philosophy and the occult sciences on Neopythagorean foundations that was produced by an anonymous coterie of Iraqi philosopher-bureaucrats and is known as the *Rasā'il Ikhwān al-Ṣafā'* ("Epistles of the Brethren of Purity"); and the famous compendium *Ġāyat al-ḥakīm* ("The Goal of the Sage"), which circulated anonymously but appears to have been written by the Andalusian Maslama al-Qurṭubī (d. 964 CE) and would become known in the Latin world as the *Picatrix*.[75]

A figure of great importance for the history of esotericism is the Iranian thinker Shihāb al-Dīn al-Suhrawardī (1154–1191 CE), known as the founder of a Neoplatonic school in philosophy usually translated as Illuminationism. Having studied Peripatetic philosophy and theology in the tradition of Ibn Sīnā (Avicenna), he was wandering through northern Syria and Anatolia when Aristotle himself appeared to his inner gaze in a luminous vision. The revelation left Suhrawardī convinced that true knowledge could not be gained through rational thought or scientific demonstrations but required an unmediated experience of spiritual Light to which he referred as "knowledge by presence." In his magnum opus, *Ḥikmat al-ishrāq* ("The Philosophy of Illumination"), he claimed that this supreme truth had been passed on through an initiatic chain of wisdom teachers that had begun in Egypt with Hermes Trismegistus and had reached him through Dhū l-Nūn and his successors. Thus Suhrawardī is a strong example of how the tradition of Platonic Orientalism not just continued in an Islamic context but expanded massively from West Africa to Southeast Asia, with multiple local adaptations that remain unexplored by scholars.[76]

A second towering figure is the Andalusian Sufi teacher Muḥyī al-Dīn Ibn al-'Arabī (1165–1240 CE), who is sometimes called "al-Shaykh al-Akbar" ("the Supreme Master") and responsible more than anyone else for theorizing sainthood in relation to both prophethood and empire. He was born in Murcia but, due to the *Reconquista*, emigrated east to Egypt, Syria, and Anatolia, spending the final part of his life teaching in Damascus.[77] A staggering number of writings have been attributed to him, with contents that range from Sufi practice, metaphysics, the nature of the soul and of time, prophecy, poetry, and prayers to impressive dreams and visionary experiences. A fusion of Ibn 'Arabi's theosophy with Suhrawardī's Illuminationism became the dominant form of Neoplatonism in the Persianate part of the Greater West.[78] One particular passage about the *'ālam al-mithāl* ("world of the image" or *mundus imaginalis*) that appears in his largest and most famous work, *Al-Futūḥāt al-Makkiyya* ("The Meccan Openings," originally in thirty-seven volumes),[79] became famous in modern European contexts during the 1970s, because of an extremely influential article written by Henry Corbin[80] – to such an extent that this *mundus imaginalis* is often believed to be the essence of Ibn 'Arabī's esotericism. In fact, it is just one particular aspect of a multifaceted oeuvre that is designed to be inaccessible to noninitiates and can therefore be very hard to understand even for Arabic readers.[81]

Ibn 'Arabī and an important Andalusian contemporary, Abū al-'Abbās Aḥmad al-Būnī (d. around 1225–33), introduced a new discipline to the Islamicate East that had already been under developments for some time in the relatively isolated West and was initially known as *'ilm al-ḥurūf wa-l-asmā'*, "the science of letters and names," or simply Lettrism ("letter science") in later centuries—the coeval twin of Jewish kabbalah.

Al-Būnī's seminal importance has been recognized just very recently.[82] The later grimoire *Shams al-ma'ārif al-kubrā* ("Greater Sun of Gnoses"), incorporating original material, was attributed to him, and became even more popular than the *Ġhāyat al-ḥakīm* (*Picatrix*), remaining the ultimate icon of Islamic magic today.[83] In the period after the Mongol invasion of Baghdad in 1258, lettrism became central to what can be called an Occult-Scientific Revolution[84] that spread throughout the Afro-Eurasian ecumene between the fourteenth and seventeenth centuries CE. Described in recent scholarship as a golden age of "Islamic occult humanism" on Neopythagorean and Neoplatonic foundations, well in advance of and then parallel to Italian Renaissance humanism and the European Scientific Revolution, it has been severely neglected and still remains largely unexplored.[85]

With explicit reference to their famous tenth-century predecessors (see above), these intellectuals appear to have thought of themselves as the New Brethren of Purity, to signal the similarity between that earlier project and their own, inspired by pseudepigrapha such as notably the *Sirr al-asrār* (see above).[86] Among a large group of Persianate intellectuals,[87] three authors stand out as particularly significant pioneers in this domain. Ṣā'in al-Dīn 'Alī b. Muḥammad Turka Iṣfahānī Khujandī (d. 1432), known as Ibn Turka, was the foremost occult and explicitly Pythagorean philosopher of Timurid Iran.[88] 'Abd al-Raḥmān al-Bisṭāmī (d. 1454) was of similar importance in the context of the Ottoman Empire. Maḥmūd Dihdār Shīrāzī (fl. 1576), who served the Safavids, was the most prolific Persian author on lettrism in the sixteenth century. All three were influential figures at Islamic courts, whose work played a major role in shaping early modern imperial cultures in the Islamicate world.[89]

Practice of the occult sciences in these contexts had to be combined with spiritual regimes such as ritual purity and seclusion, sensory and sleep deprivation, mantras, fasting, and a vegetarian diet, so as to achieve altered states of consciousness in which new experimental designs and even entire new sciences could be revealed by means of visions and dreams.[90] A similar focus on altered states continued to be central also in the Illuminationist tradition, which generally embraced the occult sciences, especially lettrism. An excellent example is the Iranian Twelver Neoplatonic philosopher Sayyid Muḥammad Bāqir Ḥusaynī Astarābādī (d. 1631), commonly referred to as Mīr Dāmād. He has left us descriptions of dazzling out-of-body experiences through which his soul traveled beyond space and time toward the utterly transcendent "capital of being" (*miṣr al-wujūd*).[91]

Popular occultist manuals or pulp grimoires attributed to "Mīr Dāmād the Great" are still circulated in cheap paper editions and online today, which brings us to the question of modern and contemporary traditions of Islamic esotericism. This remains a badly underresearched domain, largely because esotericism and the occult sciences received bad press in Orientalist scholarship after the seventeenth century, under the impact of European Enlightenment and Christian missionary polemics, together with certain later reformist movements in the Islamic world. But other movements of Islamic reform remained explicitly occultist throughout the nineteenth century[92]; and there is no doubt that esoteric or occultist traditions and practices are very much alive in modern Islamic societies, including those that are officially hostile to such pursuits. An excellent example is the more or less New Age-ish culture of spiritual practice based on traditional Islamic esotericism in contemporary Iran.[93]

Finally, it is important to be aware that Sufi traditions became popular in European and American culture during the nineteenth century and thus embarked on entirely new careers in modern esoteric and occultist contexts inspired by such movements as the Theosophical Society, Traditionalism, or new psychological-therapeutic phenomena like Gurdjieffianism and the New Age.[94] Apart from the significant impact it has exerted on such non-Sufi esoteric traditions, Sufism itself has taken on many different shapes since the twentieth century as well. Non-Muslims may often not be aware of how large some of these communities really are, and may be surprised by their reach and influence, among immigrant communities and citizens with North African origins in Europe and indeed on a global scale. The QĀDIRIYYA BŪDSHĪSHIYYA, literally "the Brotherhood of Qādir" (i.e., ʿAbd al-Qādir al-Jīlānī [1077–1166] resp. his eighteenth-century successor, *sīdī* ʿAlī Qādirī), was founded in 1952 and expanded from a small elitist group into a mass movement that today counts its followers and sympathizers in the hundreds of thousands in Morocco and Western Europe.[95] Another large Sufi movement is the SHĀDHILIYYA DARQĀWIYYA ALĀWIYYA (a title made up of the family names of three foundational figures, as is also the case with the two further movements mentioned below). Founded in 1911 by the charismatic Algerian Shayk Aḥmad Ibn Muṣṭafā al-ʿAlawī (1869–1934), under the leadership of the "iconoclastic" Shayk Khaled Bentounes (b. 1949) it developed since 1975 as a movement marked by tolerance and deliberate openness toward the non-Muslim world.[96] The globally successful NAQSHBANDIYYA-ḤAQQĀNIYYA, founded in 1973 by the Cyprian Shayk *Nazim Nāẓim ʿĀdil al-Qubrusī* (1922–2014) and prominently present on the internet,[97] seeks to spread a message of "love, beauty and peace" very much in line with popular New Age spirituality.[98] These spiritual perspectives stand in sharp contrast with the severely anti-modernist AḤMADIYYA-IDRĪSIYYA SHĀDHILIYYA. Founded by the strict Guénonian Abd al-Wahid Pallavicini (1926–2017) during the 1980s, and strongly aligned in Italy with the political right and conservative parties, it is now opening up to other Muslim perspectives than the strict Traditionalism of its founder.[99]

The European Renaissance

As the European Renaissance was gathering momentum toward the second half of the fifteenth century, a series of creative and influential thinkers took up the task of synthesizing Platonism and other major traditions of ancient "pagan" philosophy with the newly discovered Jewish kabbalah and the occult sciences that had been cultivated and partly invented in the Islamic world—all in a cultural context that took for granted that Christian theology must be wholly superior to Jewish and Islamic religious beliefs.[100] This became the basis for what modern scholars have called the "basic referential corpus" of esotericism in modern European culture.

This impressive wave of intellectual exploration and creative innovation was in fact a side effect of military conquests and geopolitical changes involving the three great monotheistic religions and, more in particular, the shifting balance of power between Christianity and Islam. We have seen that the Christian *reconquista* of the Iberian Peninsula, with the fall of Toledo in 1085 as a pivotal event, led to a flood of translations from Arabic sources that were to revolutionize the natural sciences in the Latin West. A few centuries later, the armies of the Ottoman Empire were advancing from the East, culminating in the conquest of Constantinople in 1453 that brought Byzantium under Islamic dominion. In response to the political expansion of Islam, great numbers of ancient Greek manuscripts were brought from Byzantium to Italy, thus kick-starting the momentous revival of Platonic and Hermetic speculation that is central to the European Renaissance and modern European esotericism. Meanwhile the Catholic monarchs Isabella I of Castile and Ferdinand II of Aragon, who had married their kingdoms together in 1469, were pursuing a virulent anti-Jewish and anti-Muslim policy that culminated in the expulsion of the Jews from Spain in 1492 and of the Muslims in 1609. All of the Muslims and many Jews migrated south or east to the Ottoman realm. As for kabbalists from Spain, as political pressure on them was mounting, many arrived in Italy already during the century's final decades. In a nutshell, the phenomenon of "Renaissance esotericism" resulted from the eagerness of Christian intellectuals to learn from all this newly available pagan and Jewish (but not Islamic)[101] literature in multiple languages, while attempting to integrate it all in a Greek neoclassicizing framework that remained deeply grounded in Roman Catholic theology and philosophy.

The story of Renaissance esotericism is dominated by a core group of influential intellectuals, surrounded by extensive networks of lesser thinkers who adopted their ideas and developed them further. Among the indispensable founding figures, the earliest one is the Byzantine philosopher GEORGIOS GEMISTOS (1355/60–1452?), who came to call himself PLETHON.[102] He arrived in Florence in 1437, as part of the Byzantine delegation that had sailed to Italy to attend the great Council of Ferrara and Florence. Politicians and theologians from East and West were coming together in a desperate but ultimately unsuccessful attempt to overcome their differences and unite against the threat of Islam.[103] Plethon was around eighty years old at that time. He made a big impression in the humanist circles of Florence, due to his personality and his superior firsthand knowledge of Plato and Aristotle. Calling special attention to the *Chaldaean Oracles* (discussed under theurgy, above), he extolled them as supreme examples of the ancient religion that had been continued by the Platonists. More precisely (but incorrectly, as we know today), he claimed that the Oracles had been written in very ancient times by none other than Zoroaster, the ancient chief of the Zoroastrian Magi. All of this made Plethon appear to his contemporaries as a prophet and living embodiment of Platonic Orientalism—a Platonist who actually came from the East and taught that the legendary Persian sage and inventor of magic had been the original fount of true spiritual wisdom. Plethon had no other choice than to present himself as a Christian, but most modern scholars believe that he was a Hellenistic pagan at heart, who hoped that the ancient religion of Zoroaster and Plato would soon replace the Christian church. Plethon's appearance in Florence was the opening shot in a long history of fascination with Zoroaster, who was widely imagined to have been a supreme authority of ancient wisdom.[104]

The second crucial figure is MARSILIO FICINO (1433–99), a humanist who had fallen in love with Platonic philosophy and whose great talents were discovered around 1460 by the ruler of Florence, Cosimo de' Medici (1389–1464). Having met Plethon at the time of the Council, Cosimo had been deeply impressed by his advocacy of Plato and the ancient wisdom. When a complete manuscript with Plato's dialogues arrived from Byzantium, Ficino was ordered to translate them into Latin. The task was finished in 1468, after which Ficino went on to summarize the essence of Platonic philosophy in a commentary on Plato's "Symposium" titled *De amore* ("On Love"), presenting it as eminently compatible with Christian truth.[105] With these and other seminal works, Ficino laid the groundwork for a large-scale revival of Platonism—or more precisely, Platonic Orientalism, based on the idea of a supreme ancient wisdom (known as *prisca theologia*, the ancient theology) that had come to Europe from the East. During the rest of his career, Ficino would translate a whole range of later Platonic authors as well, including Plotinus and Iamblichus. He also published a multivolume *Platonic Theology* that presented Platonism as the key to a project of Christian reform, revival, and renewal. The title itself was very daring, since it suggested that a pagan thinker like Plato was not just relevant to philosophy but should be accepted as an authority even by Christian theologians.[106]

Having just begun his labors on Plato, Ficino also translated the *Corpus Hermeticum*, from an incomplete manuscript that contained its first fourteen treatises.[107] First published in a clandestine version in 1471, it would be reprinted, translated, and retranslated in many new editions throughout the sixteenth century.[108] All of this was new and deeply exciting for Christian intellectuals all over Europe. Thanks to Ficino's activities as a translator and commentator, they now had access not just to Plato's complete works but also to what was widely believed to be the most ancient source of Egyptian wisdom, revealed by the legendary Egyptian sage Hermes Trismegistus. Interestingly though, Ficino himself stuck to Plethon's original perspective, by presenting not Hermes but the Persian Zoroaster, the supposed author of the "Chaldaean Oracles," as the most ancient and hence most authoritative wisdom teacher. During his later career, especially in an influential text known as *De Vita Coelitus Comparanda* ("On How to Harmonize Your Life with the Heavens," the third volume in his *De Vita*, "On Life"), he did pay considerable attention to Hermes as a teacher of astral magic, whose work could be used for the beneficial purposes of medical and psychological healing.[109]

The remaining treatises of the *Corpus Hermeticum* were translated, from another manuscript, by Ficino's younger contemporary LODOVICO LAZZARELLI (1447–1500). This minor humanist poet from San Severino was in fact an important and fascinating figure in his own right. He believed that the Hermetic Poimandres was identical to the divine *Logos* who had incarnated as Jesus Christ *and* had now returned to earth in the person of GIOVANNI "MERCURIO" DA CORREGGIO (1451?–after 1512). This wandering apocalyptic preacher had made a spectacular public appearance as the "Hermetic Christ," in the streets of Rome on Palm Sunday 1484. Lazzarelli also wrote a small masterpiece of Christian Hermetic literature, the *Crater Hermetis*, a spiritual dialogue about the pursuit of true felicity that would become a major influence on the much more famous Cornelius Agrippa (see below).[110] Neither of these works became available during Lazzarelli's lifetime, but they were printed by the humanist intellectuals JACQUES LEFÈVRE D'ÉTAPLES (c. 1450–1536) and SYMPHORIEN CHAMPIER (1471–1538) during the early sixteenth century and thus became part of the standard Renaissance corpus of Hermetic literature. Many authors now began to pick up the notion of a profound inner unity between the ancient pagan wisdom from the Orient, Platonic philosophy, Hermetic spirituality, and Christian theology. One prominent example is the Vatican librarian AGOSTINO STEUCO (1497/8–1548), who published the foundational Renaissance treatise on "perennial philosophy" (*De philosophia perennis*) in 1540. Another was FRANCESCO PATRIZI (1529–97), the author of a grand Platonic-Orientalist synthesis with the grandiose title *Nova de Universis Philosophia* ("New Philosophy of Everything"). It was published in 1591 but condemned by the Vatican three years later.

The third crucial innovator, next to Plethon and Ficino, was GIOVANNI PICO DELLA MIRANDOLA (1463–94). This intellectual prodigy created a much-publicized sensation in 1486. He wanted to invite intellectuals from all over Europe to engage him in a large public debate, presided over by no one less than the pope himself, about no fewer than 900 theses that he had written.[111] They demonstrated Pico's wide-ranging familiarity with all the major traditions of learned speculation in philosophy, theology, and science, including the "ancient wisdom" of the pagan philosophers, the occult sciences of the Arabs, and, most innovatingly, the Jewish kabbalah. But nothing ever came of the project. To Pico's alarm and great disappointment, Pope Innocent VIII responded by censoring thirteen theses and eventually condemning all of them, with special emphasis on those perceived as "renovating the errors of pagan philosophers" and those that were "cherishing the deceits of the Jews."

Pico's ambition had been to demonstrate that all the intellectual disputes between different philosophical and theological schools, including the rival systems of Platonism and Aristotelianism, could be resolved in a grand intellectual symphony of universal wisdom and truth. His project culminated in a sensational claim. All the foundational doctrines of Christianity could already be found, in a hidden "esoteric" fashion, not just in the ancient traditions of the pagan nations but also, most surprisingly and controversially, in the secret tradition of Jewish kabbalah that God had revealed to Moses at Mount Sinai. Regardless of his deep interest in pagan and Jewish as well as Arabic traditions, Pico's stated intention was to demonstrate the superiority of Roman Catholic doctrine once and for all. At the end of the great debate, as he must have imagined it in his mind, the pagan sages would be seen as bowing down symbolically before the truth of the gospel. Moreover, the Jews would convert quite literally, as it would dawn on them that Jesus was in fact the messiah who had been proclaimed by their own secret traditions all along. Pico's opening speech remained unpublished until after his death, when it appeared with a newly invented title that didn't come from him but that made his work famous: "Oratio on the Dignity of Man." Quoting the Hermetic *Asclepius* on its first page, Pico wrote in tones of great exaltation about the unique freedom of human beings to choose their own destiny for better or worse. Later generations would see his speech as a supreme manifesto of the new world-affirming mentality that was seen as typical of the Renaissance and modern liberal culture. In fact, Pico's Oratio as a whole is far more strongly indebted to traditional Christian values (combined with a remarkably perceptive understanding of Hermetic spirituality) than its countless later admirers have cared to admit.[112]

Pico stands at the origin of at least two new and distinct but intimately related developments in Renaissance esotericism. One of them is the complex speculative tradition of NUMBER SYMBOLISM, not to be confused with "numerology" as a divinatory practice. Much indebted to Neopythagorean traditions, but easily combined with Jewish-kabbalistic and Arabic-Lettrist forms of speculation, it assigned *qualitative* meanings or virtues to the first ten decimals, which could then be interpreted (somewhat similar in that regard to the ten kabbalistic *sefirot*) as constitutive of reality in all its dimensions.[113] During the early years of what would become known as the scientific revolution, such speculations were enormously attractive to intellectuals in search of universal patterns and hidden structures. Some of them believed they might be the key to a universal hermeneutics that would allow humanity to decode God's own handwriting both in Scripture and the work of Creation.

The other major tradition that flourished in the wake of Pico's work is known as CHRISTIAN KABBALAH. In their efforts to understand the hidden dimensions of Creation and Scripture, Jewish kabbalists had developed a set of unique concepts and approaches, such as the system of ten *sefirot*, while popularizing exegetic techniques such as *gematria*, based on the assignment of numerical values to the letters of the Hebrew alphabet. Christian intellectuals after Pico began using these elements in their own religious frameworks. Similar to the case of number symbolism, these novel techniques allowed them to perceive previously unsuspected but quite sensational mysteries and hidden structures, not just in their own sacred scriptures but even in the natural world all around them. Such a perspective resonated quite naturally with older beliefs that divine truth could be found in the two parallel "books" of divine revelation, Holy Scripture and the Book of Nature. The chief pioneer of Christian kabbalah after Pico was the German JOHANNES REUCHLIN (1455–1522), famous as the most prominent Christian Hebraist of his day. In his early volume *De verbo mirifico* ("On the Word That Works Miracles," 1494), he claimed that the Tetragrammaton (יהוה YHWH) concealed the name of Jesus as its hidden secret, because by adding the vowel *shin* in the middle, it could be read as יהשוה YOSHUA. Reuchlin's most important work, *De arte cabalistica* ("On the Art of the Kabbalah," 1517), went straight against the strong anti-Jewish tenor of this period, by casting a fictional Jewish kabbalist in the positive role of a teacher of wisdom. As the first systematic treatise of kabbalah written by a Christian, it has been called "the bible of the Christian kabbalists."[114]

As a new, extremely rich, but also very difficult intellectual and exegetical tradition, Christian kabbalah was of enormous interest to major thinkers throughout the sixteenth and seventeenth centuries.[115] Here I will mention just a few names. The French polymath GUILLAUME POSTEL (1510–81), a linguistic virtuoso and messianic prophet who believed he had discovered the messiah incarnated as a woman, was deeply involved in both the symbolism of numbers and Christian kabbalah.[116] The German Hebraist CHRISTIAN

Knorr von Rosenroth (1636–89) is best known for his extremely influential large volume *Kabbala Denudata* ("The Kabbalah Unveiled," 1677–8), one of the most important sources of kabbalistic materials for later non-Jewish esoteric and occultist authors. He was closely associated with Francis Mercury van Helmont (1614–1698), an important Christian kabbalist involved in intellectual networks that ranged from Anne Conway and Henry More to John Locke and Leibniz.[117]

The most famous and influential attempt at integrating both the philosophical and scientific traditions of antiquity in a comprehensive Christian-kabbalistic framework was published by the German humanist Heinrich Cornelius Agrippa (1486–1535/6) under the title *De occulta philosophia libri tres* ("Three Books of Occult Philosophy," 1533).[118] This work has often been dismissed as little more than a compendium or *summa* of all the available traditions of ancient learning (an encyclopedic overview that could be plundered at will for arcane information), but it was quite a bit more than that. Agrippa's three books were dealing with the three "worlds" or domains of reality according to the prevailing Ptolemaic system, which described the material cosmos as a gigantic sphere. The earth was located in its center, with the moon and the other planets circling around it, while the stars and astrological constellations were fixed on its interior surface. Agrippa's first book dealt with everything pertaining to our sublunar world made from the four elements of Aristotelian natural philosophy. The second book was about the more abstract realities pertaining to the "middle realm" of the planetary spheres in-between the moon and the fixed stars. Finally, the third book discussed the angelic and divine realities that were believed to exist beyond the cosmic globe. While Agrippa's first two books of Occult Philosophy were based on all the available knowledge from ancient and medieval sources, this final book was entirely dominated by Christian kabbalah. Agrippa would be remembered by later generations as a black magician in league with the devil (a model for Goethe's Faust), but in fact he was a deeply pious Christian who believed that only faith in Jesus Christ gave access to true knowledge.[119] Strongly influenced by Lazzarelli's Christian Hermetism, his true intention was to show a way of spiritual ascent that would lead the soul from the world of matter through all the heavenly spheres up to its final rebirth and unification with divinity.[120]

The young Agrippa had been strongly influenced by the Benedictine Abbot Johannes Trithemius (1462–1516), an important Renaissance pioneer of cryptography, demonology, and angelic magic. Although Agrippa's own work was a theoretical treatise rather than a practical manual (in contrast to an anonymous *Fourth Book of Occult Philosophy* that was later ascribed to him), it became an inspiration for occult practitioners who were working along similar lines. A notable example from a later generation is the Elizabethan magus and polymath John Dee (1527–1609), next to his collaborator Edward Kelley (1555–97/8).[121] Dee combined his studies of the natural sciences with an obsessive fascination for angelic invocations by means of visionary trance. He and Kelley, who had a talent for entering altered states, used a mantic technique known as "scrying" through which angelic beings would appear on the surface of a black mirror to answer questions and engage in lengthy conversations about religious, philosophical, and scientific matters. A particularly spectacular outcome of these sessions consisted in a completely new "Enochian" language that has remained a source of fascination for occultists to the present day.[122] Another major synthesizer of Renaissance occult philosophy and all its related traditions, notably alchemy and Christian kabbalah, was the German HEINRICH KHUNRATH (c. 1560–1605). He is best known for a masterful compendium of wisdom traditions with a series of spectacular illustrations, *Amphitheatrum Sapientiae Aeternae* ("Amphitheatre of Eternal Wisdom").[123]

Agrippa's great synthesis was still based on the traditional geocentric cosmos. But toward the end of the sixteenth century, due to the discoveries by Copernicus published in his *De revolutionibus orbium coelestium* ("On the Revolvings of the Celestial Spheres," 1543), the closed world of the middle ages began to give way to our modern vision of an infinite universe with an infinite number of solar systems. Because all the ancient and medieval philosophers and scientific thinkers had taken the pre-Copernican model for granted, this cosmological revolution was bound to have a major impact on how Renaissance thinkers looked at the authoritative claims of ancient authorities.

This can be seen in exemplary fashion in the work of GIORDANO BRUNO (1548–1600), perhaps the most brilliant and innovative thinker among all the Renaissance figures discussed in this section. Bruno realized that if the universe is infinite, this must have enormous implications for how we think about God and his relation to humanity and the cosmos. Had someone asked Agrippa, "where can I find God?," he would have pointed his finger to the sky above—for simply by moving upward through the seven planetary spheres that surrounded the earth, and then further beyond the sphere of the fixed stars, our souls were bound to arrive in the eternal heavenly world of angelic and divine realities that were believed to reside beyond the material cosmos. But in Bruno's infinite post-Copernican universe, such an answer was clearly no longer possible. Having left the earth's atmosphere and our solar system, the soul would keep traveling through empty space for all of eternity, without ever exiting the cosmos to meet God or the angels! All one could ever expect to encounter was a never-ending series of further solar systems. If this was true, then what had happened to God and his angelic heavens? *Where had they gone*? For many centuries, their presence had been taken for granted. But now, all of a sudden, there was no space left in the universe where they still could exist.

Bruno's large and multifaceted oeuvre is based on a persistent and radical attempt to rethink all the ancient and medieval philosophical and scientific traditions, systematically and from the bottom up.[124] Thus in *De gli' eroici furori* ("On the Heroic Frenzies," 1585), a brilliant multimedia work of creative speculation that combines philosophical dialogues with poetry, mythology, and emblematic imagery, divinity appears as a universal feminine reality that is invisibly present in the world of the senses.[125] In *Spaccio della bestia trionfante* ("The Expulsion of the Triumphant Beast," 1584), we read how the Greek gods intervene in the world by rearranging the astrological constellations.[126] Yet other texts by Bruno are dealing with magic, such as *De vinculis in genere* ("On Bonds in General," 1591),[127] and many of them are related to the so-called "Art of Memory" or traditional mnemonics, next to the original system of the Catalan author RAMON LLULL (1232/3–1316).[128] For a radical thinker like Bruno, it was not an option to stop at the sacred truths of Christian orthodoxy. He was arrested by the Venetian Inquisition in 1592 and spent eight years imprisoned in Rome. After a famous heresy trial, Bruno was burnt at the stake in public at the Campo de' Fiori on February 17, 1600. To pursue the path of "rejected knowledge" was not just a matter of theoretical reflection—sometimes it could literally cost you your life.[129]

Naturphilosophie and Christian Theosophy

All the Renaissance thinkers discussed above were deeply erudite intellectuals, engaged in the bookish project of synthesizing pagan, Jewish, and Arabic traditions with Christian theology and contemporary philosophy or natural science. This tradition emanated from humanist Italy as its intellectual heartland, was dominated by Roman Catholic authors, and typically took the shape of learned commentaries on the writings of ancient and venerable thinkers from antiquity and the middle ages. We now move to a second major tradition in early modern esotericism that is based on entirely different foundations. It was dominated by *German* thinkers who often wrote not in the Latin of the learned but in their own native language. Rather than appealing all the time to authorities from the ancient past, they came up with new, original, often highly creative speculative worldviews based on the authority of their *own* lived experience. More specifically, three key sources of knowledge moved to the center of attention. The first was *the bible*, the Word of God. The second was *Nature*, often referred to as a second "book," full of information from the Creator himself and written in a secret symbolic language. The third was a practice of silent *prayer and meditation*. God could make his will known to individuals in the innermost sanctuary of their hearts, by means of intimate visions or voices, illuminations or inspirations. The emphasis in this lineage shifts very clearly, although certainly not exclusively, from Roman Catholics to Protestant (mostly Lutheran) authors.

Next to the term "Theosophy" ("divine wisdom"), it is customary in this context to use the German term *Naturphilosophie* rather than its literal equivalent in English (which could just as easily refer to entirely different traditions in the "philosophy of nature"). Without any doubt, the foundational author is Theophrastus Bombastus von Hohenheim (1493/4–1541), a Swiss physician and chymical pioneer who called himself Paracelsus. Deeply influenced by alchemical literature and traditional "folk" medicine, he launched a frontal attack against the medical establishment of his time and its blind reliance on the outdated theories of Galen (129–c. 216 CE). Paracelsus told his colleagues that they should learn their craft not from dusty books but directly from Nature herself, by means of personal investigation and experimental methods. In his efforts to revolutionize medical practice, he introduced a new terminology that expanded on the traditional Aristotelian elements ("earth, water, air and fire") by adding a new triad of "mercury, sulphur and salt." But Paracelsus did not stay with medicine alone. As Luther's Reformation was sweeping through Europe, he also began writing about religious and theological questions, motivated as always by a radical drive toward innovation. As he wrote deliberately in German, not the Latin of the intellectual elites, he has sometimes been called the "Luther of medicine" who caused a "reformation" all of his own. The Paracelsian tradition, also known as the "Chemical Philosophy," gathered countless adherents during the sixteenth and seventeenth centuries. Spreading beyond Germany to France and England, it became a major force of innovation in medicine and alchemy (or rather, "chymistry") as well as religion and spirituality. The development of esotericism in the early modern period would be unthinkable without Paracelsus.[130]

From around 1600 on, PARACELSIANISM also took the shape of an alternative religious current in conflict with the established churches. Sometimes referred to as "Theophrastia Sancta," it eventually became known as WEIGELIANISM, with reference to the dissenter VALENTIN WEIGEL (1533–88).[131] Paracelsus himself was cast in the role of a divinely inspired visionary who had revived a perennial tradition that had been practiced already by the apostles. From a somewhat similar perspective, the Silezian cobbler and merchant JACOB BÖHME (1575–1624) produced an oeuvre of impressive depth and originality that laid the foundations for a central current in the history of European esotericism, CHRISTIAN THEOSOPHY.[132] Driven by a heartfelt desire to understand how a benevolent God could have created a world so full of evil and suffering, Böhme had an impressive experience of divine illumination in 1600, followed by a second one ten years later. In his attempts to understand these powerful visions and work out their implications, he developed a dramatic spiritual cosmogony filled with alchemical and Paracelsian references and symbolism. God had not created the world out of nothing but had himself been born from the unfathomable primal mystery of the *Ungrund* (the "Unground"). God's body, also referred to as "Eternal Nature," was depicted as a luminous substance composed of two complementary "Principles"—an original dark and wrathful core (the First Principle, associated with God the Father) was eternally redeemed and rendered harmless by the force of Light and Love (the Second Principle, associated with God the Son). Lucifer, the greatest of the angels, had been born as a perfect creature of Light in the midst of Eternal Nature. But in a catastrophic attempt to rise even higher, by forcing himself to be "reborn" like God, instead he found himself reborn from the Light as a creature of Darkness. This demonic reversal known as Lucifer's Fall destroyed the harmonious integrity of the divine world of Light and led to the birth of the material world in which we are living—the Third Principle. Instead of a perfect "Eternal Nature" beyond change and corruption, this is a fallen nature that has come under the dominion of time and space. In this world, the Wrath of the First Principle is now unleashed as a dark destructive force, in mortal combat with the Second Principle, the divine power of Light. Human beings are born as flawed and sinful entities in this dark and threatening world but have the potential to be reborn as creatures of Light. Thus our spiritual calling is to achieve an inner transmutation, modeled on the primordial birth of God, in a reversal of the Fall and its destructive effects. By being reborn as "sons of God" in subtle bodies of Light, we will not just be saving our own souls—as active participants in the great process of universal Reintegration, we will be assisting in nothing less than the restoration of God's own body to its original state of wholeness.

Written in a strange German filled with flashes of poetic vision, Böhme's works were widely disseminated already during his lifetime and caused him much trouble with the Lutheran authorities. Later during the seventeenth century, many spiritual dissenters took inspiration from Böhme's work and carried it into new directions. A major role in this respect was played by Böhme's biographer ABRAHAM VON FRANCKENBERG (1593–1652), his pupil or "spiritual and philosophical son" GEORG LORENZ SEIDENBECHER (1623–63), and the latter's acquaintance FRIEDRICH BRECKLING (1629–1711), a millenarian thinker who stood at the center of a large network of Christian-Theosophical enthusiasts. Many of these Böhmian freethinkers came to the Netherlands, because of its comparatively tolerant climate, resulting in small Theosophical communities around Breckling in Zwolle, JOHANN WILHELM ÜBERFELD (1659–1732) in Leiderdorp, and JOHANN GEORG GICHTEL (1638–1710) in Amsterdam, whose group was known as the *ENGELSBRÜDER* ("Angelic Brethren").[133] Much remains unclear about exactly *how* these people were giving shape to their spiritual convictions on a daily basis, but we hear about intense ecstatic and visionary group experiences, often expressed in remarkably explicit erotic language, including experiences described as sensuous-spiritual "marriage" of the entire community with the divine Sophia, the feminine embodiment of wisdom.[134]

Of key importance in the transmission of Böhmian Theosophy to England was DIONYSIUS ANDREAS FREHER (1649–1728), who lived for a while with Überfeld in Leiden but later moved to London. He produced important works in English, based on Böhme's Theosophical system,[135] but is famous most of all for his extremely impressive visual images. WILLIAM LAW (1686–1761) would later use them as illustrations to what remains the standard English edition of Böhme's writings.[136] In England, a group that is known as the PHILADELPHIAN SOCIETY took shape around the Christian Theosophers JOHN PORDAGE (1607/8–1681) and JANE LEADE (1623–1704)—an early example of female charismatic leadership in European esotericism. Ecstatic and visionary experiences with a strong erotic dimension were central to these communities as well, reflecting an emphasis on gendered dynamics that was already evident in Böhme's works and runs through all these Christian-Theosophical traditions.[137] The most extreme example is an obscure German group around EVA VON BUTTLAR (1670–1721) that called itself the *Christliche und Philadelphische Soziëtat* ("Christian and Philadelphian Society") but is better known as the *BUTTLARSCHE ROTTE* ("Buttlarian Gang"). Amazingly, all its male members seem to have practiced ceremonial sex with "Mother Eve," to reenact the spiritual marriage of earthly man with the heavenly Sophia.[138]

The most important Christian Theosopher of the eighteenth century was FRIEDRICH CHRISTOPH OETINGER (1702–82). A Lutheran pastor with strong convictions, he was deeply distressed by the rising tide of philosophical rationalism and idealism associated with Gottfried Leibniz and Christian Wolff. Whereas these modern philosophies and scientific theories were based on a concept of pure disembodied reason, sharply opposed to matter and the body, Christians should insist on the core doctrine of divine *Incarnation*—the Word had become flesh. Oetinger's deeply incarnational Theosophy was based on Böhme and the kabbalah, both Christian and Lurianic. He also took a deep interest in the work of Immanuel Swedenborg (to be discussed below), until he discovered to his alarm that the Swedish visionary was defending precisely those post-Cartesian idealist doctrines to which he objected so much! Oetinger's alternative to the philosophical idealism of conventional Enlightenment thought consisted in a radicalization of Böhme's *Geistleiblichkeit* ("Spiritual Corporeality").[139]

The tradition of Christian Theosophy entered its "second golden age" by the final decades of the eighteenth century and continued further into the era of Romanticism and German Idealism. The French author LOUIS-CLAUDE DE SAINT-MARTIN (1743–1803, known as *le philosophe inconnu*, "the unknown philosopher") and the German FRANZ VON BAADER (1765–1841) were perhaps the most important creative thinkers in an emerging European network of Christian Theosophers who were rediscovering the works of Böhme while interpreting him in new ways, under the influence of contemporary developments such as German Idealist philosophy and the vogue of Mesmeric somnambulism (see below).[140] Saint-Martin and von Baader are profound and subtle authors, and their works became important underground classics in the emerging phenomenon of esoteric resistance against the rise of Enlightenment rationalism. Precisely the famous Age of Enlightenment (notably the final decades of the *ancien régime*, right before the French revolution of 1789) was also an age of intense esoteric activity. The *philosophes* were thinking of *les lumières* (the standard French term for the Age of Enlightenment) as referring to the Light of Reason, but their opponents were searching for spiritual enlightenment referred to as *illumination*. Unfortunately, almost all the significant scholarly research about these key traditions in the history of modern European esotericism is still only available in French and German, with very few reliable publications in the English language.[141]

Initiatic Societies

That "ancient wisdom" or "the mysteries of nature" have been transmitted and kept alive by wise men through the ages belongs to the central tenets of esotericism in Western culture. Prior to the seventeenth century, however, it does not seem to have occurred to anyone in Western Europe that such a transmission from one generation to the next might require an initiatic *organization* of some kind. We encounter this idea in 1614, in the first of the three so-called ROSICRUCIAN MANIFESTOS, the *FAMA FRATERNITATIS* ("The Call of the Brotherhood"). This is an anonymous text written in German although it carries a Latin title. It describes a mysterious organization that is said to have been founded, well before the time when Luther had started "purifying the church," by an elusive adept called "C.R." who would later be identified as "Christian Rosenkreutz." We are told that as a young man, he traveled widely all around the Mediterranean, first to Damcar, a mysterious city in the Middle East, where he learned Arabic and received instruction in the occult sciences, then through Egypt and all along northern Africa to Fez in Marocco, and from there to Spain. He returned to Germany as a deep initiate in occult knowledge from "the Orient" and five years later decided to create a small brotherhood. In due time, its members decided to spread all over Europe, after having taken a vow to devote all their time to healing the sick without payment. Each member of the brotherhood should transmit his wisdom to a suitable successor, who in turn should pass it on to the next generation. In this manner, the initiatic chain of transmission would never need to be broken.

After one hundred years had passed, a member of the brotherhood is said to have discovered a secret crypt in Christian Rosenkreutz's house, with a tomb that held his body in a state of perfect preservation. The brotherhood now decided to come out into the open, announcing its existence to the general public by means of the *Fama Fraternitatis*. One year later, in 1615, it was followed by a *Confessio Fraternitatis* ("The Confession of the Brotherhood," this time written in Latin). It predicted an imminent new Reformation that would thoroughly transform the whole of European culture. As Luther's Reformation had led to doctrinal fragmentation and horrific bloodshed, a peaceful new attempt should now be made, this time by integrating the Hermetic sciences into Lutheran Christianity. A third and final manifesto, published in 1616, was quite different in nature. *Die Chymische Hochzeit Christiani Rosenkreutz* ("The Chymical Wedding of Christian Rosenkreutz") is a subtle and complex allegory of Christian transformation and spiritual rebirth, grounded deeply in alchemical and number symbolism. Its fictional protagonist was Christian Rosenkreutz, but the brotherhood played no role in it.[142]

We have no historical evidence that a Rosicrucian brotherhood really existed, let alone that Christian Rosenkreutz was a historical personality. Today the manifestoes are seen as a literary invention by the Lutheran theologian Johann Valentin Andreae (1586–1654) and his circle of friends in Tübingen. But they were eagerly read and widely discussed, because all of it was not just new but obviously very exciting! Could it really be true that a brotherhood of adepts was secretly active in Europe, a mysterious order of initiates endowed with superior wisdom and wielding awesome occult powers? We have a stunning number of published responses that cover the entire spectrum of possible opinions. While sceptics denounced the brotherhood as a hoax, others were convinced of its real existence. True believers praised the wisdom of Christian Rosenkreutz, while critics denounced his followers as dangerous heretics who must be in league with the devil. Many others were simply curious and would love to meet those mysterious brethren. One particular result of this entire Rosicrucian furor was that important authors in the field of ancient wisdom and the occult sciences, such as Robert Fludd (1574–1637) or Michael Maier (1569–1622), began identifying themselves as "Rosicrucians."[143] Ever since, esotericists who claim some special kind of hidden knowledge have kept following their example.

Fludd and Maier are both known for the impressive symbolic imagery that can be found in their published writings—combined even with poetry and music in Maier's multimedia volume *Atalanta Fugiens*.[144] Such well-known authors apart, it seems that some marginal groups involved in alchemical or related occult practices began calling themselves "Rosicrucian" as early as the later seventeenth century or the first half of the eighteenth, but the evidence is vague and ambiguous. The first irrefutable case of a Rosicrucian organization is the initiatic Order of *Gold- und Rosenkreuzer* ("Gold- and Rosicrucians"). It flourished in Germany in the second half of the eighteenth century and placed much emphasis on alchemical practice (whence the mention of gold in their name).[145] As the process of separation between church and state was gathering momentum, it now became possible for new religious or spiritual organizations to be more openly active, side to side with the established churches or even in competition with them. Ever since this period, new initiatic groups have come into existence that think of themselves as "Rosicrucian" and usually claim to be in possession of the true secrets of ancient wisdom.[146]

As regards their ritual and organizational frameworks, most of these new initiatic Orders took inspiration from FREEMASONRY. In Scotland by the end of the sixteenth century, the medieval guilds of stonemasons (connected originally to large building projects such as the gothic cathedrals) were transformed into a new kind of organization, with special rituals for the admission of new members and elaborate legends about the Craft's ancient history. In addition to the original membership of masonic workmen, so-called "Gentlemen Masons" began to be admitted over the course of the seventeenth century. As part of that development, the basic masonic repertoire was converted into a symbolic language for talking about spiritual and humanitarian pursuits. For instance, by thinking of themselves as humble yet important "stones" in the magnificent temple of the world, Freemasons could feel a personal responsibility to "work on themselves"—that is, to keep "polishing" and cultivating their characters or interior selves. As far as religion was concerned, they could think of God as the Grand Architect who had built the Universe on the basis of geometrical laws. It is important to realize that, at least up to the first decades of the eighteenth century, Freemasons were widely perceived by the general public as "Rosicrucians" and practitioners of alchemy. Quite obviously, this made their brotherhood a favorite object of curiosity and gossip—could it be that they had preserved the mysterious wisdom of antiquity, including the secret of the philosophers' stone?

Under the impact of Enlightenment thinking, Freemasons in England took their distance from such arcane interests and pursuits. Starting with the foundation of the Premier Grand Lodge of England, in 1717, they shaped their brotherhood into a social organization based on rational principles and humanitarian ideals. This type of Freemasonry has remained dominant in the Anglophone world, including the United States. But in other countries, most notably in France, alchemical and other "Hermetic" ideas or practices kept flourishing widely in masonic contexts. Having been initiated into the three standard degrees of Freemasonry ("Apprentice," "Fellowcraft," and "Master Mason"), masonic brethren could make further progress through elaborate systems of "higher degrees" that were full of esoteric symbolism. Many such higher-degree systems were created during the later eighteenth century, so for anybody who wanted to learn about hidden mysteries and ancient secrets, joining Freemasonry became the logical thing to do.[147]

Christian-Theosophical speculations in the tradition of Böhme enjoyed a new wave of popularity in such higher-degree systems during the Age of Reason, a phenomenon that is known as ILLUMINISM. Particularly important here was JEAN-BAPTISTE WILLERMOZ's (1730–1824) *RITE ÉCOSSAIS RECTIFIÉ* ("Rectified Scottish Rite") and its backgrounds in an initiatic order created by MARTINEZ DE PASQUALLY (1727–74), known as the *ELUS COËNS* ("Priests Elect")."[148] Very much in opposition to the *Zeitgeist* of rationalist philosophy and materialistic science, a large European network of Masonic-illuminist *hommes de désir* emerged during the decades before and after the Revolution.[149] Occultist movements from the late nineteenth and the twentieth centuries would later claim to continue these traditions, referred to as MARTINISM or MARTINEZISM in reference to Saint-Martin and Martinez de Pasqually. As for the Rectified Scottish Rite, it was revived in French Freemasonry and is still being practiced there today.[150]

Importantly, during the later eighteenth century, the prevailing class system was suspended in masonic lodge meetings; for instance, a member of the upper nobility might well be initiated by a Master who belonged to the working classes. As a result, the order of Freemasons became an attractive safe space for experimentation with the "dangerous" new ideas of social egalitarianism and democracy. As Freemasonry spread far beyond the Western world in the age of colonial expansion, it also functioned as an effective international network for travelers far from home, who could always be sure to find some local lodge where they would be welcomed by their fellow brethren. All of this made Freemasonry look like a society within public society, a supranational organization protected from the scrutiny of outsiders by its cultivation of secrecy. Not surprisingly, this evoked the suspicion of political authorities. In some cases, notably Adam Weishaupt's famous or notorious Order of *ILLUMINATEN* (a vehicle for radical politics and revolutionary ideas), there was some justification to such concerns.[151] We will return to that topic later.

Freemasons have always found it important to endow their order with an impressive historical pedigree—sometimes the institution of Freemasonry was traced as far back as Noah and his sons after the Flood! More in particular, many lodges developed an obsession with speculative historical lineages that would connect the ancient sects of the Essenes and Therapeutae to the medieval order of the KNIGHTS TEMPLAR. Because masonic ritual is grounded in architectural symbolism, with Solomon's Temple in Jerusalem as an ideal model of the perfect building, it is not surprising that Freemasons were interested in the medieval chivalric organization (created c. 1119) that had been charged with the Temple's defense. The basic storyline was that during the times of the crusades, Templar Knights in the Holy Land must have established contact with surviving branches of the Essenes or Therapeutae that had preserved ancient Oriental knowledge, including the supreme Pythagorean art of geometry that was essential to architectural work. After the dramatic dissolution of the Order in 1307, followed by the public execution of its last Grand Master Jacques de Molay in 1314, surviving Templars were believed to have carried its secrets with them to Scotland, often seen as the homeland of Freemasonry. This is how the ancient wisdom was supposed to have been passed on in secret through the ages, from ancient Pythagorean brotherhoods to the Essenes or Therapeutae, from there to the Knights Templar, and finally to the Freemasons—always opposed by the authoritarian forces of the religious and political establishment. This influential Templar legend led to the creation of not only special Templar degrees within Freemasonry but also non-masonic neo-Templar organizations that have flourished to the present day—not to mention a spectacular Templar mythology in popular literature, from Umberto Eco to Dan Brown and beyond.[152]

After the French Revolution, Freemasonry and other secret societies became a favorite target of CONSPIRACY THEORIES, beginning in 1797 with the conservative French Catholic Abbé Augustin Barruel and the British scientist John Robison.[153] They were blaming the spectacular collapse of traditional religious and political authority (based on the political union of "altar and throne") on subversive plots and machinations by sinister organizations such as the Freemasons and Weishaupt's *Illuminaten*.[154] This was the beginning of a long and extremely complicated history of esoteric and anti-esoteric conspiracy theories that has continued to the very present. We will see that new forms of esotericism and occultism became more prominent over the course of the nineteenth century, leading to widespread anxieties among the general public about what these groups might be up to in secret. For an excellent example, see the famous mystifications by LÉO TAXIL (ps. of Marie Joseph Gabriel Antoine Jogand-Pagès, 1854–1907) about Freemasonry as a worldwide diabolical cult opposed to the Roman Catholic church.[155] Due to the alarming rise of anti-Semitism during the later decades of the nineteenth century, Jews became major targets of suspicion as well, resulting in the influential myth of a Jewish-Masonic (but also occultist and diabolical) conspiracy.[156] The most notorious example of anti-Semitic conspiracy theory, an originally Russian forgery known as the *Protocols of the Elders of Zion*, had a major impact on Hitler and the Third Reich and remains disturbingly popular today.[157]

The Modernist Occult

With the "media revolution" of the eighteenth century, and the dwindling ability of church and state to censor voices of dissent, all the bodies of traditional literature that I have been discussing became available to larger and larger audiences. Next to a stream of skeptical literature that dismissed "the occult" as just a bunch of ridiculous superstitions, publishing entrepreneurs began catering to the public's curiosity about ancient secrets and forgotten mysteries.[158] The "modernist occult" is marked by complicated, multifaceted, and often paradoxical attempts to combine ancient and premodern sources or traditions with new ideas that come from post-Enlightenment science and rationalism. In other words, while occultists resisted the "disenchantment of the world," yet they felt deeply attracted by modern scientific models.[159] As society was moving with ever-accelerating speed into unpredictable new directions, they were bound to ask themselves whether the progress of humanity required a radical break with Tradition or, instead, a more complex transformation that would allow ancient truths to be perceived in a new light.

Not by any chance, the two most influential movements of innovation in esotericism during the nineteenth century had their origin in the work of Enlightenment scientists. The Swedish naturalist EMANUEL SWEDENBORG (1688–1772) studied philosophy, mathematics, physics, and applied mechanics and went on to produce an impressive oeuvre in the physical and organic sciences. Trained in the Cartesian philosophy of his day, with its strict separation between matter and spirit, he experienced a deep religious crisis in 1744. Forced to admit to himself that all his scientific explorations were leading him straight to the "abyss" of pure materialism and atheism, he prayed to God to save his soul and was granted a vision of Christ. After this pivotal event, he spent the rest of his life writing visionary works, in Latin, on the true meaning of the bible and the spiritual realities of heaven and hell. Deeply influenced by the Pietist distinction between "internal" and "external" truth, Swedenborg's theory of correspondences claimed that visible realities mirror invisible ones without any need for causal relations between the two. His works were filled with matter-of-fact descriptions of visionary travels to heaven and hell, including incredibly detailed conversations with spirits and angels. Followers created a Swedenborgian "New Church" after the visionary's death, which remains active today, but the influence of Swedenborg is by no means limited to that religious community. He has inspired a wide range of major writers, poets, painters, and even composers, and his basic ideas were picked up and developed into new directions by spiritualist, occultist, or metaphysical authors and practitioners throughout the nineteenth, twentieth, and twenty-first centuries.[160]

The second major movement of innovation came from the work of a German physician, FRANZ ANTON MESMER (1734–1815), who invented a theory and practice of healing known as ANIMAL MAGNETISM or MESMERISM. Mesmer claimed that an invisible "fluid" of subtle energy permeated all organic bodies, and illness was caused by disturbances or blockages in the flow of this universal life force. By making manual "passes" over the patient's body, the normal circulation of energy could be restored. The resulting transition to health and normality was typically marked by a short but violent "crisis" in which the patient would make uncontrollable movements and sounds. One of Mesmer's many followers, Amand-Marie-Jacques de Chastenet known as MARQUIS DE PUYSÉGUR (1751–1825), discovered that mesmeric treatment could result in a miraculous condition of sleeplike trance. All of a sudden, countless patients would display "paranormal" abilities and enter visionary states during which they claimed to be in contact with spiritual beings on other levels of reality. Known as ARTIFICIAL SOMNAMBULISM, this phenomenon would have an enormous influence on the development of esotericism during the nineteenth century.[161]

No fewer than three major new esoteric movements have their origin in Mesmerism, often combined with Swedenborgian concepts of the afterlife and the "unseen world." First of all, somnambulist trance was of key importance to the vogue of SPIRITUALISM. In the wake of an American media hype in 1848, around the Fox sisters in Hydesville who claimed to be in contact with a poltergeist, spiritualist séances became a popular pastime all over the United States and Europe. The simple techniques of somnambulic trance induction made it possible for average citizens, without mediation by the church or its authorities, to satisfy their curiosity about the "invisible world" and the soul's survival after death. Much of spiritualism was a practical affair with little theoretical depth, but influential authors such as ANDREW JACKSON DAVIS (1826–1910), who was strongly influenced by Swedenborg's writings, or the French spiritualist ALLAN KARDEC (ps. of Hippolyte Rivail, 1804–69), whose work would eventually inspire major religious traditions in Brasil, developed full-blown theologies and cosmologies on spiritualist foundations. Scientific curiosity about the physical phenomena and spectacular claims of spiritualism also led to the development of PSYCHICAL RESEARCH, later known as PARAPSYCHOLOGY.[162]

Secondly, physicians discovered that the techniques of artificial somnambulism opened up unheard-of possibilities for studying the human soul and its mysterious powers by means of empirical and experimental methods. This insight led to novel disciplines that are known as PSYCHOLOGY AND PSYCHIATRY today. The key psychological concept of "the unconscious" emerged in the context of German Romantic Mesmerism during the first half of the nineteenth century, originally under such labels as *Die Nachtseite der Natur* (the "nocturnal side of nature"), in sharp opposition to the sober "daylight" consciousness of Enlightenment rationality. The historical development of psychological investigation based on somnambulism can be traced from these early beginnings straight to the experimental psychology of Jean-Martin Charcot or Théodore Flournoy toward the end of the nineteenth century, and from there to Carl Gustav Jung and his school.[163] For more than a century, the emerging academic disciplines of psychology and psychiatry were inextricably entwined with the empirical study of "occult phenomena." Only during the twentieth century, under the impact of new schools such as psychoanalysis and behaviorism, did academic psychology cut its ties with esotericism and the occult (leading to streamlined and deeply anachronistic official histories of psychology in which such dimensions are typically pushed to the margins and discredited as pseudo-science).[164]

Thirdly and finally, the American career of artificial somnambulism gave birth to a large movement of religious innovation that is known as NEW THOUGHT and is based on a radical doctrine of "mind over matter." This tradition had its origin in the work of an American Mesmerist called PHINEAS P. QUIMBY (1802–66), who abandoned Mesmer's "fluidic" theory as the explanation for somnambulic healing in favor of a radical emphasis on the universal and limitless power of *belief*. This was a natural fit with American Protestant ideas about the miracles of faith. Eventually, New Thought enthusiasts were claiming not just that any illness could be cured by means of changing one's beliefs, but any other negative condition, including poverty, could be cured as well. Also known as MIND CURE, these doctrines became the basis of influential new religious organizations such as Christian Science and many similar churches. In the course of the twentieth century, they became deeply ingrained in American popular culture, as seen for instance in the case of self-help gurus such as NORMAN VINCENT PEALE (1898–1993), who had a remarkable impact even on a figure like Donald Trump. In contemporary "New Age" contexts, the doctrine of New Thought has led to a never-ending production of commercial books, all based on the claim that we "create our own reality" by means of our beliefs and should therefore be able to "manifest" literally anything that we want in our lives.[165]

Typical Enlightenment figures such as Swedenborg and Mesmer therefore laid the foundations, somewhat paradoxically, for new esoteric traditions that were looking for alternatives to the dominance of "science and rationality." The important philosophical and artistic movements known as GERMAN IDEALISM and ROMANTICISM played a key role in this development.[166] When German thinkers of this period (including major figures such as Goethe or Schelling) spoke about *die Geisterwelt*, they did not mean just some vague "spiritual reality" but were referring quite specifically to Swedenborg's "world of spirits."[167] In his famous critical philosophy, known as transcendental idealism, Immanuel Kant declared that any such "noumenal" world must be forever beyond the reach of reason—a conclusion that most later Idealist philosophers did not wish to accept.[168] Both Mesmerism and somnambulism had a deep impact on German Romantics and Idealist philosophers, as seen with particular clarity in the case of the second-generation Romantic physician JUSTINUS KERNER (1786–1862), the philosopher CARL AUGUST ESCHENMAYER (1768–1852), and their patient FRIEDERIKE HAUFFE (1801–29), known as "the Seeress of Prevorst"—probably the most famous among countless somnambulic visionaries with spectacular psychic abilities.[169]

The ancient, medieval, and Renaissance traditions focused on esotericism and the occult remained a vital part of German intellectual culture during the first half of the nineteenth century. In England and France, by contrast, they were usually seen as little more than quaint objects of curiosity about the "weird beliefs" of bygone ages. But after mid-century, they began to be rediscovered and reconceptualized, by individuals and groups that were deeply influenced by spiritualism and somnambulist practice and were looking for a "third path" between the dogmas of traditional Christianity and positivist science. This new phenomenon was known as OCCULTISM and comes in different shapes and varieties. French occultism was strongly influenced by Roman Catholicism. Here we encounter remarkably large numbers of *abbés*, pretended or real, who clearly felt a need to process the traumatic legacy of the French Revolution and its sensationally successful assault on all traditional authorities. Their political perspectives went from deeply conservative to radically progressive, but they all shared an obsessive nostalgia for the lost unity of a universal Tradition that had formerly expressed itself by means of spiritual symbolism.[170]

A particularly important example was ELIPHAS LÉVI (ps. of Alphonse-Louis Constant, 1810–75). Originally trained as a priest, he became a Catholic revolutionary deeply influenced by French socialism; but after the deception of the 1848 revolution, he achieved esoteric fame with a series of foundational books about magic and kabbalah, most notably *Dogme et rituel de la haute magie* ("Dogma and Ritual of High Magic," 1556) and *Histoire de la magie* ("History of Magic," 1860).[171] Because Lévi was a remarkably creative thinker and a gifted writer, his works were widely read and core ideas were taken up by many later occultists. A second key figure is PAPUS (ps. of Gérard Encausse, 1865–1916), an extremely active networker and popular author sometimes referred to as "the pope of occultism." He played a central role in the confusing network of occultist organizations that were active in France during the fin de siècle and whose ideas deeply influenced the visual arts, literature, and even the music of that period.[172] We already saw that the esoteric traditions linked to Papus are sometimes labeled MARTINISM, with reference to the Illuminist legacies of Saint-Martin and De Pasqually.[173] A few other authors whose work became important to the development of French occultism were the neo-Pythagoreans ANTOINE FABRE D'OLIVET (1767–1825)[174] and JOSEPH ALEXANDRE SAINT-YVES D'ALVEYDRE (1842–1909), whose speculations about a secret spiritual elite (next to the attractive fantasy of a mysterious underground city known as Agartha) would have a significant impact on later esoteric conspiracy theories.[175] A particularly flamboyant figure was "Sâr" JOSÉPHIN-AIMÉ PÉLADAN (1858–1918), the author of a great number of novels and plays filled with esoteric themes, but best known for his ORDRE DU TEMPLE DE LA ROSE + CROIX ("Order of the Temple of the Rose + Cross") and his important exhibitions of Symbolist art that were marketed as SALONS DE LA ROSE + CROIX ("Salons of the Rose + Cross").[176]

French occultists were generally fascinated by any movement or figure that had been condemned by the Roman Catholic church as heretical or demonic. For instance, JULES DOINEL (1842–1902) founded an ÉGLISE GNOSTIQUE ("Gnostic Church") in 1890,[177] naming himself Tau Valentin II after the second-century teacher Valentinus. The poet and occultist STANISLAS DE GUAITA (1861–97) published books with provocative titles such as *La clef de la magie noire* ("The Key of Black Magic") and *Le Temple de Satan* ("The Temple of Satan"). Interpreted not as the principle of evil but as a Romantic rebel against despotic divine authority, or a symbol of human emancipation, the figure of Satan became an object of deep fascination for many poets, artists, and occultists during this period.[178] As for the social history of SATANISM, it is dominated by spectacular but mostly fictional stories about underground satanic organizations and their sinister activities, such as the famous Black Mass described in an influential novel by Joris-Karl Huysmans, *Là-bas* (1891). Ever since this period, there have been groups and individuals presenting themselves as satanists. While some of them believe in Satan as a real metaphysical entity (notably Michael Aquino's TEMPLE OF SET, founded in 1975), for many others (such as Anton LaVey's notorious CHURCH OF SATAN, created in 1966) he functions rather as a symbol of transgression and rebellion against establishment morality.[179]

The deep concern with Tradition, so typical of French occultism, found its most extreme expression in the work of RENÉ GUÉNON (1886–1951). During his younger years in Paris, he was active in a whole range of esoteric or occultist orders, but he ended up rejecting them all. In two volumes about spiritualism and modern Theosophy, he argued that occultism was no more than a spiritually corrupt product of compromise with the destructive forces of modernity.[180] Guénon's mature work revolves around the idea of one universal spiritual Tradition, based on metaphysical "first principles" that are wholly beyond refutation or critical debate.[181] He completely rejected the modern world and all its values as the absolute antithesis of Tradition and spent the final decades of his life as a Sufi recluse in Egypt.[182] Guénon's many writings are at the origin of an independent esoteric tradition known as TRADITIONALISM (sometimes PERENNIALISM).[183] Ironically, precisely its extreme rejection of modernity makes Traditionalism a typical product of the modern world! In such cases as the major Traditionalist author JULIUS EVOLA (1898–1974), a deeply elitist contempt for modern democracy and social egalitarianism led to an enthusiastic embrace of Fascist and National-Socialist politics.[184] In other cases, such as the important Traditionalist guru FRITHJOF SCHUON (1907–98), it inspired new organizations and communities that allowed their participants to follow Traditionalist lifestyles in relative seclusion. Other postwar Traditionalists, such as notably SEYYED HOSSEIN NASR (b. 1933) and HUSTON SMITH (1919–2016), are known as vocal defenders of Traditionalism in academic settings.[185] Traditionalism has been making a remarkable popular comeback since the early 2000s, especially in far-right circles, as seen for instance in the case of the influential Russian philosopher Aleksandr Dugin (b. 1962) and his radical rejection of Western liberalism.

Compared to their counterparts in France, occultists in the anglophone world were generally more open to liberal-progressive values such as democracy, individualization, sexual reform, feminism, women's emancipation, and anti-colonialism.[186] Their type of occultism was strongly indebted to an anti-Christian mythographical tradition that had been created by Enlightenment libertines such as Richard Payne Knight (1750–1824), Charles François Dupuis (1742–1809), and Constantin-François de Volney (1757–1820). These thinkers rejected the theological concept of divine revelation and replaced it by comparative studies of religion as a wholly *natural* phenomenon that had emerged from solar and phallic worship.[187] From such a perspective, occultism could be perceived as a superior wisdom grounded not in biblical monotheism but in ancient pagan traditions, and sharply opposed to the dogmatic exclusivism of establishment Christianity. Erstwhile spiritualist mediums and pioneers of occultism such as Emma Hardinge Britten (1823–99) and Helena P. Blavatsky (1831–91) became disillusioned with what they saw as the intellectual poverty of spiritualist doctrines and began searching for inspiration in all the major "Hermetic," "occult" and related traditions prior to Swedenborg.[188] In their view, the "occult science" of the ancients that had flourished both in the East and in the West should be revived in the modern world, as an alternative to the narrow materialism of positivist science.

The early Theosophical Society was created in Blavatsky's apartment, New York City, on September 7, 1875. At that time, she and Britten were in the process of finishing large books that would become classics of the occultist movement. Britten's occult novel *Ghost Land* (1876) revolved around somnambulist practice and was situated partly in Europe and partly in India, while the companion volume *Art Magic* (also 1876) was focused on occultist theory and traced the ancient wisdom from the ancient Hindu *Vedas* to contemporary Spiritualism.[189] Blavatsky's *Isis Unveiled: A Master-Key to the Mysteries of Ancient Theology and Science* was published in two large volumes just one year later (1877) and became an immediate bestseller. India was looming large in early Theosophical discourse, as the cradle of civilization and the source of occult wisdom, but this was still very much the exotic India of the Orientalist imagination as perceived by Western occultists. The Theosophical Society itself began as a tiny group of practitioners focused on such "Western" topics as "the Kabbalah of the Egyptians" and theurgical rituals for the invocation of Paracelsus's "elemental beings." Much of this had its origin in literary sources from the Victorian period, notably Edward Bulwer Lytton's occult novel *Zanoni* (1842).[190]

All of this began to change decisively when Blavatsky traveled to India in 1879, together with Henry Steel Olcott (1832–1907), a talented organizer and public speaker who would play a major role in the spectacular expansion and transformation of the Theosophical Society from a small occultist group into a major organization with many international branches. Blavatsky and Olcott were welcomed with great enthusiasm by the *bhadralok*, the Bengali educated elites, because they shared similar agendas of emancipating Indian religions such as Hinduism and Buddhism (seen as the cradle of occult wisdom by Theosophists) against the Christian agendas of the missionaries and the Orientalist prejudice of colonial administrators. As is evident from Blavatsky's second major book, *The Secret Doctrine* (1888), modern Theosophy now developed into an extremely ambitious worldview based on a doctrine of universal spiritual evolution that sought to combine Indian and European traditions in a "higher" occultist synthesis. Theosophy became a powerful and extremely well-organized new religious movement on a global scale. Its large following consisted not just of Europeans and Americans but of countless Indian members who took occultist beliefs into new directions based on their own traditions and often in their own languages.[191] To a much larger extent than they have traditionally been given credit for, Theosophists made important contributions to the comparative study of religions and the ongoing enterprise of getting classic Indian texts translated into English and other Western languages.

Theosophy entered its second phase of development under the leadership of ANNIE BESANT (1847–1933), a well-known socialist and advocate of women's rights who had converted to Theosophy after meeting Blavatsky in 1890, and the former Anglican priest and self-declared clairvoyant visionary CHARLES WEBSTER LEADBEATER (1854–1934).[192] Under their influence, Theosophy began moving away from comparative studies of religion on occultist premises, toward a new kind of East-West Esoteric Christianity based upon the clairvoyant "observations" of Leadbeater in particular. All of this culminated in a period of messianic fervor around a young Indian man, JIDDU KRISHNAMURTI (1895–1986), who was raised as the coming "World Teacher" but publicly rejected that role in 1929. Largely in response to the Krishnamurti cult, combined with major controversies over Leadbeater (who was accused of pederasty), the large majority of German Theosophists broke away in 1910 and followed the charismatic Austrian clairvoyant and occultist philosopher RUDOLF STEINER (1861–1925). The result was a new organization, the ANTHROPOSOPHICAL SOCIETY. Again, it was based on a Christian interpretation of Theosophical doctrine but strongly informed in this case by German Idealist philosophy and bolstered by Steiner's claims of superior clairvoyant access to "the spiritual world." Anthroposophy became the inspiration for a whole series of innovative ventures such as the Waldorf Schools, biodynamic agriculture, alternative medicine, and new directions in architecture and the visual arts.[193]

Occultists after the mid-nineteenth century began developing new forms of magical practice as well. While often claiming ancient roots and relying on the standard corpus of European texts and traditions, such as Christian kabbalah and the Occult Philosophy of the Renaissance, these new forms of occultist practice were often highly innovative. An important pioneer was the black American practitioner PASCHAL BEVERLY RANDOLPH (1825–75), the first major spiritualist and occultist who argued that sexual energy and psychoactive substances could be harnessed for the ends of "magical" self-development.[194] In England by the end of the nineteenth century, an initiatic Order called THE HERMETIC ORDER OF THE GOLDEN DAWN began practicing ceremonial magic based on an extremely sophisticated system of symbols and ritual practices that revolved around the kabbalistic structure of the ten sefirot. It was created by SAMUEL LIDDELL MACGREGOR MATHERS

(1854–1918) and has become the model for countless later forms of occultist magic up to the present day.[195]

While women such as Blavatsky, Britten, or Besant played leading roles in early Spiritualism and Theosophy, the Golden Dawn had female members in central positions as well, such as the actress and musician FLORENCE FARR (1860–1917), the revolutionary activist and actress MAUD GONNE (1866–1953), or the artist MINA BERGSON (1865–1928), sister of the famous French philosopher.[196] In this context, I should also mention the British anti-vivisectionist and women's rights campaigner ANNA BONUS KINGSFORD (1846–88), one of the first women to obtain a degree in medicine and the founder of a HERMETIC SOCIETY in 1884. In these occultist contexts, the adjective "Hermetic" usually signaled a wish to keep focusing on specifically "Western" traditions, such as (Christian) kabbalah and the European *philosophia occulta*, rather than on the "Oriental" spiritualities of Hinduism or Buddhism that were being promoted by Theosophy.[197]

The most notorious occultist magician of the twentieth century, ALEISTER CROWLEY (1875–1947), broke away from the Golden Dawn to join the ORDO TEMPLI ORIENTIS, a magical order created by the German THEODOR REUSS (1855–1923). Having assumed leadership of this organization (often abbreviated as the O.T.O.), he turned it into a vehicle for the ceremonial practice of sexual magic. Rebelling against his strict Christian upbringing in the Plymouth Brethren, Crowley enjoyed stylizing himself as the "Great Beast" of the Apocalypse whose new religion THELEMA (based on a revelation received from an Egyptian deity "Aiwass" in 1904) was destined to replace Christianity as the new world religion of the future. Crowley's systematic experimentation with every conceivable form of transgression has made him controversial even among occultists, but the impact of his writings has been enormous, and several initiatic orders that claim to continue the original O.T.O. remain active today.[198]

Flourishing before and after the Second World War, occultist organizations can be seen as responding to the "process" or "problem" of disenchantment in modern secular societies.[199] By cultivating the powers of the human imagination, they seek experiential access to parallel realities of magical enchantment.[200] In these contexts, the focus is ultimately on the magician's individual inner development rather than on attempts to influence the outside world (although the latter is certainly not excluded). Evidently under the impact of popular psychology, the very concept of "magic" therefore acquires new shades of meaning. As regards this focus on "inner development" in an esoteric context, I should finally mention the enigmatic Greco-Armenian teacher GEORGE IVANOVITCH GURDJIEFF (1866–1949) and his Russian pupil PIOTR DEM'IANOVICH OUSPENSKY (1878–1947). Gurdjieff developed an independent and quite original esoteric system that includes a neo-gnostic cosmology and a complicated system of personal training designed to liberate the mind from social control and attain spiritual freedom.[201] Gurdjieffian techniques were adopted by various esoteric teachers and movements after the Second World War and have become an important dimension of the post-1960s concern with "self-realization."

Esotericism after the Second World War

Most esoteric activities discussed in the previous section can be understood as manifestations of an emerging CULTIC MILIEU or, in more recent terminology, of a popular phenomenon known as OCCULTURE.[202] These terms refer to what has clearly become a permanent feature of modern and contemporary liberal societies. Countless citizens today are receptive to esoteric ideas or experiential practices because they do not feel satisfied by the dominant worldviews, approaches to knowledge, or ways of living that are promoted by mainstream educational institutions and official channels of information. They feel that something is missing—there must be something else, something different, some other source or foundation of meaning. This search for alternatives takes the form of multiple fluctuating and continually evolving networks, of groups and individuals who are looking for inspiration and deeper fulfilment in their lives but also for explanations of what seems puzzling or incomprehensible in history and world events. While exploring spiritual traditions from all over the world, including those "esoteric" ones that used to be marginalized and discredited in Western culture, they will take their information from wherever they find it. As the so-called "culture industry"[203] gained dominance in postwar capitalist societies, this resulted in huge commercial markets for spiritual products of any kind, from books and journals or material objects (for instance crystals, incense, or symbolic imagery) to training programs, workshops, or retreats. In these contexts, we see a constant process of recycling, repackaging, and creative reinterpretations (or misinterpretations) of all those traditional esoteric and occultist materials that are dismissed as "rejected knowledge" by the dominant culture.

This postwar cultic milieu, or popular occulture, developed in Europe and the United States during the 1950s and became impossible to ignore with the emergence of the so-called COUNTERCULTURE of the 1960s and 1970s. During these decades, many people began to see themselves as parts of a momentous spiritual revolution that was on the verge of transforming the dominant culture and would lead humanity into a new spiritual era of harmony and light—the famous "Age of Aquarius" or AQUARIAN AGE. This millenarian idea of an imminent spiritual transformation had emerged in Theosophical circles in England, associated with the popular writings of ALICE BAILEY (1880–1949), and flourished in alternative communities such as Findhorn in Scotland.[204] It was closely connected to the new postwar fascination with flying saucers or UFOs—a popular phenomenon that, among other things, led to new esoteric communities whose members believed that extraterrestrials would soon appear in their spaceships to save the world.[205] All of this was seen as belonging to the realm of "the unexplained"—that is of everything, from mystical visions to paranormal phenomena, that had no place in the materialist worldview of official science. Largely based on modern Theosophy and related forms of occultism, these powerful esoteric imaginaries were marketed on a massive scale now, also through popular media such as science-fiction and superhero comics.[206]

An important new development in esoteric pop culture can be traced to a bestseller published by the French authors LOUIS PAUWELS (1920–97) and JACQUES BERGIER (Yakov Mikhailovich Berger, 1912–78) in 1960, *Le matin des magiciens* ("The Morning of the Magicians"). Translated into multiple languages soon after its appearance, it was so successful that a new popular journal *Planète* was launched in 1961 to further capitalize on its central themes, leading to parallel commercial journals published in various other language domains as well.[207] The *Planète* phenomenon was grounded in a specific form of FANTASTIC REALISM that deliberately blurred the boundaries between real and imaginary while focusing on weird and wondrous phenomena, enigmas, or mysteries that science could not explain.[208] For perfectly obvious reasons, this opened the doors to exploring all the traditional "occult sciences" or any esoteric traditions that had been neglected by the academic mainstream; but it also led to a never-ending stream of pseudohistorical narratives about secret traditions and sinister conspiracies, such as the myth of *The Holy Blood and the Holy Grail* (linked to "the mystery of Rennes-le-Château") and its transformation into fiction by Dan Brown in his mega bestseller *The Da Vinci Code* (2003).[209] Particularly important, in view of later developments, was Pauwels's and Bergier's fascination with "vanished civilizations" such as Atlantis or Lemuria (a theme that goes back to the late nineteenth century and had been popularized by Blavatsky[210]), the sensational fantasy of Hitler and the Nazis as occultists or black magicians,[211] and speculations about the awesome but yet underdeveloped superhuman potentials of "that infinity called Man."[212]

A standard ingredient of this esoteric genre is that official authorities, including historians and academics, cannot be trusted—they are either just naïve and blind to the evidence or in league with the authorities to hide the truth from the common people. What truth? In one way or another, it always has to do with the existence of sinister conspiracies and a Manichaean battle between "good and evil" that is going on behind the screen of official historical and political events. I already discussed this kind of thinking at the example of the Knights Templar, the Freemasons, the Order of the Illuminaten, the Jesuits, and the Jews. These and many other CONSPIRACY THEORIES received a powerful new boost in the wake of Pauwels's and Bergier's bestseller in 1960, leading from there to a never-ending series of conspirational narratives in which elements from the older stories are mingled with new ones such as the assassination of John F. Kennedy, US government plots to conceal the truth about UFOs from the general public, underground satanic and pedophile networks that sacrifice children, the terrorist attacks of 9/11 as an "inside job," plans for a New World Order steered by a hidden elite of wealthy Jews and/or Illuminati, David Icke's theory of politicians as shape-shifting reptilians, the Covid-19 pandemic as part of a sinister plan to enslave the world by means of vaccines and techniques of digital control, the QAnon conspiracy about politicians as blood-drinking pedophiles, and so on and so forth.[213] Not all these conspiracy theories contain elements from the history of esotericism, but many of them do. And of course, they could all be seen as "esoteric" or "occult" in the specific sense of a deep obsession with secrets and hidden or concealed knowledge.

Next to this general phenomenon of popular occulture, with its constantly changing features and topics of interest, a wide variety of somewhat more stable new esoteric movements or traditions emerged after the Second World War as well. A major new phenomenon that came out of the 1960s counterculture is known as *(NEO)PAGANISM*.[214]

It originated in England, with a new religion created in the 1950s by GERALD GARDNER (1864–1964) but presented by him as the revival of a European underground cult based on pagan nature worship. Referred to as WICCA, or "the Old Religion" of Witchcraft, it combined occultism in the tradition of Aleister Crowley with a fascination for ancient fertility cults. Wicca spread from England to the United States during the 1960s, where it moved into entirely new directions. Feminist activists such as STARHAWK (ps. of Miriam Simos, b. 1951) or SZUSZANNA BUDAPEST (b. 1940) interpreted Wicca as GODDESS RELIGION, by highlighting the female principle in nature as an alternative to the male deity of monotheism. From this period on, (neo)paganism has developed into many new directions, often based on the wish to revive specific regional pagan traditions such as DRUIDRY and similar forms of Celtic revivalism, or movements such as ÁSATRÚ that focus on the ancient Germanic and Scandinavian pantheons. Today, pagans exists in many countries as a vital subculture that celebrates diversity and emphasizes natural and ecological lifestyles. But in line with broader cultural and political shifts over the past decades, significant sections of these milieus (notably those that focus on "Nordic" traditions) have taken a clear turn toward the right or the far right,[215] resulting in considerable tensions with their left-leaning pagan counterparts. Finally, it is clear that all things connected to "paganism" or "witchcraft," next to other "occult" pursuits, have become extremely popular online and among young people.[216]

Many other new religious movements and traditions based on esoteric beliefs developed after the Second World War as well, and it would be impossible here to list them all. A Theosophical belief system was central to new esoteric organizations such as the CHURCH UNIVERSAL AND TRIUMPHANT (or SUMMIT LIGHTHOUSE), which made headlines during the 1980s by building bomb shelters in Montana, because the ascended masters had predicted a nuclear conflict prior to the arrival of the New Age.[217] Another major new esoteric organization is L. Ron Hubbard's (1911–86) SCIENTOLOGY, which combines a variety of esoteric and occultist beliefs with elements of science fiction and is notoriously surrounded by legal and media controversies.[218] A variety of new Rosicrucian organizations with roots in the prewar period have been active in Europe and the United States after the Second World War, notably the ROSICRUCIAN FELLOWSHIP founded between 1909 and 1911 by MAX HEINDEL (ps. of Carl Louis von Grasshoff, 1865–1919), the Dutch LECTORIUM ROSICRUCIANUM (founded in 1935) under the leadership of JAN VAN RIJCKENBORGH (ps. of Jan Leene, 1896–1968) and CATHAROSE DE PETRI (ps. of H. Stok-Huizer, 1902–90), and the ANCIENT AND MYSTICAL ORDER ROSAE CRUCIS (AMORC) created in 1915 by HARVEY SPENCER LEWIS (1883–1939).[219]

An extremely different family of esoteric groups and organizations emerged from the rebellious and anarchistic spirit of the American counterculture, continuing from there into punk and other alternative scenes in England. The various traditions of DISCORDIANISM are based on a "holy book" titled *Principia Discordia: Or, How I Found Goddess, and What I Did to Her When I Found Her*, published in 1963 by Malaclypse the Younger (ps. of Greg Hill, 1941–2000) and Omar Khayyam Ravenhurst (ps. of Kerry Wendell Thornley, 1938–98). It was quoted extensively in another key discordian text, *The Illuminatus! Trilogy* (1975) written by Robert Shea (1933–94) and Robert Anton Wilson

(1932–2007), a key satirical novel about the extremes of American esoteric-occultist conspiracy thinking. Yet another related movement is the CHURCH OF THE SUBGENIUS, a "parody religion" created by Ivan Stang (ps. of Douglas St. Clair Smith, b. 1953) and Philo Drummond (dates unclear), focused on an invented prophet called J. R. "Bobb" Dobbs. They all seek to disrupt the dominance of capitalist-consumerist media culture by techniques of subversion referred to as "culture jamming." Sometimes referred to as "invented religions," they have also been described by such labels as "the Psychedelic Church Movement" or PSYCHEDELICISM, defined by the belief that human consciousness can be expanded to higher levels of awareness—with the help of psychedelics but also by means of various other mind-altering techniques.[220] An extremely productive and influential esoteric author who came out of these milieus was PETER LAMBORN WILSON aka HAKIM BEY (1945–2022), famous for coining the anarchist concept of a "Temporary Autonomous Zone" (T.A.Z.).[221] Many discordian ideas and attitudes flourished in England since the 1970s in occultist milieus known as CHAOS MAGICK, strongly influenced by the work of the occultist artist AUSTIN OSMAN SPARE (1886–1956) and by the new culture of postmodernism that was becoming popular at this time.[222] Out of these same milieus came radical activist groups such as THEE TEMPLE OV PSYCHICK YOUTH, with as its central figure GENESIS BREYER P-ORRIDGE (ps. of Neil Andrew Megson, 1950–2020), and connected to musical collectives such as *Throbbing Gristle* and *Psychic TV*.[223]

Another esoteric tradition grounded in social resistance against the status quo emerged in African-American communities since the early parts of the twentieth century. As early as the 1920s, an organization known as the MOORISH SCIENCE TEMPLE was created in Chicago by a certain Timothy Drew (1886–1929). He called himself NOBLE DREW ALI and claimed to have received occult initiations in Morocco and Egypt, notably by an Egyptian priest in the Pyramid of Cheops. Drew published a text called the *Circle 7 Koran*, clearly indebted to popular Theosophical texts about the secret life of Jesus,[224] next to Freemasonry, especially the African-American tradition knowns as the "black Shriners." The Moorish Science Temple had a catechism, which pointed out that dark-skinned Americans came from the "Arabian" lineage of the angels, whereas people with a "pale" skin had descended from Adam and Eve after they had caused "discord in the Holy city of MECCA and were driven out."[225]

Many aspects of the Moorish Science Temple were carried over into another organization, THE NATION OF ISLAM, founded in Chicago in 1930 by WALLACE D. FARD (dates unclear: he appeared on the streets of Detroit in 1930 and vanished again four years later).[226] He taught that the God of the Christians was invented by the devil to oppress and manipulate the masses, and the only true living God was the black man. The Nation of Islam became a major organization under his successor, ELIJAH MUHAMMAD (Elijah Poole, 1897–1975), who claimed that Fard had been Allah himself appearing in human form and Elijah was His new messenger. The foundational mythology of the Nation of Islam reversed ideologies of white supremacy by stating that "the original man is the Asiatic Black man" whereas "the Colored man is the Caucasian (white man)."[227] In fact, the white race consisted literally of blue-eyed devils, artificially created about 6,600 years ago by a "big-headed" young scientist called Yacub (modeled after the Biblical Jacob, who stole Esau's birthright). Fard would soon return in a spaceship, to wipe out the white race and establish a black utopia. The Nation of Islam became a large and powerful movement during the 1960s, largely due to the charisma of its spokesman Malcolm X (Malcolm Little, 1925–65), who famously opposed Martin Luther King and was assassinated after breaking with the Nation of Islam and, impressed by the *hajj* in Mecca, with its anti-white ideology.[228]

Fard had claimed that 85 percent of the general population consists of "uncivilized" manipulated masses, 10 percent consists of wealthy "Blood Suckers of the Poor," but the remaining 5 percent are "the poor, righteous Teachers" whose eyes have been opened to the fact that the supreme being is the black man of Asia.[229] This is why an offshoot of the Nation of Islam, created in Harlem after 1963 by CLARENCE 13X (Clarence Ernest Smith, 1928–69), called itself the FIVE PERCENT NATION (or Five Percenters), although it is also known as the NATION OF GODS AND EARTHS.[230] Its central message is that all black men are really Gods in the flesh, while black women are referred to as "Earths." Amusingly, the greeting "what's up, G" originally meant God (not gangsta). But much more seriously, it is clear that for young men from the ghettos, who looked up to Clarence 13X as a father figure, it was deeply empowering to think of themselves as "not just another poor black kid but a God . . . the 'original man of all civilization'." As formulated by the rapper RZA of Wu Tang Clan, "Hearing that when you're a kid, you're like, 'Whoa, Who, me?' It was power."[231] The Five Percenters became highly popular, but were always controversial, and typically portrayed in the media as "a dangerous street gang dedicated to crime, violence, and general mayhem."[232] Particularly interesting for our concerns is its sophisticated system of esoteric symbolism and coded language, based on what is known as the Supreme Mathematics and the Supreme Alphabet.[233] Part of a strategy of "semiotic guerilla warfare"[234] directed against the oppression of white society, it developed into a kind of stylized coded slang that plays a central role in the musical genres of hip-hop and rap during the 1980s and 1990s. This is an excellent example of how esoteric secrets may be hidden in plain sight.[235]

As the excitement about an imminent Aquarian Age began calming down toward the end of the 1970s, the term "New Age" was being picked up by the popular media as a convenient label for all those countless "alternative" ideas and practices that were flourishing in the cultic milieu, whether or not they included a millenarian component.[236] Next to esoteric/occultist currents and Oriental spiritualities, popular fascination with the NEW PHYSICS was an important part of the mix as well.[237] The radical paradoxes of quantum mechanics and relativity theory seemed to confirm that the old scientific ideologies were breaking down, together with religious dogma, thus making way for a new spiritual and holistic worldview in harmony with the ancient wisdom of East and West. As business entrepreneurs discovered the market for spiritual products during the 1980s—the age of rapid neoliberalization—the NEW AGE became a major growth industry. As an inevitable result of commercial success, many of its ideas (such as reincarnation, the belief in other spiritual dimensions, or cosmic visions of spiritual evolution) have become more acceptable to countless consumers in mainstream society.

The original countercultural critique of mainstream society, with its hopeful vision of radical spiritual transformation, remains very much alive in many branches of the cultic milieu. This is particularly evident in the context of (NEO)SHAMANISM.[238] In an enduring bestseller published in English in 1964 (French orig. 1951), Mircea Eliade presented "shamanism" as a universal spiritual tradition grounded in the induction of altered states of consciousness for purposes of healing and visionary insight.[239] The American anthropologist of Peruvian descent CARLOS CASTANEDA (1925–98) produced enormously popular books about his alleged initiations by a Mexican shaman, a certain Don Juan, who worked with mind-altering "power plants" such as Peyote.[240] After the beginning of the War on Drugs under the Nixon presidency toward the end of the 1960s, MICHAEL HARNER (another anthropologist, 1929–2018) started an extremely successful tradition of "core shamanism" based on rhythmic drumming for inducing altered states.[241] For similar reasons concerned with legality, the transpersonal psychologist and pioneer of LSD psychotherapy STANISLAV GROF (b. 1931) developed "holotropic breathing" as yet another technique for inducing altered states in therapeutic group settings.[242] With the emergence of Rave Culture and the rapid proliferation of new information technologies during the 1990s, these traditions entered a new psychedelic phase sometimes referred to as TECHNO-SHAMANISM. Exemplified by large utopian lifestyle festivals such as Burning Man (Black Rock Desert, Nevada) or Boom (Portugal), charismatic leaders such as TERENCE MCKENNA (1946–2000) or DANIEL PINCHBECK (b. 1966),[243] not to mention the global spread of Amazonian traditions of shamanic healing based on the indigenous brew Ayahuasca,[244] it is clear that such new shamanic spiritualities and forms of ENTHEOGENIC ESOTERICISM have become a major phenomenon in contemporary alternative culture.[245]

Esoteric millenarianism remains a major theme in these contexts. It went through several phases after the prediction of an Aquarian Age during the 1960s–1970s, via the widespread belief in a HARMONIC CONVERGENCE that should have occurred on August 16–17, 1987, to the new date of December 21, 2012 (the end of the Mayan Calendar proclaimed by José Argüelles, coinciding with the "eschaton timewave" calculated by Terence Mckenna), and the expected arrival of "the Singularity," when the entire planet would move toward a higher level of spiritual vibration.[246] While the eschaton did not arrive, there's no doubt that in the wake of the 9/11 attack on the World Trade Center and the US-led wars on Iraq and Afghanistan, the world was hit by an accumulating series of serious crises roughly around this time—the financial crisis of 2008–9 and its aftereffects, large-scale campaigns of extremely publicized violence by Islamist terrorist groups such as Al Qaida and Islamic State, pressures on liberal democracy with the international resurgence of far-right populism and authoritarian strongmen, aggressive culture wars and identitarian polarization fueled by the new phenomenon of social media, a headlong increase of technology-driven "surveillance capitalism,"[247] the acceleration of climate change, the Covid-19 pandemic, Vladimir Putin's war on Ukraine and Western liberalism, the war between Israel and Hamas after October 7, 2023, and the rise of AI (these lines are written in the summer of 2024). Against these backgrounds, it can be no surprise that contemporary esotericism often assumes darker, more aggressive, and more pessimistic shades. Evident examples are the new attraction of "gnostic-dualistic" or Manichaean worldviews that think of the world as a malevolent cosmic prison ruled by evil elites, the enormous popularity of extreme conspiracy theories that feed on such fears and feelings of paranoia, and a remarkable resurgence of far-right Traditionalist movements whose adherents would like to "restore sacred order'" by destroying liberal democracy.[248]

The obvious conclusion is that contemporary esotericism is very much alive in popular culture, on the internet, and now on social media as well. Its basic concepts, ideas, or terminologies are no longer tied to any specific religious or intellectual tradition but can be freely recycled, repackaged, and reinterpreted by anybody who takes an interest, without regard for their original meaning or historical context. No matter how bizarre and mistaken such adaptations may often seem, especially to historians who are familiar with the original sources and traditions, they are fascinating as contemporary products of the esoteric imagination. The overwhelming presence of esoteric or occultist themes in popular novels, comics, music, film, art, or videogaming still tends to be studied mostly on a case-by-case basis, and it may be too early to formulate any general, systematic, or synthetic conclusions about these latest outgrowths from the history of esotericism. What this wealth of popular references has to teach us about the "sub-zeitgeist"[249] of contemporary culture and society remains very much an open question. In any case, contemporary esotericism has ceased to be an object of historical research altogether and must be seen as a vital dimension of the very present.

3 Internal Eurocentrism

> For habit is truly a violent and treacherous schoolmistress. Gradually and stealthily, she slides the foot of her authority into us; but after this gentle and humble beginning, once she has planted it firmly within us by the aid of time, she then shows us her furious and tyrannical face, against which we no longer have the liberty even just to lift up our eyes.
>
> (Michel de Montaigne, *Essays*)[1]

Ideas do not live in a social vacuum, as topics of polite conversation among disembodied minds. In intellectual history or the study of religion, we are always dealing with flesh-and-blood people who care deeply, often passionately, about defending their own convictions and criticizing those of others. These two basic activities—*apologetics* on behalf of one's own ideas and *polemics* against those with which one disagrees—mutually imply one another. By denouncing the doctrines of others as false, you assert your own claims to orthodoxy and orthopraxy; and conversely, to defend your own position means questioning or even attacking the position of others.[2] Moreover, ideas do not just exist in people's heads or in the pages of books. They become embodied in social institutions, such as churches or political organizations, that may have a lifespan of many generations and are deeply invested in consolidating and maintaining their own identity by any means available to them. Whether by tradition and socialization or deliberate choice or conversion, individuals may either commit themselves to what such institutions stand for or criticize and reject them. If so, they may give their allegiance to alternative and competing ones. Whatever side you are on, the most effective strategy for establishing and cementing your own identity is always to create the image of a negative "other." To make clear what *we* are all about, *they* (whoever they are) must be clearly depicted as our antithesis.

What is really at stake in such rhetorics is *power*. For our present purposes, it may be defined as the ability of a discourse and of those who dominate it to decide what will and will not be accepted as valid and true. Once a discourse attains a certain degree of such power, it may be converted into real political or coercive power—that is, the ability to enforce its ideas while silencing, suppressing, or discrediting dissenting voices. Such measures can be highly effective over long periods of time, because those who dominate the discourse in any given society will be able to educate new generations in conformity with their own beliefs. Yet they are never final and secure. It is true that any dominant movement or trend may use the rhetorical weapon of "othering" to dismiss its opponents as despicable heretics, dangerous subversives, or ridiculous fools—thereby implicitly confirming its own identity as orthodox, reliable, or reasonable. But those at the receiving end of such polemics may use the same weapon against their opponents. They may depict them as arrogant and blind oppressors or mindless bureaucrats who have to rely on coercion because they lack the arguments to convince—thereby promoting their own identity as champions of freedom, tolerance, and reason. If they manage to muster enough support for their narrative, this may affect the balance of power and lead to larger or smaller intellectual, social, and even political revolutions.

In the context of Western culture and its history, the modern perception of a field referred to as "esotericism" (but which, as we have seen, has been known by a variety of other names as well) is the outcome of deep discursive processes involving complex polemical and apologetic debates that can be traced back to the period of Late Antiquity. To a much larger extent than most people realize, "esotericism" stands for the sum total of *rejected knowledge* against which mainstream monotheist cultures and their modern or secular successor societies (including our current academic institutions) have always been establishing their own normative identity. Even today, it remains their principal discursive Other, like a dark canvas that allows them to paint their own messages in shining colors of light and truth. The implication is that our Western societies and their intellectual representatives have a vested interest in keeping the canvas dark—otherwise their own messages would be more difficult to decipher.

We have every reason to be deeply suspicious of the dominant narratives about "esotericism" that circulate widely in contemporary society. Quite simply, there is an enormous gap between the ways in which everything that pertains to this field tends to be *depicted* in common discourse, or appears in the polemical (or, for that matter, apologetic) *imagination*, and what we actually find if we study the historical sources or investigate contemporary practitioners at firsthand. To give just one simple example, Cornelius Agrippa has been remembered since the sixteenth century as a black magician and a model of the Faust figure who sells his soul to the devil; yet if you take the time to study his writings, you will discover an extremely pious Christian, who saw unquestioning faith in Jesus Christ as the exclusive foundation of any reliable knowledge.[3]

To get a handle on such discrepancies between reality and imagination, it is useful to draw a distinction between HISTORY and MNEMOHISTORY.[4] In simple terms, "history" refers to what happened in the past, while "mnemohistory" refers to how we remember what is supposed to have happened in the past. It follows that the attempt to write the history of what has actually happened may be referred to as HISTORIOGRAPHY, which means that MNEMOHISTORIOGRAPHY would be the attempt to describe the genesis and historical development of what a given culture imagines or believes to have happened. If we stick to our example, a historian will want to know who Agrippa really was and what he really believed, whereas a mnemohistorian is interested in analyzing how Agrippa has been remembered and imagined by later generations up to the present. Her focus is on tracing the chain of reinterpretations, distortions, misunderstandings, and creative inventions that have come to be attached to Agrippa's name—and which are mainly responsible for his continuing fame and notoriety!

We are confronted here with a basic truth that has deeply troubling implications. Because reliable historical accounts tend to be messy, complicated, and not necessarily all that exciting, they almost always lose the battle for popular attention. It takes so much time to read them carefully, and we tend to forget all those countless details! By contrast, mnemohistorical narratives are typically more simple, with a clear storyline about who was "right" and who was "wrong," and this makes them far easier to remember ("Agrippa? You know—that guy who sold his soul to the devil!"). For this reason, efficient mnemohistorical narratives can exert great power over their readers' imagination *regardless* of whether they have any basis in demonstrable facts. Even the wildest historical fantasies, or outright lies, may often have a much stronger impact than the carefully documented reconstructions by professional historians. At the end of the day, what really seems to count is not whether such stories are true but whether they are remembered and believed.

After the previous chapter, which focused on *history*, I will turn in this chapter to the *mnemohistory* of "esotericism" in Western culture. How did "it" come to be constructed as a reservoir of rejected knowledge in (and by) the polemical and apologetic imagination of mainstream European intellectuals and the wider public? And why did that happen? To understand this process, we will have to look more closely at three central historical contexts: (1) Pre-Reformation Christianity, (2) European Protestantism, and (3) Modernity.[5] What ultimately came out of these mnemohistorical developments was a potent narrative about *The West* that remains extremely influential in our societies and our educational institutions. It is based on systematic patterns of excluding, marginalizing, misrepresenting, or discrediting a wide range of ideas and practices that, in actual fact, were always part and parcel of Western culture but did not fit a narrow ideological agenda of what that culture was supposed to be all about. The title of a famous older book by the historian Norman Cohn, *Europe's Inner Demons*, captures this quite precisely—the politics of establishing a European identity required that its "internal enemies" (in this case heretics, witches, and magicians) would be identified, set apart, demonized, and finally exorcized.

I will refer to this as the *INTERNAL*-EUROCENTRIC narrative of Western culture. It is the culturally dominant story of what we've been told to see as *central* to the identity of Europe and the West. By the same token, it is also the story of what we've been instructed, tacitly or explicitly, to dismiss as *marginal* to that identity. We are dealing here with a grand narrative in the true sense of the word: a foundational *myth* about "where we came from," "who we are," and "where we should be going." Once we understand its nature and its manner of operation, we will understand why "esotericism" is commonly perceived as a separate field, a domain of otherness and weirdness. It will also become easy to see why intellectual or religious elites have so often depicted it as a subversive and dangerous threat to foundational Western values or, with even greater effect, as a laughable and silly fools' asylum. Eventually, as I will argue in Chapter 9, this polemical narrative would become the chief template for *external*-Eurocentric perceptions of non-Western cultures and peoples as "primitive," "superstitious," "irrational," "immoral," "backward," "uncivilized," or otherwise "inferior." Insofar as the modern study of esotericism exposes the deep ideological structure of Internal Eurocentrism and its effects on a global scale, I therefore see it as a profoundly *decolonial* project. It seeks to break the power of the dominant narrative on which claims of Western superiority have historically been built; and it seeks to restore the victims of marginalization and exclusion, together with their "rejected" modes of knowledge, to a status of normality and legitimacy.[6] Therefore what needs to be rejected is not Western culture itself but, rather, a narrow Eurocentric story that we have been told about the West.

Early Christianity and the Church of Rome

Our story begins in late antiquity, with the early Christians, who had to establish their identity on two different fronts. They were concerned with demarcating themselves against Judaism, while simultaneously taking position against the dominant "pagan"[7] religion of their wider environment in the Roman Empire. From his Jewish upbringing, the apostle Paul inherited an absolute abhorrence of any worship that would direct human attention away from the one invisible God and toward "images resembling mortal man or birds or animals or reptiles" (Rom. 1:23). Thus the quintessentially Jewish rejection of IDOLATRY, the worship of images, was adopted by the Christians as well. Both religions agreed that it was the ultimate sin, "the thick wall that separated the non-pagans from pagans."[8] The *cultic* practices of pagan religion could therefore be rejected, clearly and unequivocally, as worship of evil demons. But the *philosophical* systems of the gentiles were a different matter altogether. Some early fathers of the Church found them incompatible with Jewish and Christian monotheism, as seen from a famous statement by Tertullian, "What indeed has Athens to do with Jerusalem, the Academy with the Church, heretics with Christians?"[9] But many other Christians saw room for a constructive dialogue, particularly with the Platonic traditions that were so widespread among intellectuals in the Hellenistic culture of the Roman Empire. The consequences would prove to be enormous, not just for the history of Christianity but also for what we now refer to as "esotericism" in the West.

The Apologetic Fathers

In their attempts to convince pagan intellectuals about the superiority of their new faith, apologists for Christianity were faced with a serious problem. It was a general conviction of their age that no religion or philosophical system could claim to be authoritative *unless* it was rooted in very ancient and venerable traditions. In other words, everybody (including the Jews) agreed that no religion could be both new *and* true.[10] Yet Christians claimed that their faith had originated very recently, with a Jewish prophet called Jesus Christ—a ridiculous idea in the eyes of their pagan critics. Thus a second-century philosopher called Celsus was making fun of those Christians, a people without roots who "wall themselves off and break away from the rest of mankind": "I will ask them where they come from, or who is the author of their traditional laws. Nobody, they will say!"[11] One century later, the Neoplatonic philosopher Porphyry was quite as deeply puzzled by this community of believers. How could they possibly think that it was possible to just start from scratch, to "cut out for themselves a new kind of track in a pathless desert"?[12]

Christians took such accusations seriously and felt they needed to provide an answer. They found it in a doctrine that modern scholars refer to as PLATONIC ORIENTALISM[13]—the widespread belief that Plato had taught not just a rational philosophy that began in fifth- to fourth-century Greece but a much more ancient spiritual wisdom that had come from venerable sources in the "barbarian" Orient. Egyptians were bound to highlight Hermes Trismegistus as the original fountain of this "ancient theology"; Persians would point to Zoroaster, the legendary inventor of *mageia* ("magic"); and Greeks could refer to such ancient sages as Orpheus or Pythagoras. But CHRISTIAN APOLOGISTS (notably Justin Martyr, Tatian, Clement of Alexandria, Origen, and Eusebius of Caesarea) had found another and better candidate—they argued that all those pagan philosophers and sages had ultimately been dependent on the ancient wisdom of the Hebrews. It had been codified by Moses at Mount Sinai, as told in the book of Exodus, and had now attained its final splendor in the religion of Jesus Christ.

This argument against the pagans meant that Christianity was *not* radically new. It had to be a revival (after a long period of decline since the biblical Fall, when evil demons convinced the pagans to worship them as "gods") of the true ancient religion that was rooted in Mosaic wisdom. From the very beginning, this universal religion of mankind had been inspired by the eternal *Logos*, the divine Word—even long before it was finally "made flesh, and dwelt among us" in the person of Jesus Christ (John 1:1-14). A particularly eloquent statement of this position comes from St. Augustine himself:

> The very thing which is now called the Christian religion was with the ancients, and it was with the human race from its beginning to the time when Christ appeared in the flesh: from when on the true religion, which already existed, began to be called the Christian.[14]

This doctrine had far-reaching implications. It meant that Christians could expect to find nuggets of true wisdom not just in the Jewish and Christian scriptures but even in the writings of pagan sages. Venerable authorities, such as the Egyptian Hermes Trismegistus or Plato himself, could have drunk from the wells of the Mosaic revelation. Even without their conscious awareness, they could also have received direct inspiration from the divine *Logos*. In other words, these pagan authorities could be seen as "unconscious Christians" through whose writings God had gently been preparing humanity for the glorious advent of the gospel. What makes this theory so important is the fact that it opened up all the philosophical writings of antiquity as potential sources of pious inspiration for Christians. Powerful support could also be found in Paul's mission to the Greeks. Referring to an altar in Athens that was devoted to "the unknown God," the apostle had famously told the Athenians that "whom you ignorantly worship, him I declare unto you" (Acts 17:23).

It would be hard to overstate the importance of this early apologetic tradition, not just for the history of Christianity but also for the conceptualization of "esotericism" in Western culture. Rather than following in Tertullian's footsteps (by rejecting any pagan philosophy as incompatible with Christian belief), countless theologians found they could make sense of the Christian message by adopting Platonic and other Greek philosophical frameworks or concepts. An extremely authoritative example is Augustine himself, who stated that "no one has come closer to us [that is, the Christians] than the Platonists" and affirmed that true doctrines might have been held by wise men or philosophers of other nations, "be they Atlantic Libyans, Egyptians, Indians, Persians, Chaldaeans, Scythians, Gauls, or Spaniards."[15] A particularly impressive example of how intimately Platonic philosophy would become integrated with Christian theology is the anonymous fifth-/sixth-century author known as Pseudo-Dionysius the Areopagite ("pseudo" because he was misidentified as a much earlier Greek intellectual converted by St. Paul at the occasion of his Areopagus speech to the Athenians, mentioned above; see Acts 17:34). The extremely influential writings of this Pseudo-Dionysius were full of Neoplatonic metaphysics, lending further plausibility to the alliance between Platonism and Christian theology.

Prisca Theologia and *Philosophia Perennis*

After the great medieval wave of translations from Arabic to Latin (see the previous chapter), Plato was largely eclipsed by Aristotle in the dominant philosophical theology known as scholasticism. But Platonism made a spectacular comeback during the European Renaissance. Most of the relevant sources (Plato's complete dialogues but also the *Corpus Hermeticum*, the *Chaldaean Oracles*, and a wide range of texts by Neoplatonic authors such as Plotinus, Iamblichus, or Proclus) became available in Latin translation as well, largely thanks to the labors of Marsilio Ficino. Moreover, the invention of printing meant that they could be diffused now on an unprecedented scale. The resulting revival of Platonic Orientalism in the European Renaissance is known as *prisca theologia* ("the ancient theology") or *philosophia perennis* ("the perennial philosophy")—two terms that have often been confused but do not exactly have the same meaning.

In a period that was rife with millennial and apocalyptic fervor, the program of PRISCA THEOLOGIA carried revolutionary implications of spiritual reform and Christian renewal. That all the ancient sources of religion and philosophy were becoming available all of a sudden, precisely in this period, was believed to be more than just coincidence. Intellectuals like Ficino saw the hand of Providence at work—as the Ottoman armies were knocking on the door of Europe, God himself was telling the Christians how to reconnect with the original fountains of divine revelation! Much of the excitement about the new Platonic philosophy had to do with such hopeful perspectives of imminent spiritual renewal. In this regard, it is important to note a peculiar aspect of Ficino's program. Although his Christian motivations were undoubtedly sincere, yet he followed in the footsteps of Gemistos Plethon (the crypto-pagan from Byzantium) by highlighting not Moses but Zoroaster as the most ancient authority of ancient wisdom. This meant that even the religion of the Hebrews had ultimately come from a pagan sage—and worse than that, in the eyes of critics, precisely the one who was believed to have invented magic.

Giovanni Pico della Mirandola's program of Christian kabbalah looks like a deliberate attempt to correct such a belief in pagan anteriority, by leading the genealogy of ancient wisdom back into a more orthodox direction. Just like the original patristic apologists, but unlike Ficino, he pointed to Moses as the earliest authority of ancient wisdom on whom all the pagan sages had depended. But that was not all. He claimed to have made a sensational discovery that provided new and even more convincing arguments for the patristic point of view. Moses at mount Sinai had received not just the tablets of the Law, intended for the great multitude of believers, but also a secret teaching reserved for the chosen few. This "secret wisdom" was the Kabbalah, and it was from *this* supreme source that all the pagan sages had taken everything of enduring value in their teachings. The kabbalah had been jealously preserved by the Jews and remained unknown to the Christians. But as the first Christian to ever study these Hebrew sources in their original language, Pico claimed, he had discovered a secret to which the Jews themselves were blind—all the essential Christian doctrines were contained already in the kabbalistic scriptures. They even mentioned the name of Jesus! Needless to say, this argument finds absolutely no support in modern research of Jewish kabbalah, but it opened the gates for subsequent developments of Christian kabbalah as a specific form of *prisca theologia*. Pico's program was even more revolutionary than Ficino's, because it implied not just a concordance between pagan wisdom and Christian doctrine but should even convince the Jews to accept the Messiah and convert to Christianity—an event that was widely expected to be the prelude to Christ's return.

Of course, none of these high expectations were to be fulfilled. A few decades after the deaths of Pico and Ficino, a very different kind of Reformation would succeed where theirs had failed. Martin Luther was calling for a "return to the sources" too, but Protestantism would prove to be more hostile to "pagan wisdom" than Catholicism had ever been. The notion of a PHILOSOPHIA PERENNIS, highlighted by Agostino Steuco in 1540, must be seen against this background. In contrast to the revolutionary implications of *prisca theologia*, Steuco's understanding of ancient wisdom carried a deeply conservative message. Far from suggesting any need for "return" or "reform," he stated that the universal and eternal truth had always been available to mankind and would always remain so. Steuco was on a first-name basis with the Pope, and his book appeared on the eve of the Council of Trent (1545–63), at which Roman Catholic theologians tried to find an answer to Luther's Reformation. By emphasizing the universal concordance of all ancient wisdom with Catholic doctrine, Steuco was making a final attempt to preserve the unity of the One Church as the divinely instituted repository of everything that had ever been true in religion and philosophy. The message was that no reform was necessary or even possible, because the truth had never been lost. The Roman Catholic church had preserved the ancient wisdom intact and inviolate and kept offering it to all Christians for the salvation of their souls. Thus we see that in a Roman Catholic context, the Renaissance revival of Platonic Orientalism could have either revolutionary or conservative implications.

The Anti-Heretical Position

If apologetics are inseparable from polemics, as we have seen, it can be no surprise that these agendas of *integrating* "good" paganism into Christianity were the reverse mirror image of equally powerful agendas of *exclusion*. First of all (and no matter how hard Protestant polemicists would later try to suggest the opposite), of course it would be a mistake to think that all Catholics were positive about traditions of "pagan wisdom." Even the patristic apologists had not accepted all of them but only what they saw as compatible with Christian doctrine and dependent on the Mosaic revelation. Other Fathers of the Church (Tertullian was already mentioned) were far more skeptical, preferring to highlight rather than minimize the differences between pagan and Christian religion. As far as cultic practices were concerned, we have seen that no compromise could ever be possible with pagan idolatry. When Christianity achieved dominance from the fourth century on, the countless divinatory or related practices (such as the reading of signs and omens, visions, dreams, oracles, astrology, or necromancy) that had been flourishing in the Roman Empire were prohibited. Usually grouped together under pejorative labels such as *magia* or *superstitio*, they were now seen as forms of idolatry involving contact with evil demons. Only during the later Middle Ages did this perspective begin to change, as we have seen, with the emergence of *magia naturalis*.

The most potent legacy passed on by early Christian polemicists to the Roman Catholic tradition was their conceptualization of HERESY. As nicely formulated by Karen L. King (in line with the mainstream of modern research), anti-heretical strategies "were devised not in the face of a clear external enemy, but to deal with an internal crisis of differentiation. . . . The polemicists needed to create sharp lines of differentiation because in practice the boundaries were not so neat."[16] Early Christianity had always been a highly diverse phenomenon, with doctrinal interpretations that varied widely along a spectrum between "gnostic" and what we have learned to see as "orthodox." In their attempts to create doctrinal unity, Church fathers such as Irenaeus, Hippolytus, and Epiphanius told their readers that the Christian church was under threat from a kind of counter-Church of heretics who called themselves "gnostics." This anti-gnostic polemic is a classic example of identity formation by means of creating a negative "other." Until quite recently, it was accepted at face value even by modern scholars,[17] due to a persistent Protestant bias that (as will be seen) is deeply ingrained in modern intellectual culture.

A particularly effective polemical strategy involves the creation of historical genealogies that depict all forms of heresy as having sprung from one single demonic origin. Thus Irenaeus described Simon Magus (Acts 8:9-24) as the original arch-heretic and instrument of the devil; and during the sixteenth century, this narrative was adopted by many anti-witchcraft authors and critics of heresy, beginning with JOHANN WEYER:

> From Simon, as though from a seed pod, there sprouted forth in long succession the monstrous Ophites, the shameless gnostics . . ., the impious Valentinians, Cardonians, Marcionists, Montanists, and many other heretics.[18]

In Weyer's heretical imagination, Simon himself was heir to an even older genealogy of pagan idolatry that originated with Noah's son Ham and his son Misraim, believed to be identical to Zoroaster, the inventor of magic.[19] Such alarmist GENEALOGIES OF DARKNESS became a staple of later anti-witchcraft literature. They show how paganism and gnostic heresy could be conflated to a point of virtual identity by means of a Platonic Orientalism-in-reverse: the narrative of divine wisdom originating with Moses is now replaced by one of demonic infiltration originating with Zoroaster. Plato and later Platonists remain essential to such stories, now as the chief channels of transmission through which heresy was able to infect the Christian religion. Historically, the relation between "pagan" Hellenistic influences and the religious perspectives associated with "gnosticism" is extremely complicated; but as already noted, the simplifications of mnemohistorical narrative are usually much more effective than the careful reconstructions of historians. Simply because "pagan idolatry" and "gnostic heresy" were negative concepts that stood for Christianity's radical "other," they converged in the polemical imagination as ultimately just one single phenomenon of demonic error and spiritual darkness.

On the eve of the Reformation, two very different perspectives on "paganism" were therefore operative in Roman Catholic culture. An *inclusive* perspective accepted ancient pagan wisdom as participating potentially in Christian truth. An *exclusive* counter-perspective rejected all pagan influences as forms of demonic infiltration that could only result in heresy. With this conflictual situation, the stage was set for the second act in the historical drama that led to our modern concepts of "esotericism."

Protestantism

From its very inception, the Renaissance revival of Platonic Orientalism provoked a strong anti-Platonic reaction. As early as 1458, the Aristotelian GEORGE OF TREBIZOND described Plato as the source of every imaginable depravity and the fountainhead of all heresies.[20] The dramatic idea of a "genealogy of darkness" (coming from the pagan Orient and leading through Platonism to Christian heresies such as those of the gnostics) flourished especially in the new genre of anti-witchcraft literature. By the end of the sixteenth century, this tradition of anti-Platonism culminated in a large work by GIOVANNI BATTISTA CRISPO (c. 1550–c.98), *De Platone caute legendo* ("On the Need to Read Plato with Caution," 1594), where Plato was depicted as the chief agent of corruption in the Church. How could it have happened, Crispo was asking himself and his readers, that this dangerous virus of Platonic paganism had been allowed to infect the healthy organism of Christian theology? His answer was clear—the fault lay with the so-called apologetic Fathers. Through an excess of kindness and naïvety, they had accepted Plato's teachings and thus allowed them to slowly poison their own minds. There is a deep irony here. Crispo was a counter-Reformation theologian who moved in the highest circles of the Catholic hierarchy, and all he wanted was to fight the danger of Protestant heresy. It seems he never realized that with this critique of the Christian apologists, he was handing his opponents a perfect weapon to use in their battle against the Church of Rome.

Protestant polemicists were already arguing that the Church had badly gone astray between the apostolic period and the present time. A classic example is the massive multivolume church history known as the *Magdeburg Centuries*, published between 1559 and 1574 by Mathias Flacius Illyricus (1520–75) and a team of collaborators. As elegantly formulated by a modern specialist,

> In this protestant delineation, the church starts in the apostolic age in perfect purity, and is perverted by a process of slow canker, till it has become changed into its opposite, and is now the church not of Christ, but of anti-Christ, an instrument not for saving men but for destroying them.[21]

For the authors of the *Magdeburg Centuries*, the institution of the Papacy had been the chief agent of corruption. But toward the end of the sixteenth century, more and more authors began arguing that the "hellenization of Christianity" was the true origin of evil. It was the patristic apologists, beginning with Justin Martyr, who had made the fatal mistake of opening up a dialogue with paganism instead of rejecting it entirely. A flood of heresies had been the result. Of course, the Renaissance revival of Platonic Orientalism was bound to be seen as particularly dangerous from such a perspective. It had led to a positive appreciation of pagan teachers such as the Persian Zoroaster and the Egyptian Hermes; it was bound up with pagan "idolatrous" practices such as astrology, magic, and witchcraft; and last but not least, devoted Christians were now meddling in the abstruse kabbalistic speculations of the Jews, the traditional enemies of Christ! None of this, Protestant hardliners were arguing, had anything to do with the gospel. That Catholic intellectuals could seriously defend such teachings was perfect proof of how badly they were out of touch with what the Christian faith should be all about.

Anti-Apologeticism

In Germany during the second half of the seventeenth century, this line of argumentation led to a school of Protestant thought that is known as Anti-Apologeticism.[22] As this modern label shows, its representatives attacked the patristic apologists for having allowed the virus of paganism to infect the Church of Christ. Importantly, as will be seen, it so happens that the anti-apologetic argument was intimately interwoven with the emergence of *history of philosophy* as a new academic discipline. It all began with the work of Jacob Thomasius (1622–1684), whose central argument in a key text titled *Schediasma Historicum* (1665) would be picked up and developed further by a line of important successors. The eventual result was an entirely novel conceptual framework that became extremely influential during the Enlightenment. As I will try to show, it ultimately became decisive for modern perceptions of "esotericism" as a field of research.

Thomasius's innovation consisted in a novel way of distinguishing between biblical religion and pagan philosophy. In typical Protestant fashion, he claimed that the former had been revealed straight by God and carried absolute authority. Because the biblical revelation is infallibly true, it cannot change and therefore does not have a history. Moreover, because God's Word is utterly superior to human reason, it cannot be subjected to philosophical analysis either. One must simply believe it. By sharp contrast, the philosophical systems of the pagans rely on the weak and fallible instrument of human reason and all share one central assumption: that the world is eternal and, therefore, has not been created by God out of nothing. In actual fact, this famous doctrine of *creatio ex nihilo* is not biblical (it was introduced by Theophilus of Antioch and Tatian in the second century),[23] but Thomasius was not aware of that. He believed that the bible distinguished sharply between God and the world (Creator and creation), whereas pagans made the world coeternal with God himself. All heretical beliefs came from that single core error—the doctrine of emanation (souls or intelligences are not newly created by God out of nothing but pour forth from his eternal essence), dualism (form and matter, or God and matter, are equally eternal), pantheism (the world is God), and materialism (God is the world). In the end, all these heresies led to the *deification* of creation at the expense of its Creator.

Through the devil's machinations, these doctrines had infiltrated Christianity in the form of Platonic and Aristotelian philosophies. For Thomasius, any such continuation of pagan philosophy in the shape of Christian theology must be rejected as a case of SYNCRETISM, and thus of heresy—regardless of whether it occurred in the Fathers and in Roman Catholic doctrine or in the many gnostic heresies and other sectarian movements that had sprouted forth from the "arch-heretic" Simon Magus. Thomasius's argument implied nothing less than that, prior to the Reformation, the *entire* history of the Church was synonymous with the history of heresies! Worse than that, it had not stopped even with the Reformation—in spite of Luther's revolution (the most serious attempt, so far, to lead Christianity back to the gospel), the pagan heresies of Platonism were now infiltrating Protestantism in the form of heterodox spiritualities. These were the many "spiritualist" and theosophical sects that flourished during Thomasius's lifetime, the seventeenth century. What they all had in common was an extreme emphasis, known as ENTHUSIASM (*Schwärmerei*), on strictly personal religious experience at the expense of doctrinal belief. Thomasius insisted that just like all other heresies, they too were based on the one central error at the heart of pagan darkness: the false belief that God had *not* created the world out of nothing, at the beginning of time, but it had been in existence for all eternity. These Protestant heresies were just new variations on the old Platonic doctrine of emanation and restitution; human souls were not created *ex nihilo* either but participated forever in an eternal spiritual substance, the divine light-world or *pleroma*. Therefore they had a natural capacity to rediscover their true essential oneness with God, by attaining direct experiential knowledge of their own divine essence. In short, it was always the same quintessential "gnostic" doctrine of auto-salvation and deification by means of an ecstatic state of *gnōsis*.

From an intellectual point of view, Thomasius's argument was a stroke of genius. It created a razor-sharp distinction between what he saw as "true" Christianity and its pagan or heretical "other," and it showed how all doctrinal errors (whether in Patristic theology or its gnostic opponents, in Roman Catholicism or any form of Protestant heterodoxy) could be understood as based on one single principle, the eternity of the world. The argument was even more impressive because it pertained both to ontology (the nature of being) and epistemology (the nature of knowledge) at the same time: by denouncing the general philosophical worldviews of all pagans and heretics (from dualism to monism and everything in between), it also denounced their opinions about salvation through *gnōsis*. In short: by focusing on "the eternity of the world" as the core principle of error, Thomasius had found a way to kill not just two birds but the whole family of heretical birds with one single stone.

Thomasius's work was picked up by a belligerent Lutheran minister, Ehregott Daniel Colberg (1659–98), who used it as the conceptual basis for an extreme attack on heresy that got published in two volumes: *Das Platonisch-Hermetisches Christenthum* ("Platonic-Hermetic Christianity," 1690–1). For the first time in European intellectual history, it covered all the traditions and ideas that we would nowadays associate with the field of "esotericism." Based on a systematic theological analysis of their central doctrines and beliefs, Colberg presented them all as belonging to one single "family tree" of dangerous heresies. For him, the core error of this "Platonic-Hermetic Christianity" lay in the misguided attempt of feeble human intellects to apply rational methods to matters of divine revelation. Whenever human beings are so presumptuous as to "fathom the nature of the revealed mysteries about which God's Word keeps silent,"[24] the result is a syncretism with pagan delusion. In Colberg's heresiological imagination, the many "sects" of Platonic-Hermetic Christianity were like a filthy breed of vermin that had all come crawling from the "Platonic egg."[25] This is yet another example (like the "seed pod" of Simon Magus, mentioned above) of how vivid images of horror can be combined with historical genealogies to dehumanize "the enemy" while tracing all forms of otherness back to one single demonic origin. All heresies that focused on the nature of the soul were described by Colberg as basically "Platonic," while those that focused on the study of nature (notably alchemy and Paracelsianism) were understood as "Hermetic." Conceptually, all were grounded in Thomasius's view of paganism as one single unified tradition that rejected the Christian doctrine of creation out of nothing.

The Pietist Reaction

Before continuing the story of anti-apologeticism, we need to pay some attention to its counterpart during the same period. We have seen that in the context of early Christianity and the church of Rome, the assimilation of pagan philosophies by patristic apologists was sharply opposed by anti-pagan polemicists. Something similar happened in the Protestant context: next to these radical anti-apologetic polemicists, we also find a more irenic apologetic tradition that refused to think of paganism in black-and-white terms.

As the Reformation split off from the Roman Catholic church, its representatives began to quarrel among themselves about the correct interpretation of the Christian faith. The result was an increasing fragmentation of Protestantism into larger and smaller churches, "sects," and spiritual communities, including many believers who felt appalled by the dogmatic intolerance of "orthodox" hard-liners and heresy hunters. They felt that true Christians should try to emulate the original apostolic community. Instead of fighting like cats and dogs over doctrinal matters, they should better concentrate their energies on cultivating an exemplary life of pious virtue, in harmony with one another and with the moral teachings of Jesus. These circles were generally more receptive than their "orthodox" Protestant counterparts to Platonizing tendencies or alchemical and Paracelsian speculation, leading eventually to Christian Theosophy and a fascination with Rosicrucian ideals. Of course, that is precisely why Colberg was attacking them under his rubric of "Platonic-Hermetic Christianity." Toward the end of the seventeenth century, similar accusations began to be leveled at the circles of PIETISTS. The latter had ideas of their own about the true nature of faith, and thus about the history of true Christianity, leading to yet another novel perspective that would influence modern perceptions of what "esotericism" is all about.

Here the central figure was a radical Pietist, GOTTFRIED ARNOLD (1666–1714), the author of a famous *Unparteyische Kirchen- und Ketzer-Historie* ("Impartial History of Churches and Heretics," 1699–1700). Other Pietists who are largely forgotten today, such as Balthasar Köpke or Johann Wilhelm Zierold, had responded to anti-apologetic critics with somewhat ambiguous defenses that came close to the patristic-apologetic perspective. Arnold's response was different and considerably more sophisticated. Interestingly, he had found a way to use the anti-apologetic argument as a weapon to *defend* the "heretics." He began by agreeing with Jacob Thomasius that there could never be any concord between pagan philosophy and Christian faith. In line with Tertullian's rhetorical question, "what indeed has Athens to do with Jerusalem, the Academy with the Church, heretics with Christians?," therefore, he saw no need to pay even the slightest attention to Platonism or other gentile philosophies in his own history of Christianity.

On a deeper level, he had found the most vulnerable spot in the anti-apologetic argument. As Protestant historians were getting better at identifying any trace of pagan philosophy in traditional Christian doctrine, they had begun to discover how little of it was actually free from such influence. You simply couldn't build a consistent theological system on the bible or the words of Jesus alone—sooner or later, in one way or another, you always needed the help of Greek philosophy. In their obsession with erasing all forms of "pagan contamination" from the Christian tradition, the anti-apologists had therefore been busy cutting the branch on which they themselves were sitting, undermining those very doctrines that they wanted to defend. Entirely against their intentions, they ended up giving new strength to their Pietist opponents, who could respond with an I-told-you-so: "hadn't we told you that the bible is all about practical piety, not theological doctrine?"

On these foundations, Gottfried Arnold was changing the rules of the game. He built his history of Christianity *not* on the opposition between biblical Christianity and pagan heresy but on the opposition between true Christian piety and doctrinal theology. As a result, the question of pagan philosophies and their historical influence ceased to be of any relevance. The only valid criterion was whether an author's works exemplified the spirit of humble faith, love, unity, peace, and practical piety that Arnold believed had been practiced by the original apostolic community. All who did so were true Christians, regardless of whether the official church might see them as "heretics." The true heretics were those dogmatic theologians with their endless disputes about doctrinal details; it was *they* who were responsible for turning the Church of Christ into a filthy "cesspool" of quarrelling, slandering, violence, and vain ambition.[26] Against the depressing spectacle of historical Christianity and its never-ending bickering over doctrine, Arnold placed a supra-historical principle of *direct spiritual experience* grounded in Sophia, God's Wisdom. Any such experience of internal illumination, he insisted, was the true work of God in the human soul. Its contents could never be expressed in words, for the hidden mysteries of faith would reveal themselves only in the humble intimacy of the pious heart. Against the "visible church" with its doctrinal quarrels, bigotry, intolerance, and violence, such divine illumination provided access to the INVISIBLE CHURCH in which all true Christians are united. The former was just an "external" phenomenon of history; but the latter was an "inner" phenomenon of the spirit.

With this development, the basic outlines begin to emerge of how modern scholars would come to think of "esotericism." Thomasius and Colberg were pioneers in its eventual conceptualization as a *historical* phenomenon grounded in the "hellenization of Christianity." By contrast, Arnold turns out to be the chief pioneer of "esotericism" understood as *inner traditions*—a perspective that is central, as we have seen, to modern "religionist" and "perennialist" approaches. Historical research concerned with such questions as "how did pagan philosophies influence the development of monotheistic religions" becomes ultimately meaningless in such a context, because the focus moves from external historical and social factors toward a nonhistorical spiritual reality sui generis.

Modernity

We have now reached the third and final act of our historical drama. In the first act, as we have seen, *Christianity* established its identity against Judaism and paganism. In the second act, *Protestantism* carved out a new Christian identity for itself against its enemies, the "pagan heresies" that had infected the Roman Catholic church and kept flourishing in sectarian movements as well. In this third act we will see how *Enlightenment* thinkers took up these Protestant arguments and developed them further, in ways that would lead them eventually to break loose from Christianity altogether. In each act of the drama, we see how an ideological movement succeeds in gaining dominance at the expense of its rivals, who get excluded and marginalized as much as possible. These losers in the game of intellectual and religious history were, essentially, the pagan traditions from late antiquity. Under conditions of monotheistic and (eventually) rational-scientific dominance, they managed to survive by means of creative adaptation. This is the core pattern of how a specific domain of religious thought and practice, nowadays referred to by scholars as "esotericism," has come to be set apart and perceived as "other" in dominant modern narratives.

The History of Philosophy

German intellectual culture is central to the third act of our drama. CHRISTIAN THOMASIUS (1655–1728), the much more famous son of Jacob Thomasius, used the critical tools of his father in the context of a new intellectual project. He wanted to liberate the history of philosophy from its theological dependencies and turn it into an autonomous academic discipline. Instead of rejecting the systems of the pagan thinkers altogether, he argued, we should simply recognize them for what they were on their own terms—honest attempts to understand the world by means of our strictly human cognitive faculties, unaided by divine Revelation. In this manner, philosophy and Christian theology could be seen as parallel but separate paths instead as competitors in the same domain. Christian Thomasius is seen traditionally as "the Father of the German *Aufklärung* (Enlightenment)." He disliked syncretism just as much as his father did, but argued that pagan philosophy could be purified from religious prejudice and superstitions. The result would be a practical and useful philosophy entirely free from metaphysics. The method promoted by Thomasius would become known as ECLECTICISM. Instead of just describing all the claims of the various philosophical schools indiscriminately, the historian of philosophy should take an active role. Like a kind of referee in the intellectual game, he must dare to use his own faculty of rational judgment to "separate the wheat from the chaff," accepting reasonable ideas wherever he found them while rejecting unreasonable ones.

Eclecticism was of key importance to German intellectual life during the period of the Enlightenment.[27] It was widely used by Enlightenment thinkers, as their central tool for distinguishing "reason" from "superstition"—in fact, even those authors who were still attracted to "Platonic-Hermetic" philosophies used it as well, to highlight what *they* saw as reasonable. Most immediately relevant for our concerns is the radical Enlightenment eclecticism represented by the pioneering historian of philosophy CHRISTOPH AUGUST HEUMANN (1681–1764), sometimes dubbed "the Thomasius of Göttingen." Heumann felt very strongly that the history of philosophy could not be established as a legitimate academic discipline *unless* it would be cleaned of any remaining "pagan superstitions." He made the point in his new journal *Acta Philosophorum* in 1715, where he provided a set of criteria to distinguish "true" from "pseudo" philosophy. As became perfectly evident from his discussion, what he had in mind was the entire lineage of "ancient wisdom" on Platonic-Orientalist foundations—all of it was nothing but "foolishness" in his eyes. And thus, in a unique passage of supreme contempt, he was cheerfully waving them goodbye forever:

> So adieu, dear *Philosophia Chaldaeorum, Persarum, Egyptiorum* [philosophy of the Chaldaeans, Persians, Egyptians], &c, that one usually makes such a fuss about, out of blind veneration for Antiquity. . . . I am certain that all these *Collegia sacerdotum Aegyptiorum, Orphaicorum, Eumolpidarum, Samothracum, Magorum, Brachmanum, Gymnosophistarum* and *Druidum* [priestly colleges of the Egyptians, Orphics, Eumolpians, Samothracians, Magi, Brahmans, Gymnosophists, and Druids] which Morhof[28] sometimes calls *occulta* then again *arcana*, or *secreta* and *secretiora* [occult,

> arcane, secret, most secret] . . . that all of these were schools, not of Wisdom, but of Foolishness, which attempted to bring *superstitio in formam artis* [to turn superstition into an art form] and sought to draw profit from deceiving the people. . . . So nobody should hold it against me if I have not the slightest respect for all those *Collegia philosophica secreta* [secret philosophical colleges], but judge that the passing of time has quite rightly made a secret of these mysteries, by dumping them into the sea of oblivion; and that even if the writings of these *philosophorum barbarorum* [philosophers of the barbarians] were preserved by posterity, they would deserve to be sent *ad loca secretiora* [to the most secret places] right away, for superstitious idiocies belong in no better library.[29]

Heumann was announcing the final disappearance of what we nowadays call "esotericism" from official philosophical discourse and academic discussion. Authors such as Jacob Thomasius or Ehregott Daniel Colberg had still seen these pagans and heretical thinkers as serious and dangerous opponents, but Heumann simply dismissed them as a bunch of fools and idiots. They had no right to be taken seriously, and their worthless writings deserved no place in academic libraries or anywhere else. They should be dumped into "the sea of oblivion," to be forgotten forever. The sad truth is that academic research after the eighteenth century would essentially follow Heumann's advice.

By far the most influential representative of Enlightenment eclecticism was JOHANN JACOB BRUCKER (1696–1770), an immediate successor of Heumann and the author of a monumental six-volume *Historia critica philosophiae* ("Critical History of Philosophy," 1742–1744, revised and expanded edition 1766–1967). Brucker's name should be much better known than it is today. His work became the standard reference on history of philosophy from the age of Enlightenment to the time of Hegel and even beyond; in fact, most of the entries on philosophical subjects in Diderot's famous *Encyclopédie* (and many other less famous reference works, such as the *Grosse Zedler*) were basically paraphrased or plagiarized from Brucker's *Historia critica*. It would be hard to overemphasize the importance of this publication. Based on the anti-apologetic principles of Jacob Thomasius and the eclectic method of Christian Thomasius and Christoph August Heumann, Brucker presented a gigantic encyclopedic survey of the entire history of human thought. True to the principles of eclecticism, his aim was to separate the philosophical "wheat" from the masses of pseudo-philosophical "chaff." As a result, his magnum opus in fact consisted of two intimately interwoven strands—a history of true philosophy (labeled *philosophia eclectica*, "eclectic philosophy") against a history of false philosophy (*philosophia sectaria*, "sectarian philosophy"). We have seen that Colberg had already published what may be seen as the very first "history of esotericism," in 1690–1. Brucker's discussion of *philosophia sectaria* was the second and much more ambitious one—in fact, it may be the most extensive and detailed single survey that has ever been published. Brucker made a general distinction between three general periods, modeled on the history of Christianity:

1. The Chaldaean / Zoroastrian / Egyptian philosophies from before the Birth of Christ.

2. The two central systems described as "Neoplatonism" and "Kabbalah" during the era of Roman Catholicism.
3. The system of "Theosophy" that had emerged after the Reformation.

Since Brucker combined Heumann's rational convictions with a staunch profession of Protestant orthodoxy, it should be obvious that the *historia critica* was not just critical but extremely hostile toward all these currents of thought. Yet it was also marked by an acute sense of historical criticism. Rather than just dismissing the "sectarian philosophy" out of hand, Brucker took the trouble to study each and every thinker or system seriously and in great detail, based on an impressive command of the primary sources. He knew very well what he was talking about.

In Brucker's synthesis, the domain that we would nowadays recognize as "esotericism" may be defined as *the continuation of pagan religion concealed as Christianity*. Just like philosophy, it is grounded in paganism; but contrary to philosophy, it is not based on reason. Just like Christianity, it is a form of religion; but contrary to Christianity, it is a false religion without any basis in divine Revelation. In short, Brucker saw it as *a third domain*—the domain of pagan error that had been developing, in countless forms, next to rational philosophy and the Christian religion. One reason why Brucker's work is of such importance is that he wrote it at a pivotal moment. The historical memory of all these currents and ideas was still intact among intellectuals of this time, but he provided them with compelling reasons to dump all of it into Heumann's "sea of oblivion." After Brucker, academic historians of philosophy had understood the point—if all this "weird stuff" was really no more than *pseudo*-philosophy and *pseudo*-Christianity, no need to give it any further serious attention in the history of *true* philosophy or the history of the church.

This is why, after Brucker's time, his *philosophia sectaria* began to vanish from standard academic textbooks and narratives. Because no other discipline took it up, the field became "academically homeless." During the nineteenth and much of the twentieth century, scholars and intellectuals even tended to pride themselves on not knowing anything about such "occult stuff," and learned ignorance about these traditions became deeply ingrained in academic culture. With just very few exceptions, what we now call "esotericism" became the domain of amateur scholars without proper historical training, resulting in a hybrid type of literature full of errors and misconceptions. The doubtful quality of such publications further strengthened common perceptions of "the occult" as a domain that was far below the dignity of serious thinkers. This downward spiral continued far into the twentieth century. Only in recent decades have scholars seen the need again to get educated about these traditions of "rejected knowledge."

We have seen how Protestantism established its identity against the "pagan" heresies that had infected Roman Catholicism. The Enlightenment then built further on these same Protestant polemics, to establish its own identity against "superstition" and "prejudice." The popular assumption is that Enlightenment rationalists were attacking the irrationality of Christian belief and practice, but this is just half the truth—their true target was the *paganism* that had become part of Christianity. For instance, take the figure of Voltaire. In a well-known witticism, this famous icon of the Enlightenment wrote that superstition was born from religion "as the very foolish daughter of a wise and intelligent mother." Religion, understood as "the worship of a supreme Being and the submission of the heart to his eternal orders," was therefore wise and reasonable enough for Voltaire. The problem for him lay elsewhere: "Born in paganism, adopted by Judaism, superstition infected the Christian church from the very beginning."[30] It was against *this* historical infection by "occult" prejudice, and not just against Christianity, that the Enlightenment defined its core identity. Peter Gay's famous reference to the Enlightenment as "The Rise of Modern Paganism"[31] was therefore spectacularly off the mark but illustrates how deeply the modern academy has forgotten its historical origins.

The Romantic Reaction

If we turn now to the intellectual reaction against Enlightenment rationalism in Romanticism and German Idealism, we encounter a similar case of mnemohistorical amnesia. The importance of these cultural and philosophical movements is very well known, but the general trend of eclectic historiography has resulted in highly selective pictures of what they were all about. Most relevant for our concerns is the impact of Mesmerism and somnambulism during the first decades of the nineteenth century. The remarkable powers of vision and cognition displayed by somnambules in a state of trance were widely discussed in contemporary society; and especially among second-generation Romantics, this led to a full-blown counter-metaphysics directed against Enlightenment rationalism.[32] The shallow "daylight" world of the rationalist, who reduces everything to cold logic and discursive prose, was placed in sharp contrast with the profoundly meaningful "nocturnal" world of the somnambules who expressed themselves through symbols and poetic language. These Romantics argued that when the bodily senses shut down and we descend into dream or somnambulic trance, our soul wakes up to the larger spiritual world that is its true home. Therefore it's the rationalist who is truly asleep, unconscious of reality as it really is. Out of sheer ignorance, he dismisses "higher" human faculties such as supranormal cognition and occult powers as mere superstitions.

Far from rejecting science, these Romantics insisted that somnambulism revealed *empirical facts* about nature and the soul that were blindly ignored by Enlightenment ideologues. On this basis, they promoted an "enchanted" organic worldview congenial to Paracelsianism and Christian Theosophy. This new perspective had far-reaching implications, not just for studying the natural world but for the history of human thought as well. All those marvelous phenomena (magic, divination, clairvoyance, symbolism, occult powers) that had been consigned to the wastebasket of history by Enlightenment historiographers were dug up again by the Romantics. They saw them as natural manifestations of the soul and its hidden powers and, in fact, as absolutely central to the development of human culture and civilization. Popular authors such as JOSEPH ENNEMOSER (1787–1854) began publishing comprehensive histories of "magic," based on the idea that external historical events were just the reflections of deeper "internal" events of the soul and its mysterious powers. They were combining German Idealist concepts of human evolution (notably Hegel's famous thesis that the Spirit comes to self-realization and self-knowledge through history) with a Pietist emphasis on interiority that was indebted to earlier thinkers such as Gottfried Arnold. In these new historical narratives, the ancient world was idealized as a "golden age" of the Spirit, when humanity had still understood the mysterious language of Nature. The original home of "ancient wisdom" had been in the Orient. All these elements would become standard ingredients of popular "esoteric" views of human history that remain a staple of New Age literature today.[33]

As we have seen in the previous chapter, there is a straight historical continuity between Mesmeric somnambulism and the experimental psychology and psychiatry that flourished during the decades around 1900. The psychology of CARL GUSTAV JUNG had deep roots in these German-Romantic Mesmeric traditions, and his approach to history was built on the same foundations.[34] Jung's concepts and beliefs would have an enormous impact on what "esotericism" came to mean in popular culture after the Second World War. He popularized the idea of a continuous spiritual tradition that led from Gnosis and Neoplatonism in late antiquity, via medieval alchemy to Renaissance traditions such as Paracelsianism, all the way to German Romantic Mesmerism and Jung's own modern psychology. Jung was at the center of a new and extremely influential intellectual tradition that, in deliberate opposition to dominant modern trends such as rationalization and disenchantment, combined psychological exploration with a deep fascination for symbolism and myth.

From 1933 on, intellectuals and scholars who sympathized with such agendas came together at a famous series of annual conferences in Ascona (Switzerland), known as the ERANOS meetings.[35] Most of them shared a deep conviction that human beings cannot live their lives by Enlightenment reason alone, as naïvely assumed by Enlightenment and positivist thinkers, but need to maintain a healthy balance with the nonrational, "savage," or "primitive" energies of the psyche. If these were not allowed to express themselves consciously but were suppressed into the "unconscious," due to social taboos in a society built only on rational science, they were bound to break through to the surface sooner or later. This was held to be true not just for individuals but for human collectives as well. The violent catastrophes of the two world wars were seen as evident examples of what happens if these powerful nonrational energies are repressed by the dominant culture instead of being allowed to express themselves.

Eranos after the Second World War became the annual meeting place for an impressive new generation of scholars and intellectuals, including the pioneering historian of Jewish kabbalah GERSHOM SCHOLEM (1897–1982), the scholar-philosopher of Islamic esotericism HENRY CORBIN (1903–78), and the religious comparativist MIRCEA ELIADE (1907–86). They all shared a deep concern with the vital importance of gnosis, myth, and symbolism. Their intellectual sympathies lay mostly with traditions that were indebted to German Idealism (especially Schelling) and Romanticism, often combined with specific esoteric currents such as French Illuminism or Traditionalism. Eranos is of key importance for the influential movement and perspective that I have referred to as RELIGIONISM. Very similar to Gottfried Arnold's rejection of historical approaches in favor of a "universal" spiritual experience, religionism looks at history not in terms of external events but of its internal meaning for the human soul. In the famous case of Mircea Eliade, this experiential dimension became the only real means for *homo religiosus* to escape from "the terror of history."[36]

This European intellectual tradition spread to the United States during the 1960s, when countless publications by Eranos intellectuals were translated from German, French, or Romanian into English. Jung and Eliade, in particular, attained an iconic status during this period, as cultural heroes and modernist critics of the materialist-positivist mainstream. Other Eranos luminaries, such as Scholem and Corbin, made their readers aware of previously unknown traditions in Western culture such as Jewish kabbalah and Islamic "mysticism"; yet others, such as D. T. Suzuki (1870–1966), focused on Oriental traditions such as Zen Buddhism; and the same Eranos traditions were further promoted by a new generation of American authors such as Joseph Campbell (1904–87) and James Hillman (1926–2011). During his tenure as a famous professor at the University of Chicago, Eliade even came to dominate the academic study of religion in the United States. Eranos-style scholarship appealed not just to a new generation of academics but also to a very wide audience of readers.

The specific "religionist" approaches of the Eranos school were widely adopted, as more or less self-evident, by many scholars who began turning their attention toward "Hermetic," "occult," or "esoteric" topics from the 1960s and 1970s on. Scholem dominated the new wave of research into Jewish esotericism. Corbin did the same for the study of esoteric dimension in Shiʿi Islam. As for the Christian dimension, the most prominent example would be Antoine Faivre, a friend of Eliade and Corbin whose work became known internationally since the 1980s.[37] Faivre took distance from Eranos religionism during the 1990s, but his famous definition of "Western esotericism" (still strongly indebted to that tradition) would play a major role in the emergence of esotericism as a new field of research during that period.

Conclusion

I have focused in this chapter on a series of polemical and apologetic battles that dominated much of the history of European culture from late antiquity to the post-Second World War period. They are not about the actual *history* of all those ideas, traditions, and practices that are currently studied under the "esotericism" label but about the MNEMOHISTORY of how those ideas, traditions, and practices have been imagined and remembered. The first and second acts of this drama were all about the conflict between Christianity and paganism, in the contexts of Roman Catholicism and Protestantism. The situation changed in modernity, the third act. Enlightenment thinkers now converted the standard pattern of Protestant anti-paganism into a blanket dismissal of "magic," "the occult," or irrational "superstition." Particularly in the context of German culture, this dominant Enlightenment perspective caused a strong reaction by Idealist philosophers and Romantic thinkers, leading to highly influential religionist approaches to "esotericism" that have remained dominant in popular culture to the present day. The first histories of "esotericism" were written by its critics and enemies, notably Colberg and Brucker, who wanted to show which historical traditions should be rejected as "histories of error." Those who disagreed, such as Gottfried Arnold, argued that history should not be described in terms of external events at all—they promoted a "history of truth" that should be all about direct *internal* experiences of a timeless spiritual dimension.

Mnemohistory is about how we remember and imagine the past. If we follow the dominant narratives, based upon Christian anti-paganism and a fight of reason against superstition, we end up with an extremely well-known Eurocentric narrative of "Western superiority." Reaching its pinnacle in the ideology of PHILHELLENISM that dominated classical studies and the humanities during the nineteenth century, it says that European or Western culture is ultimately all about the traditions of "Greek rationality" and "biblical morality," as opposed to its inferior opponents ("Oriental superstitions," the immoral practices of "barbarian peoples," etc.). With the beginning of the colonial age, the battle against "Europe's Inner Demons" that I have tried to sketch in this chapter became the template for a global assault on Europe's *Outer* Demons as well, as will be further explored in Chapter 9. This entire Eurocentric vision, both internal and external, rests on the presumed superiority of Christian over Pagan religion and of Greek rationality over Oriental superstition. This is how most Europeans were told to remember their cultural history and imagine the identity of the West.

The alternative does not consist in a counter-mnemohistory of pagan superiority that would simply reverse the roles, by casting biblical monotheism and scientific rationality in the role of the villains (a perspective that we do encounter in some modern esoteric traditions, notably Neopaganism and Traditionalism). Rather, it suggests a consistent and thoroughly ANTI-ECLECTIC historicization of Western culture itself.[38] Such a new historiography of the West should refuse to categorize historical information in terms of ideological distinctions such as "central versus marginal," "superior versus inferior," "right versus wrong," or "good versus bad." The West is just what it is—a continually transforming historical formation of much greater complexity than one would infer from the normative mnemohistories promoted by defenders and critics alike. The task is to correct the historical record, by restoring the balance between those well-known dimensions of Western culture that used to be highlighted as central and all-important *and* all those other "esoteric" traditions that have been marginalized and suppressed. For the moment, it remains almost impossible to imagine what such a future history of Western culture will look like, but it will certainly be extremely different from anything we have seen.

4 Worldviews

> . . . the knowledge of who we were, what we have become, where we were, where we were placed, whither we hasten, from what we are redeemed, what is birth, and what is rebirth.
>
> (Clement of Alexandria, *Excerpta ex Theodoto*)[1]

Who am I? What am I doing here? Where have I come from? What is this world in which I find myself? Why am I here at all? What are we supposed to be doing in this world, what is our calling, what is our destiny? What is the point of it all? And what will happen to us when we die? Is this all there is, or is there something more, something different, something greater? In one way or another, whether directly or indirectly, these ultimate questions have been asked by all historical traditions that fall under the esotericism umbrella. They all want to know (or claim to know) the true nature of reality, the bigger story of what life is all about, and the ultimate meaning or purpose of existence. If we look more closely at these questions and answers, we can see that they are all about three different but interrelated dimensions of reality. Firstly, there is the world of sense experience, our material cosmos or universe in time and space. Secondly, a spiritual or divine dimension is believed to exist beyond the reach of the physical senses, an ultimate reality that must in some way not be spatial and temporal but infinite and eternal. And finally, there is us—human beings who seem to participate simultaneously in those two worlds of spirit and matter.

There are many ways of describing this basic triangle, analyzing the relation between the three dimensions, and answering the question of ultimate meaning. Hence there is no such thing as "the" esoteric worldview—if we travel from one century to the next, we encounter an enormous variety of different, sometimes sharply conflicting beliefs. Nevertheless, if we zoom out from the intricate details of actual esoteric worldviews, we find that they fall within a limited number of structural patterns. I will refer to the first one as METAPHYSICAL RADICALISM. Metaphysical radicals insist on sharp "either/or" distinctions between spirit and matter, resulting in worldviews that are either monistic (nondual) or dualistic. I will refer to the second pattern as METAPHYSICAL MEDIATION. Metaphysical mediators take a "both/and" approach, because spirit and matter for them are not sharply separate realities but come together on the intermediary level of human beings and the natural world. Metaphysical mediation in esoteric contexts may take two specific forms as well, which I will call Platonic and Alchemical. In this chapter, I will illustrate these structural patterns by just a few specific examples that could easily be expanded with many others.

Metaphysical Radicalism

In a short story by the American writer J. D. Salinger, we find a famous description of radical nonduality, monism, or pantheism.

> "I was six when I saw that everything was God, and my hair stood up, and all that," Teddy said. "It was on a Sunday, I remember. My sister was only a tiny child then, and she was drinking her milk, and all of a sudden I saw that she was God and the milk was God. I mean, all she was doing was pouring God into God, if you know what I mean."[2]

Salinger's pantheism was not based on esoteric traditions of Western provenance but reflected the Hindu philosophy of Advaita Vedanta as expounded by Sri Ramakrishna (1836–1886). It says that the "world of division" or duality in which we live our lives is ultimately an illusion of the mind. We make distinctions in space between "here" and there," distinctions in time between "before" and "after," we see ourselves as "individuals" who are distinct from other individuals, and so on and so forth. But none of these distinctions is ultimately real—including the one between spirit and matter, or God and the world. If we can manage to dispel the illusion of duality, we will discover that All is One.[3] But please note that even this claim of radical oneness could be criticized as subtly dualistic. If there is just one single reality, this implies that we should not even draw any distinction between "reality" and "illusion," as if the former would be more real than the latter.[4]

Responding to Clement of Alexandria's list of existential questions, with which I began this chapter, radical nondualists will state that we have not "come" from anywhere at all and do not need to "go" anywhere either—we are forever one with God or ultimate reality. All we need to do is wake up to the fact. This doctrine has been popular in New Age circles ever since the 1960s, in a culture strongly marked by the impact of Oriental spiritualities. For instance, we might think of the classic "channeled" text known as *A Course in Miracles*, first published in 1975 and seen as a holy scripture by its devotees. Its more than 1,100 pages are based on one single opening statement of RADICAL NONDUALITY: "Nothing real can be threatened. Nothing unreal exists. Herein lies the peace of God."[5] Similar perspectives have been expressed by many other influential spiritual teachers after the Second World War, such as JIDDU KRISHNAMURTI (1895–1986) or DEEPAK CHOPRA (b. 1946). In a somewhat less explicit manner, it also informs the so-called quantum mysticisms of FRITJOF CAPRA (b. 1938), DAVID BOHM (1917–92), and a whole range of similar authors.[6]

Prior to the "Oriental Renaissance" of the nineteenth century, it is somewhat less easy to find radical nonduality in Western culture. Pantheism existed certainly as a technical philosophical doctrine, notably in Spinoza; and we also find it in certain Christian mystics, such as Meister Eckhart (c. 1260–c. 1328); but on the whole, at least in cultural contexts dominated by monotheism, we seldom encounter it as a salvational doctrine that tells us to dispel the illusion of the world. A metaphysics of radical nonduality does, however, lie at the heart of pagan metaphysical systems as found in Plotinus's *Enneads* or the original Hermetic writings from Roman Egypt. The anonymous visionary in *Corpus Hermeticum* I (the Poimandres) is told that his own *nous* is perfectly identical with the divine *Nous*—in their true essence, both are nothing but limitless divine Light.[7] Experiential phenomena that appear to our senses are therefore ultimately just delusions. Interestingly, however, this does not lead the Hermetic authors to embrace an attitude of world-denial. On the contrary, they insist that our task as human beings is not to escape from this world of division but to achieve an interior rebirth. This will allow us to function as embodied channels of divinity that infuse noetic Light into the phenomenal world. This Hermetic doctrine is perhaps indebted to Parmenides, finds strong support in Plato's *Symposium*, and is strikingly similar to the Neoplatonic theurgy of Iamblichus as well.[8]

Nonduality is more than just a matter of abstract metaphysical theory. Importantly, it responds to the existential fact of *suffering* by claiming that nothing we experience in our embodied state is ultimately real. Interestingly, the message can be one of equanimity and serene acceptance of whatever happens ("it is all just an illusion anyway") *or* its perfect opposite—a radical refusal to accept the "realities" of this world. If we are living our lives in a world of deceptive shadows, as suggested by Plato's famous metaphor of the cave,[9] it makes sense to conclude that we should leave it behind. For instance, see this passage written by two twentieth-century Rosicrucians, JAN VAN RIJCKENBORGH (ps. of Jan Leene, 1896–1968) and CATHAROSE DE PETRI (ps. of Henriette Stok-Huyser, 1902–90):

> We are pursuing a pilgrimage, deliberately and methodically. We do not want to die anymore and we do not want to live, we no longer want to be found anywhere. That is to say, we do not want to go to the mirror-sphere, nor to the sphere of matter: we want to go into "the Eternal Nothing," as the dialectical world and all her aeons and entities call it. . . . We have . . . investigated dialectical nature. We could do so because we are of this nature. With our ego-essence we were able to profoundly grasp and taste all that this world has to offer. And see, it was all trouble and misery. We have found this nature to be a nature of death, and we did not desire to sing with the blessed in front of the throne, or put any effort in trying to make this cursed order acceptable in any way. After years of experimentation, we concluded that this could not be the meaning of the true life, and that it was not good to collaborate any longer in deluding humanity in this nature of death.[10]

In such a radical dialectical vision of metaphysical alterity, what we believe to be Reality is actually Nothingness. Therefore its opposite, "the Eternal Nothing," must in some way be Eternally Real.

Such attitudes of radical world-denial or world-rejection have often been referred to as "gnostic" or Manichaean DUALISM.[11] Radical dualists do not feel at home in this world. They often experience it as alien and hostile, ruled by values they do not accept. Hence they may describe themselves as "strangers" or "exiles" who have "fallen" or have been "thrown" into the "prison" of an absurd and threatening world, a world in which they do not belong.[12] Such painful existential anguish implies a profound emotional desire to escape from the trap. If we are lost in a world that has no meaning, we must find our way toward a world that makes sense—not one of material darkness and suffering in a state of ignorance but one of spiritual Light and bliss where true knowledge (*gnōsis*) can be found. But in order to get there, first we must understand what went wrong. How do we explain our present situation of exile? Many different answers have been given to that question.

One radical narrative comes from MANICHAEISM and explains that there are two eternal worlds, one of Darkness and one of Light. Originally they were separate, and this should have remained the case; but unfortunately, they got mixed when the forces of Darkness made an attack on the world of Light. The result was a cosmic spiritual battle that continues to the present day. Sparks of spiritual light are trapped in our material bodies (or at least, of those who belong to the elect and have a chance to be saved), forever longing to escape and return to their original state of purity and bliss. One day they will succeed, and the two worlds will again be separate: "Light shall return to its place, the Darkness shall fall and not rise again."[13] Other radical dualists have claimed that there was originally just *one* single divine world of unbroken harmony, bliss, and Light. Our world of darkness and division is an accident or mistake, the result of a primordial Fall, error, or cosmic disaster—think of a cancerous growth that develops in an otherwise healthy tissue as the result of some infection or genetic defect. This sickness must be cured, so that the whole of Being may be restored to its original state of health and wholeness.

Yet other traditions claim that this material world was created *deliberately*, as a prison for the soul, by an evil or ignorant deity—the "demiurge" or world-maker. He wants to make us believe that he is the true God and no other God exists. His demonic helpers, the "archons," are trying to prevent us from waking up to our true condition. But once we do, by gaining *gnōsis* (salvational knowledge) of who we really are, we will seek to escape from the demiurge's prison to find our way back to the true world of divine Light from which we originally came and where we really belong. However, it is also possible to imagine a doctrine of salvation that implies no "return to one's origin." The early Christian followers of MARCION OF SINOPE (85–160 CE) believed that human beings are actually creatures of the demiurge, which means that this world *is* our true home. However, an "alien God" of Light and Love had sent Jesus to save them anyway, out of pure pity and compassion.

Across the spectrum from monism (nonduality) to dualism, all manifestations of metaphysical radicalism share one thing in common. *The World* in which we find ourselves (the phenomenal reality that appears to our physical senses) is experienced as a problem. Somehow it must be resolved or overcome, because it falls short of the pure perfection of divinity or spirit. Divinity means bliss; but the World is full of suffering. Divinity is pure light; but the World is full of darkness. Divinity is whole; but the World is full of division. Divinity means Being and eternal life; but the World is ruled by Becoming, time and transience, death and dissolution. Divinity is good; but the World is flawed, imperfect, or downright evil. Divinity is truth; but the World is full of error and falsity. Divinity is perfect beauty; but the World is full of ugliness. In sum, the World is a problem to which Spirit or Divinity is the answer. Metaphysical radicals think in sharp either/or terms; they refuse to settle for any compromise when it comes to solving this problem. For radical nondualists, as we have seen, the solution lies in a profound realization that all this lack and imperfection is in fact just illusion, like a dream or a nightmare. Once we have woken up to that truth, none of it can touch us anymore, because none of it is ultimately real. We were never really in trouble, we just thought that we were.

But this solution cannot be convincing to radical dualists. To them the World *is* definitely real—at the very least, as long as we are trapped in it—and so it poses a real problem that needs to be resolved. We *are* in trouble. We have to fight for our spiritual freedom against the powers of domination that want to keep us enslaved in this world. Because radical dualism distinguishes so sharply between Light and Darkness, Goodness and Evil, or Spirit and Matter, it has an enormous dramatic potential. It becomes natural to imagine the world, the cosmos, or the universe as a huge spiritual battlefield where the divine forces of Light are struggling against the demonic powers of Darkness over the liberty or captivity of human souls. Therefore it is hardly an accident that radical dualistic worldviews can lead to attitudes of militant activism resulting in violent conflicts between "sectarian" movements and the "powers of this world." One evident example would be the BOGOMIL and CATHAR heresies of the Middle Ages and their violent suppression by the authorities.[14] In a more recent period, we might think of extremist modern groups such as the neo-Rosicrucian ORDER OF THE SOLAR TEMPLE or the neo-gnostic organization HEAVEN'S GATE—in 1994 and 1997, respectively, leaders of these groups decided to "escape from this world" by committing collective suicide and murdering those who were less willing.[15] In the first edition of this book, I could still write that such forms of "spiritual extremism" seemed rather exceptional in contemporary esoteric contexts. But over the most recent decade, radical dualistic narratives of spiritual warfare against the demonic powers of this world have become disturbingly popular in online conspirituality contexts fueled by social media.

While metaphysical radicalism is based on an extreme "either/or" stance that rejects any compromise, most traditions that fall under the esotericism umbrella take a more inclusivist "both/and" attitude to divinity and the world. Human beings and the natural world are seen as participating in spirit and matter simultaneously, which means that they enjoy some kind of "middle status." The focus is not on a radical choice for spirit or divinity against matter and the world (whether by unmasking it as an illusion or trying to escape from its power) but on *mediation* between those two polar extremes—even though, admittedly, the spiritual pole is always seen as prior and superior. In esoteric contexts, we encounter two chief paradigms of mediation; one of these is grounded in Platonic theory, while the other is based on alchemical models.

Platonic Mediation

In a notable passage, the American historian of ideas Arthur O. Lovejoy (1873–1962) argued that, due to the persistent influence of Platonism, Western culture has always been torn between two different conceptions of God.

> The one was the Absolute of otherworldliness—self-sufficient, out of time, alien to the categories of ordinary human thought and experience, needing no world of lesser beings to supplement or enhance his own eternal self-contained perfection. The other was a God who emphatically was not self-sufficient nor, in any philosophical

> sense, "absolute": one whose essential nature required the existence of other beings, and not of one kind of these only, but of all kinds which could find a place in the descending scale of the possibilities of reality—a God whose prime attribute was generativeness, whose manifestation was to be found in the diversity of creatures and therefore in the temporal order and the manifold spectacle of nature's processes.[16]

The first perspective lends itself naturally to metaphysical radicalism. It suggests that from this world of division and multiplicity we must find the way back to the perfect otherworldly Oneness of the "self-sufficient absolute." This is the "alien God" of pure spirit who has nothing in common with our material world.[17] But the second perspective suggests exactly the opposite. It implies not an attitude of negation that leads us away from this world but a positive movement of creative generativity that is seen as flowing from God *toward* or *into* the world. God is conceived as the "generative Source" (*pēgē* in Greek) of all creation or manifestation, the great fountain of Life and Light.[18] Our material world therefore cannot be conceived of as the dark and negative counterpart of spirit; on the contrary, it is to be welcomed and admired as the splendid manifestation of infinite divine power and creative abundance. If Lovejoy's first God of Platonism implies a rejection or denial of the world, the second God implies a positive attitude of world-affirmation.

In the history of Platonism throughout Western culture, this concept of God as the Generative Source of Being became central to the extremely influential view of reality as a "Great Chain of Being." Out of the boundless creative depths of the divine Source flows a splendid imaginal universe full of entities and creatures of incredible diversity,[19] from the most exalted angelic intelligences close to God down to the lowest animal creatures. They have all been given their proper place in a magnificent ordered hierarchy that is stretched out between the ultimate poles of pure Spirit and pure Matter. Here the emphasis is not on conflict but on *continuity* and *universal connectedness*, for the very idea of a Great "Chain" means precisely that the emanations of Life and Light stretch down from the ultimate divine Source all the way down toward the lowest levels of manifestation. The result is a multileveled universe in which spiritual powers can travel downward while human souls may travel upward.

This medieval and early modern concept of a Great Chain of Being combined a Platonic model with biblical monotheistic beliefs about the unique status of human beings. In a famous passage, Giovanni Pico della Mirandola describes how God made the human being into "a creature with no distinct image," assigning him "a place in the middle of the world" while addressing him as follows:

> No fixed seat, no special form, nor any particular talent of your own have we given you, Adam, so that whatever seat, whatever form, whatever talent you may choose for yourself, may be yours to possess according to your own desire and judgment. All other beings are constrained by a definite nature within the laws that we have prescribed. But you, constrained by no limits, may determine that nature by yourself, using the free will under whose authority I have placed you. I have set you up as

the center of the world, so that you will be better placed to survey whatever the world contains. We have made you neither heavenly nor earthly, neither mortal nor immortal, so that on your own, as your own free maker who may honourably mold his own nature, you may fashion yourself in whatever form you prefer. You will have the power to degenerate into the lower forms of life, which are brutish. But by the judgement of your own soul, you will also have the power to be reborn into higher forms that are divine.[20]

This passage has deep Platonic resonances, notably with Socrates's famous image of the human soul as a "charioteer" whose carriage is carried by two horses—a good one that draws him upward toward the purity of the divine ideas and an unruly one that drags him down toward the lower things of the bodily senses.[21] That human beings have the power to rise up to heaven and even be reborn as divine beings, but are tempted by bodily desires that draw them down to the world of matter, is a recurring motif in Platonic and Hermetic literature. In fact, it is one of the most fundamental "deep structures" of esoteric speculation in Western culture from antiquity to the present. It could inspire passages of heroic exaltation about "human dignity," as in Pico,[22] but could also be cast in a more ironic register, as seen in Alexander Pope's *Essay on Man* (1734):

Placed on this isthmus of a middle state,
A being darkly wise and rudely great:
With too much knowledge for the Sceptic side,
With too much weakness for the Stoic's pride,
He hangs between, in doubt to act or rest;
In doubt to deem himself a God or Beast;
In doubt his mind or body to prefer;
Born but to die, and reas'ning but to err;
Alike in ignorance, his reason such,
Whether he thinks too little or too much;
Chaos of thought and passion, all confused;
Still by himself abused or disabused;
Created half to rise, and half to fall:
Great lord of all things, yet a prey to all;
Sole judge of truth, in endless error hurl'd;
The glory, jest, and riddle of the world![23]

Broadly speaking, and allowing for quite some exceptions and qualifications, concepts of God as the "self-sufficient absolute" (with all their world-denying and ascetic implications) were largely dominant in earlier phases of Christian Platonism, while the world-affirming idea of God as the "generative source" achieved greater dominance in later periods. This is part of the general historical drift, in European history, from a focus on religious salvation in the afterlife toward an increasing concern with "conquering the world" by means of reason and scientific progress.

The intermediary status of human beings in a multileveled hierarchical universe did not just imply that they could steer their chariot either upward (away from the world toward unity with God) or downward (away from God toward the pursuit of worldly pleasures). Even while pursuing an ideal of spiritual purification and rebirth, they could seek to profit from the spiritual virtues or "gifts" that were believed to emanate downward from the inexhaustible divine Source. In other words (as already suggested above), "mediation" could mean the attempt to find a balance between the upward movement of souls toward the Light of divinity *and* the downward movement of divine powers into the world. One excellent example is MARSILIO FICINO's 1489 volume *De Vita Coelitus Comparanda*, about "how to bring your life in harmony with the heavens."[24] It says that each and every second of our lives, we are subject to influences that are coming down from the stars according to the orderly movements of the astrological constellations. If we know how to attract and channel these "gifts" (for instance by sacred hymns and ceremonies, aromatic perfumes, or amulets and talismans) we can use them to our own benefit, especially to heal and protect our bodies and minds from harmful influences. But Ficino's critics were quick to point out the flip side of the argument. They pointed out that these theurgical techniques had been invented by pagan authors and might as well attract dark demonic forces.

If the *upward* movement of transcending this world and finding unity with the divine is conventionally (although problematically) associated with MYSTICISM,[25] such attempts to draw powers *down* from above are usually referred to as astral MAGIC. A classic traditional reference is the Hermetic *Asclepius*. In two notorious passages, it describes how the ancient Egyptians had learned to attract the powers of angels and demons down into their temple statues, which thereby gained the power to do good or evil.[26] St. Augustine had rejected such Hermetic practices as pagan idolatry,[27] but Renaissance humanists who admired the wisdom of Hermes Trismegistus were no longer so sure. They knew that great Christian authorities such as Thomas Aquinas had made a sophisticated distinction between "talismans" and "amulets" (material objects that, not unlike those Hermetic statues, could function as receptacles of spiritual energies channeled from above)—the former were inscribed with linguistic signs, implying the dangerous attempt to communicate with demons, but the virtues of the latter were purely natural and therefore acceptable for Christians.[28] Ficino tried to convince his readers (and himself, for he was clearly tormented by doubts) that astral magic belonged to the latter category and could safely be used for the purpose of healing.

The Platonic concept of mediation resulted, therefore, in a universal holistic worldview that combined a "magical" movement of higher powers or virtues drawn down into the world with a "mystical" upward movement of the human soul toward God. The classic *summa* of all these ideas is HEINRICH CORNELIUS AGRIPPA's *De occulta philosophia libri tres* ("Three Books of Occult Philosophy," 1533). In the first volume he described the sublunary world of the four elements; in the second volume he moved on to the intermediary world of planets, numbers, and mathematics; and in the final volume he discussed the spiritual, angelic, and divine entities beyond the material cosmos. This structure allowed him to cover the full scope of traditional information about the elementary, celestial, and super-celestial realms with all their occult virtues. The general message was that, by achieving spiritual rebirth and unification with the divine mind, human beings could even come to participate in God's own creative powers. Far from suggesting some kind of ultimate absorption or annihilation of the finite human intellect in the infinite Light of divinity, it was all about the prospect of ultimate deification.[29] Agrippa's context was resolutely Christian; but in modern occultist and New Age formulations, the core idea has been popularized and reformulated in psychological terms, as spiritual "self-realization" or finding one's "true self." Such ideals imply neither a pious submission to God's will nor an annihilation of the ego in the ocean of divinity but put all the emphasis on spiritual empowerment and the unfolding of our "human potential." The Renaissance Magus becomes the early modern model of a "fully realized human being" placed "at the center of the universe" and endowed with the power to "create his (or her) own reality."[30] In contemporary popular culture, from novels and comics to video games that (whether directly or indirectly, consciously or unconsciously) are often inspired by esoteric traditions, this core concept of human deification and access to spiritual "superpowers" has become a theme of major importance.[31]

Agrippa's Platonic worldview was still based on the traditional Ptolemaic/Aristotelian cosmos. Placed "in the middle of the universe," human beings could gaze down toward the material globe or up toward God, who resided with his angels above the sphere of the fixed stars. But the Copernican revolution after the mid-sixteenth century made such a spatial and vertical perspective untenable. As evident for the first time in the works of GIORDANO BRUNO, God could no longer be imagined as living in some place beyond the cosmos or high up "above the stars." An infinite God in an infinite universe could no longer be imagined as residing in any specific place at all—quite literally, there could be no room for him anywhere in the universe. Therefore he had to be present *everywhere* at the same time, as an invisible power or dimension that permeates all that is. A convenient term for this perspective is PANENTHEISM. Unlike pantheism (which claims that God and the world are identical), it means that God is omnipresent in the world *and* the world is contained in God. Many centuries before Bruno, we already encounter this worldview in the Hermetic literature of the first centuries CE:

> All beings are in God—not as though they were in some place . . . but in a different manner: they rest in his incorporeal imagination (*en asōmatōi phantasiāi*). . . . You must conceive of God as having all *noēmata* in himself: those of the cosmos, himself, the all. Therefore unless you make yourself equal to God, you cannot understand God. Like is understood only by like. Allow yourself to grow larger until you are equal to him who is immeasurable, outleap all that is corporeal, transcend all time, and become the *aiōn*—then you will understand God. Having perceived that nothing is impossible for you, consider yourself immortal and capable of understanding everything—all arts, all learning, the nature of all living beings. Rise higher than every height and descend lower than every depth; gather all sensations inside you of all that is made—fire, water, dry and humid. Be everywhere at once: on earth, in the sea, in heaven, before you were born, in the womb, young, old, dead, in the hereafter. If your *nous* can behold all these things simultaneously—times, places,

> actions, qualities, quantities—then you can know God. . . . On that road he will meet you everywhere, you will see him everywhere, at places and times where you least expect it, while waking or sleeping, on sea or on earth, at night or in daytime, while you speak or as you're silent—for there is nothing that he is not. So will you say "God is invisible"? Don't speak like that. Who is more visible than he is? He has made everything so that you might see him through all that is.[32]

As seen for instance in the work of RICHARD MAURICE BUCKE (1837–1902), with his famous volume *Cosmic Consciousness* (1901), Hermetic panentheism resonates strongly with the expansive Romantic worldview of American Transcendentalism.[33] Such perspectives became popular in spiritual milieus after the Second World War, as welcome alternatives not just to traditional Christian notions of ascetic otherworldliness, depravity, and sin but also to the existentialist despair and pessimism that had been dominant for decades.[34] A strong emphasis on the beauty and goodness of the universe and the capacity of human beings to experience the world as God's living body were obviously congenial to the emerging environmentalist ethic; and they also informed a whole range of spiritual movements that called attention to the unlimited possibilities of "Human Potential." We may think here of the famous ESALEN center in Big Sur, California,[35] but also of such bestselling authors as JANE ROBERTS (1929–1984) and her extremely influential series of channeled messages attributed to "Seth."[36] Human consciousness as such was seen here as the vanguard of spiritual *evolution*—a concept with deep historical backgrounds in esoteric speculation as well, as we will see in the following section.

Alchemical Mediation

The Platonic model conceives of the universe in *spatial* terms. It is imagined in the shape of a multileveled Great Chain of Being, spread out along a spectrum between the polar opposites of spirit and matter, with human beings placed in the middle. This concept carries a message of universal harmony and hierarchical order—all spiritual power and authority resides forever in the divine principle of Unity high up above, from whence it reaches downward, step by step, through all the lower degrees of Being. During the European Renaissance, this powerful paradigm had its center in Italian culture. It was obviously congenial to the idea of one universal (i.e., "Catholic") religion embodied in the Church of Rome, a strictly hierarchical organization under the central authority of the Pope. But this image of divinely instituted unity and sovereign harmony was shattered forever by the events of the Reformation. Protestant revolutionaries needed different models to make sense of their experience. The new sensitivity has been described in an eloquent formulation by the church historian FERDINAND CHRISTIAN BAUR (1792–1860):

> If for the Catholic there is no such thing as a historical movement through which the Church has become essentially different from what it was at its origin, if in the

entire development of the Church he merely sees its immanent truth coming to ever greater realization and ever more general recognition, from the perspective of the Protestant, in contrast, the Church as it exists in the immediate present is separate from what it originally was by an abyss that is so wide, that between these two points in time there must have been an immeasurable series of changes.[37]

In other words, the Protestant revolution implied a new kind of *historical* consciousness. To account for the unprecedented historical struggles in which the Reformers found themselves, the spatial concept of immutable cosmic harmony and sublime beauty (congenial to the idea of a *philosophia perennis*) had to give way to a *linear* model focused on temporality and irreversible change. Many Lutherans and Protestant Spiritualists found such a model in the alchemical core narrative of TRANSMUTATION. Out of this came a new and entirely different paradigm of mediation, centered geographically and culturally in the German-speaking heartland of the Reformation. The relation between the two paradigms could be summarized as follows:

Platonic	**Alchemical**
Spatial	Linear
Static Harmony	Dynamic Process
From Spirit to Nature	From Nature to Spirit
Fall (from Light into Darkness)	Birth (from Darkness to Light)
The Authority of Tradition	Individual Experience

The Platonic model is based on a top-down and hierarchical mode of thinking, beginning with general metaphysical principles and reaching downward from there toward lower physical realities. By contrast, the Alchemical model takes a bottom-up approach, starting with the physical world and then working its way upward from there toward the soul and spiritual realities. The Platonic model is dominated by an essentially static concept of universal harmony, starting with a vision of the whole and then assigning to everything its proper place in the "Great Chain of Being," a kind of universal depository of all that exists. The Alchemical model is inherently dynamic, linear, and dialectical; it begins with nothing else than the simple unity of primal matter and then moves forward from there, in a dramatic and painful process of birth, growth, and progressive development full of violent conflicts between opposed forces or principles. The Platonic model implies the "downward" movement of a Fall, because it needs to explain how the darkness of matter and spiritual ignorance could have emerged from the bliss and perfection of divine Oneness and Light. The Alchemical model implies an "upward" movement of generation and birth, as it tries to describe how an original state of darkness could be the matrix or womb from which superior, even divine spiritual realities come forth. Finally, the Platonic model is inherently conservative, as it is based on an accumulation of the authoritative teachings from the past. By contrast, the Alchemical model is focused far less on traditional erudition and much more on creative discovery and new insights, because it relies primarily on direct individual experience.

If the Platonic model during the early modern period had its center in Roman Catholic Italy, the Alchemical model had its cultural, geographical, and linguistic center in German culture, the heartland of the Reformation. It is not hard to see why. These linear and dynamic perspectives, with their focus on painful struggle and individual experience, simply made more sense to the lived experience of Protestant revolutionaries. They knew very well what they had done—they had broken the harmony of the Church, rejected its sacred tradition, and were in open rebellion against priestly authority. With nothing to guide them in their struggle except the Word of God and their own individual conscience, they had embarked on an entirely new adventure forward into the future, for which tradition gave them no blueprint or script. This journey began in darkness, in a frightening world of suffering and sin, not a reassuring spiritual world of harmony and light. Thus it made perfect sense for them to think of their existential situation in alchemical terms, as the *nigredo*, the initial black phase from which the Great Work must begin.

The Alchemical model is not deductive (beginning with a grand overview of the whole) but *inductive*. In an Aristotelian rather than Platonic spirit, its point of departure lies right here in the concrete and tangible realities of nature and physical bodies. In early modern Europe, the key pioneer of this new paradigm was PARACELSUS. Instead of relying blindly on ancient authorities, he insisted on direct empirical study of nature and ourselves. We should learn from our own experience at firsthand, not from dusty books. Although he never became a Protestant, it makes sense that Paracelsus is referred to sometimes as "the Luther of medicine": he wrote in the German of the common people instead of the Latin of the learned, reaching audiences much larger than just the intellectual elites, and promoted an individual approach to salvation and healing—two pursuits that, for him, were ultimately one and the same. As human beings we are vulnerable to illness because, due to the sin of Adam and Eve, we are born in a fallen state, for which Paracelsus had invented the term *cagastrum*. Therefore the attainment of health implies a process of not just bodily but also spiritual purification and regeneration or rebirth—healing means ultimately reversing the Fall.

Under the strong influence of Paracelsian concepts, the model of Alchemical mediation came to full development in the system of JACOB BÖHME. As we have seen in Chapter 2 (and in the sharpest possible contrast with Platonic models), Böhme's God is neither the primordial spiritual principle of harmony and Light nor the creator of our world. He has himself been born, in darkness and pain, out of the mystery of the *Ungrund*. From an initial state of darkness and wrath (comparable to the alchemical *nigredo*), God's body moves through a process of dialectical struggle until it attains the ultimate condition of universal Love and Light; from a frightening "hellish" world of suffering and strife (associated with the Father), it is transmuted alchemically into a luminous world of harmony called Eternal Nature (associated with the Son). Thus Light is born from darkness, love is born from wrath, and the Son is born from the Father. All this is based on an alchemical model of transmutation, with frequent reference to sexual and bodily processes of "fertilization" and "(re)generation" or "(re)birth."[38] The redemption of human beings and of the whole world of Nature, the body of God, follows the same pattern. For the salvation of humanity, Christ was born in a dark world as the Light of divinity (similar to how God himself had been born from the *Ungrund*); and he must be born once again in the inner darkness of each sinful human creature. The final goal of spiritual salvation does not consist in an escape from the body but in a transmutation *of* the body. It will be reborn as a luminous vehicle, a subtle organism made of light, that will survive the death of the gross physical body. As formulated by FRIEDRICH CHRISTOPH OETINGER in the eighteenth century, *Leiblichkeit ist das Ende der Werke Gottes* ("Corporeality is the end [i.e, the goal, or *telos*] of God's works").[39]

Precisely because the Platonic and Alchemical models of mediation are so different, even antithetical, there have been many attempts to bring them together in some kind of grand synthesis. During the early modern period, we encounter many such enterprises of creating an encyclopedic vision of the whole of creation, often expressed not just in words but in visual imagery as well.[40] Essentially, we are dealing here with grand universal "Theories of Everything" that comprise theology, philosophy, cosmology, physics, chemistry, and anthropology. For speculative minds engaged in such projects, nothing could be more tempting than the attempt to overcome the conflict between Being *and* Becoming (*Sein und Zeit*, "Being and Time"), the Oneness of "All That Is" *and* its processual development through temporality and change. Among the most important, most intriguing, but also most elusive examples is GERMAN IDEALISM and its impact on nineteenth-century evolutionist thought. Some scholars have seen the alchemical-theosophical tradition from Böhme to Oetinger, or even the entire "Hermetic Tradition," as a major key to understanding philosophers like Schelling or Hegel.[41] Others have questioned the significance of such influences, and the truth is that we are still far from any scholarly consensus. This research deficit illustrates the need for a radical interdisciplinary perspective, which should begin by recognizing that neither the proponents of *philosophia occulta* nor the philosophers of Romanticism and German Idealism would have accepted the disciplinary straitjackets that the modern academy imposes on them. They all saw their speculative worldviews as relevant equally to philosophy, religion, science, and the arts; and they felt much more free than their contemporary interpreters to draw upon anything they could use in any of these domains.

Therefore it is still not entirely clear in how far ROMANTIC EVOLUTIONISM is indebted historically to the processual dynamics of the Alchemical model of mediation. Be that as it may, there is certainly no doubt about the enormous influence of Romantic and Idealist narratives of evolution on the development of esotericism after the eighteenth century.[42] Evolutionism emerged as a dominant new paradigm during this period. It transformed not just those academic disciplines that already existed, such as biology, geology, the history of culture, or the study of religion, but was also of key importance to the newly emerging discipline of psychology. Romantic and Idealist narratives were still indebted to Christian theological models (Hegel's Absolute Spirit that comes to self-realization through the historical process must somehow be the Spirit of God); but they could easily be psychologized and transformed into narratives about the evolution of the human spirit or of human consciousness as such.[43] A perfect example is the Swiss physician JOSEPH ENNEMOSER, whom we already encountered as the author of a large *History of Magic* (1844), on Romantic and Idealist foundations. It became a crucial although largely unacknowledged source for central esoteric authors as different as Helena P. Blavatsky and Carl Gustav Jung.[44] The true impact that Idealist philosophy and its historical narratives have had on the popular practice and understanding of religion and spirituality in Western modernity still tends to be underestimated by scholars.

For our present concerns, the most important example is JUNGIAN PSYCHOLOGY and its historical backgrounds in German Romantic Mesmerism. Jung drew partly on gnostic models, describing the spiritual goal of psychological self-knowledge as an "interior sun"—the inner light of the human psyche that could give access to a numinous transpersonal reality. But his most potent models were derived from alchemy, from a perspective that was heavily influenced by German Romanticism and Idealist philosophy, including its backgrounds in Christian Theosophy and Pietism.[45] The core alchemical narrative of transmutation (a difficult and painful struggle, leading from prime matter to gold or from darkness to light, accompanied at every stage by potent imagery, loaded with numinous power) provided Jung with a perfect model to describe the psychological process of "individuation," understood as an arduous journey of self-discovery and confrontation with symbolic images that emerge from the unconscious. Here the initial state of "darkness" is no longer understood to be a state of sin, as in the original Protestant model, but rather in terms of spiritual ignorance and immaturity. There is no better illustration than Jung's record of his own *decensus ad inferos* (descent into the depths) known as the *Black Books* and their final edited version, the *Liber Novus* or *Red Book*.[46] Even in this heavily psychologized version of Theosophical salvation, the ultimate goal can only be described as deification.

A Cautious Reminder

In this chapter, I have focused not on any specific historical traditions or esoteric worldviews but on the somewhat more abstract *models* by which they are structured. It remains important to emphasize once again that, in the real world, we never encounter any pure and perfect manifestations of Radical Nonduality (or Monism, Pantheism), Radical Dualism, Platonic Mediation, and Alchemical Mediation. Structural models or ideal types are useful as hermeneutical tools for bringing some order and clarity to the infinite complexities of intellectual, religious, or social history. But they can never capture what we actually encounter "on the ground" while studying any specific sources, movements, practices, or phenomena. There have been many attempts to achieve a theoretical synthesis of some kind between these different models, usually by authors with a strong esoteric agenda of reducing the variety of different traditions to a single "true" essence. None of those attempts has been successful, and none will ever be, because they all rely on similar procedures of *reducing* the messy complexity of our actual human world to some abstract theoretical scheme that can only exist in the mind.

Once again, my advice to readers would be to not waste their time on the pursuit of an artificial chimera called "the" esoteric worldview. There is no such thing. The ultimate objective in studying esoteric conceptions of reality is not explanatory or reductionist but *hermeneutic*—it is about trying to understand, as well as possible, how people make sense of the world and their own lives in it. This business of sensemaking involves creative human attempts to find meaningful answers to existential questions, of the kinds that were formulated at the opening of this chapter.

5 Knowledge

> There *had* been a time when he had thought of nothing else, when he had stood on his rooftop watching the grimy spheres of heaven revolve around him, *Oh I see, I get it*: but to hear those notions in another's mouth, unqualified, fitted to a different kind of consciousness, made them sound at once loony and banal, too much and not enough.
>
> (John Crowley, *The Solitudes*)[1]

It has been suggested that "claims of higher or perfect knowledge" are central to esoteric discourse,[2] but it would be more correct to say that its participants *aspire* to such knowledge. They typically believe that it is possible for humans to "lift the veil of Isis,"[3] so as to gain direct access to the hidden face of reality and see *ta onta*, "the things that really are." In less monistic and more hierarchical or dualistic terms, they believe that our soul can wake up, free itself from the spell of the senses, and see the supreme spiritual reality far beyond matter and the physical world.[4] Sometimes such higher or perfect knowledge is claimed as a proud possession, but more often it is held out as a promise.

The basic worldviews discussed in the previous chapter lend legitimacy, on a theoretical level, to such hopes for discovering the ultimate truth about existence. Following the Platonic model of emanation and restitution, our soul has its origin in an eternal, divine reality to which it secretly longs to return. This implies that human beings must have an inborn (latent or dormant) capacity to know what is ultimately real and true, by gaining access to the supreme spiritual source of everything beautiful and good.[5] Therefore we are not dependent on God's initiative to reveal Himself to us, as in classic accounts of monotheism, where the mortal creature is dependent on the Creator's initiative. Nor is our capacity for knowledge limited to the bodily senses and natural reason, as in classical science and rational philosophy. In contrast to both alternatives, the very nature of our souls allows us direct access to the supreme, eternal, and universal substance of ultimate Being—even though, in some accounts, an ultimate mystery may exist even beyond Being itself.[6] In terms of the alternative Alchemical model, with its logic of linear development, the attainment of supreme knowledge cannot be a matter of "remembering" our divine origin and getting *back* to where we came from (implying a cyclical pattern of fall or decline, alienation or exile, and restitution or return) but implies a latent capacity or human potentiality that *yet* needs to be attained in the future. From such a perspective, the state of perfect knowledge lies not at the origin of the soul's journey but beckons from the future as its *telos* or ultimate goal.

Such salvational knowledge of ultimate reality is usually referred to by the Greek word *gnōsis* and has often been presented as central to esoteric spiritualities. But although its importance cannot be doubted, it would be a mistake to assume that "esoteric" traditions are concerned exclusively with higher or absolute knowledge of the soul and its spiritual salvation, to the exclusion of more conventional goals or modes of knowledge. On the contrary, many of its representatives have been deeply involved in the pursuit of learning or gaining knowledge by rational-philosophical and scientific methods, scriptural hermeneutics and exegesis of sacred texts, dogmatic theologies based on authority and tradition, and, last but not least, practical forms of "know-how" for gaining control over life events. In this chapter, I will first discuss the relation between salvational *gnōsis* and other types of knowledge that share the ambition of unveiling ("dis-covering") ultimate truths about reality. I will then turn to the pursuit of knowledge in the sense of *understanding* esoteric mysteries through interpretation or hermeneutics, and, finally, to practical "esoteric" knowledge about *how to do* things in the world.

Reason, Faith, Experience, *Gnōsis*

In this section, I will discuss claims of knowledge about "how things really are," in terms of a four-part typology that may be summarized as follows. I will explain the terminology.

	COMMUNICABLE	VERIFIABLE	
REASON	+	+	Propositional knowledge
FAITH	+	–	
EXPERIENCE	–	+	Knowledge by acquaintance
GNŌSIS	–	–	

- We are all familiar with claims of knowledge that focus on *rational analysis* and *science* or *scholarship* (unfortunately, the English language does not have one single umbrella term to cover natural sciences *and* the humanities, comparable to, e.g., *Wissenschaft* in German). To find answers to our questions about how the world works, we depend first of all on the evidence of our senses (enormously extended by technologies that allow us to study the whole of physical reality from the infinitely small to the infinitely large) combined with models of rational prediction and control. Scholars and scientists have developed sophisticated methods and instruments for studying and comparing physical data, empirical phenomena, historical sources, or human behavior. To understand or explain what they discover, they formulate theories or models and hypotheses as guides for further exploration. In doing so, they rely on reasonable arguments that are seen as consistent with the factual evidence; and they often need highly technical languages to discuss the complexity of the data as accurately as possible. Even the limits of reason and language themselves can become an object of reasoned discourse, for instance, about how the pursuit of "objective knowledge" relates to the social dynamics of power, political agendas, or subjective prejudice.

If I claim to "know" something and wish to be taken seriously in such a rational-scientific context, two minimum conditions need to be fulfilled. Firstly, I must use some clear language for *communication* so that others can understand what I am trying to tell them. Secondly, it must be possible for them to *check and evaluate* my claims independently, so as to determine whether they are true, or at least, convincing enough. In other words, I must formulate my arguments in a way that makes sense to others, and I must provide some kind of evidence or reasonable argument that can be put to the test. Without these boundary conditions, we have no science, no scholarly research, and no rational discourse. I will use the term REASON as convenient shorthand for this first type of knowledge.

- Yet we also encounter claims of knowledge that (like those of *reason*) can be communicated in clear language but *cannot* be tested independently. For instance, traditional Christian theology claims to know for certain that God is a trinity of Father, Son, and Holy Spirit, the second person of which was incarnated as Jesus Christ. Extremely intelligent and erudite theologians have been formulating these convictions with great precision, in exact discursive prose that can be studied by anybody who takes an interest. Those statements leave no doubt about what they mean: they do indeed seek to convince us that the Son of God was born as a man. But how do we find out whether these statements are true or false? Theologians have produced incredibly sophisticated arguments, but we have no independent procedures for determining whether an entity such as God exists or not, let alone whether He might have a triune nature and a Son who was born in the flesh. When all is said and done, these are statements of belief. You might accept them on the basis of authority and tradition (i.e., because you have been told that they are true), but you cannot test them independently in any way. I will use the term FAITH as convenient shorthand for this second type of knowledge.

Of course, the example of Christian trinitarian theology can be readily extrapolated to many other contexts—not just religious ones such as paganism, Judaism, or Islam but also secular ideological perspectives such as atheism ("no God exists") or materialism ("no spiritual realities exist independent of matter"). The point about *faith* is that one chooses to adopt certain claims that have been handed down by tradition or authority, thereby accepting them as valid knowledge but *without* insisting on independent verification. It is a perfectly natural thing to do. After all, most of us accept scientific claims not because we have bothered to check them ourselves but because we believe (i.e., have confidence, or *faith*) that scientists know what they are doing. As for atheists and materialists, they may be impressed by the explanatory power of physical science and rational models, but they still have no methods or instruments for *proving* the nonexistence of God or a spiritual reality.

- So far, so good. If we continue the exercise, what about claims of knowledge that (unlike those of *reason* and *faith*) cannot be communicated by discursive language but *can* be verified or tested independently? For instance, we might think of the experience of pleasure or pain. We all know what it means to get hurt. To check the reality of physical pain, all you need to do is hold your hand above a burning candle. But although we know that pain is real, and we can easily test it, there is no way of communicating the reality of pain by means of discursive language alone. You need to feel it to know what it's all about. In the rest of this section, I will use the term EXPERIENCE as convenient shorthand for this third type of knowledge.

But before moving on to the fourth and final type, at this point we must note an important distinction that is often overlooked, because of the limits of English vocabulary. Most modern European languages, for instance German or French, distinguish clearly between two different kinds of "knowledge" for which English has just one single word. The two categories that I just defined as *reason* and *faith* are concerned with *propositional* knowledge. In German this would be *wissen*, and in French it would be *savoir*. Because this knowledge takes the form of verbal propositions, it can indeed be communicated through discursive language. But my third category, defined as *experience*, consists of *knowledge by acquaintance*. In German this would be referred to as *kennen* and in French as *connaître*. If you say "I know Jeff," this does not mean that you have some information about him; it means that you know him personally and have learned from experience what kind of person he is. "I know that the flame will hurt me": that is *wissen/savoir*, propositional knowledge. "I know what it's like to feel pain," because I've experienced its reality at firsthand: that is *kennen/connaître*, knowledge by acquaintance. Please note that the former statement is about *truth*, whereas the latter is about *reality*.

- Finally, then, we reach the fourth and final combination: claims of knowledge that can *neither* be communicated by discursive language *nor* verified or tested by independent observers. Here we are dealing with such statements as "I have seen it, I have experienced it, and I know that it's real—but I can't prove that it's real, and I can't even express the experience in words." In this case, the claim about an experienced reality cannot be tested independently, as in the case of a burning flame.[7] I will use the term GNŌSIS as convenient shorthand for this third and final approach to knowledge. Again, we are dealing here with claims of reality based on immediate personal acquaintance (*kennen, connaître*). They should not be confused with propositional claims about whether something is or isn't the case (*wissen, savoir*).

Before continuing my argument, I must insert a rejoinder to avoid possible misunderstandings. The *reason-faith-gnōsis* triad (which I'm expanding here by the addition of *experience* as a fourth component) comes originally from GILLES QUISPEL (1916–2006), a Dutch scholar of gnosticism who was deeply influenced by Carl Gustav Jung and the "religionist" perspectives associated with Eranos. In line with a strong tradition in German research that speaks of *die Gnosis* as a quasi-historical category (roughly equivalent to "the Western esoteric traditions"), Quispel conceptualized gnosis as "the third component of Western culture" next to the dominant components of reason and faith. His perspective on gnosis was very similar to Jung's concept of a grand historical continuity from ancient gnosticism through medieval and early modern alchemy up to modern depth psychology. But my own way of using the *reason-faith-gnōsis* triad (and expanding it further) has nothing in common with Quispel's Jungian perspective or his religionist background assumptions. Far from referring to any historical currents or spiritual traditions, it is meant strictly as an analytical instrument for distinguishing between different categories of knowledge (or, more precisely, claims of knowledge) that can be encountered in Western culture.[8] In no way does this imply that "esotericism could be defined in terms of gnosis." In this chapter I have chosen to write *gnōsis* with an accent, reflecting the Greek letter omega, to place extra emphasis on this point: what I have in mind is a type of knowledge (i.e., an epistemological category or, more precisely, a category of epistemological claims), *not* some quasi-historical "phenomenon."

Propositional Knowledge in Esoteric Contexts

Contrary to common stereotypes about the "irrational beliefs" of esotericists or occultists, traditions that fall under the "esotericism" umbrella do not necessarily reject *reason* or *faith*. Rather, their usual argument is that such approaches are valid in themselves but have their limitations, and only knowledge of the *gnōsis* type leads to ultimate insight. A paradigmatic formulation is found in a passage from the *Corpus Hermeticum* that uses highly technical language for explaining the relation of *gnōsis* to reasoned discourse (*logos*) and faith (*pistis*). To understand this fragment, it is important to know that the Hermetic *nous* refers to a specific human faculty that allows us to attain *gnōsis* of the universal divine *Nous*, the supreme reality of spiritual Light that emanates from the ultimate "generative Source" or *pēgē*. *Nous* has therefore an epistemological *and* an ontological meaning at the same time—we might say that humans perceive the ultimate Light by means of their own inner light, but those two are ultimately one and the same. The activity of our human *nous* is called *noēsis*, a crucial but strictly untranslatable term that often gets rendered by weak equivalents such as "understanding" but actually requires a neologism such as "noeticizing." Because the exact terminology is so important in this case, I add the relevant terms here within brackets:

> If you noeticize [*ennoounti*], Asclepius, you will find all these things to be real; but they will seem unbelievable [*apista*] if you do not noeticize [*agnoounti*]. To understand noetically [*noēsai*] is to have faith [*pisteusai*], and to not have faith [*apistēsai*] means to not understand noetically [*mē noēsai*]. *Logos* [reasoned discourse] does get you to what's real; but *nous* is powerful, and, when it has been guided by *logos* up to a point, it has the means to get you all the way to what's real.[9]

To gain true noetic understanding or *gnōsis*, therefore, we must have faith and make good use of our rational faculties; but the final step can be taken only by *nous* itself and leads to a level of direct perception beyond the reach of reason. To use a metaphor, the former gets you right to the city wall, but only the latter beams you inside the city itself. The Hermetic writings keep emphasizing that if you want to attain *gnōsis*, you will first have to master the "general discourses" (*genikoi logoi*) that are concerned with rational and natural philosophy.

This basic principle is not restricted to the Hermetica alone. It is clearly evident throughout the corpus of texts that fall under the esotericism umbrella in Western culture, at least up to the European eighteenth century. For instance, Renaissance authors such as Marsilio Ficino, Pico della Mirandola, Heinrich Cornelius Agrippa, or Giordano Bruno (the list can be extended indefinitely) were erudite scholars who had mastered the entire curriculum of traditional philosophy—they knew not just the works of the Platonists or "mystical" authors such as Dionysius the pseudo-Areopagite but were deeply familiar with the more "rational" Aristotelians and scholastics as well. Key "esoteric" authors such as John Dee, Robert Fludd, Heinrich Khunrath, or Emanuel Swedenborg were deeply involved in the natural sciences of their time, such as chymistry, biology, or physics; and these scientific dimensions are indispensable to the more "esoteric" dimensions of their work. For example, Emanuel Swedenborg did not leave Cartesian philosophy and natural science behind when he entered his visionary period as a biblical exegete; on the contrary, he built his religious or spiritual worldview on those very foundations of rational philosophy.[10]

Moreover, at least up to the eighteenth century, almost all those authors who are seen as relevant to "esotericism" in European culture were devout Christians who deeply believed in the supreme authority of the biblical revelation. For instance, Cornelius Agrippa went out of his way to stress the absolute superiority of faith in Jesus Christ over any knowledge gained by the merely human arts and sciences—including the entire field of *philosophia occulta*.[11] In short, the popular modern idea (very common in contemporary esoteric milieus) that ultimate knowledge or *gnōsis* means abandoning Christian dogma, or renders it irrelevant, would have struck them as dangerous nonsense. Nor did they see themselves as opposing science and rational inquiry. All those roads toward knowledge were not just necessary but supremely important to them. The point is that they had their limits. There was always a higher level beyond the reach of *reason* and *faith*, focused on a salvational knowledge of ultimate realities that may be referred to as *gnōsis*.

In this regard, as in so many others, the European Enlightenment was a crucial caesura that changed the rules of the game. Esoteric authors after the eighteenth century tend to become much more assertive, even aggressive, in presenting their "higher knowledge" as a superior *alternative to* traditional religious and rational-scientific perspectives, rather than as an extra level *built upon* them. For instance, madame HELENA P. BLAVATSKY's bestselling *Isis Unveiled* (1877) is built on a virulent polemic against established positivist "science" (vol. 1) and Christian dogmatic "religion" (vol. 2). If many other and later occultists still presented their worldviews as Christian (from Anna Kingsford, Annie Besant, or Charles Webster Leadbeater to Alice Bailey or Rudolf Steiner), they meant their own understanding of an *esoteric* Christianity based on direct spiritual insight or *gnōsis*, not to be confused with the merely "exoteric" dogmatic beliefs of established churches and theologians. We see the same pattern in contemporary "New Age" contexts, most clearly among those who feel that the church has lost touch with the true message. Alternative forms of spirituality are then presented as *better* ways of understanding that message, for example, by focusing on the gnostic gospels (while downplaying inconvenient aspects of those texts, such as radical dualism or an ascetic rejection of sex and the body). Thus the focus is strongly on spiritual *gnōsis*; but in contrast with pre-Enlightenment contexts, very little is left of traditional Christian dogma. The point is that such esoteric understandings of Christianity are no longer seen as an extra level built upon a larger theological structure but as full-blown alternatives in which *gnōsis* must take the place of *faith*.

As far as science is concerned, the situation is somewhat comparable but slightly different. Contemporary esoteric audiences usually see traditional Christianity as old-fashioned, stuck in the dogmas of the past, and out of touch with contemporary spiritual concerns; but by contrast, the prestige and authority of science remains very high. Contemporary esotericism usually emphasizes that science and spirituality (but not religion, which mostly has negative connotations) must be brought together in some kind of higher unity. Old-fashioned types of positivist science, built on Cartesian and Newtonian foundations, are dead and buried; but radical avant-garde theories such as relativity theory or quantum mechanics are not just perfectly compatible with the belief in spiritual realities but may even provide them with a scientific foundation. The classic "New Age" example of such an argument is FRITJOF CAPRA's *The Tao of Physics* (1975), followed by a never-ending stream of similar books for the popular market. To be sure, none of this has much to do with actual scientific practice—it is really about the search for an enchanted philosophy of nature (a *Naturphilosophie*) that should close the gap between "matter and meaning."[12]

Summing up, the general pattern is that pre-Enlightenment esotericism saw *gnōsis* as pertaining to the highest level of truth, while still respecting the perspectives of *faith* and *reason* as legitimate and even necessary dimensions of the total fabric of knowledge. In post-Enlightenment esotericism, by contrast, that fabric has broken apart. Esotericism used to be integrated rather solidly in a wider religious and scientific context; but it has become a largely autonomous "counterculture" in open conflict with mainstream perspectives. *Gnōsis* is understood as a spiritual alternative to the misleading dogmas of *faith* (blind belief in religious authorities) and *reason* (narrow-minded rationalism and reductionism). This certainly does not mean that contemporary esotericists see themselves as "irrational"—on the contrary, they generally hold that it is much more reasonable to accept the evidence for spiritual dimensions than it is to deny or ignore their reality. *Gnōsis* and *reason* can be united in a higher synthesis, if only scientists will learn to abandon their bad reductionist habits. As regards the relation between *gnōsis* and *faith*, by contrast, such a future synthesis is neither expected nor seen as desirable. Unquestioning belief in tradition or authority is simply not appreciated.

There is something deeply ironic and deceptive about this constellation. The fact is that contemporary esotericists believe with quite as much devotion in their own esoteric traditions and authorities (for instance, inspired "channeled" scriptures received from spiritual entities) as traditional Christians believe in theirs. *Faith* is not at all absent in esoteric communities today—on the contrary, its reign is almost universal. At the same time, a consistent appeal to *reason* (always in the precise technical sense defined above!) is actually quite rare. For instance, as will be explored in Chapter 7, independent historical research or textual criticism is not appreciated; insofar as these approaches undermine cherished beliefs, they are rejected as "reductionist" and hostile to esoteric spirituality. It is rather easy for contemporary esotericists to accommodate natural science into their worldviews, at least to their own satisfaction; but historical methods proper to the humanities cannot be so easily appropriated. Therefore they tend to be ignored.

The conclusion about contemporary esotericism, as opposed to its pre-Enlightenment ancestors, is therefore quite peculiar. *Reason* is applauded in theory but largely rejected or curtailed in practice. Conversely, *faith* is rejected in theory but largely embraced in practice. Perception is one thing, reality is another.

Altered States of Knowledge

When it comes to *gnōsis* as a category of epistemological claims, we are faced with a strange research lacuna. Countless scholars have tried to answer the question "what is gnosticism?," but serious attempts to explain "what do we mean by *gnōsis*?" are extremely scarce. It would be easy to fill a library with learned studies about the mythology, doctrinal contents, cultural context, historical sources, and cultural influence of the "gnostic" and Hermetic currents of late antiquity, but specialists rarely have much to say about the salvational knowledge that was undoubtedly central to these spiritual milieus.[13] This deafening silence among scholars has everything to do with the claim of radical incommunicability that is central to the very concept of *gnōsis*. Gnostic and Hermetic practitioners insist that they are unable to say in clear language what it is that they have seen and discovered, and this seems to have discouraged most specialist from trying to say much more. André-Jean Festugière finished his 1,700-page standard work on the Hermetica by admitting that "the historian knowns only what he is being told. He does not penetrate the secret of the heart"; and Garth Fowden concluded his own standard work by stating that the Hermetic way of *gnōsis* remains "immune from the scrutiny of philologist, philosopher, and historian alike."[14]

But is this really all that can be said? It is certainly true that classical references to *gnōsis* are deeply puzzling. When it comes to the highest levels of absolute knowledge about ultimate reality, we typically read stammering expressions of amazement and awe about thoroughly impressive spiritual experiences that are said to defy any verbalization and can only be hinted at indirectly. As a perfect example, consider what the Hermetic pupil Tat has to say about the out-of-body experience in which he perceives the universal Light of the *Nous* and even glimpses the *pēgē*, the ultimate Source of all that is:

> I see, yes, I see unspeakable depths! . . .
> I also see a *Nous* that puts the soul in movement.
> In a state of sacred ecstasy I see him who moves me!
> You give me power . . .
> I see myself!
> I want to speak—but fear holds me back.
> I have found the origin of the Power above all powers, who has no beginning.

> I see a fountain bubbling with life! . . .
> I have seen . . . It is impossible to express this in words.[15]

It is a matter of consistency, and not a sign of deliberate obscurantism, that those who claim to have beheld such things insist that you must have experienced them yourself to understand what they are talking about. For example, the Islamic Platonist SUHRAWARDĪ (a direct heir of these traditions from late antiquity)[16] tried to convince the Aristotelian philosophers of his time that, since rational knowledge is restricted to the lower and secondary realm of "darkness" that is our world, it cannot be expected to grasp the superior and primary reality of pure spiritual "Light" from which everything has been born:

> That there are dominating lights, that the Creator of all is a light, that the archetypes are among the dominating lights—the pure souls have often beheld this to be so when they have detached themselves from their bodily temples. . . . Whose questions the truth of this—whoever is unconvinced by the proof—let him engage in mystical disciplines and service to those visionaries, that perchance he will, as one dazzled by the thunderbolt, see the light blazing in the Kingdom of Power and will witness the heavenly essences and lights that Hermes and Plato beheld.[17]

Therefore we are told that, in order to attain *gnōsis* of the ultimate noetic Light, we must learn how to detach ourselves from the body, our "bodily temple." If we read these texts with the gaze of an anthropologist or a psychologist, while paying close attention to textual detail, we may note that they often refer to specific *bodily conditions* combined with unusual states of consciousness. For instance, in the *CORPUS HERMETICUM* we find this passage (emphases added):

> Only then will you see it, when you no longer have anything to say about it—for the *gnōsis* of this is divine silence and *suppression of all the senses*. He who has once come to this knowledge [*noēsai*] can know nothing else, he who has *seen* it can *see* nothing else, he cannot *hear* of anything else, nor can he *move his body* at all. He is immobile, all *bodily perceptions and movements* forgotten.[18]

Many similar hints and references to unusual bodily states can be found throughout the Hermetic literature, beginning with the opening lines of CH I. The fact is that an extremely rich technical vocabulary existed in antiquity for describing such conditions and distinguishing between their different modalities (e.g., *ekstasis, alloiōsis, kinēsis, entheos, enthousiasmos, daimonismos, theiasmos, apoplexia, ekplēxis, mania*).[19] The experiences and bodily phenomena that such terms tried to capture must therefore have been common and well-known. In the Hermetic literature we read how exemplary seekers such as Hermes Trismegistus and his pupil Tat are being initiated, step by step, through a series of unusual states of consciousness. It all begins with *words*, that is, verbal philosophical instruction during an ordinary state of consciousness. From there, initiates move toward knowledge imparted through *imagery*, that is, by means of direct visions of transcendent entities and realities perceived in trance-like altered states. Next, when pupils are ready, they may be purified of the dark astral forces that keep their consciousness chained to the physical senses. This means being literally reborn in a new body made of noetic light, endowed with nonphysical "higher senses" that allow them to perceive literally everything that exists, has existed, or will yet exist in the physical cosmos. At the final stage of the initiatory process, their consciousness may rise even beyond the cosmos toward the Ogdoad and the Ennead (the eight and the ninth spheres beyond the seven planetary spheres) where they are granted ultimate ecstatic *noēsis* of the universal noetic Light and participate in ineffable "hymns sung in silence."[20] With that final step, they have attained the ultimate condition of perfect *gnōsis*.

Unusual states of consciousness and the bodily conditions in which they occur have been documented in considerable detail by anthropologists and historians of religion, but there is little agreement about how to study them or even about basic terminological conventions. Some scholars speak of "trance," others of "ecstasy," yet others of "dissociation" or, indeed, "altered states of consciousness." Moreover, often such terms refer to broader theoretical frameworks that are riddled with ideological assumptions and moralistic agendas, notably "mysticism," "magic," and "shamanism."[21] Ever since the eighteenth century at least, reports of ecstatic experiences (especially in combination with strange or erratic patterns of behavior) have been associated with the presumed "irrationality" of "primitive savages" or romanticized in terms of a primordial "archaic" mentality. Whether seen as threatening and dangerous or attractive and desirable, they always marked the "otherness" of peoples and cultures seen as far removed in time or in space from the "normative" standards of modern Western intellectual culture. As for Western culture itself, from antiquity to the present, the abundant textual evidence concerned with nonordinary states of consciousness or bodily conditions has been largely ignored, marginalized, or presented in heavily distorted ways. Again, they did not fit the normative standards of what "good religion" or "rational thought" were supposed to be all about. Of course, all of this exemplifies the apologetic/polemical dynamics of Western identity politics described in Chapter 3. As for the impact of normative standards, that is a topic to which I will return in Chapter 9.

To steer clear of this terminological and theoretical minefield, as much as possible, I prefer to speak of ALTERATIONS OF CONSCIOUSNESS.[22] The original terminology "altered states of consciousness" (ASCs)[23] implies the existence of a baseline state, a "normal" standard condition of consciousness, compared to which altered states must then be seen as "abnormal" or "supranormal." But because our consciousness is never entirely stable, it is doubtful whether any such baseline exists. Rather than imagining radical shifts from a state of normality to "altered" states, it may therefore be more helpful to think of consciousness as a *spectrum* that allows for subtle shifts and gradations. An additional issue is that the "altered states" terminology was promoted actively by the countercultural generation of the 1960s and is still associated quite strongly with agendas of psychedelic activism. As a result, psychoactive drugs tend to dominate the popular perception of what ASCs are all about, although in reality there are many other factors that may change a person's state of consciousness in subtle or more radical ways. In terms of a well-known typology,[24] major examples are sensory deprivation or sensory overload and hyperalertness or hypoalertness.[25] All of these may function as deliberate techniques for inducing altered states, in ceremonial contexts or private rituals; but one can also be thrown into an altered state unintentionally, as it were "spontaneously," for instance by violent and painful emotions or deep psychological trauma.[26]

To speak of "alterations of consciousness" is a simple way to acknowledge the full breadth and diversity of experiences, or experiential dimensions, that are potentially available to human beings.[27] If the basic source materials of esotericism describe transcendent visions, angelic or demonic voices, ecstasies, or unitive states, in no way does this conflict with established knowledge about consciousness and reality.[28] Some of these accounts may strike us as very weird, and one might even be tempted to dismiss them as "impossible" (I will return to those adjectives in the final chapter) but in fact there is usually no good reason to dismiss them out of hand as "irrational" or "crazy" delusions. Specific types of unusual experiences and bodily phenomena are exactly what can be expected if you expose a person to specific psychophysiological conditions or experiences, for instance in the context of spiritual ceremonies or individual exercises. Particularly if such practices are embedded in a comprehensive symbolic system,[29] such as the Platonic or Alchemical worldviews discussed in the previous chapter, there is no cause to be surprised if the experiences will be seen as confirming those worldviews and will make a deep impression on the individuals involved.

If we accept alterations of consciousness as perfectly *normal* phenomena that are known to occur under certain conditions, this leads to a new way of reading the sources of esotericism in Western culture. Many things that would be dismissed as irrelevant or unimportant from traditional internal-Eurocentric perspectives (i.e., as "marginal" compared to what is held to be "central" to Western culture) turn out to be perfectly relevant and obviously important. For instance, in PLATO's famous dialogue *Phaedrus*, we find an influential description of four types of *mania* ("frenzy") that allow the true philosopher to gain access to divinity but look like madness to the common crowd: "Standing aside from the busy doings of mankind, and drawing near to the divine, [the true philosopher] is rebuked by the multitude as being deranged, for they do not know that he is full of God."[30] One type of *mania* is believed to bestow the gift of prophecy, and the three others are linked by Plato to specific triggers or conditions. Poetry (and music), ceremonial practices of purification, and love or erotic desire (*erōs*) can powerfully affect our state of consciousness, detaching our souls from consensus reality and bringing them closer to the divine. Plato's authoritative discussion of *mania* (translated as *furor* in Latin) became deeply attractive for Renaissance philosophers relevant to esotericism, such as Marsilio Ficino or Giordano Bruno, who needed a terminology to speak about "higher or absolute" knowledge attained in a state of divine exaltation.[31] The term *gnōsis* was not yet available to these authors at that time, because even for them, it was still associated with despicable "gnostic" heresies. Therefore Plato's concept of *mania* was used instead, to discuss powerful alterations of consciousness in which ultimate knowledge could be attained.[32]

How do alterations of consciousness correspond to esoteric worldviews? In terms of the Platonic paradigm, it is natural to see such states of *mania* as experiential symptoms of the soul's liberation from the body (in fact, even modern accounts of "near-death experiences" still fall within that pattern). But according to the logic of the Alchemical model, they would rather be seen as bodily signs or anticipations of interior rebirth. In the former case, we are dealing with a circular concept of alienation and return, whereas the latter thinks in terms of linear progress. A classic example is JACOB BÖHME. In a famous passage, he describes how he had been "wrestling with God" to enlighten his soul about why there is so much evil and suffering in the world, until finally,

> my spirit [has] broken through the gates of hell and into the innermost birth of the Godhead, where it was received with love, the way a bridegroom embraces his dear bride. But this triumph in the spirit I cannot express by the written or spoken word; indeed it cannot be compared with anything but the birth of life in the midst of death, and with the resurrection of the dead. In this light, my spirit has right away seen through everything, and in all creatures, even in herbs and grass, it has seen God: who he is, how he is, and what his will is.[33]

This breakthrough experience to direct *gnōsis* must have come after a lengthy regime of intense and anguished prayer. Presumably, it was this emotion-laden practice that finally triggered Böhme's altered state of spiritual illumination. During the later history of Christian theosophy, in spiritual groups and communities such as the PHILADELPHIAN SOCIETY or the ANGELIC BRETHREN, spectacular visions in conditions of trance became quite common, combined with strange patterns of behavior that could be easily dismissed by outsiders as madness. In the context of heterodox spirituality and Pietist conventicles, such phenomena were known as ENTHUSIASM (*Schwärmerei* in German); and again, practitioners were known for extreme forms of bodily expression such as fits, convulsions, trembling, swooning, shrieking, or what looked like possession by alien spirits. The history of such "ecstatic spirituality" can be traced through the eighteenth and nineteenth centuries, up to the phenomena of "hysteria" studied by early clinical psychology.

In my opinion, alterations of consciousness are essential to understand what is being referred to in countless esoteric claims of "higher or absolute knowledge." So far, I have tried to illustrate this point by referring to pre-Enlightenment traditions (the Hermetica, the Platonic frenzies, Böhme's experience of illumination) in which *gnōsis* is seen as the highest level in a hierarchy of knowledge that also includes *reason* and *faith*. In post-Enlightenment situations, where *gnōsis* is placed in polemical opposition against *reason* and *faith* (understood negatively as the dogmatisms of established religion and science), it tends to absorb the claims of knowledge that used to be seen as the latter's domain. Now *gnōsis* is no longer just the ineffable cherry on the cake of *reason* and *faith* but becomes the whole cake! From that perspective, you no longer believe in spiritual beings such as angels or demons on the basis of faith in the authority of traditional religion. You now either believe in them because you have seen and encountered them yourself or because you trust the reports from those who claim to have done so—that is to say, claims of *gnōsis* become objects of esoteric *faith*. Immediate spiritual experiences are now presented as empirical proof, not just of the ineffable Absolute but also of spiritual realities that can more easily be described in verbal communication. Spiritual techniques, such as meditation or a variety of other methods for inducing altered states, are now promoted as quasi-scientific tools for exploration, testing, and verification. In short, alterations of consciousness become empirical methods for studying anything, communicable or not, that is believed to exist on other planes of reality than the physical one.

The paradigmatic example of this new development is EMANUEL SWEDENBORG, with his meticulous verbal descriptions of "things heard and seen" in heaven and hell.[34] The other main movement of innovation in esotericism since the Enlightenment, MESMERIC SOMNAMBULISM, was based quite as strongly on alterations of consciousness. But whereas Swedenborg claimed to be unique as the Lord's elected visionary prophet, mesmerism consisted of simple techniques for trance-induction that could be tried out by anybody. Similar to Swedenborg, somnambulic patients described spectacular visionary journeys. They claimed to explore the realm of spirits and angels, other planets in the universe, as well as more "interior" or abstract dimensions of reality as such.[35] The basic patterns of experiential religion established by mesmeric somnambulism have become key to the modern development of esoteric practices for gaining knowledge,[36] such as "astral travel," past life explorations, clairvoyant "investigations" of the human aura, "occult chemistry," reading of the "akasha chronicles," visionary exploration of "higher worlds," psychedelic visions, or the "channeling" of spiritual entities existing in other worlds or other dimensions.[37]

In terms of my basic typology, many such claims about knowledge obtained through consciousness alteration would actually fall under the heading of *faith* rather than *gnōsis*: clairvoyant visionaries such as Swedenborg or the Theosophist Charles Webster Leadbeater provide meticulous verbal descriptions that can readily be communicated, although they cannot be checked independently and must ultimately be taken "on faith." Therefore we must differentiate between knowledge (or information) *obtained by means* of an altered state and knowledge that is deemed *specific to* an altered state. This radical concept of "state-specific" knowledge, which by definition cannot be translated or transmitted toward another state, is indebted to Charles T. Tart and would seem to come closest to what we mean by *gnōsis* in the strict typological sense of the word.[38]

Knowing How

All types of knowledge discussed so far have a certain finality about them, in the sense that their goal is to uncover "the truth" or "the nature of reality" in some ultimate sense. Such an aspiration to "higher or perfect knowledge" is *not* specific to esotericism, as has often been claimed,[39] nor is it typical just of those who aspire to *gnōsis*. Think about it—very much the same ambition drives classical scientists as well as rational philosophers (*reason*),[40] and dogmatic theologians, no less than clairvoyant theosophists (*faith*).[41] But the term "knowledge" does not just mean some final discovery of "how things really are," resulting in an ultimate conclusive insight ("now I know!"). It is also concerned with the never-ending process of *learning* or the more practical knowledge of *how things must be done*. Both approaches to the pursuit of knowledge are highly relevant to esotericism as well and must therefore be mentioned in this chapter as well, although I will keep the discussion brief.

First of all, enormous amounts of literature that fall under the "esotericism" umbrella are concerned with HERMENEUTICS, the art of interpretation.[42] For instance, Jewish and Christian kabbalistic exegesis, or their equivalents in Quranic exegesis, consist of highly technical methods for reading sacred scripture and discovering layer upon layer of profound spiritual meaning. These hidden scriptural mysteries might be just as infinite as their author, God himself. If so, "higher or perfect knowledge" will always be out of reach for mere human interpreters. There will always be more to learn. In these contexts, to be knowledgeable does not mean that you have made some ultimate discovery of "how things really are," after which all books might as well be closed because nothing more will ever be found. Rather, it refers to *knowing how* to read Scripture.[43] An expert level of hermeneutic skill requires deep (and sometimes highly technical) learning, considerable experience built up over time, and a powerful intelligence. Having "intelligence" means much more than just being smart—etymologically, the word refers to a natural talent for *understanding* and discernment that cannot strictly be taught but can certainly be honed and developed through careful practice and training.

The skillful art of hermeneutics can be applied not just to scripture but potentially to the whole of reality, as suggested by traditional references to "reading the book of nature." From a kabbalistic perspective, the very letters of the Hebrew alphabet were the building blocks of creation, suggesting that the deep structure of the world is essentially linguistic.[44] But even without making such an assumption, the phenomenal world as a whole can certainly be understood (!) as a mystery that will never be grasped in any final and conclusive sense although—precisely for that reason—it *does* require interpretation. By "knowing how" to conduct such an ongoing hermeneutical project, we can make progress in our understanding of reality, in the specific sense not of propositional knowledge but of knowledge-by-acquaintance (*kennen, connaître*). Just as we may "get to know" or understand our friends or loved ones on ever deeper and more intimate levels, there is always more that we can "get to know" or understand about scripture or about reality or about the universe in which we find ourselves, without ever attaining "ultimate knowledge" in the sense of "finally discovering the truth." In contemporary society, with its very strong emphasis on science and technology, this crucial difference between *explanatory* and *hermeneutic* types of knowledge is easily forgotten. This makes it all the more important to be aware that much of esoteric literature, especially in earlier periods, has less to do with explaining the world than with understanding it.

Secondly, many pursuits that fall under the "esotericism" umbrella are concerned neither with ultimate knowledge nor with hermeneutic understanding but with such practical matters as knowing how to predict, control, or manipulate life events.[45] Many of these "esoteric practices" have traditionally been referred to as "magic," but for reasons that will be explained in the next chapter, I try to avoid that label. Just as the development of hermeneutic expertise requires learning, experience, and intelligence, esoteric practices are based on learning by imitation, practical experience, and the application of skills such as attention and discernment. Esoteric practices in Western culture may be fruitfully compared to similar practices in other parts of the world and would seem to have at least four basic components.[46] Firstly, their concern is with learning how to identify and influence present and future life events (for instance, drawing up a horoscope, making astrological prognostications, or healing an illness). Secondly, they require some kind of specialized expert knowledge, including strategies of secrecy and concealment (the power to influence life events by such means as spells or enchantment should not be accessible to just anybody but must be carefully preserved). Thirdly, they are based on forms of ritual efficacy that work with causes that are considered "occult," in the sense that their operation is hidden partly or completely from the physical senses (for instance, consecrated amulets, talismans, or so-called "voodoo dolls"). Fourthly and finally, they tend to be contested and precarious, because no generally accepted explanation exists for how these practices work and how to account for their effects (hence the idea of "occult sciences" as distinct from "normal" physical science).

The different dimensions of "esoteric practice" will be discussed in the next chapter. At this point, I just want to emphasize that we are dealing with special skills of *knowing how* that, like hermeneutics, require a certain level of practical training, expertise, and skill. In this sense, the knowledge of esoteric practitioners does not differ in any structural manner from the knowledge of medical specialists such as ophthalmologists or brain surgeons. They all know what must be done and they know how to do it. This is true not just for practices that have traditionally been categorized as "magical" or "occult" but also for "spiritual exercises" or ceremonial procedures focused on inner development or the attainment of *gnōsis*. For instance, think of how Hermes Trismegistus leads his pupil Tat through a process of exorcism and purification that may culminate in an ecstatic journey toward the ultimate noetic realm[47] or how a Sufi master may guide his pupils along the path toward purity and knowledge of Allah.

6 Practice

Insist on the thought that this is what it is all about. . . . Zum-zum-zum-zumbaba. Zumbaba. Zumbaba. Really, that's all there is to say.

(Mattijs van de Port, *Ecstatic Encounters*)[1]

Just like religion, esotericism consists of much more than belief. It is not just about holding certain worldviews, asserting to doctrinal propositions, or making claims about the true nature of reality. To a very large extent, as already suggested in the final part of the previous chapter, it is about *doing* things. People pray or meditate, go to church or visit a masonic lodge, confess their sins or pronounce ceremonial formulas, light candles or burn incense, listen to sermons or receive instructions from spiritual masters, sing hymns or participate in *dhikr* recitations, dance together or go on pilgrimages, celebrate religious holidays or seasonal festivals, partake of the Eucharist or drink ayahuasca, practice penitence or ceremonial sex, attempt to heal illness or harm their enemies, study scripture or decipher Qdrops on the internet, fight against unbelievers or participate in psytrance festivals, and so on and so forth.[2] Doing certain things, but also refusing to do other things, belongs to the very core of what it means to be religious or spiritual. And this is true, regardless of whether practitioners are all that clear in their own minds about the exact nature of their beliefs or their reasons for holding them. Since the "esotericism" rubric covers large parts of religion and spirituality in Western culture, while also participating in such domains as philosophy and science, as we have seen, no overview can be complete unless it pays attention to these practical dimensions. What do people involved in esotericism actually *do*? Perhaps no other dimension of the field is so difficult to study and understand, for a whole number of reasons.

- First, there is THE PROBLEM OF SOURCES. Because beliefs and convictions are usually written down at some point, information about them is transmitted to posterity much more easily and with more precision than information about practices. There is often no great need to describe exactly what is being done and how it is done—in most cases, practitioners learn by oral instruction, daily experience, or observation and imitation, and they may have little need of written reminders about what everybody already knows. The result is that we are usually better informed about esoteric beliefs than about esoteric practices.
- Second, there is THE PROBLEM OF LANGUAGE, that is, of verbal description. Practices are inherently more difficult to describe than theories or doctrines. Every ceremonial act is overdetermined by countless details that impinge on all the senses

simultaneously. Even simple ceremonial procedures that are easily learned by observation and imitation may be very difficult to capture adequately in words. As a result, even if we have sources about esoteric practices, they are almost inevitably incomplete.

- Third, there is THE PROBLEM OF (CRYPTO)PROTESTANT BIAS. Classical approaches to the study of religion were influenced heavily by Protestant assumptions, including an implicit polemics against Roman Catholicism as crypto-"pagan" practice,[3] resulting in a structural overemphasis on doctrine and belief and a corresponding lack of attention to ritual and other forms of practice. As a result, most scholars concentrate on the history of esoteric ideas or the study of esoteric discourse while giving scant attention to esoteric practice. Even when studying contemporary currents firsthand, they often still tend to avoid engaging the relevant practices directly.[4]
- Finally, there is THE PROBLEM OF METHOD. Even if the importance of practice is acknowledged in principle, it is not easy to decide on appropriate methodologies for studying it. Anthropologists have built up much experience with participant research and have become increasingly interested in contemporary forms of esotericism,[5] but attempts to apply anthropological approaches to historical materials still remain relatively rare.

As a result of all these factors, we still know much less about esoteric practice than about the history of esoteric ideas or organizations. There are as yet no general synthetic studies. Given that situation, I cannot do much more in this short chapter than make an initial attempt to map largely uncharted territory. I will discuss the wide range of practices that seem relevant to esotericism under eight headings, by concentrating on *their intended goals*: (1) Control; (2) Knowledge; (3) Amplification; (4) Healing; (5) Progress; (6) Contact; (7) Unity; (8) Pleasure. These categories will be further explained below, but I want to emphasize from the outset that they are *not* meant to be mutually exclusive. For example, specific kinds of *knowledge* may be pursued in an effort to gain *control* over one's environment or *heal* oneself of an illness; but they may also be seen as belonging to a certain stage of spiritual *progress*. Again, by trying to *contact* spiritual entities such as angels or demons, one may hope to gain *knowledge*, *control*, or *healing* advice. And so on.

Before embarking on a short discussion of each category, it is important to get rid of one major obstacle in the study of practice. This is the concept of MAGIC as a universal reified *etic* category, usually pitted against RELIGION and SCIENCE.[6] The idea that certain practices are inherently "magical," as opposed to inherently "religious" or "rational/scientific," was created by armchair anthropologists and sociologists between the mid-nineteenth and mid-twentieth century (notably the schools of Edward B. Tylor/James G. Frazer and Marcel Mauss/Emile Durkheim). They were doing so against the background of Enlightenment polemics against "superstition" that, in turn, were heavily indebted to Protestant polemics against "paganism" and "heresy." Grounded as it is in this far-ranging and incredibly influential discourse of exclusion, which I analyzed in Chapter 3, the famous MAGIC–RELIGION–SCIENCE triad is riddled with deep ethnocentric and moralistic prejudice. The problem is that to think in these terms has become deeply intuitive to most Western readers and scholars but leads to systematic distortions and misinterpretations in the history of religion both in Europe and in other parts of the world. In the former context, the triad reflects and lends further support to the basic ideological structures of Internal Eurocentrism. In the latter context, the same triad gets projected on to non-Western peoples, resulting in the pervasive externalization of internal-Eurocentric prejudice that is typical of the colonial age (see Chapter 9). I believe that no other second-order or *etic* concept has been more harmful to an adequate understanding of "esotericism" in Western culture and to the general study of "religion." Dismantling the magic-religion-science triad and its ideological presuppositions should therefore be seen as the first order of business for a global study of religion on decolonial foundations, including the modern study of esotericism in Western culture.

Meanwhile, due to the enormous influence of this conceptual triad in popular and academic discourse, the fact is that most practices that will be discussed on the following pages still tend to be perceived almost automatically as somehow inherently "magical"—with the essentialist implication or subliminal suggestion that they must be inherently different from "genuine" religion (usually a code for "Christianity" or, even more specifically, "Protestantism"), not to mention "genuine" science. It would be hard to think of a better example of why it's so important in scholarly research, but in general parlance as well, to be aware of the critical distinction between "second-order" or *etic* and "first-order" or *emic* language. The term magic and its cognates (*mageia*, *magia*, etc.) have acquired a whole series of culturally specific *emic* meanings over the course of European history,[7] all of which must be recognized for what they are, carefully distinguished from one another, and studied contextually on their own terms. The problem does not lie in such research of *emic* meanings but in the assumption that somehow there *is* such a thing as "magic" in a general and theoretical *etic* sense, and that it's different in some essential manner from other presumed "phenomena" (in the literal etymological sense of things that make their "appearance" in reality) such as "religion" and "science." The truth is that all three terms are just *imaginal formations* that get reified in our minds almost automatically, due to a deep but deceptive human proclivity known as "psychological essentialism,"[8] although they have no actual existence anywhere else than in our collective imagination.[9]

Thus there is no good reason, for instance, to describe the practice of invoking angels or demons as a specifically "magical" as opposed to a religious or spiritual activity. Again, if medieval practitioners of *magia naturalis* are studying the hidden (occult) forces in nature, there is no reason to deny them their historical status as practitioners of early science or natural philosophy. Separating such practices from religion or spirituality and from science or rationality, by placing them apart in a third category labeled "magic," serves no other purpose than to endow certain practices with an aura of legitimacy while labeling others as illegitimate in some unspecified sense—a normative and subjective pursuit that should have no place in scholarship and historical research and is deeply complicit in the long history of Eurocentric and colonial prejudice. Please note that this argument about reification and *etic* categorization applies not just to traditional ways of using the term "magic" as a *negative* category for excluding the false or evil "Other." In principle, it also applies to later projects of turning it into a *positive* category, for example, when "the magical worldview" is embraced and promoted as a beautiful and enchanted alternative to religious dogmatism or materialist science.[10]

On the following pages, I provide a short sketch of my eight categories. Again, this overview is meant to be exploratory and heuristic, not exhaustive or definitive in any way. My intention is just to give an initial impression of the wide spectrum of esoteric practices. For each category I will discuss just a few examples as illustration, but countless other choices would have been possible.

Control

This first category is concerned with practices for gaining some kind of power or influence over reality. Many of them have their origin in the basic fact of human vulnerability. To a greater or lesser extent, we are all at the mercy of external circumstances that might harm us in some way at any moment, and it's perfectly natural that human beings respond to this fact by looking for ways to exercise control in a threatening world. One obvious example is the widespread use of consecrated AMULETS or TALISMANS for purposes such as personal protection against natural dangers, notably illness or death, but also against the malicious intentions (imagined or real) of demonic entities or other humans.[11] After all, it is not just that people may feel a need to protect themselves against harm—they may also take the initiative and try to harm their enemies by means of malicious charms, curse tablets, or "voodoo dolls."[12] Still, inflicting harm on others or protecting oneself against it is just one possible motivation for engaging in practices of control. For example, men and women have always been using charms or potions to make other men or women fall in love with them or consent to sex,[13] and similar techniques have been applied to such goals as the pursuit of power or wealth, for instance, finding hidden treasures. Explanations for why such practices are expected to work range from *natural* causes, such as hidden or occult powers and cosmic forces of sympathy or antipathy, to intentional assistance from *supernatural* agents such as demons or angels.

Most of these practices could be described as a kind of "self-help religion" for individuals, without deeper intellectual pretentions. Popular techniques such as charms or incantations and the wearing of amulets or talismans are certainly not restricted to premodern times but have continued into the very present. Popular ancient and medieval practices for gaining control have their direct counterparts in a contemporary multimillion dollar industry, from countless how-to manuals (techniques and prescriptions for getting love, happiness, or wealth) to crystals and gems that are for sale in New Age shops. On a higher intellectual level, too, the search for control is certainly far from absent in "esoteric" contexts—and how could it be otherwise, since desire for power is among the most common human motivations? Still, among modern self-identified "magicians" and occultists, it plays a somewhat less prominent role than one might perhaps expect. The case of Aleister Crowley may serve as an example. At first sight, his famous definition of magic ("the Science and Art of causing Change to occur in conformity with Will") might seem like a perfect illustration of the occultist's lust for power over the outside world. But in fact, the wide range of "magickal" practices that Crowley experimented with during his lifetime were not aimed at goals so naïve as acquiring Harry Potter-like abilities. Rather, they ultimately served a spiritual purpose of individual self-realization, described as finding one's "true Will" (and, as such, might be more congenial to the category of "progress" discussed below).

On the whole, and allowing for a number of specific exceptions, the sensational topos of untrammeled lust for power and control over others has more to do with stereotypical imaginations of "magic and the occult" (pertaining strictly to mnemohistory) than with the actual historical sources of esotericism in Western culture. More commonly, the idea is that while human beings are unconsciously manipulated on a daily basis by forces that seem stronger than themselves, it is possible by means of esoteric training to gain control over one's own life. For instance, Hermetic practitioners sought liberation from the harmful energies of daimonic entities linked to the zodiac.[14] Followers of Gurdjieff "work on themselves" to wake up from the habitual machine-like condition of average human beings. And contemporary practitioners might want to break the addictive power of social media, to win back control over their own mind and imagination. In all such cases, it is about getting oneself back into the driver's seat as "the master of one's fate, the captain of one's soul."[15]

Knowledge

A second category is concerned with practices for acquiring information. For example, an important group of medieval texts known as the *ARS NOTORIA* focused on the acquisition of perfect knowledge of the several liberal arts and related gifts such as rhetorical skill. Referring to the authority of the bible, where God grants King Solomon *sapientia*, *scientia*, and *intelligencia* (II Chron. 1:9-12), they claimed that such "wisdom, knowledge and intelligence" could be readily acquired through complicated rites and purifications, including the taking of confession, the drawing of figures (*notae*) and prayers, orations and invocations, including strings of obscure words or names (*verba ignota*).[16] The *ars notoria* was not sanctioned by the Church, and practitioners might be prosecuted, but the number of surviving manuscripts shows that it must have been remarkably popular. In Richard Kieckhefer's terms, its primary audience seems to have belonged to a "clerical underworld" of monks who had sufficient education to produce, read, and copy such texts.[17] The tradition continued right into the Renaissance and survived until as recently as the seventeenth century. John Dee's famous practices of angel conjuration served the same essential goal of knowledge acquisition—the idea was that angelic entities should be able to provide information in the domains of natural philosophy and science that could perhaps not be gained by other means. Dee's ritual practice was derived from the Solomonic tradition of *ars notoria*,[18] but also included the use of a "scryer" (Edward

Kelley) who claimed that the angels appeared to him in the surface of a black mirror while he himself was in a state of trance. In terms of the typology in Chapter 5, this is an excellent example of how alterations of consciousness in a ritual context may result in claims of knowledge that pertain to the domain of *reason* (natural science in this case) rather than *gnōsis*.

The attempt to acquire knowledge (about the past, the present, and especially the future) is no less central to a wide range of practices that are known as DIVINATION or the divinatory arts.[19] The concept itself is derived from Isidore of Sevilla's extremely influential *Etymologiae* (early seventh century) but is actually quite vague. To a very large extent, it consists of practices for distilling meaning from observable patterns or signs that sceptics might regard as meaningless. Examples are the casting of lots, reading a person's destiny from his physiological appearance (PHYSIOGNOMY) or from the lines of his hand (CHIROMANCY), interpreting patterns of apparently random figures according to standardized procedures (GEOMANCY), reading the cards of the tarot deck, and even the interpretation of dreams (ONEIROMANCY). Other techniques rely essentially on alterations of consciousness induced by gazing at a reflective surface. Edward Kelley's visions in John Dee's black mirror are an example of mirror-divination (CATOPTROMANCY), but of course we also have the famous practice of gazing at crystal balls, which appears to have been popular even during the heyday of occultism in the nineteenth century.[20] Finally, there is ASTROLOGY, partly as a technique for predicting events or deciding on the best moment for initiating some course of action, based on the future constellations of the heavenly bodies, but also as a way of acquiring knowledge about a person's psychological potentials by interpreting his or her birth horoscope. As an additional note, it should not be forgotten that practitioners of *magia naturalis*, alchemy, and astrology were often engaged in the business of studying nature by means of empirical observation and practical experimentation. In such cases, we are actually dealing with early modern science or natural philosophy.

Amplification

This third category is concerned with practices for expanding or maximizing the range or quality of one's natural powers and abilities. For example, Marsilio Ficino published a famous treatise titled *De vita coelitus comparanda*, "On how to bring your life in harmony with the heavenly bodies." Usually categorized as ASTRAL MAGIC, its central practices are concerned with maximizing a person's exposure to beneficial influences from the stars, by using the cosmic dynamics of sympathy and antipathy (see the quotation from Plotinus in Chapter 7).[21] Ficino's pupil Francesco Cattani da Diacceto (1466–1522) has left us a wonderful description of what such a practice would look like:

> If for example [the practitioner] wishes to acquire solarian gifts, first he sees that the sun is ascending in Leo or Aries, on the day and in the hour of the sun. Then, robed in a solarian mantle of a solarian colour, such as gold, and crowned with a mitre of laurel, on the altar, itself made of solarian material, he burns myrrh and frankincense,

> the sun's own fumigations, having strewn the ground with heliotrope and suchlike flowers. Also, he has an image of the sun in gold or chrysolite or carbuncle, that is, of the kind they think corresponds to each of the sun's gifts. . . . Then, anointed with unguents made, under the same celestial aspect, from saffron, balsam, yellow honey and anything else of that kind . . . he sings the sun's own hymn . . . He also uses a threefold harmony, of voice, of cithara, and of the whole body, of the kind he has discovered belongs to the sun. . . . To all these he adds what he believes to be the most important: a strongly emotional disposition of the imagination, by which, as with pregnant women, the spirit is stamped with this kind of imprint, and flying out through the channels of the body, especially through the eyes, ferments and solifies, like rennet, the kindred power of the heavens.[22]

This unique description describes a ritual practice through which all the bodily senses, as well as one's inner imaginal world, are deliberately flooded with solarian powers or energies. The intention is to improve a person's spiritual, mental, and bodily well-being. Ficino's prescriptions could be read as a remarkable prefiguration of contemporary methods of "holistic health" as pioneered by Human Potential centers such as ESALEN in California: it's all about exposing oneself to healing energies while avoiding negative ones.

Ficino's astral magic sought to maximize a person's "human potential" by manipulating environmental conditions in a controlled ceremonial setting, on the assumption that all human beings are constantly exposed to astral influences. Other practices consist essentially of techniques for training and developing a person's abilities. For instance, Giordano Bruno was a recognized expert in ancient and medieval MNEMONICS, the "art of memory," a body of traditional techniques for memory improvement that require systematic training of a person's faculty of VISUALIZATION.[23] The ability to visualize, which Bruno seems to have perfected to a stunning degree, became extremely important in the context of occultist ritual magic toward the end of the nineteenth century. In the Hermetic Order of the Golden Dawn, visualization is essential to such core practices as the "Middle Pillar Ritual" (in which practitioners align themselves to the kabbalistic Tree of Life, visualizing how the "universal energy" descends as iridescent light through all the ten sefirot that are seen as corresponding to their own body) or astral travel (where practitioners are told to visualize a hexagram that then becomes a "doorway" through which they can enter into another world of the reified imagination and encounter angels or other spiritual entities).[24] In a classic study of contemporary occultism in London, the anthropologist Tanya Luhrmann has shown that systematic training of one's ability to visualize is central to the process of "interpretive drift" that allows initiates to enter the world of ritual magic.[25] In New Age contexts today, the practice of visualizing spiritual "light" for purposes of healing and personal transformation is virtually omnipresent.

Here it may be important to note that modern and contemporary esotericists tend to distinguish between mere fantasy (however enjoyable) and true IMAGINATION. The latter is often seen as an actual *faculty of perception*, in addition to the five physical senses, providing access to spiritual worlds that are ontologically real in some sense. This assumption is actually central to Antoine Faivre's concept of "imagination/mediation" and Henry Corbin's famous doctrine of the *mundus imaginalis*.[26] It means that by learning to expand our powers of visualization, we are actually training our ability to receive true visions of other times and other worlds.[27]

Healing

This fourth category is concerned with practices for curing bodily or mental illnesses. Healing is an important dimension of esotericism and obviously overlaps with all the previous categories—illness may be attributed to the malice of others and one may try to cure it by using amulets or charms ("control"), the search for "knowledge" is often focused on medical information, and Ficino's astral magic ("amplification") was intended especially for intellectuals whose health was endangered by the harmful influence of Saturn and the occupational hazards of the scholarly life. A remarkably large number of important figures in the history of esotericism have been physicians, psychologists, or psychiatrists. Ficino, the son of a physician, liked to think of himself as a "doctor of souls"; and one of the key figures of sixteenth-century esotericism, Paracelsus, was a major innovator in the history of medicine. There are very important differences between their medical systems, but they both saw physical healing in a much larger context than that of the physical body alone. Human beings are subject to illness and death because, due to the sin of Adam and Eve, they find themselves in a fallen state—referred to as *cagastric* by Paracelsus. Therefore the only real and lasting method of healing has to consist in spiritual regeneration, or rebirth, and the soul's salvation from mortal sin. In a Christian context, this made Jesus Christ into the ultimate healer. Through large parts of its history, the practice of alchemy is inseparable from medical experimentation. Quite obviously, the elixir of life would be the perfect universal medicine. In the wake of Paracelsus, during the seventeenth century, such medical alchemy became known as IATROCHEMISTRY. It is not surprising that in the *Fama Fraternitatis* of 1614, the Rosicrucians are described as a brotherhood of healers whose mission it is to cure the sick without asking for payment.

Franz Anton Mesmer's innovative practice of ANIMAL MAGNETISM was presented as a universal method of healing. We have seen that after De Puységur turned it into a method for inducing "somnambulic" states, the range of applications was expanded from healing the body to healing the mind as well. Yet another physician, Justinus Kerner, published a series of influential books about his somnambulic or demonically possessed patients, with detailed information about a whole range of treatment methods—including even such traditional ones as the use of amulets and talismans.[28] This German Mesmeric tradition in a Romantic context stands at the origin of what has been called "the discovery of the unconscious," leading straight to the emergence of modern PSYCHOLOGY and PSYCHIATRY.[29] Carl Gustav Jung's analytic psychology comes from that lineage, to such an extent that this therapeutic practice might be described as a highly sophisticated and innovative form of applied esotericism.[30] Next to Jung, other new therapies such as NEW

Thought were developed out of Mesmeric origins as well. These various traditions of alternative healing have been flourishing, like never before, in the various "holistic health" movements since the 1960s. In these modern and contemporary contexts, we find the complete scope of traditional esoteric methods, in new and often commercialized forms, from crystals and gems to various kinds of trance induction, from natural or herbal remedies to techniques for influencing the mind through positive "affirmations," and from neo-Mesmeric practices such as Reiki to entheogenic plant medicine such as ayahuasca.

Progress

This fifth category is concerned with practices for advancing or moving forward in one's personal spiritual development. The idea of moving toward a spiritual goal is naturally expressed by the imagery of travel, as in John Bunyan's famous *The Pilgrim's Progress* (1678) or, somewhat earlier and closer to the domain of esotericism, Jan Amos Comenius's *Labyrinth of the World and Paradise of the Heart* (1623 and several revisions). As for practices intended to accompany and stimulate such spiritual progress, think of structured regimes or cycles of prayer and meditation, in organizational contexts such as monasteries and spiritual communities but also in a person's individual life. In medieval and early modern Europe, it would often be hard to distinguish such forms of esoteric practice from Christian practice more generally. For example, Christian-Theosophical communities such as the English Philadelphians or Johann Georg Gichtel's Angelic Brethren may have differed from other Christian groupings less by the nature of their devotional practices than by the specific contents of their beliefs and experiences, although quite some mysteries remain about what exactly they were doing.[31]

More obvious examples of the "progress" category can be found in the ceremonial practices of Freemasonry and many esoteric organizations inspired by masonic ritual. The ceremonial movement through a series of progressive initiations, staged as ceremonial "dramas" (Apprentice, Fellowcraft, Master, perhaps followed by a series of higher esoteric degrees), is based on the idea that masonic brethren are progressing in orderly fashion from a state of profane ignorance to ever more exalted states of spiritual insight. This is not supposed to be just a matter of acquiring new knowledge but rather of "polishing" oneself as a human being so as to become more useful as a "stone" in the great building of the world. The idea of initiation was derived from the model of mysterious ancient brotherhoods, such as the Pythagoreans. It is based on the notion that higher spiritual truths must be reserved for those who are worthy to receive them and capable of understanding them. In the eighteenth century, all of this resonated with contemporary ideas of human progress by means of education, as in Jean-Jacques Rousseau's *Emile* (1762) or Gotthold Ephraim Lessing's *Education of the Human Race* (1780).

The ideal of "working on yourself," making spiritual progress by means of disciplined practice or training, has become part and parcel of esotericism and occultism since the nineteenth century. As can be easily seen in such new traditions as modern Theosophy and Anthroposophy, it developed in tandem with the much broader popularity of evolutionist thinking,[32] for if human consciousness is supposed to evolve to ever higher levels, then it makes sense that individuals should try to evolve on a personal level as well. Such progress may find symbolic expression in initiatory rituals, as in the masonic context, but may also be a persistent pursuit in a person's individual life. Quite simply, it can mean that you try to "live consciously," in a responsible manner, making consistent efforts to discipline your daily thoughts and actions in accordance with your beliefs. This can naturally lead to the cultivation of specific practices, such as daily meditation or a variety of other spiritual techniques. Teachers such as Gurdjieff or Steiner have developed elaborate systems for helping pupils "advance along the path," and a stunning number of training programs are offered by esoteric entrepreneurs today.

Contact

This sixth category is concerned with practices for getting in touch with entities that are claimed to exist beyond the normal range of the physical senses. Throughout the history of esotericism in Western culture, from antiquity to the present, this has been an extremely popular pursuit. It begins with ritual practices such as Neoplatonic THEURGY, which were directed at "disposing the human mind to participation in the gods."[33] During the middle ages, many kinds of CEREMONIAL MAGIC aimed to establish contact with angels or demons. The demonic variety was often referred to as NECROMANCY or NIGROMANCY and included the drawing of magical circles, animal sacrifices, strange words and formulas, cryptic signs and characters, suffumigations, and so on.[34] The angelic variety contained many elements of the *ars notoria* (discussed above, under "knowledge") and worked with lengthy prayers addressed to God, Christ, the Holy Spirit, and the angelic orders, combined with such practices as fasting, confession, and periods of silence and meditation. This is a particularly clear illustration of why the category of "magic" is so problematic, for of course such practices might as well be described as religious. Medieval traditions of demonic and angelic invocation continued right into the Renaissance, as is evident from personalities such as Johannes Trithemius or John Dee.[35] It bears repeating that these famous "big names" are merely the tip of an iceberg that consists of many lesser figures who have mostly been forgotten but were engaged in similar pursuits.

Emanuel Swedenborg claimed to be in daily contact with spirits and angels but saw this strictly as a gift from God—except for some inconclusive references to "circular breathing," we know almost nothing about the practices or techniques through which his visions may have been induced.[36] By contrast, Mesmeric techniques of trance induction were a reliable way of establishing contact with spirits and other entities, as in the paradigmatic case of Justinus Kerner's *Seeress of Prevorst* (1829). During the vogue of SPIRITUALISM after 1850, similar methods were used to bring mediums in a state of trance. With the spread of Theosophy toward the end of the nineteenth century, and under the influence partly of independent occultists such as Paschal Beverly Randolph, the possible range of "entities" that could be contacted expanded far beyond the traditional categories of angels, demons, or spirits of the departed. Randolph spoke of a sevenfold hierarchy of "Spirits/Angels, Seraphs, Arsaphs, Eons, Arsasaphs, Arch-Eons, and Antarphim,"[37] but that was just the beginning—in many later traditions of occultism and esotericism, the range of possible entities that are there to be contacted seems to have become almost limitless. According to countless trance mediums or "channels" who are currently active in New Age contexts, we are living in a multidimensional universe with a very wide spectrum of possible forms of consciousness. In the words of one of them:

> There are many levels of guides, entities, energies, and beings in every octave of the universe. There are those who are lords, just like there were Grecian lords on one octave of reality, and ascended masters on another octave of reality. There are lords of the universe, the galactic frequencies. They are all there to pick and choose from in relation to your own attraction/repulsion mechanisms.[38]

One channel even claimed to be in contact with "The Committee," described as a geometrical consciousness comprised of a line, a spiral, and a multidimensional triangle![39] In this bewildering contemporary scene, the boundaries between esotericism and fantasy or science fiction are blurred to an unprecedented degree[40] – whatever we are able to imagine is not just real but can be contacted and asked for information. The result is a never-ending flood of messages and spiritual teachings that are being received by means of practices and techniques for consciousness alteration, from meditation and visualization or breathing techniques to the use of entheogenic substances.[41]

Unity

This seventh category is concerned with practices for overcoming duality or separation. In the context of esotericism, total unification with divinity could perhaps be seen as a boundary case, depending on how far we are willing to expand the field to include practices commonly classified as MYSTICISM. The comparison is tricky for several reasons. Most of the "classical" mystics describe a much wider range of unusual experiences than just unity with God (for instance, Teresa of Avila is known for her elaborate visions of an "interior castle" and many medieval ascetics experienced deeply erotic encounters with Jesus Christ). Moreover, the "mysticism" category has been so heavily theologized by Christian and especially Roman Catholic authors that it is often more about doctrinal distinctions between supposedly "true" and "false" types of religion than about the actual experiences reported by religious ecstatics.[42]

In the wider context of esotericism, the search for perfect union with the divine seems most typical for a minority of metaphysical radicals (Chapter 4). Jewish, Christian, and Islamic cultures have always been marked by a strong doctrinal tension between the core monotheistic principle that God created the world and is therefore distinct from his creations, on the one hand, and influential (neo)Platonic concepts of ultimate nonduality, on the other. Whether Jewish kabbalah has room for mystical unity is deeply contested among experts; and when the Sufi Al-Ḥallāj seemed to declare himself identical with Allah, it cost him his life. In Christian contexts, the role of Christ or the Logos as mediating between God and humanity often made it more natural for esoteric thinkers to focus on a middle realm of "imagination and mediation"[43] where opposites could meet. In more recent esoteric traditions, such core modern values as individualism and personal autonomy are somewhat hard to reconcile with spiritual ideals of self-annihilation in which the human soul is compared to a drop of water that should aspire to be swallowed by the ocean of the One. And yet, the neurobiology of ecstatic states suggests quite strongly that practitioners may have strong experiences of union regardless of their personal theology or philosophical convictions.[44]

Since panentheist (rather than pantheist) worldviews seem to predominate in "esoteric" contexts, God tends to be seen not as a remote spiritual entity who exists "elsewhere" beyond our material world but as an invisible power or energy who is present *in* the cosmos or the universe as a whole. When our habitual condition of separation is overcome, the result must therefore be an experience of "cosmic" unity with all that is rather than of an acosmic unity with the One, an awareness of our inseparable connection with the whole of reality rather than an annihilation of individual consciousness. Hermetic spirituality in Roman Egypt was based on a metaphysics of radical NONDUALITY, because there was ultimately no distinction between the inner Light of the human *nous* and the primordial Light of the divine *Nous*.[45] However, when the Hermetic pupil achieved rebirth, he experienced perfect unity not with the inner spiritual essence of God but with God's "cosmic" consciousness of everything that exists in the world of space and time: "I am in heaven, on earth, in water, in the air; I am in animals, in plants; in the womb, before the womb, after the womb, everywhere. . . . Father, I see the All, and I see myself in the *nous*."[46] Remarkably similar experiences have been reported also by modern authors, such as the Canadian transcendentalist RICHARD MAURICE BUCKE (1837–1902)[47] or the transpersonal psychologist JEAN HOUSTON (b. 1937):

> suddenly the key turned and the door to the universe opened. I didn't see or hear anything unusual. There were no visions, no bursts of light. The world remained the same. And yet everything around me, including myself, moved into meaning. Everything . . . became part of a single Unity, a glorious symphonic resonance in which every part of the universe was a part of and illuminated every other part. . . . Everything mattered. Nothing was alien or irrelevant or distant. The farthest star was right next door and the deepest mystery was clearly seen. It seemed to me as if I knew everything. It seemed to me as if I was everything.[48]

Admittedly, Bucke's and Houston's experiences of unity happened spontaneously rather than as a result of previous practice; but precisely because they are so impressive, they typically become the reason why those who have them embark on a search for practices that might cause them to return.

Pleasure

This eighth category is concerned with practices that are not a means to an end but an end in themselves. One does not necessarily engage in them to attain something (power, knowledge, amplified abilities, healing, a next step in one's spiritual progress, contact with invisible entities, or unification with divinity or the universe) but simply because one likes practicing! Again, of course, there is a degree of overlap with some other categories. For example, it is inherently pleasurable for us to increase our well-being, to notice that we become capable of things that we couldn't do before, or to have experiences of cosmic unity. But apart from all this, practice as such may be a pleasure in itself.

The primary example of this final category is RITUAL. It is certainly true that Freemasons are supposed to "make progress" during the course of successive initiations, as we have seen, but there can be no doubt that many of them simply take a lot of pleasure in this "serious play" of dressing up in ceremonial costumes and performing their well-defined roles in what amounts to an elaborate ritual theater. The pleasure may be further enhanced by the welcome opportunity to escape, temporarily at least, from the constraints of your everyday life and your normal social roles. For example, the illuminist Jean-Baptiste Willermoz earned his living as a simple silk merchant, but his talents as an organizer and administrator made him one of the most powerful and influential personalities in the parallel universe of Freemasonry.[49]

The same thing is true for countless other esoteric organizations and ritual systems that exist in modern and contemporary society. They all result in parallel universes with their own forms of sociability and collective rituals, in a more general context that is known as the "cultic milieu." For example, participants in contemporary Wicca or other forms of paganism often emphasize how good it feels to be among likeminded people, to participate in a community that shares the same essential worldviews and values, and to perform rituals that both express and further enhance a sense of community and common purpose. Singing or dancing together is a pleasure, and many modern witches will confirm that even invoking the gods can be a lot of fun.

I would like to repeat what I wrote at the outset—this short discussion of practices, ordered in eight basic categories, is just a preliminary attempt to chart the enormous variety of "things that are being done" in esoteric contexts. It would be an understatement to say that the list of examples is far from complete, and there is definitely a need for much more research. The scholarly significance of studying esoteric practices in detail lies in the fact that it greatly expands and transforms traditional understandings of what "religion" in Western culture is all about. I have emphasized that many of these practices have been placed traditionally in an artificial special category, that of "magic," to keep them apart from supposedly more "serious" or "respectable" forms of religious worship. Such a distinction is normative and misleading. If we discard it, we discover that most of what used to be seen as magic may as well be described as religion, or sometimes even as science or natural philosophy, whereas what used to be seen as "true" religion is full of practices formerly categorized as magic.

7 Modernization

> True, history may at bottom be an illusion, but an illusion without which no perception of the essence is possible in time.
>
> (Gershom Scholem, "A Birthday Letter to Zalman Schocken")[1]

There has always been a strong tendency, not just among committed insiders but even among influential scholars in the field, to think of "esotericism" as a universal phenomenon or an enduring spiritual perspective that is in some sense above time and historical change.[2] I have been pushing back against such a perspective throughout this book—as you will have noticed, I advocate an empirical, bottom-up historical approach that always begins with giving full attention to whatever is there to be studied or observed, in as much detail as possible and preferably with a minimum of preconceived ideas. This means that I always prioritize such things as the historical *uniqueness*, the irreplaceable *specificity*, and the sometimes remarkable *originality* of individual thinkers or practitioners and historical trends. I do this because a primary focus on what all "esoteric" materials supposedly have in common usually goes at the expense of paying close attention, first of all, to everything they do *not* have in common.

Essentialist concepts of a "universal esotericism" simply do not jell with the historical fact of cultural *difference*. The deeply conservative belief that only that which never changes can ever be truly important militates against a recognition of human inventiveness and sheer creativity. For my part, in this book, I am interested in learning *new* things and asking how we might gain *new* insights into history and human culture: if we already know in advance which "universal truths" we are looking for, we will hardly expect to discover anything new that could possibly challenge our prior assumptions. And therefore we will certainly not find it. But in advocating historicity, I am not just pushing back against perspectives of cultural conservatism, in the sense of a search for "eternal wisdom" that disregards historical context, for anti-historical modes of theorizing are just as common among secular academics who are deeply committed to social progress. The present-centered ethnocentric gaze can be a powerful blinding force that subverts historical awareness, insofar as it measures everything that comes into its purview by the tacitly assumed superiority of its own theoretical frameworks and assumptions. In doing so, it conveniently ignores the (admittedly) troubling fact that the latter, too, like everything else, are strictly contingent and historically situated.[3]

My goal in this chapter is to illustrate the importance of *difference and historicity* at the example of modernization. Traditional scholarship tended to emphasize *continuity* at the expense of *discontinuity*, for instance by describing esotericism as a "form of thought" that would always have to remain the same.[4] By contrast, I focus on the dramatic processes of irreversible change, historical transformation, and radical discontinuity that are captured by such terms as MODERNIZATION, SECULARIZATION, and DISENCHANTMENT.[5] They are of central importance to the field as a whole, as will be seen. But to understand them properly, first of all, we must zoom in on the concept of HISTORICITY as such. Why is it that so many scholars of esotericism and of religion, including self-described "historians," show such strong resistance against the power and implications of historical method?

The Resistance against History

A first reason is quite straightforward, although at first sight it might seem counterintuitive. *There is no greater threat to religious or esoteric conviction than the practice of historiography.* If you wish to evaluate esoteric truth claims from a critical perspective, it is *not* natural science or analytical philosophy that will provide you with the "hardest" evidence and the most incisive critical arguments but precisely the study of historical sources as practiced in the supposedly "softer" disciplines of the humanities! Philosophical rationalists and natural scientists have come up with sophisticated strategies both for refuting *and* protecting belief in the existence of God or a spiritual dimension of reality, and no end to such debates seems to be in sight.[6] By contrast, the results of critical historiography and textual-philological research are often final and conclusive, because they can make it impossible to keep holding certain beliefs without sacrificing your intellect.[7] This is true for instance in such mainstream domains as biblical studies, where textual and linguistic criticism since the early modern period basically destroyed the possibility of seeing the bible as the Word of God.[8] In the field of esotericism more specifically, a famous example is the dating of the *Corpus Hermeticum*. Throughout the fifteenth and sixteenth centuries, Ficino's *Pimander* was widely believed to be among the most ancient and therefore most authoritative sources of ancient Egyptian wisdom. Its status came close to "holy scripture" among believers in the *prisca theologia* or *philosophia perennis*. But doubts about the great antiquity of the Hermetic corpus began to be raised toward the end of the sixteenth century. In 1614, the great philologist and textual critic ISAAC CASAUBON (1559–1614) published a conclusive demonstration, based on strict linguistic evidence, that it could not have been written earlier than the first centuries of the Christian era.[9] His discovery dealt a heavy blow to the intellectual credibility of Renaissance Hermetism, from which it basically never recovered. This example demonstrates how a grand (mnemo)historical narrative with deep spiritual implications can sometimes be utterly destroyed by strict historiographical analysis focused on tiny textual details.

A second reason for the resistance against historicity is more general in nature. In the context of the Eranos meetings, from which the religionist study of esotericism emerged after the Second World War, the de(con)structive potential of HISTORICISM was recognized as a very major issue. For influential scholars such as Jung, Eliade, or Corbin, the problem was larger than just the fact that cherished esoteric beliefs may sometimes be refuted by historical discoveries. Their profound concern was with the necessarily antithetical relation between History and Truth. In the wake of Friedrich Nietzsche, a towering influence on their generation,[10] they understood that strict historical thinking (concerned with temporality and change) necessarily relativizes all metaphysical values (concerned with an eternal reality) and would therefore undermine the foundations of belief in any deeper meaning to human existence. Perhaps no scholar experienced this more painfully than MIRCEA ELIADE.[11] If "everything passes," and anything that happens (the worst historical atrocities next to the most inspiring victories) might just as well have happened differently, or not at all, then history ceases to be a "story" with some kind of plot that gives meaning to the human quest. In a formulation by John Masefield, famously quoted by Arnold Toynbee, history gets reduced to just "One Damned Thing After Another"—an apparently pointless series of random contingencies without any deeper significance, goal, or direction, beginning with nothing and leading nowhere, for no particular reason at all. Eliade referred to this nihilist specter as "the terror of history" and spent his life battling against it. After the Second World War, his anti-historicism resonated strongly with the feelings of a generation that was growing up in the shadow of horrors—two successive world wars, the holocaust, the nuclear bomb, the war in Vietnam. History seemed like a nightmare from which they yearned to escape.[12]

The problem that Eliade saw is very real and extremely important. It is not surprising that many scholars in the study of esotericism, and in the study of religion more generally, would like to find an antidote of some kind against historical relativism. Also, it is not just consoling but very exciting to think that some kind of "hidden hand" must be at work, some kind of providential design, something that gives purpose and direction, some kind of higher guidance, some kind of narrative plot that lends ultimate meaning to historical events. It can provide a deep sense of spiritual relief to feel personally "captured" or existentially "addressed" (*ergriffen* in German, *interpellé* in French) by some numinous presence that, in spite of everything, speaks to us from the beyond, through the medium of symbols or archetypal images.[13] And it is very attractive to believe that there are universal esoteric truths, a hidden Tradition of eternal wisdom that has never changed and remains as valid today as it was in ancient and primordial times.

The sober truth, implicitly recognized by the entire Eranos tradition, is that none of these spiritual beliefs or desires can ever find support in the documented evidence that is accessible to historians *qua* historians.[14] We need no hidden designs or more-than-human influences to account for the emergence of "esoteric" currents or ideas and their development through time. Straightforward historical interpretations and explanations are more than sufficient. To be sure, it will always be possible to believe that some numinous reality exists beyond normal sense experience—we can neither prove nor disprove its existence, and there's nothing "irrational" or otherwise disreputable about being personally convinced of its presence, for instance on the basis of profound spiritual experiences.[15] We just shouldn't expect *historians* to provide us with arguments or evidence in support of such convictions, because that is not what their methods are able to do (remember the metaphor of "tools" in Chapter 1).[16] Nothing that historians can know about historical events suggests the idea of a universal Tradition or an unchanging esoteric worldview, with its hidden implication (which defenders tend to overlook or play down) that individual creativity is of no importance and originality should be discouraged.

What we find in the history of "esotericism" is precisely what we find everywhere else: contingent events and coincidences, creative inventions, continual change, and surprising transformations that could never have been anticipated or predicted in advance. All this activity is carried by the actions and desires of human-all-too-human beings just like ourselves. Some of them make grandiose claims of superior knowledge, but they are not necessarily any wiser or more perceptive than we are. As formulated by Foucault, the history of human culture consists of an ongoing "series of interpretations."[17] Throughout history, human beings have kept revising and reformulating earlier ideas and traditions or coming up with new ones, always in response to challenges in their intellectual, religious, cultural, and social environments. If any divine or sacred presence is at work in these historical events, it does an excellent job at staying out of sight!

In short, the relativist and potentially nihilist implications of critical historiography are real enough. It is easy to understand the emotional resistance against "historicizing everything" or to sympathize with the initial feelings of disappointment that beginning students may sometimes experience when they take a peek behind the official surface of awe-inspiring traditions or charismatic personalities.[18] But whether for better or for worse, respect for demonstrable evidence and the force of arguments remains the *sine qua non*, not just of scholarly research but, quite simply, of our ongoing human attempts to understand the world a bit better. In addition, it is important to be reminded that, even though historicity comes at a price, its denial comes at a price as well. Critical historiography and philological expertise are not just instruments of destruction but have always been potent forces of *emancipation* and *liberation* from establishment propaganda and authoritarian narratives. In modern Western societies, we owe them much of our freedom from theological dogmatism and ecclesiastical control.

If we are open to the evidence for continuous change and innovation in the history of esotericism, we can begin to appreciate the creativity and originality of its best representatives. Whether we see them as genuinely inspired or deluded (or both, for that is perfectly possible!), at least they had the courage to think for themselves and follow their own lights—sometimes at great personal costs, from public ridicule even to death. For my part, I sympathize with those independent spirits who dare to think for themselves and who can be seen as converging in what has been called the Embassy of the Free Mind.[19]

Many key historical transformations that are central to the field of "esotericism" should already be evident from the overviews in Chapters 2 and 3. I began this story in the "pagan" Hellenistic culture of late antiquity, but its further development turned out to be extremely complicated. Even a very incomplete list of transformative developments would at least include the following: • the emergence of Christianity; • the theological campaign against pagan idolatry and other forms of "superstition"; • the birth and spread of Islam and its creative interaction with (Neo)Platonism and the Occult Sciences; • the flourishing of science and natural philosophy in medieval and early modern Islam; • the invention of Jewish kabbalah; • philosophical innovations such as the rise of nominalism and scholasticism; • the Crusades and the rise of military orders, such as the Johannite and Templar knighthoods; • successive Jewish diasporas, including notably the expulsion of the Jews from Spain; • cultural and intellectual innovations such as Italian humanism; • the dawn of printing; • the advent of the Reformation and Protestant sectarianism; • colonial expansion and the encounter between Europeans and non-European cultures; • radical new philosophies such as Spinozism, Cartesianism, or Kantianism; • the so-called Scientific Revolutions; • the Enlightenment; • the emergence of capitalist modes of production; • the invention of Freemasonry; • the French Revolution; • the rise of conspiracy theories; • the increasing separation between church and state, finally leading to a "religious supermarket"; • industrialization and the expansion of technology; • Romanticism in literature, art, philosophy, and religion; • the rise of historical consciousness; • the new philosophies of evolution; • socialism and Marxism; • the emancipation of women; • the birth of academic psychology and psychiatry; • the study of so-called "primitive" cultures by yet another new discipline, anthropology; • the "death of God"; • existentialism; • the interconnected political phenomena of anti-Semitism, imperialism, and totalitarianism; • neoliberal marketization and globalization; • philosophical revolutions such as post-structuralism and deconstruction; • or the rise of information technology, the internet, virtual realities, social media, and AI. Again, this list is anything but complete! Each and every one of these changes and innovations is either heavily involved with "esotericism" or has strongly impacted the historical development of its various components, moving them into ever-new directions that would have been impossible to predict. Without any need for additional arguments, I believe that this long and yet quite selective list should be sufficient to refute the idea of one Universal Esotericism or an unchanging spiritual Tradition of Ancient Truth.

Even if change and transformation have always been the rule, some revolutions are more radical than others. As I already suggested in Chapter 1, the general process of "modernization" might be the most decisive of all. This is why (as outlined in Chapter 1) some scholars think of "esotericism" as the prototype of premodern enchantment, others as an essentially modern phenomenon, while yet others believe that it promises a way of escape from (post)modernity to timeless realms of the spirit. In the rest of this chapter, we will take a closer look at the historical transformations from pre- or early modernity to modern, postmodernity, and perhaps even meta-modernity.[20]

Instrumental Causality

A first crucial transformation has to do with ideas about how the world or the universe is functioning and is closely connected to the rise of modern science. In pre-Enlightenment periods, we can draw a distinction between three different perspectives. The first one looks at reality as a grand, harmonious, and organic whole in which all the parts correspond to one another *without* a need for intermediary links or chains of causality.

This idea, which comes ultimately from Stoicism, is described in a classic passage by PLOTINUS:

> This whole universe is in a state of sympathy, and is like one living creature; and what is far away is yet close—just like, in a living creature, a nail or horn or finger or another limb that does not lie immediately next to it. What is at distance is affected, although nothing is felt by what lies in between; for things that are similar do not lie next to one another but are separated by things that are different, and yet they are subject to the same influences due to their similarity, and therefore something that is done by a part that does not lie next to it must necessarily reach what is distant. For it is all one living thing and part of one unity, and no distance is so great that things would not still be close enough to be in mutual sympathy as part of this one living being.[21]

This concept says that even the remotest parts of the universe may correspond (or co-respond) to one another by means of some kind of secret sympathy based on their inherent similarity or likeness (*similitudo*). It was extremely widespread and has been promoted by Antoine Faivre as the first intrinsic characteristic of "Western" esotericism—CORRESPONDENCES. It is inseparable from similar concepts that have been discussed under rubrics such as "analogical thinking," "correlative thinking," "*ressemblance*," "signatures," "participation," or "synchronicity."[22] While many scholars have seen it as essential to the worldview of the Renaissance,[23] critics of "the occult" have often described it as the essence of magical superstition.[24]

In many authors from the Renaissance period, beginning with Ficino, a holistic worldview of noncausal correspondences was closely aligned to a second perspective. This one assumes that different parts of the universe *do* in fact influence one another, even at great distances, by what might be called OCCULT CAUSALITY.[25] A classic reference is the medieval Islamic philosopher al-Kindī and his famous doctrine that all things and events in the universe send out invisible "rays."[26] Ficino used al-Kindī's work to explain astral influences, while also postulating the existence of a universal *spiritus*—a kind of subtle substance or invisible fluid that was believed to permeate the whole of the cosmos. Described as "a very tenuous body, as if now it were soul and not body, and now body and not soul,"[27] it was the ideal medium for explaining causal connections between bodies and souls that could not be explained in terms of visible and material chains of causality. Which brings us to the third perspective, that of INSTRUMENTAL CAUSALITY. This is the familiar "mechanical" or billiard ball model in which one thing can influence another only by means of physically demonstrable and theoretically predictable chains of material cause and effect. With the development of modern science, from its original Newtonian foundations to new perspectives such as relativity theory, quantum mechanics, or string theory, this model has been developed in extremely sophisticated new directions but without sacrificing the essential assumption—that it should be possible to explain everything that happens in the world as resulting from strictly material causes, in terms of natural laws that function with strict regularity, and that in principle, the human mind must be able to discover those laws and principles.

Because these three models were all deeply rooted in classical sources, intellectuals were referring to them widely before the eighteenth century. They were often mixed in confusing ways, as scientists might try to explain the world partly in terms of instrumental or occult causality and partly in terms of correspondences. But as the Scientific Revolution was gathering steam, the lines of opposition hardened, and correspondences and occult causalities began losing the battle against instrumental causality. Meanwhile it began to dawn on European scientists, including deeply convinced Christians such as Isaac Newton or Robert Boyle, that if "mysterious and incalculable forces"[28] would truly disappear from the world, then angels or demons would vanish as well, until there would ultimately be no room even for God himself! A seminal "esoteric" figure such as EMANUEL SWEDENBORG can only be understood against these backgrounds. His work was based on a theory of correspondences but one that crucially differed from the Plotinian model: it did not function as an alternative to instrumental causality but as a way to *preserve* causality in the natural world without needing to sacrifice the independence of spirit. Swedenborg's spiritual world was separate from, but in perfect sync with, a world of matter that answered entirely to the laws of post-Cartesian physics. No occult forces or subtle influences connected this spiritual world with its material counterpart. And yet everything in the physical world reflected or corresponded to the spiritual, because that was how the Lord had ordained it. Swedenborg's worldview was not a continuation of the kabbalah or other forms of premodern esotericism, as has sometimes been assumed. As a creative new departure grounded in up-to-date science and natural philosophy, it is an excellent example of esoteric innovation.[29]

And it was highly influential. The basic notion of two "separate-yet-connected" levels of reality became a bedrock assumption of modern spiritualism and occultism, because it served to protect spiritual realities from scientific falsification and disenchantment.[30] These modern traditions were no longer grounded in the holistic universe of Plotinian or Renaissance correspondences but in an essentially dualistic world modeled partly on René Descartes's famous concept of *res cogitans* and *res extensa* and partly also on Immanual Kant's key distinction (itself inspired by Swedenborg!)[31] between a noumenal and a phenomenal world. Still, it remained possible for occultists and even for scientists to think in terms of occult causality. The new science had not truly rejected the key notion of *qualitates occultae* ("occult qualities") as such but rather the assumption that such forces were "hidden" and unknowable by definition. As famously formulated by the early pioneer Julius Caesar Scaliger (1484–1558), the ambition was to take them out of the "asylum of ignorance" and turn them into genuine objects of scientific research.[32]

For instance, such phenomena as gravity, magnetism, or electrostatics used to be seen as "occult forces" but have become perfectly normal parts of science and technology. Whenever we use our cell phone or watch the internet, we are making connections by means of an invisible medium (electromagnetic radiation) that would have been seen as occult by our pre-Enlightenment ancestors. Other claims of occult causality did eventually lose their scientific prestige, but it sometimes took a long time. For instance, theories of an invisible "ether" remained part of mainstream scientific discourse until far into the twentieth century but were retrospectively written out of the history books after relativity and quantum mechanics had emerged victorious.[33] But before that happened, and even afterward, the fact that they could serve as a permeable medium between spirit and matter allowed them to mediate between religious and scientific concerns as well.

Yet other claims of occult causality, such as thought transference or healing at a distance, never gained a serious foothold in mainstream science but were widely dismissed as superstition. The basic argument has always been that (in contrast to such hidden forces as magnetism or electricity) they cannot meet the basic requirement of experimental reproducibility, and that neither their actual occurrence nor an "occult" medium of transmission has been conclusively demonstrated. Against these mainstream patterns of rejection, a new field of study emerged, known as PSYCHICAL RESEARCH and (eventually) PARAPSYCHOLOGY.[34] Many psychical researchers have tried to demonstrate empirically that "anomalous" phenomena do in fact occur and can be explained in terms of scientific mechanisms of instrumental causality. Others insist that the phenomena are real but might be difficult or even impossible to demonstrate in those terms and therefore require us to expand our scientific models. In a more recent period, for instance, the English biologist RUPERT SHELDRAKE developed a theory called "morphic resonance" that postulates the existence of "morphic fields."[35]

Finally, the correspondences model has by no means vanished either. Its most sophisticated formulation comes from Carl Gustav Jung, who was collaborating with the Nobel-Prize-winning physicist Wolfgang Pauli (1900–58). With copious references to pre- and early modern "esoteric" traditions, and in deliberate opposition to positivist science, they coined the concept of SYNCHRONICITY as a noncausal principle that connects nature and the psyche.[36] References to synchronicity have become incredibly popular in postwar esotericism and New Age contexts. This not only reflects an instinctive rejection of instrumental causality and its nihilist implications but also shows the enormous impact of psychology on contemporary concepts of how the world works. We will turn to that topic below.

In terms of the basic argument in this chapter (the key importance of historical discontinuity and creative innovation in the history of esotericism), we may conclude that the dominance of instrumental causality since the Enlightenment resulted in multiple attempts at avoiding its materialist and reductionist implications by developing some new kind of enchanted *Naturphilosophie*.[37] Whether in esoteric contexts or anywhere else, the social and discursive authority of modern science is now so overwhelming that it rarely gets rejected as such—although admittedly, there are signs that this may be changing in our current post-truth world of social media, conspirational theories, and alternative facts. Modern and contemporary esotericism has often been dismissed as a regressive phenomenon, based on the misguided dream of returning to premodern worldviews and ancient superstitions. But if we look more closely, we encounter multiple attempts at negotiating a compromise of some kind between the conflicting options of instrumental causality, occult causality, and correspondences. These projects are driven by a sense of spiritual urgency, for if we cannot find a solution, that would seem to condemn us to living in a thoroughly disenchanted world driven just by technology and money. The very difficulty of resolving this vital "problem of disenchantment" without sacrificing one's intellect[38] remains a powerful incentive for spiritual creativity and conceptual innovation.

Globalization

A second crucial transformation has to do with the religious and cultural horizon of "esoteric" forms of religion or spirituality. I have been tracing them back to the period of "pagan" Hellenism, from where they developed into new directions in the context of Jewish, Christian, and Islamic monotheisms that remained dominant until far into the European eighteenth century. The widespread belief in an ancient wisdom handed down from nonbiblical Oriental sages, such as the Egyptian Hermes or the Persian Zoroaster, did not need to imply a superiority of paganism over monotheism. It could also suggest that the power and wisdom of the true God had already been available, at least partly and as a matter of principle, to the gentile nations before the advent of Christ or Muhammad. Even in the nonproselytizing monotheism of the Jews, the divine powers of Life and Light were held to be present and active in the entire created world.

Although Platonic-Orientalist traditions sometimes mentioned the Indian Brahmins or gymnosophists, known from contacts along the silk roads, their cultural horizon did not seriously extend beyond Persia in the East. As formulated in a standard work by Wilhelm Halbfass, here focusing on the early Greek perspective,

> The relationship between Greek thought and the world outside of Greece, the Orient, is marked by a particular ambivalence. It is precisely the openness for the possibility of alien sources, the readiness to learn and the awareness of such readiness which sustains the Greek claim of being different from the Orient. In fact, ιστορια [*historia*] implies "openness for the alien, the other." Claiming such openness is a means of Greek self-identification and self-definition. . . . Unlike other "Orientals," Indians did not actively participate in the shared culture of late antiquity. Nor is there anything like an ongoing dialogue between India and the Hellenic or hellenized world. . . . The Greeks of antiquity did not like to learn foreign languages, and they did not favor translating into their own tongue. They never opened themselves to a foreign religious and literary tradition in a manner comparable to the comprehensive acquisition and translation of Indian Buddhist texts by the Chinese or Tibetans.[39]

As for the Islamic world, although Muḥammad's religion did extend far into India, Halbfass explains, "the Muslims, whose religious beliefs and social institutions sharply contrast with those of the Hindus, resisted the process of absorbtion," and for most of them, India remained essentially "a strange and exotic land."[40] On the whole, when missionaries or colonizers from monotheistic cultures such as Christianity encountered the religious practices of faraway continents, such as Eastern Asia but also sub-Saharan Africa or the New World, they seldom saw much more in them than typical instances of paganism and idolatry. They certainly didn't consider them as serious alternatives to the Christian revelation.[41]

These basic patterns began to change toward the end of the seventeenth century, and decisively during the eighteenth. The Christian churches were slowly losing their grip on society, and Western scholars became curious about the vast religious literature from cultures beyond the Old World. The result, at least as seen from Europe, has been famously described as an ORIENTAL RENAISSANCE.[42] During the original European Renaissance in fifteenth-century Italy, humanists had been exploring the sources of Greek and Roman antiquity, including newly available manuscripts relevant to Platonic Orientalism. But as new waves of ancient Asian texts became available for scholars, they began to move the original sources of "Oriental wisdom" much further toward the East. This process began with the pioneering work of Abraham Hyacinthe Anquetil-Duperron (1731–1805), who went to India in the 1750s and came back with a great number of Avestan, Middle Persian, and Sanskrit manuscripts. As beautifully formulated by Raymond Schwab in his standard work on the subject,

> [W]ith his translation of the Upanishads, [Anquetil-Duperron] dug an isthmus between the hemispheres of the human spirit and liberated the old humanism from the Mediterranean Basin. . . . Before him, Latin, Greek, Jewish, and Arab writers were the sole sources of knowledge about the distant past of the planet. The Bible appeared as an isolated rock, a meteorite. People believed that text contained the whole universe; hardly anyone seemed to imagine the immensity of the uncharted territories. . . . He cast a vision of countless and ancient civilizations, an enormous mass of literatures into our schools, which to this day arrogantly keep the door shut behind the narrow legacy of the Greek-Latin Renaissance.[43]

During the nineteenth century, the comparative study of religions developed into a powerful new discipline closely interwoven with the study of ancient and oriental languages. This led to the widely accepted paradigm of an "Indo-European" cultural and linguistic matrix that could be brought to light with the technical methods of comparative philology.[44]

This new wave of fascination with Oriental religions was congenial to Enlightenment and Romantic agendas alike, although for different reasons. Rationalist skeptics and anti-Christian libertines developed radical theories of myth and symbolism to undermine biblical and theological dogma. They argued that religion in all its forms, including Christianity itself, had not originated in a divine revelation but came from "primitive" ritual practices addressed to the life-giving powers of nature, notably the sun ("solar worship") and the sexual organs ("phallicism"). The remnants of solar and sexual symbolism could still be discovered everywhere, in European Christian culture and the religions of India.[45] European Romantics were impressed by the rich mythology and symbolism of Oriental religions and their mystical aspirations. In the wake of Friedrich Schlegel's *Über die Sprache und Weisheit der Indier* ("On the Language and Wisdom of the Indians," 1808), Hinduism was idealized as a noble tradition of great antiquity grounded in a universal spiritual wisdom from which Westerners had much to learn. Buddhism took a bit longer to be discovered by Europeans. At mid-century it was still widely perceived as a "gloomy religion of negation,"[46] but in the wake of the popular success of Sir Edwin

Arnold's *The Light of Asia* (1879) and Theosophical concepts of "esoteric Buddhism," it became a source of inspiration for Europeans and Americans.

The enormous expansion of comparative studies in religion, mythology, and ancient languages, driven by a popular fascination with the spirituality of the Orient, all occurred in a broader political-economic context dominated by European imperialism and colonial rule. According to the complicated dialectics of the Orientalist imagination, famously placed on the agenda by Edward Said,[47] European audiences defined their "Western" identity against the "Otherness" of the East. Negative stereotypes (such as the supposed passivity or lasciviousness of "the Oriental mind," the "dark pagan idolatry" of Hinduism, or the "bleak otherworldliness" of atheist Buddhism) served to extol the superiority of European attitudes and values. But Europe or the West could also be criticized in positive-Orientalist terms, for instance, by presenting India as the original home of ageless Wisdom and deep spirituality, while contrasting it with narrow-minded Christian orthodoxy and its obsession with sin or with Western materialism and shallow notions of secular "progress."

All these elements (the comparative study of religions, the Indo-European model, mythographic theories of phallicism and solar worship, India as the home of ancient wisdom and a superior spirituality, the dialectics of Orientalism) are of fundamental importance to understand what happened to esotericism during the nineteenth century. Modern THEOSOPHY was not just a "revival of ancient wisdom," as its followers liked to claim,[48] for in many ways, it was a radical *new* synthesis grounded in theories and concerns that were typical of the nineteenth century. Blavatsky's original referential corpus consisted of Western esoteric traditions described by Theosophists as "the oriental kabbalah," but although India was often seen as the cradle of occult wisdom, this was still the India of the popular Western Orientalist imagination.[49] This changed decisively after 1879, when Blavatsky and Olcott arrived in Bombay and began collaborating directly with Hindus and Buddhists who, obviously, had access to their own sacred scriptures in the original languages. In the wake of these encounters and productive exchanges, the Theosophical Society emerged as a powerful international organization with countless Indian members that began publishing English translations of Hindu and Buddhist scriptures.

As a logical result, Theosophical doctrine was being transformed into a unique amalgamation of Eastern and Western concepts, not just by Blavatsky herself but by many other Theosophists from India and Europe. As part of these complicated processes of mutual projection and appropriation, in a colonial context marked by unequal power relations, influential Indian authors could use concepts of Western provenance to promote the superiority of their own traditions, just as Western Theosophists were using concepts of Eastern provenance to promote *their* occultist perspectives.[50] While all participants in these debate were laying claims to the true and "authentic" ancient wisdom, in fact these exchanges resulted in *modern* creative reinterpretations or mutations of both Indian and European traditions.[51] Far from being just a one-sided process of diffusion in which Western esotericism gets exported to the East,[52] complex patterns of influence were moving in all directions driven by the agency of both Indian and European Theosophists.

The agendas of the former did not necessarily align with those of the latter, but they were all operating in a wider context that was permeated by spiritualist or occultist elements and widely shared background assumptions about their relation to "Western science."

The notion of "karma" might be a particularly good example of how Theosophists were able to adopt *and* reinterpret key concepts from Asian traditions, bringing them to the attention of countless readers on a global scale.[53] There is no doubt that Theosophy was a major force of innovation, creating many of the basic foundations of twentieth-century esotericism, as also demonstrated for instance by such practices as Yoga and Tantra.[54] In all these contexts, we see how Western esoteric traditions were "orientalized" and their Oriental counterparts "occidentalized" in an ongoing creative process of mutual fertilization. While Theosophy was particularly important in this regard, it certainly did not stand alone. In the American context, TRANSCENDENTALISM was another key movement that enabled mediation and exchange between Oriental spiritualities and esoteric traditions of Western provenance.[55] Without Theosophy and American METAPHYSICAL RELIGION, profoundly indebted to Transcendentalism,[56] it would be hard to imagine the massive "turn towards the East" that occurred in Western societies since the 1960s or, for that matter, the New Age movement that developed in its wake.

India may have been particularly popular, but esoteric audiences in the modern West have always been busy adopting, appropriating, integrating, reinterpreting, and repackaging many elements from other Asian traditions as well. For example, think of the enormous popularity of the Chinese I Ching, with Carl Gustav Jung as an important pioneer, or the Japanese Zen Buddhism inspired by D. T. Suzuki—both of them speakers at the Eranos meetings, that crucial academic cauldron from which so much of postwar esotericism has taken its cue. It would seem that the impact of African religions on esotericism in modern Western societies remained a bit more limited, except in the predominantly American milieus of Black or AFRICANA ESOTERICISM. Important instances are the Black spiritualist churches, the Nuwaubian Nation, the Nation of Islam, the Nahziryah Monastic Community, or influential figures such as Ishmael Reed and Sun Ra.[57] If esotericism long used to be seen as predominantly white,[58] this has been corrected more recently by a new generation of scholars, who also call attention to the implications of a normative "whiteness" bias in previous and contemporary research.[59]

As for Native American spiritualities and Latin American SHAMANISM, both have been recognized as significant factors of innovation in esotericism since the 1960s.[60] In esoteric milieus, they tend to be seen as "wisdom traditions" grounded in deep traditional knowledge of the mysteries of nature that Western societies have sadly lost. They have also been crucial to yet another innovative tradition that can be referred to as ENTHEOGENIC ESOTERICISM.[61] Natural psychoactive substances or "plant medicines" (notably peyote, ayahuasca, or psilocybin mushrooms) are seen as avenues toward "higher knowledge" in the context of neo-shamanic mixtures between esoteric traditions of Western provenance and indigenous Latin American cultures. In all these contexts, we are dealing with complicated reciprocal patterns of influence and appropriation or negotiation, both in Western and non-Western societies, between Western and non-Western agents.

For European or American authors, it may seem natural to imagine all these processes of "esoteric globalization" in terms of a progressive *expansion* of intellectual horizons beyond the traditional borders of the Christian West, but that is not how the situation will appear from other parts of the world. If you are born and raised in modern China or Brasil, to give just two random examples, naturally you will not think in such Eurocentric terms of a global expansion from the "center" toward the "margins" but rather in terms of having been invaded by powers that came from somewhere else. Again, if there are concepts in your own language that seem equivalent to anglophone "esoteric" vocabulary, there is no need for you to think of your culture as having "received" Western esoteric teachings from abroad. You might as well say that this foreign vocabulary enables you to express *your* beliefs in such terms that people from other cultural spheres may understand what they mean.[62] In post-nineteenth-century global contexts, after more than two centuries of intensely creative exchange between traditions of European and non-European provenance, it may no longer make much sense to speak of "Western" esotericism in non-Western countries. Even though, historically, contemporary esoteric discourse may have been the product of creative encounters between Europeans and non-Europeans, its current manifestations are usually neither Western nor non-Western. They are now a global phenomenon in its own right.

None of this contradicts the fact that Europeans, from their perspective, did experience a spectacular broadening of vision after the period of the eighteenth century. Having expanded its horizon, first from Christian Europe to "the mystic East,"[63] and eventually to the rest of the globe as well, in more recent years the esoteric imagination has been casting its gaze even beyond our solar system or our galaxy! In earlier phases of historical development, the mythical appeal of the Orient had much to do with a European need for "orientation"—you needed to situate yourself, or define your position, with reference to some center or origin that was "Other" in respect to yourself.[64] For Europeans this was the Orient, the direction of sunrise, hence the term orientation. Today, of course, all parts of the globe have been mapped and explored, thereby losing much of their mysterious aura of infinite promise and possibilities. Yet our current "Google Earth" generation may still feel a need to avoid "disorientation" by defining an original spiritual center of ultimate cosmic wisdom. In the contemporary esoteric imagination, deeply influenced by science fiction, it may therefore be placed no longer on earth but in some physical location elsewhere in the universe, with Sirius and the Pleiades as popular favorites.[65] Esotericism has definitely come a long way!

Evolution

A third crucial transformation has to do with conceptualizations of time and history in relation to the story of humanity. The concept of evolution is extremely familiar today but did not exist before the eighteenth century. Next to standard concepts of divine providence in a monotheistic culture, the influential model of a *prisca theologia* implied a process of degeneration or corruption instead of evolution, whereas the concept of a *philosophia perennis* implied that nothing new should be expected because the truth had always been available and always would be. Against all these traditional approaches, evolution was something new.

I already suggested that the emergence of evolution may have been indebted historically to the Alchemical Paradigm that took shape in the sixteenth century.[66] By mediation of Christian Theosophy in the tradition of Jacob Böhme, it reached the philosophers of Romanticism and German Idealism. Another (but not necessarily conflicting) account would connect the birth of evolutionism rather with the Platonic Paradigm. In his classic study about the Platonic "Great Chain of Being," Arthur Lovejoy called attention to the important concept of *plenitude*, based on the idea that everything that *could* possibly exist *does* in fact exist, somewhere in the grand universal hierarchy of existence. Lovejoy explains how, in the eighteenth century, this great chain of being came to be interpreted in terms of temporality: "The *plenum formarum* [fullness of forms] came to be conceived by some, not as the *inventory* but as the *program* of nature, which is being carried out gradually and exceedingly slowly in the cosmic history."[67] In this manner, the static model of universal harmony and cosmic order was giving way to a dynamic model of gradual unfoldment. This led eventually to a doctrine of evolutionary development through time, according to which new and higher phenomena emerge organically and in orderly fashion from lower ones, guided by some kind of hidden teleological or providential design. Already during the later eighteenth century, we encounter stories of "natural history" in which life forms are being imagined as climbing an evolutionary stairway that begins with primitive organisms, moves upward from there to animals, and finally culminates in Man.[68]

Such evolutionary models came to full development in the work of the German Idealists, notably Schelling and Hegel, and were popularized by Romantic poets and philosophers in many other countries such as France, England, and America.[69] Because the grand narrative of Christianity (from God's creation of the world to the Fall of Man and the expulsion from paradise, followed by the incarnation and sacrificial death of Jesus Christ, and culminating finally in his future return at the End of Time) was losing credibility in this period, a different story was needed to explain "the meaning of history"—where have we come from, what are we supposed to be doing here, and where is it all going? Perhaps the most powerful philosophical answer came from HEGEL. He invented a seductive grand narrative about world history, depicted as a deeply painful but ultimately glorious process of spiritual liberation driven by the power of reason (*die Vernunft*), by means of which the World Spirit (*der Weltgeist*) finally attains to perfect self-consciousness.[70]

Such philosophical theories of *SPIRITUAL* EVOLUTION could be seen as the backdrop to scientific theories of *BIOLOGICAL* EVOLUTION. With hindsight, it is clear that they paved the way for Charles Darwin's revolutionary narrative in *The Origin of Species* (1859) and *The Descent of Man* (1871). The new super-story said that life had been unfolding over enormous stretches of time, by the mechanisms of natural selection, in an upward evolutionary movement from the lowest and simplest organisms to the birth of the human species. But humanity itself had been evolving as well, from "primitive" modes of consciousness exemplified by the "lower races" to the highly civilized consciousness of Modern Western Man. Anthropological theories about "primitive cultures" seemed to lend hard scientific support to this obviously racist and sexist vision. The founder of cultural anthropology Edward Burnett Tylor (1832–1917) in his two-volume *Primitive Culture* (1871), and his successor James G. Frazer (1854–1941) in an enormously popular series of volumes titled *The Golden Bough* (1900), described the progress of human civilization in terms of an upward evolutionary development: from *magic* (typically associated with the dark superstitions of dark-skinned peoples) by way of *religion* (typically associated with white European Protestantism) to modern *science* (obviously dominated by European gentlemen as well). All these theories of evolution reflected the obviously ethnocentric perspective of white European males during the high colonial period, who were happy to think of themselves as the pinnacle of the entire evolutionary process.

Inevitably, such visions brought up the question of where humanity might be heading next. Hegel thought that the historical process had reached its highest and final evolutionary stage in his very own philosophy. A similar notion of "the end of history" has been proclaimed even in far more recent times, by popular authors who saw Western liberal democracy and global neoliberal capitalism as the final stage in the evolutionary process—although, admittedly, it could also end with the depressing specter of Nietzsche's "last man," described as small-minded herdlike humans "hopping around on the earth like flies," who have lost the ability to even imagine anything higher than simple sensory gratification.[71] For Nietzsche, the only hope to avoid such a bleak finale would lie in the appearance of a superior type of human or superhuman species, the famous *Übermensch*. Whether inspired by Nietzsche or by other thinkers, many "esoteric" authors since the nineteenth century (with prominent names such as Sri Aurobindo, Louis Pauwels and Jacques Bergier, or the contemporary academic Jeffrey J. Kripal) have imagined a continuing evolutionary process reaching far into the future, by means of which humans will develop higher and more exalted types of consciousness, god-like abilities or superpowers, and superior levels of spiritual understanding.[72]

Once again, almost all these radical new concepts in modern esotericism have their origin historically in German culture. As early as Gotthold Ephraim Lessing's famous *Die Erziehung des Menschengeschlechts* ("The Education of the Human Race," 1777–80), the story of humanity was compared to the growth from childhood to maturity, under the providential guidance of God in the role of a benevolent Father. Other influential German thinkers, notably Johann Gottfried Herder (1744–1803), described world history in terms of the successive achievements of "peoples" (*Völker*) such as the Orientals, the Egyptians, the Greeks, the Israelites, the Romans, and the Germans. These different trends all came together in the work of a Tyrolean physician and Mesmerist, Joseph Ennemoser (1787–1854). His *Geschichte der Magie* ("History of Magic," 1844) is a model example of esoteric evolutionist historiography in the German Romantic tradition,[73] and counts among the most important influences on Helena P. Blavatsky.[74]

Blavatsky's Theosophical system is of key importance, not just for the "orientalization" of esotericism and the impact of comparative religion (discussed in the previous section) but also for the emergence of new esoteric systems modeled on grand evolutionary schemes. In deliberate opposition to Darwin, Blavatsky built an ambitious cosmology on her concept of seven "root races" (each further subdivided into seven subraces) that represented the successive evolutionary stages of humanity's earthly spiritual advancement. In perfect concordance with Ennemoser's emphasis on the "Germanic people," and against the background of current Indo-European speculations, she claimed that we had advanced to the fifth "Teutonic" subrace of the fifth "Aryan" root race. Blavatsky integrated most of the "ancient oriental wisdom" within the history of this fifth root race: the "Teutonic" had been preceded by the "Hindu," "Arabian," "Persian," and "Celtic" subraces. She expected that the next "Australo-American" subrace would take over during the course of the twentieth century.

Finally, in the context of modern and contemporary esotericism, evolutionist visions of the history of humanity are closely connected to ideas about further spiritual progress after death. Already Lessing had surprised his readers by ending his book on the education of the human race with speculative references to reincarnation. In doing so, he could fall back on a long tradition in Western culture, from Pythagoras and Plato to the Jewish and Christian kabbalah or the work of Giordano Bruno.[75] As for Helena P. Blavatsky, she clearly came out in favor of reincarnation in her second great book, *The Secret Doctrine* (1888), written after she had traveled to India. Her way of defending it is inseparable from her grand evolutionary design *and* her discovery of karma. Its great attraction lay in the concept of a universal and impersonal "natural law" of moral retribution, as a welcome scientific alternative to Christian notions of sin and punishment.[76]

In the wake of Blavatsky's Theosophy, reincarnation has made an enormous career in modern and contemporary esoteric milieus. With the extremely influential "Seth" books written by Jane Roberts (1929–1984) as a major example, it became the central core assumption of spectacular science-fiction-like cosmologies, in which the soul is seen as a boundless creative energy that evolves through an infinite series of spiritual dimensions, leading far beyond our planet and solar system toward supreme metaphysical realities that utterly transcend our current faculties of understanding.[77] Without any doubt, a grand narrative of cosmic spiritual evolution is central to these perspectives. In the previous section, we have seen how the original *Western* horizon of esotericism expanded to embrace a *global* vision since the nineteenth century; and in the present section, we have now seen how its original horizon of *time and history* expanded as well, from monotheistic-providential models grounded in biblical narratives (also normative for Muslims) toward *cosmic* evolutionary visions of infinite spiritual development.

Psychology

A fourth major transformation is concerned with human consciousness, usually seen as residing in the soul, and its relation to divine or spiritual realities. A core belief in almost all traditions that fall under the "esotericism" umbrella, from antiquity to the present, is that our soul has a natural although frequently clouded or forgotten capacity for seeing the truth and attaining ultimate salvational knowledge (*gnōsis*). We have seen that the Hermetic writings contain radical statements of nonduality, to the effect that there's no distinction between our inner noetic light of spiritual understanding and the ultimate noetic Light of divinity itself.[78] Whereas these texts were unambiguously pagan, cultures dominated by biblical monotheism usually tend toward hierarchical models of some kind, based on the ontological primacy of God or ultimate spiritual reality. It then becomes more natural to imagine human souls as sparks of divine Light that have become separated from the great Source and long to return to where they came from. As this sense of separation gets emphasized more strongly, it can result in strong dualistic concepts of painful alienation and material entrapment. Across the entire spectrum of possibilities, from nonduality to radical dualism, the source of spiritual salvation or liberation is ultimately present in our own soul. PSYCHOLOGY means literally a discourse about the soul but may refer directly or indirectly to many related concepts as well, such as the Greek *nous*, the English "spirit," the German *Geist*, or our modern "consciousness" and its equivalents in other languages.[79]

As modern psychology developed during the nineteenth century, it began pushing back against monotheistic concepts based on the ontological primacy of God the Creator, by directing attention toward the soul as the central core of the human experience. For obvious reasons, during the heyday of positivism, this led to major intellectual struggles not just with theology but also with naturalist and materialist worldviews; and as everybody knows, the relation between "mind and matter" has remained a core concern in modern philosophies of consciousness.[80] A crucial pioneer during the early period was the philosopher LUDWIG FEUERBACH (1804–1872), author of a controversial bestseller about "the essence of Christianity" (1841),[81] who radically "reversed" or "inverted" the core assumptions on which Christian theology had been based—instead of God having created Man in his image, he insisted, human beings had created "God" (or gods) in *their* own image.[82] Feuerbach was a major influence on Karl Marx, Friedrich Nietzsche, and Sigmund Freud, the famous "masters of suspicion" who attacked the foundations of Christian culture.[83] As the century progressed, the once so revolutionary idea that God, gods, or any other spiritual realities might be just psychological projections of human wishes and desires lost its radical edge and became widely accepted. Today it is a popular commonplace in secular culture.

These developments had a very major impact not just on the social decline of Christianity in Europe and the United States but also on the development of esotericism from the nineteenth century up to the present. Starting with Mesmerism and somnambulism, human consciousness and its hidden potentials moved to the center of attention in esoteric practices, theoretical speculations, and empirical science (notably in the context of psychical research). In the earlier phases of Romantic Mesmerism, focused on the "nocturnal" side of nature and the human soul, a Christian metaphysics was still largely dominant in the background. If somnambules in a state of trance experienced themselves as entering a spiritual world, that world was still modeled on traditional Christian or Swedenborgian concepts of a heavenly reality beyond the senses, with God at its very center. But more radical psychological perspectives were already announcing themselves discreetly. For instance in JUSTINUS KERNER's seminal publication *Die Seherin von Prevorst* ("The Seeress of Prevorst," 1829), the somnambulist's visions depicted not just the physical stars and the moon but even intelligent spirits or angelic beings and the mysterious divine Source itself as located *inside* the inner world of her own mind.[84]

As somnambulist visions became ever more spectacular, with elaborate descriptions of invisible spiritual realities "from India to the Planet Mars," including space travels and encounters with spiritual entities and the inhabitants of other planets,[85] it could become difficult even for esoteric enthusiasts to accept it all at face value. Some kind of a middle position would have to be found between the extremes of accepting such accounts as straightforward empirical descriptions of objective realities or dismissing them as simple subjective delusions or hallucinations. Jeffrey J. Kripal has argued that precisely such an ambiguous state, intermediary between acceptance and rejection, is of key importance to how "the paranormal and the sacred" function in contemporary spiritual consciousness.[86]

The psychologization of esotericism in modern Western culture may be described in terms of a double dialectics. Realms of experience or belief that used be seen as pertaining to "the Sacred" (or, for that matter, the demonic) are frequently interpreted in psychological terms, according to the basic Feuerbachian principle of reversal or inversion. Yet this does not need to result in skepticism or disenchantment, because simultaneously the psyche *itself* gets sacralized and is now seen as endowed with all those numinous powers and wondrous abilities that used to be attributed to the divine! This dialectics allows esoteric practitioners to talk about divine realities while really meaning their own psyche and about their own psyche while really meaning the divine. A concept of "the Spiritual" can mediate nicely between God and the soul.

Undoubtedly the central author in this entire process of historical transformation—the psychologization of the sacred and the sacralization of psychology—is CARL GUSTAV JUNG. After the posthumous publication in 2009 of his *Liber Novus* ("the Red Book"), which I would count among the most important primary sources of esotericism in the twentieth century, it has become clear that Jungian psychology as a whole was grounded in intense visionary experiences that basically deconstruct the very distinction between mind and matter, consciousness and reality, or internal and external worlds. In a key passage, Jung turned the Feuerbachian procedure of reversal or inversion on its head. He describes how in one of his visions, he saves the life of the great hero God Izdubar, who has literally been poisoned by Western science with its exclusive focus on external things. He does this *not*, as one might expect, by proving that the god is real but precisely by declaring him a fantasy, a figment of the imagination! "This tangible and visible world is the one reality, but fantasy is the other reality."[87] Jung's *Liber Novus* is a sustained attempt to find an answer to the Death of God, announced by Feuerbach and Nietzsche, by showing how (just like Izdubar in this visionary narrative) the Sacred may be resurrected intact from the soil of human consciousness itself. The individual and collective imagination, whether working consciously or unconsciously, becomes a reality sui generis—the spiritual arena in which our souls must conduct their struggles for human meaning and moral values.

Psychologization is a powerful force of secular transformation; but precisely because the psyche itself may be endowed with numinous powers, it is possible to keep believing in supernatural forces independent of the human mind. For instance, occultists in Victorian England introduced pioneering psychological techniques of guided visualization, and Aleister Crowley's secretary Israel Regardie interpreted the rituals of the Hermetic Order of the Golden Dawn from a perspective informed by Freudian psychoanalysis. Nevertheless, Crowley himself ultimately insisted on the independent metaphysical reality of the spiritual entities that were being contacted in magical ritual.[88] Again, contemporary Chaos Magickians are using radical post-structuralist arguments to dismiss the very distinction between fiction and reality as a modernist myth. This means that the traditional (quasi-Feuerbachian) argument that "it's all just in your mind" loses its reductionist sting. The invocation and worship of gods that have been deliberately and consciously *self-invented,* for instance the creatures of horror from H. P. Lovecraft's Cthulhu mythology, becomes just as reasonable or unreasonable as any other kind of religious activity.[89]

Finally, the psychologization of esotericism and sacralization of psychology is part of a much broader trend that moves away from theoretical and theological concerns toward an emphasis on *experiential practice.* For many practitioners in contemporary esoteric spirituality, online or offline, it may ultimately not be all that important whether those "entities" or "realities" "really" "exist" in some ontological manner "out there," independently from their own minds (the common impulse of bracketing all these words, as shorthand for writing "so-called" or "what is conveniently referred to as," precisely illustrates my point). If the very distinction between matter and mind is felt to be questionable anyway, if no difference seems to exist between fiction and reality,[90] if we spend ever larger parts of our lives traveling through virtual realities, and if the imagination is seen as a reality sui generis, then all that really matters [sic!] to countless practitioners is *whether it works* for them to enter such altered realms of experience and communicate with its inhabitants.

The Spiritual Supermarket

A final key transformation is grounded in the deep political and economic revolutions that have transformed our world during the modern age. Especially in Europe and the United States, the legally encoded separation between church and state made it possible for religious minorities to establish themselves as new organizations or communities next to the traditional Christian churches. The result was an entirely new situation of religious or spiritual competition, in the context of an emerging "free market" based on modern liberal principles of individual choice and autonomy. In such a socioeconomic situation, citizens become spiritual consumers who follow their personal tastes in picking and choosing whatever they like.

As the range of available options began to expand since the eighteenth century, it did not remain limited to more or less stable religious organizations similar to churches or sectarian movements, with clear doctrinal demarcations and membership criteria. Like never before, individuals were free to make their own individual choices in matters of religion or spirituality, not just by committing themselves to specific groups and their doctrines to the exclusion of others but also by "shopping around" and combining any practices or ideas that they might find personally attractive—or dropping them again if they lost interest. The result has been described as a highly fluid "cultic milieu" of spiritual seekers and consumers. In a famous article that introduced this concept, Colin Campbell distinguished between "cults" and "sects."[91]

Cult	*Sect*
Individualistic	Collectivist
Loosely structured	Tightly structured
Few demands on members	Many demands on members
Tolerant	Intolerant
Inclusivist	Exclusivist
Transient	Stable
Undefined boundaries	Clearly circumscribed
Fluctuating belief systems	Stable belief systems
Rudimentary organization	Stable organization
Highly ephemeral	Persisting over time

Most scholars today avoid the pejorative term "sect" in favor of the more neutral "new religious movement" (NRM), but the basic distinction makes perfect sense. In the postwar period, a few random examples of esoteric NRMs would be the Lectorium Rosicrucianum, the Church Universal and Triumphant (Summit Lighthouse), Scientology, or the Raelians. Such organizations are usually created by one or more charismatic individuals and may continue to exist over longer periods of time. By contrast, the point about "cults" (always in Campbell's understanding) is that "new ones are being born just as fast as the old ones die," and there's "a continual process of cult formation and collapse which parallels the high turnover of membership at the individual level."[92] But while specific cults come and go, the cultic *milieu* in which they participate is a permanent feature of modern and contemporary society.

To get a further grip on the spiritual supermarket, it may be helpful to distinguish analytically between RELIGION, RELIGIONS, and SPIRITUALITIES along the following lines:

Religion
Any symbolic system
which influences human action
by providing possibilities
for ritually maintaining contact
between the everyday world and a more general
meta-empirical framework of meaning

A Religion
Any symbolic system
embodied in a social institution
which influences human action
by providing possibilities
for ritually maintaining contact
between the everyday world and a more general
meta-empirical framework of meaning

A Spirituality
Any human practice which maintains contact
between the everyday world and a more general
meta-empirical framework of meaning
by way of the individual manipulation
of symbolic systems

This framework is based on a famous definition of religion proposed by the anthropologist Clifford Geertz in 1966,[93] but with an additional distinction between "religions" and "spiritualities" (plural). For our present concerns, my point is to clarify a major transformation of "religion" under secular conditions, and of "esotericism" more specifically. All esoteric systems are examples of *spiritualities*. For example, Marsilio Ficino's Platonic Christianity or Jacob Böhme's Christian Theosophy resulted from their own personal and creative manipulation of symbolic systems that were available to them. In Ficino's case, these were Platonic Orientalism and Roman Catholicism; and in Böhme's case, they were Paracelsianism, alchemy, Christian mysticism, and Lutheran theology. But before the period of separation between church and state, any such spirituality had to be grounded in a specific *religion*, in this case a Christian one—Ficino was a Roman Catholic who developed his own peculiar understanding of what Christianity should be all about, whereas Böhme was a bible-based Lutheran with his own unique way of interpreting Holy Scripture. In other words, esoteric *spiritualities* were embedded in *religions*, both of which could be seen as instances of the generic category *religion*.

This situation changed dramatically as a result of the separation of church and state in modern secular societies, which made it possible for esoteric *spiritualities* to separate themselves from any organized *religions*. You might say that they now had the option to set up shop for themselves and become entirely independent. They could do so by becoming New Religions or NRMs themselves, taking the shape of what Colin Campbell called "sects," by embodying their particular symbolic system in a social institution. But they could also exist now as individual syncretic formations without any organizational structure whatsoever, that is, as *spiritualities* independent from any *religions*, while still remaining recognizable as forms of *religion*. It is interesting to see that the sociologist Emile Durkheim began perceiving that trend by the turn of twentieth century and already realized that it challenged his own theory of religion as an inherently social phenomenon. Early on in his foundational study *The Elementary Forms of Religious Life* (1912), he mentioned the newly emerging concept of "individual religions that the individual institutes for himself and celebrates for himself alone" and even predicted that this new phenomenon might develop into the religion of the future:

> Some people today pose the question whether such religions are not destined to become the dominant form of religious life—whether a day will not come when the only cult will be the one that each person freely practices in his innermost self.[94]

Of course, religious organizations or "churches" have remained very significant factors in Western society, but Durkheim's prophecy was largely correct. As the "spiritual supermarket" became ever more dominant in liberal democracies after the Second World War, most decisively with the rise of Neoliberalism after the 1970s, individual *spiritualities* became entirely independent from any *religions*—including esoteric NRMs such as the Theosophical Society, Anthroposophy, Rosicrucian or Occultist Orders, and so on. In other words, much of contemporary esotericism takes the shape of ad hoc spiritualities, created by individual consumers from whatever raw materials they happen to encounter on the market, online or offline. The current esoteric landscape might therefore be captured analytically by distinguishing between three dimensions:

1. Esoteric religion: the sum of all "esoteric" ideas and practices that are currently available for anyone to pick and choose from.
2. Esoteric religions: larger or smaller organizations based upon some specific esoteric doctrine.
3. Esoteric spiritualities: individual mixtures of esoteric or any other elements, fine-tuned to the personal needs and interests of individual consumers.

The "supermarket" metaphor could be taken quite literally. Once upon a time, just a few large international companies were monopolizing the religious food market. Roman Catholicism provided white grain, Protestants brown wheat, Sunni or Shiʿa Islam brown and white rice, and so on—but choices were pretty limited, and the available options depended largely on the country or city where you happened to live. Enterprising individuals kept trying to bring variety to the menu, by adding ingredients of their own, and this often got them into trouble with the big companies. But by and large, even such creative innovators still had to work with the basic materials that everybody was using. But see what happened! Today, a truly stunning variety of different foods is available on the market, and much of it comes ready-made for immediate consumption. We may try out many fascinating alternatives to those old-fashioned options of bread or rice, even though we may often have no idea what it really is that we are eating or from where it has come. Many types of spiritual food claim to be good for your health or at least promise to satisfy your hunger and sustain you through the day, but lots of cheap junk food are floating around as well. Some products claim to come from ancient companies with a reliable reputation, others are advertised precisely for their novelty, or seek to attract customers by promising weird and exotic taste sensations.

In any case, no matter how rich or confusing the supply may be, the bottom line is that *it is up to you* to decide what you put in your trolley at any given time.

This radical autonomization and individualization of esoteric *spiritualities*, in contrast to their traditional embeddedness in established *religions*, is a final innovation that has radically changed the landscape of esotericism in the West. Nothing escapes from this new phenomenon, which has been described as "the heretical imperative," referring to the original Greek meaning of the word *haeresis*, "choice."[95] We are all heretics now, for in liberal-democratic societies based on the separation of church and state, even the most well-established traditional religions are no longer the self-evident foundation of how we choose to live our lives. They have become an optional choice next to others, and even deeply orthodox believers may feel at liberty to play around with some ideas that their community officially rejects. Finally, of course, the supermarket metaphor is more than just that. Esotericism has very literally become a multimillion market in the real-world neoliberal economy on a global scale.

8 Esoteric Transdisciplinarity

> I'm a fiction that can enter your dreams, possess her creators, talk through them to you. I'm an idea. But I'm a *real* idea. I'm the idea of the human *imagination* . . . which, when you think about it, is the only thing we can really be certain *isn't* imaginary.
>
> (Alan Moore, *Promethea*)[1]

The study of esotericism is not just relevant to the study of religion but to all disciplines in the humanities and the social sciences. Among the most rewarding things about this field is its thorough *transdisciplinarity*, by which I mean that it transgresses all the conventional boundaries that are usually drawn between religion, spirituality, philosophy, science, the visual arts, literature, music, and even politics. An entire book could be devoted to any of these disciplines. Once again, in this chapter, we will just be scratching the surface.

Religion, Philosophy, Science

Within the general field of esotericism as outlined in this book, the boundaries between religion, philosophy, and science are often extremely fuzzy. As so often, this is particularly evident for the period before the eighteenth century, for reasons that have been discussed in Chapters 3 and 7. When the modern academic disciplines began to establish themselves during and after the Enlightenment period, they had to define their identities much more sharply than before. Partly they did so by drawing boundaries of demarcation against one another and partly by drawing a common boundary against the "other" that they all agreed was beyond the pale—whether they called it "heresy," "superstition," "magic," "mysticism," "the occult," "irrationality," or used any other similar term of rejection. By and large, grudgingly or not, academic theologians, philosophers, and scientists have usually been willing to accept one another's legitimacy as long as everybody pleased to stay on their own turf. By contrast, they were quite united in condemning the "esoteric" category of rejected knowledge as unworthy of respect and serious study. Predictably, this process of discursive and institutional exclusion resulted in alarming levels of academic ignorance about major dimensions of religion, philosophy, and science. If you do not take the trouble to study these things, and if students are never told about them as part of their education, you end up with a situation where nobody has even the slightest notion of what it's all about. A useful comparison is with premodern maps of the world, where only the domains of "civilization" would be filled in whereas all the rest was left blank, a mysterious domain of "the unknown" that seemed to be inhabited by fabulous monsters—*hic sunt dracones.*[2]

The core problem is that standard histories of "religion," "philosophy," and "science" as separate disciplines are all based on deeply normative patterns of sharp opposition between what is supposed to be "true" and "correct" religion, philosophy, or science, on the one hand, and their "false" or "fake" counterparts, on the other. In the case of *religion*, this standard procedure resulted in deeply misleading perceptions of "religion" (= true) as distinct from "magic" (= false).[3] More specifically, it resulted in multiple histories of Judaism, Christianity, and Islam that were written entirely from the perspective of socially dominant orthodoxies and their doctrinal theologies. In the case of *philosophy*, too, it led to highly selective overviews and educational programs, many of which suggest that philosophy really got going only after the time of Descartes. As for standard historiographies of *science*, almost all of them were based on a profoundly anachronistic distinction between real and "pseudo" science that in fact makes it impossible to understand how the study of nature developed historically between antiquity and the present.[4] The basic pattern was always the same. Following a principle known as ECLECTICISM, historians focused on what they themselves saw as interesting and important, while paying scant attention to the full complexity of what you actually encounter in the historical record.[5]

As academics were exploring the garden of history, they usually operated like *gardeners*, intent on cultivating their own favorite flowers and plants while silently removing the weeds as much as possible. By the sharpest possible contrast, the "new historiographies" that developed decisively since the 1990s[6] look at the garden of history from the perspective of a *biologist* who studies a complicated ecological system. Biological organisms such as weeds or mushrooms are just as important as those cultivated plants and flowers. This is not just a question of personal choices. Perhaps you like the gardener's perspective, for reasons of aesthetics or personal taste, but that does not change the fact that your preference for that beautiful garden is a strictly subjective judgment. Objectively, it is demonstrably wrong. If you closely examine the garden of history, instead of just looking at what the gardener would like you to see, you discover that even its most artificially cultivated parts are full of weird and wondrous organisms. You will encounter weeds and fungi, frogs and worms, predators and creeping insects. They are all worthy of your attention. None of them is any "better" than any other. All are vital parts of the garden's ecological system. And no attempt at cultivating the garden can ever be fully successful. To preserve the illusion that this is otherwise, you have to ignore or suppress the evidence for all those things you don't want to see.[7]

Therefore students or scholars in the fields of religion, philosophy, and science must make up their minds. Will you be a gardener or a biologist? If you prefer the former, then the study of esotericism is not for you. But if you choose the latter, you'll need to train your awareness of *difference* and learn to recognize the distortive effects of normative cultivation. If you get better at this, you'll start noticing the deep and subtle mechanisms by which standard academic disciplines and educational programs serve to confirm the normative agendas of the gardener. This counter-normative sensitivity, as I propose to call it (and to which I will return in the final chapter), has been making headway in the academy since the 1960s, but it is a slow and difficult process. Traditional patterns of discursive dominance just do not change overnight; some cultural biases are so deeply ingrained in our social and educational institutions that it may take several generations for them to start losing their power; and their hold over your consciousness may run much deeper than you think. As long as this remains the situation, my advice to students in religion, philosophy, and science is to always approach standard academic textbooks and educational programs with a healthy dose of suspicion. What is it that these authoritative conveyors of official information are silently omitting? What is there that we overlook, not because it's hidden or invisible but just because we fail to register its presence?

Many of the central figures discussed in Chapter 2 have been condemned, by traditional historiography, to a kind of ghostly existence in a liminal space halfway between "philosophy" and "religion." This happened not by any fault of their own but because those modern categories are far too narrowly defined. As for history of "science," the great relevance of such fields as *magia naturalis*, alchemy, and astrology should by now be perfectly clear; and again, their boundaries with "religion" and "philosophy" have always been fuzzy. Moreover, next to the limited number of famous "big names" in all these fields, almost limitless amounts of unexplored materials written by thoroughly forgotten figures are still waiting in libraries and archives for someone to take an interest. Such research expeditions into the unknown may lead to unexpected new discoveries that force us to question and reconsider what we knew—or thought we knew. But to discover *which* new horizons they might open up for us, and what they'll allow us to see and understand, first the work must be done. This is why I believe we need an empirical, historical, bottom-up approach inspired by an attitude of openness to new discoveries, with a minimum of preconceived notions or theoretical assumptions a priori about what might be waiting for us out there.

The Visual Arts

Visitors to Iran who enter the spectacular SHAYKH LUṬF ALLĀH MOSQUE in Isfahan (built in 1617–18) may not be aware that everything in this sacred space is meant to be a visual expression of ultimate transcendent realities understood in terms of IBN TURKA's Islamic Pythagorean science of letters (*ʿilm al-ḥurūf*). As explained by Matthew Melvin-Kouskhi, the spectacularly beautiful dome of this mosque represents the cosmos

> constellated not by *taskhkīk al-wujūd*, the transcendental modulation of being . . . but by the transcendental modulation of the letter as uncreated, all-creative light (*taskhkīk al-ḥarf*), gradually emanating down from the One in extramental (*ʿaynī*), mental-mathematical (*lubābī iḥṣāʾī*), spoken-aural (*kalāmī*) and finally written-visual (*kitābī*) form . . . number-letters of light radiating from the One of the central dome to mathematically and then linguistically constellate the Many. . . . A number of the accompanying poetic inscriptions were composed by Shaykh

> Bahā'ī (d. 1621)—the Safavid Chief Juris-consult (*shaykh al-islām*), philosopher, mathematician, astronomer and architect who is famed to this day as the most powerful practicing mage of his generation, and student in lettrism of the New Brother [of purity] Maḥmūd Dihdār.[8]

A case like this does not just illustrate the arbitrariness of our contemporary distinctions between religion or spirituality, philosophy, science, and the occult but also shows how core esoteric worldviews could be encoded in visual art.

Particularly since the early modern period, many artists in Western culture have taken inspiration from ideas and traditions that fall under the "esotericism" rubric, and many esoteric practitioners have tried to express their spiritual convictions by means of visual art. In this domain, smartly titled books for the commercial market can be extremely useful, even if their textual commentaries may often be unreliable or out of date. An enormous treasure of visual imagery is on display for instance in Richard Cavendish's (1930–2016) famous multivolume *Man, Myth & Magic* (orig. 1970)[9]; Émile-Jules Grillot de Givry's (1874–1929) *A Pictorial Anthology of Witchcraft, Magic & Alchemy* (1958; later also published as *The Illustrated Anthology of Sorcery, Magic and Alchemy*, 1973)[10]; Fred Gettings's *The Occult in Art* (1978)[11]; Stanislas Klossowski de Rola's *The Golden Game: Alchemical Engravings of the Seventeenth Century* (1988)[12]; or more recently, Alexander Roob's *Alchemy and Mysticism: The Hermetic Museum* (1997, with many reprints) and Peter J. Forshaw's splendid volume *Occult* (2024).[13] All this expressive and sometimes very beautiful imagery should be sufficient in itself to show the great artistic relevance of esotericism, and of alchemy more in particular. The intricate symbolism of alchemical emblematics and other forms of "Hermetic" art is often very difficult to decipher and interpret, but we have quite a good number of scholarly commentaries written by reliable experts. Some instances are Barbara Obrist's pioneering volume *Les débuts de l'imagerie alchimique (XIVe–XVe siècles)* (1982)[14]; Jacques van Lennep's *Alchimie: Contribution à l'histoire de l'art alchimique* (1985);[15] Heleen M. E. de Jong's *Michael Maier's Atalanta Fugiens* (1969; new edition 2002);[16] and, last but not least, Peter J. Forshaw's brand-new four-volume study of Heinrich von Khunrath and his *Amphithreatrum sapientiae aeternae* (2025).[17] A very useful online resource for alchemical imagery is the enormous website by Adam MacLean.[18]

The early modern revival of Platonic Orientalism had a considerable impact on the high art of the Italian Renaissance. For instance, Ficino's work inspired such famous works as Botticelli's "Primavera," Raphael's "The School of Athens," and several works by Michelangelo.[19] During the seventeenth century, next to the high tide of alchemical imagery during the Baroque period, a unique and particularly impressive work of art is the Christian-kabbalistic *Lehrtafel* (educational tableau) of Princess Antonia of Württemberg (1659–63) in the church of Bad Teinach, Germany, which inspired one of the most important books by the Christian Theosopher Friedrich Christoph Oetinger.[20] From the next century and after, the enigmatic art of William Blake (1757–1827) shows how this extremely original and fiercely independent thinker created a complete mythological system more or less from scratch, although deeply influenced by Platonic, "gnostic," and Swedenborgian models.[21]

The remarkable influence of Swedenborg on the visual arts (as well as on literature and music) is well-documented and belongs mostly to the idealist tradition in Romanticism,[22] but it confronts us with a hermeneutical problem similar to the case of German Idealism.[23] Even though the relevance of broadly Platonic and Christian Theosophical models might seem pretty evident, even to casual observers, in the absence of clear and explicit references it may still be difficult to *demonstrate* conclusively. To a lesser extent, the same is true for the darker stream of "Gothic" Romanticism,[24] with its evident debts to traditional Christian imaginaries of demonism and "the occult." The impact of standard theological fearmongering about pagans, heretics, witches, and demon-worshippers may be just as important here as any direct influence from authors or traditions that fall under the "esotericism" rubric.

When we reach the DECADENT ART of the fin de siècle, with Paris as its cultural center, such hesitations become less relevant. It is very well-known how deeply many artists during this period were attracted by occultism or Martinism, were flirting romantically with Satan (imagined as a heroic rebel against divine authority), or mingled in neo-Rosicrucian circles around charismatic esoteric figures such as Stanislas de Guaïta or Joséphin Péladan. Perhaps more than in any other historical period, occultism was fashionable, edgy, and progressive. Even so, much remains unclear about the exact relations between French occultism and major visual artists such Aubrey Beardsley, Edward Coley Burne-Jones, Gustave Moreau, Jan Toorop, Jean Delville, Carlos Schwabe, Arnold Böcklin, Franz von Stuck, Félicien Rops, Fernand Khnopff, Albert von Keller, Alfred Kubin, or countless other sometimes largely forgotten artists. The cultural importance of occultism during the European fin de siècle is impossible to deny but remains difficult to read properly, because art historians are often not so well-equipped to interpret its symbolic repertoire and recognize esoteric references for what they are. Moreover, scholars who *do* make a laudable effort at decoding occult symbolism do not always manage to avoid the trap of overinterpretation. Once you start looking for "hidden messages" in art, be aware that you may find it hard to decide where to stop—the mental labyrinth of paranoid semiotics (or conspirational hermeneutics) has many entrances but no exit.[25] Not every cup is an alchemical vessel and not every arrangement of ten visual elements is a sefirotic tree.

Moving on to the twentieth century, in the surrealist movement around ANDRÉ BRETON, the impact of esotericism kept increasing over the course of several decades. Focused originally on somnambulism as a means of exploring altered states, surrealism became deeply imbued with alchemical symbolism and other strands of esotericism before and after the Second World War, often combined with Freudian approaches that sharply rejected supernatural beliefs.[26] Important figures in this French context, who became highly relevant to Louis Pauwels's and Jacques Bergier's key bestseller *Le Matin de Magiciens* (1960), were the specialist of alchemy René Alleau (1917–2013) and the mysterious practical alchemist Fulcanelli (fl. 1920s) with his student Eugène Canseliet (1899–1982).[27] Largely due to their influence, many esotericists came to believe that the mysteries of alchemy were encoded in the architecture and symbolic imagery of the Notre Dame de Paris and other great Gothic cathedrals.

In 1986, an important exhibition at the Los Angeles County Museum of Art created considerable controversy, by demonstrating the central importance of esotericism and occultism to the history of ABSTRACT ART.[28] That such ideas and traditions could have any relevance to the rise of abstraction was experienced as shocking and offensive by the then dominant school of "formalist" art criticism associated notably with Clement Greenberg. Today, it is perfectly evident that all the well-known pioneers of abstract art (for instance, Malevich, Kandinsky, Mondriaan, Arp, Klee, or Duchamp, but also less famous ones such as the more recently rediscovered Italian artist LUIGI PERICLE[29]) saw their work as inseparable from their personal esoteric perspectives. The key importance of esotericism is evident for instance in KANDINSKY's treatise *Über das Geistige in der Kunst* ("On the Spiritual in Art," 1911) or MALEVICH's Russian manuscripts about *Suprematism* (1922).[30] Moreover, the earliest abstract works did not actually come from these famous male artists at all but from several forgotten female painters who were deeply inspired by esoteric convictions and saw themselves as channeling spiritual entities. The earliest of these pioneers was GEORGIANA HOUGHTON (1814–1884),[31] followed by the now widely celebrated HILMA AF KLINT (1862–1944).[32]

Apart from the relevance of esotericism to famous and less famous modern artists, modern esotericists often used visual art to express their spiritual beliefs. An excellent example is RUDOLF STEINER. He designed his Goetheanum in Dornach as an architectural representation of his anthroposophical worldview, produced large sculptures of spiritual entities, and developed a theory of colors (influenced by Goethe) that became basic to the instantly recognizable anthroposophical style of painting. In fact, it is often impossible to tell the esotericist apart from the artist. A few examples are the Theosophically inspired landscape paintings by the Russian NICHOLAS ROERICH (1874–1947), the Tarot Garden in Toscany created by the French-American artist NIKI DE SAINT PHALLE (1930–2002), the occultist art of ITHELL COLQUHOUN (1906–1988), the unique surrealist and magical-realist oeuvres of LEONORA CARRINGTON (1917–2011) and REMEDIOS VARO (1908–1963), the visionary magical-realist art of JOHFRA BOSSCHART (1919–1998), or the psychedelic-spiritual paintings of ALEX GREY (b. 1953).[33]

Contemporary art is a veritable fancy fair of the spiritual, the esoteric, and the occult. JOSEPH BEUYS (1921–1986) and ANSELM KIEFER (b. 1945) are just two examples of major artists who draw in subtle way on traditions such as alchemy or shamanism. Again, such art may present us with deep hermeneutical ambiguities. For instance, it has been playfully suggested that PIERO MANZONI's notorious work *Merda d'artista* (1961) could be read as an alchemical statement, insofar as these ninety cans that are supposed to be filled with the artist's own feces are now so valuable that he actually succeeded in making gold![34] In the postmodern context, where anything goes, such allusions no longer need to imply any adherence to esoteric beliefs or worldviews. They may just as well be intended in an ironic register, and sometimes this very ambiguity can be the whole point of an artistic statement. For instance, think of BRUCE NAUMANN's (b. 1941) neon artwork "The True Artist Helps the World by Revealing Mystic Truths" (1967).[35] The sum conclusion: particularly since the end of the nineteenth century, esotericism has become an indispensable core dimension of modern and contemporary art, whether or not it gets advertised as such. Its rich store of symbolism, imagery, and mythical narratives gets used and recycled by artists at will, with or without acknowledgment, and with or without any intentional spiritual agenda.

Literature

Whereas the role that esotericism plays in the visual arts is now accepted rather widely, its importance to literature has seldom received the attention it requires and deserves.[36] Again, there have been very significant advances since the 1990s, but much of the work remains to be done. By now, the basic pattern will sound familiar. The role of esotericism in the work of well-known poets and literary writers has often been overlooked or misinterpreted because specialists were unfamiliar or uncomfortable with the relevant traditions and ideas. As Leon Surette admitted in 1993, in an important study that began making a break with these attitudes but was still "pervaded with a sense of palpable distaste for esoteric beliefs,"[37] most scholars were used to carrying "the blinkers that continue to protect the scholarly community from any exposure to the occult components of literary modernism."[38] The resulting strategies of neglect or dismissal were not necessarily their fault, because the unsatisfactory state of academic research in this field made it difficult to find reliable and historically grounded scholarship that could help them interpret literary references to esoteric symbols or ideas.

In tracing the relevance of esotericism to literature, we could go back as far as antiquity, looking for instance at APULEIUS' *Metamorphoses* (better known as *The Golden Ass*, second century CE), a particularly clear example of a novel inspired by magical traditions and mystery cults. At least from the perspective of later esoteric traditions, we should also include the medieval production of chivalric literature, including romances about the quest for the Grail such as WOLFRAM VON ESCHENBACH's *Parsifal* (thirteenth century). A major title from the European Renaissance is the *HYPNEROTOMACHIA POLIPHILI* (1499), attributed to an elusive author by the name of Francesco Colonna and famous as one of the most beautiful books in the history of printing. The hallucinatory story of Poliphilus's "dream-quest" for his beloved Polia is set in a deeply pagan atmosphere that reflects the contemporary revival of ancient myth and symbolism.[39] The *philosophia occulta* and its fascination with ancient sciences is reflected in many literary writings from the sixteenth and seventeenth centuries, including such famous titles as CHRISTOPHER MARLOWE's *The Tragical History of the Life and Death of Doctor Faustus* (1592/3), WILLIAM SHAKESPEARE's *The Tempest* (c. 1610–11), or BEN JONSON's satirical *The Alchemist* (1610).[40] The new vogue of Hermeticism also led to a rich production of alchemical poetry, sometimes combined with emblematic imagery as discussed in the previous section.[41]

One of the key texts of Rosicrucianism, *THE CHYMICAL WEDDING OF CHRISTIAN ROSENKREUTZ* (1616) is written in the form of a novel filled with alchemical and arithmological references. The emergence of Rosicrucianism and Freemasonry led to a remarkably large production of pulp fiction and initiatic novels about mysterious secret brotherhoods and their benevolent or sinister activities.[42] This literature has been almost completely forgotten today. For instance, who has ever heard of CAJETAN SCHINK's *Geschichte eines Geistersehers* ("History of a Spirit-Seer," 3 vols., 1790–3), WILHELM FRIEDRICH VON MEYERN's *Dya-Na-Sore* (3 vols., 1787), or VEIT WEBER's "Die Teufelsbeschwörung" ("Summoning the Devil") and "Brüder des Bundes" ("Initiated Brethren") in his *Sagen der Vorzeit* (1792)? In view of its later influence, a particularly important novel is HENRI DE MONTFAUCON DE VILLARS's earlier *Comte de Gabalis* (1670). It caused a popular wave of fascination with "elemental beings" that is reflected not just in literature and art but also in theater and even opera through the eighteenth and up to the twentieth century.[43]

Many Christian Theosophers and Illuminists were writing fiction next to their theoretical work. A few examples are JACQUES CAZOTTE's *Le diable amoureux* ("The Devil in Love," 1772), JOHANN HEINRICH JUNG-STILLING's *Heimweh* ("Nostalgia," 1794), KARL VON ECKARTSHAUSEN's *Kostis Reise* ("Kostis' Journey," 1795), or LOUIS-CLAUDE DE SAINT-MARTIN's *Le crocodile* ("The Crocodile," 1799). The genre of "initiatic novels" deeply influenced by esoteric speculation includes such famous cases as NOVALIS's *Heinrich von Ofterdingen* and *Die Lehrlinge zu Saïs* ("The Pupils at Sais," 1802) or GOETHE's enigmatic *Märchen* ("Fairy Tale," about the Green Snake and the Beautiful Lily, 1795) next to his poem "Die Geheimnisse" ("The Mysteries," 1795). And then of course there are the two parts of Goethe's great *Faust* tragedy, replete with references to alchemy, witchcraft, and *occulta philosophia*, with Agrippa as an obvious model of Faust himself. The theme of secret initiations and hidden brotherhoods had an evident potential for thrilling stories, resulting in a very large genre of novels around such mysterious organizations as the Knights Templar or the Illuminaten, from an early case such as ZACHARIAS WERNER's *Die Söhne des Thals* ("The Sons of the Valley," 1802–4) up to modern and contemporary novels such as UMBERTO ECO's *Foucault's Pendulum* (1988) or pulp fiction bestsellers such as DAN BROWN's *Da Vinci Code* (2003).

Many occultists have been enthusiastic novelists. EMMA HARDINGE BRITTEN's novel *Ghost Land* (1876, published anonymously, and claimed by its author to be nonfictional) must be highlighted here as an important key source for the early phase of occultism in the context of British colonialism.[44] Many other novels with occult themes were written by major esoteric personalities such as Anna Kingsford, Josephin Péladan, Paschal Beverley Randolph, Charles Webster Leadbeater, Aleister Crowley, Dion Fortune, G. I. Gurdjieff, P. D. Ouspensky, or Raymond Abellio. This list is obviously incomplete and could easily be expanded with many more names. The category of esotericists or occultists who tried their hand at literature, as a vehicle for their spiritual beliefs, morphs almost imperceptibly into that of literary writers whose work was influenced by esoteric or occultist themes. On this side of the spectrum, among the most important names are HONORÉ DE BALZAC with his Swedenborgian/Illuminist stories *Louis Lambert* (1832) and *Séraphita* (1834); EDWARD GEORGE BULWER-LYTTON's key esoteric titles *Zanoni* (1842), *A Strange Story* (1862), and *The Coming Race* (1871);[45] JORIS-KARL HUYSMANS's notorious novel about fin de siècle occultism and satanism, *Là-bas* ("Down There," 1895)[46]; the very important literary-esoteric oeuvre of GUSTAV MEYRINK,[47] including *Der Golem* (1914), *Das Grüne Gesicht* ("The Green Face," 1916), *Walpurgisnacht* (1917),

Der weisse Dominikaner ("The White Dominican," 1921), and *Der Engel des westlichen Fensters* ("The Angel of the West Window," 1927); the popular writer of exotic adventure romances H. RIDER HAGGARD, with such titles as *She* (1887), *Cleopatra* (1889), and *Love Eternal* (1918)[48]; a spiritual writer linked to surrealism such as RENÉ DAUMAL, notably *Le Mont Analogue* ("Mount Analogue," 1952); famous Nobel Prize winner WILLIAM BUTLER YEATS, who was involved for a while with the Hermetic Order of the Golden Dawn (see especially *A Vision*, 1925); other towering modernist poets such as EZRA POUND in his *Cantos* and T. S. ELIOT in *The Waste Land*;[49] RAINER MARIA RILKE's magnificent poetry and prose, much more deeply indebted to contemporary spiritualism and occultism than one might perhaps imagine;[50] the occult fiction of CHARLES WILLIAMS, including *Shadows of Ecstasy* (1925–32) and *The Greater Trumps* (1932)[51]; the great Portuguese writer and poet FERNANDO PESSOA, whose works are permeated by esoteric themes[52]; or the "archontic spirituality" and magical practices of the major beat generation writer WILLIAM BURROUGHS.[53] Again, there is no end to the titles that could be mentioned.

The importance of esotericism to major poets and novelists does not depend on whether they endorse its ideas or worldviews. A good example is UMBERTO ECO, whose bestselling *Foucault's Pendulum* is based on a profound critique of esoteric semiotics and its potential for conspirational paranoia. In the great modernist novels of Thomas Mann, alchemical symbolism and grail mythology is used in a characteristically ironic register along with multiple references to the god Hermes.[54] Especially in the post-Second World War period, and quite similar to what we see in the visual arts, the entire esoteric repertoire tends to be used pragmatically as an inexhaustible source of interesting references, personalities, and ideas. For instance, in her impressive novel *L'oeuvre au noir* (translated as *The Abyss* in English, but more appropriately in Dutch as *Het Hermetisch Zwart*, since the title alludes to the alchemical phase of the *nigredo*) MARGUERITE YOURCENAR uses the model of the sixteenth-century *magus*, from Agrippa or Paracelsus to Giordano Bruno, who keeps wandering restlessly through Europe and is always in danger of being persecuted as a heretic or Black magician. The German writer HELMUT KRAUSSER, too, relies on Renaissance magic as a central theme in his major novel *Melodien* (1993). The Dutch novelist HARRY MULISCH used elements of alchemy, kabbalah, Pythagorean arithmology, and other esoteric currents in many of his works, notably *Voer voor psychologen* ("Food for psychologists," 1974), *De ontdekking van de Hemel* ("The Discovery of Heaven," 1992), and *De procedure* ("The Procedure," 1998). My favorite example of postwar literature based entirely on Hermetic scholarship, with central roles for Giordano Bruno and John Dee, is the four-volume *Aegypt* cycle written by the American writer JOHN CROWLEY.[55] Some modern writers delve deeply into the history of esotericism for writing novels of historical fantasy, as in Philippe Cavalier's impressive while gruesome four-volume cycle *Le siècle des chimères* ("The Century of Chimeras," 2005–2008).[56] Countless other authors use the medium of literature to convey some kind of esoteric message, as in the immensely popular novels by PAULO COELHO, notably *The Alchemist* (1988), or to convey the magical worldview of modern paganism, as in MARION ZIMMER BRADLEY's *The Mists of Avalon* (1983). Yet other writers seem to be using literature, partly at least, as a medium for initiating readers into some deeper *gnōsis* about the human condition. One good example would be the impressive novel *The Chymical Wedding* (1989) by the British writer LINDSAY CLARKE, based on the alchemical oeuvre of Mary Anne Atwood and her father.[57]

Music

A major classic in the history of Renaissance esotericism, published by FRANCESCO GIORGI DA VENETO (1466–1540) in 1525, was titled *De harmonia mundi*, "On the Harmony of the World." In the wider context of what I have referred to as the "Platonic Paradigm," and against the background of Pythagorean notions of the music of the spheres, the entire cosmos was seen as grounded in divine order and universal harmony. As early as late antiquity, Hermetic devotees developed a practice of vocalizing the seven musical tones connected to the seven vowels of the Greek alphabet and the seven planets, to accompany the soul's ceremonial ascent from the world of phenomena to the ultimate spheres of noetic Light.[58] Cosmology was intimately related to what has been described as SPECULATIVE MUSIC.[59] In terms of the theory of correspondences, all parts of the universe could be seen as resonating with one another, like the strings of a great musical instrument tuned by God, as visualized very literally in some famous illustrations to the work of Robert Fludd. These hidden (occult) relations could be deciphered by means of Pythagorean number symbolism and kabbalistic hermeneutics. The words and letters that God had been using to create the world could ultimately be reduced to numbers, and numerical relations could be made audible as sounds. Speculative music was intimately related not just to kabbalah and the symbolism of numbers but also to magic, astrology, and alchemy in the early modern period. This close relation between music and *philosophia occulta* continued straight into the "scientific revolution" of the seventeenth century. All of this makes the field of esotericism into a fruitful domain of study for musicologists.[60]

Joscelyn Godwin mentions the paradox that although the eighteenth century was a high point in European music, it was also a period of decline for these traditions of musical esotericism, which ran counter to the spirit of Enlightenment rationalism.[61] The few exceptions, such as the role of Freemasonry in the libretto of MOZART's opera *The Magic Flute*, are more anecdotal than substantial. A revival of the speculative tradition began with Romanticism, in the work of such authors as Johann Friedrich Hugo von Dalberg, Antoine Fabre d'Olivet, Charles Fourier, Hoëne Wronski, R. F. G. Lacuria, Louis Lucas, Edmond Bailey, and Saint-Yves d'Alveydre.[62] Pythagorean traditions of speculative music were carried into the twentieth century by HANS KAYSER and his pupils, notably Rudolf Haase and Werner Schulze. Apart from this central speculative tradition, with its roots in antiquity and the Renaissance, the occultist milieus of fin de siècle Paris were attractive not just to painters, poets, and novelists but occasionally to composers as well. A notable example is ERIK SATIE, who was strongly involved with Sâr Joséphin Péladan's Rosicrucian milieu but eventually broke with him. He founded an organization of his own, the "Église Metropolitaine d'Art de Jésus Conducteur" ("Metropolitan Church of Art of Jesus the Conductor"), with Satie himself as its high priest and sole member! From these backgrounds came piano music inspired by esoteric themes, such as Satie's "Sonneries de la Rose+Croix," "Le Fils des Étoiles," and a mystical ballet titled "Uspud."[63] We have seen that in the decades before and after the First World War, spiritual and esoteric themes were very much in the air. RICHARD WAGNER's great musical dramas were sometimes interpreted from esoteric perspectives, and strong esoteric influences are perfectly explicit for instance in the work ALEXANDER SCRIABIN.[64]

Esotericism is of great importance to the birth of atonality and the system of "dodecaphony" or twelve-tone music associated with the SECOND VIENNESE SCHOOL of Arnold Schönberg, and his pupils Alban Berg and Anton Webern. In a fascinating parallel to the birth of abstraction in the visual arts, esoteric speculation played a decisive role in this breakthrough from late Romanticism to modernity in musical composition. Next to Schönberg's fascination with Jewish kabbalah, and Webern's devotion to Goethe's speculative theories of plant morphology and the color spectrum, Swedenborg's doctrine of correspondences was a key factor in the theoretical conceptualization of dodecaphony as a universal system for organizing "musical space."[65] For these radical innovators, the structural laws of musical composition must be grounded in a hidden spiritual "Law" (which Schönberg associated with Moses and the Ten Commandments)[66] that informed the whole of reality on a deep spiritual level. Music could be imagined as an autonomous world made of sounds, reflecting the basic laws of the macrocosmos and corresponding closely with the hidden structures of ultimate reality.

The relevance of esoteric speculation to "total serialism" and other forms of radical experimental music after the Second World War remains virtually uncharted territory. KARLHEINZ STOCKHAUSEN (1928–2007) stands out in this context as a particularly impressive composer, an iconic figure whose oeuvre is deeply and explicitly embedded in esoteric speculation.[67] Reaching rock-star status during the 1960s and 1970s (his face appears on the cover of the Beatles' *Sergeant Pepper's Lonely Hearts Club Band*), Stockhausen deeply absorbed that period's spirit of radical experimentation and countercultural innovation.[68] Soaking up many spiritual traditions from East and West, he was particularly impressed by *The Urantia Book* (1955), a modern channeled text received in Chicago between the 1920s and 1950s.[69] Stockhausen's spectacular seven-part opera cycle *Licht* is based entirely on an esoteric cosmology, reminiscent of science fiction and strongly influenced by the Urantia message, with a grand mythical narrative that pits the masculine hero Michael (modeled on the composer himself) and the "eternal feminine" Eve against their tragic adversary Lucifer.[70]

Of course, the emergence of classic ROCK MUSIC coincided with the popular vogue of alternative spiritualities, occultism, and oriental religions that took off in the 1960s. In spite of their enormous popularity, there have been comparatively few attempts to study the esoteric or occultist dimensions of song lyrics, the esoteric-psychedelic imaginaries combined with fantasy and science fiction that were on full display in symphonic and psychedelic rock bands during the 1970s, or the role of Crowleyan occultism, Satanism, and Chaos Magick in the subculture of heavy metal.[71] Again, quite a lot of popular esoteric culture may be "hidden in plain sight," as in the case of 1970s–80s HIP-HOP and RAP lyrics that are full of coded Five Percenters references. Yet there are some cases of musicians or bands whose esoteric or occultist interests are impossible to miss. A particularly good example from the context of punk and industrial music would be the musical activist, transgender pioneer, and radical "esoterrorist" GENESIS BREYER P-ORRIDGE (ps. of Neil Andrew Megson, 1950–2020), the founder of COUM Transmissions, lead vocalist of Throbbing Gristle and Psychic TV, and founding member of Thee Temple ov Psychick Youth.[72] Finally, there is some good research on the spiritual dimensions of contemporary Rave and Festival culture, although hardly from a perspective of esotericism studies per se.[73]

The Social Sciences

We already looked at the contemporary phenomenon of a "spiritual supermarket" and its relation to the Cultic Milieu. In recent years, social scientists have also been using a new term, OCCULTURE, invented originally by Genesis Breyer P-Orridge (mentioned above). As pointed out by Christopher Partridge in a programmatic discussion of this topic, the important point about occulture is that it's precisely not a social anomaly but a perfectly *ordinary* feature of society—not just in the contemporary world, he insists, but even in earlier historical periods.[74] It covers many types of popular practice and belief that have always been part of the normal lives of men and women but were typically perceived as inferior, possibly even dangerous, by the intellectual and political elites. To this I would make one additional remark. The hegemonic power of a free-market economy in contemporary neoliberal societies means that such traditional elite opinions about popular (oc)culture no longer result in government campaigns of marginalization or suppression but rather the opposite. Today it would seem that the prevalence of esotericism, spirituality, or the occult in popular culture is actually more than welcome, not because of any interest in its contents but simply because it creates opportunities for business and commercial exploitation.[75]

This de facto normalization of popular occulture in neoliberal mass societies is driven by a powerful culture industry.[76] It produces an enormous daily supply of popular books, comics, movies, internet sites, YouTube videos, or video games, next to music and visual art, in which esoteric or occultist elements play a significant role. To be sure, many larger or smaller entrepreneurs who work in these fields are driven by genuine spiritual convictions and personal motivations, but there is virtually no way for them to escape from the capitalist matrix. Even major countercultural or psychedelic festivals such Burning Man or Boom need to *market* themselves as "temporary autonomous zones" opposed to a mainstream culture based on that very same market![77] Whether all these spiritual activities and products can still be covered under the general "esotericism" label is a moot point. Scholars who associate the term primarily with some specific historical prototype(s) might be tempted to answer in the negative, objecting that such popular mass-produced stuff isn't *real* esotericism anymore! But if "esotericism" is really just a pragmatic label of convenience (as I have been arguing throughout this book), not a historical "phenomenon" defined by some immutable "essence," then clearly no such normative distinctions are available to keep the "real" or "authentic" article apart from its "fake" or "pseudo" simulacra.[78] Personal judgments about depth or quality are legitimate enough, to be sure, but should not be confused with definitional criteria.

Next to studying the Cultic Milieu or its occultural manifestations, sociologists have been focusing much of their attention on specific *esoteric organizations*. This is where the study of esotericism overlaps significantly with the study of NEW RELIGIOUS MOVEMENTS (NRMs). Its focus is on the enormous variety of larger and smaller organizations or churches based on esoteric systems of belief and practice—from older ones, such as the Theosophical Society, the Anthroposophical Society, or the neo-Rosicrucian Lectorium Rosicrucianum, to newer and sometimes controversial ones, such as the Church of Scientology, New Acropolis, the Raelian movement, the church of Santo Daime, and countless others. In this enormous domain of research, crucial work has been done by the Italian scholar Massimo Introvigne in collaboration with a large network of specialists including J. Gordon Melton, Eileen Barker, James R. Lewis, Jean-François Mayer, Susan J. Palmer, and many others. Next to a flood of publications, they have created scholarly organizations to provide reliable information about NRMs, particularly in view of popular anxieties about the perceived dangers of "cults" or "sects."[79]

This scholarly field comes with challenges of its own. As NRMs became more prominent and visible since the 1960s, this led to the emergence of secular *ANTI-CULT* MOVEMENTS as well as more religiously motivated *COUNTER-CULT* MOVEMENTS, all devoted to the fight against "dangerous cults."[80] It is well known, of course, that serious problems may sometimes occur in any larger or smaller religious organization, from abuse of power or financial malversations to violence against members or even terrorist activities. Esoteric or occultist organizations are no exception, as painfully demonstrated by such cases as the collective suicides and murders in the neo-Rosicrucian *Order of the Solar Temple* (1994) and the neognostic New Age movement *Heaven's Gate* (1997).[81] What makes anti- or counter-cult perspectives problematic is not the fact that sometimes things go seriously wrong in specific religious or spiritual communities. Rather, it lies in a default assumption that minority religions with unfamiliar beliefs or practices are not "real" or "genuine" religions but something else—dangerous "pseudo-religious" *cults* that probably brainwash their members and commit other immoral acts, such as financial extortion or sexual abuse. There are many problems with this popular perspective. Firstly, the distinction between true "religions" and pseudo-religious "cults" is entirely arbitrary.[82] Secondly, there is no scientific basis for the dramatic concept of cultic brainwashing or mind control, whereas coercive countermeasures known as "deprogramming" are actually in conflict with the law.[83] Thirdly, based on the core principle of freedom of religion that lies at the heart of liberal-democratic societies and the rule of law, any individual practitioner or religious organization should be considered innocent until proven guilty in a court of law. This means that NRMs and their leaders or members should not be harassed or persecuted by media or the police just because their beliefs or practices seem weird to others. Without any doubt, the overwhelming majority of religious minorities or spiritual communities, whether esoteric or not, consist of perfectly normal people who abide by the law and deserve to be left in peace.

Scholars who insist on such straightforward principles of demonstrable evidence and due process have often clashed not just with anti- or counter-cult activists but even with powerful governmental institutions. Politicians and administrators are easily swayed by popular rhetoric about "dangerous cults" and tend to ignore the advice of academic experts whenever they find it inconvenient.[84] A standard suspicion is that if academics are so eager to defend NRMs, this means that they must be "cult apologists" in disguise whose opinions cannot be trusted. The disingenuity of that argument should be evident. Experts of NRMs are committed to standard criteria of scholarly and legal practice, such as respect for reasonable arguments and demonstrable facts that can be evaluated by independent observers. In dealing with controversies about any specific NRM, serious scholars will rely on their expertise and their critical judgment to evaluate the evidence to the best of their ability. If an accusation is false or not supported by sufficient evidence, it is their moral duty to point that out so that innocent people may not get hurt. This often requires quite a bit of courage, for the reality is that "cult battles" can get very ugly. Scholars who venture into this arena may find themselves the target of public attacks that are designed to destroy their reputation by any means available. Not everybody is able or willing to take such personal risks, and those who do deserve our respect.

As regards methodology, sociological studies in the field of contemporary esotericism tend to be qualitative, but there are interesting cases to show the value of quantitative methods as well.[85] A lot of solid sociological research focused on esoteric NRMs can be found in leading academic journals such as *Nova Religio* or the *Journal of Contemporary Religion*. Next to sociology, anthropology of religion is a discipline of major importance to the study of contemporary esotericism. A early landmark book that set standards for anthropological fieldwork in this field was Tanya M. Luhrmann's study of ritual magic in England; a very different but useful model was Michael F. Brown's research of channeling in New Age milieus; and a much more recent key example is Susanna Crockford's monograph on contemporary utopian spiritualities in the United States.[86] This is obviously just a small sample. As the study of esotericism became more widely known in academic contexts, anthropologists began discovering it as a field of research. Meanwhile, the community of esotericism studies has been expanding its perspectives from historiography toward ethnographical and related approaches.[87]

In sum, the relevance of contemporary esotericism to the social sciences and the study of popular culture is perfectly obvious. In my opinion, this type of research can only achieve its full potential by cultivating optimal connections with historical scholarship about the spiritual and intellectual traditions under investigation. It is simply not possible to understand contemporary esotericism and NRMs properly, unless we take their worldviews and ideas seriously and are well-informed about their provenance and historical development.[88] By paying attention to ideas and practices in the *longue durée*, rather than just in our immediate present, we can see how they have been modified, transformed, and put to new uses under the impact of unprecedented new developments such as modernization and secularization.

Politics

How relevant is esotericism to politics, or politics to esotericism? This partly depends on definitions. If we understand "politics" in the broadest terms, as covering social processes of allocating values and distributing resources on all levels of society,[89] almost *everything* could be seen as political. But even if we understand politics as concerned more precisely with institutions of government, the relevance of esotericism is perfectly clear. For instance, in early modern Islamicate cultures there is fascinating evidence of occult scientists who worked as valued advisors to imperial rulers and engaged in projects of "political magic."[90] There are countless parallels in Christian culture as well. For instance, think of Ficino's deep involvement with the ruling elites of Florence; Johannes Reuchlin's courageous advocacy of Jewish literature in the midst of virulent anti-Semitic campaigns; Agostino Steuco's *De perenni philosophia* as a political instrument of Counter-Reformation propaganda; John Dee's role as personal advisor to Queen Elizabeth (not just about magic but also about such issues as global navigation that were obviously important to the British Empire); the controversial topic of Rosicrucianism as a radical reformist movement in the early modern conflict between Lutheranism and the Holy Roman Empire; conspirational narratives about Freemasonry or the *Illuminaten* as a sinister political threat to the established powers of Church and State; the remarkable story of Swedenborg's impact on anti-racist policies and the abolition of slavery; or the role of QAnon and other conspiracy theories in contemporary American politics.[91] As always, the list could go on.

Many esotericists after the French Revolution saw themselves as cultural revolutionaries and were aligned with LEFT-WING, SOCIALIST, or PROGRESSIVE agendas. There are strong historical connections between esotericism and early socialism,[92] and this intellectual legacy may perhaps be helpful to explain the initially somewhat puzzling fact that influential Marxist philosophers (think of Walter Benjamin, Ernst Bloch, or Georg Lukács) were fascinated by kabbalah and a wide variety of other esoteric traditions.[93] We already saw that many esoteric and occultist movements were actively involved in progressive social causes, such as women's emancipation and voting rights, anti-vivisectionism, gender reform, sexual liberation, and anti-colonialism.[94] The most influential modern esoteric organization of the late nineteenth and early twentieth century, the Theosophical Society, promoted a worldwide program of social reform that should lead to "the Universal Brotherhood of Humanity, without distinction of race, creed, sex, caste or colour."[95] That this was not just theory is shown by the very strong presence of women and South Asian Theosophists in the leadership and publications of this global organization.[96] After the Second World War as well, much of the popular esotericism that flourished in the counterculture since the 1960s was leaning decidedly toward the left, for instance in its support for the civil rights movement, sexual liberation, or opposition to the Vietnam War and other manifestations of Western imperialism.

However, we can observe a gradual shift of emphasis in the history of modern esotericism over time, from broadly liberal-modernist and progressive critiques of traditional religious and political authority during the long nineteenth century toward mounting critiques of liberal modernity itself during the twentieth and twenty-first centuries. While typically modern developments such as individualism, capitalism, and liberal democracy were on the rise in Europe and America, spreading widely across the globe in the broader context of colonialism and Western imperialism, their shadow sides became more obvious as well. After the successive catastrophes of two World Wars, which dealt an enormous blow to popular confidence in rationalization and social progress, we see increasing levels of concern about such effects of modernization as the decline of traditional social hierarchies, the disintegration of local communities, extreme environmental degradation, shocking levels of economic exploitation and social injustice, a weakening of commitment to shared moral values, feelings of confusion about whether there are any standards of truth, a deepening sense of alienation and nihilism with respect to the meaning of human existence, growing doubts about whether history has any kind of direction or evolutionary purpose, and, indeed, profound doubts about the very future of human civilization. In regard to all these challenges, a wide variety of modern esoteric currents or personalities have come up with alternatives of their own. These run across the entire political spectrum, from the left through the middle to the right, so it may be helpful to discuss them roughly under those three headings.

Toward the FAR LEFT of the spectrum, we find progressive and often anarchistic forms of radical esoteric militancy. Typically, their concern is to "Fight the System" of global control and social injustice by creating alternative spiritual undergrounds, or "Temporary Autonomous Zones," following the basic principle of "turning on, tuning in, and dropping out."[97] Of great importance here is the iconoclastic Hip Psychedelicist esotericism that emerged from the neo-"gnostic" spiritualities of the Beat generation and the general psychedelic ferment of the 1960s counterculture, exemplified for instance by Discordianism and various other "parody religions" that engaged in playful subversive practices called "culture jamming."[98] After the prohibition of psychedelics, this kind of leftist esotericism continued in an underground Zine Scene of radical amateur publishing, circulated through the mail, with Hakim Bey (Peter Lamborn Wilson) as a particularly iconic figure. Another evident example of far-left activism, more aligned to the British milieus of Punk and Chaos Magick, would be the "esoterrorism" of Genesis Breyer P-Orridge and *Thee Temple ov Psychick Youth*. Very different traditions of left-leaning esotericism, directed especially against the patriarchy and environmental destruction, have always been prominent in pagan circles. Feminist witches such as Starhawk and Szuszanna Budapest were pioneering examples, and many similar types of paganism have kept flourishing up to the present. Much of contemporary neoshamanism and global psychedelic counterculturalism is inspired by a somewhat similar ethos of living in harmony with nature and its invisible energies as opposed to the spiritual alienation created by the dominant culture of capitalist consumerism.

Intermediary between the political left and right, many political agendas in postwar esoteric milieus are in some way indebted to the ERANOS tradition. This might be seen as somewhat ironic, because most Eranos scholars were intent on presenting their work as *non*-political—to which their critics tend to respond by placing politics precisely at the center of their analyses.[99] Be that as it may, what was really at stake in the Eranos context was not a choice or a preference for any specific political system or ideology but rather a process of intellectual reflection about *the price of modernity*. Scholars like Jung, Eliade, Scholem, or Corbin felt deeply concerned about such developments as the death of God, the disenchantment of the world, the rise of rational-scientific quantification, or the vanishing sense of symbols and mythology as numinous vehicles of spiritual meaning. These worries may certainly be described as "conservative" in the sense that they reflected a wish to *conserve* (i.e., to preserve and protect) a living sense of the Sacred as present in the world. These Eranos intellectuals felt strongly that desacralization would result in severe pathologies on the level of the individual psyche and the social collective as a whole, as demonstrated by two successive world wars.[100] But interestingly, as their work became enormously popular in English translation since the 1960s, the younger generation experienced it all as wonderfully *progressive*! They were rebelling against the conservatism of *their* parents' generation, grounded in a modern "scientific" rationalism that had clearly failed to avoid destructive war and environmental devastation while leaving no room for spiritual values or the numinous powers of the imagination. From such a perspective, the search for "ancient wisdom" or "archaic worldviews" (including the study of mysticism and magic, esotericism, or the occult) was anything but reactionary. Precisely those traditions of "rejected knowledge" that modernity had neglected and forgotten might teach humanity how to move *forward* again, beyond the tired dogmas of establishment religion and establishment science, toward a new and better future.[101]

It is on the FAR-RIGHT sight of the esoteric-political spectrum that we encounter truly reactionary agendas of "Restoring Sacred Order."[102] Contemporary far-right esotericism comes in three basic varieties, which may overlap and intermingle in various ways. Firstly, there is the radical *Traditionalism* associated most famously with Julius Evola and a range of other declared opponents of liberal democracy who are popular in such interlocking contemporary milieus as the European New Right and their American counterparts, Aleksandr Dugin's Eurasianism, far-right esoteric publishers such as Arktos, or heavily racist "white nationalist" websites such as Counter-Currents.[103] Modern *paganism* (or neopaganism) is the second main field where conservative-traditionalist and reactionary far-right ideas have become more prominent in recent decades (leading to controversies with those many pagans who lean toward the liberal left and support progressive agendas such as feminism and environmentalism). Right-wing pagans tend to emphasize "masculine" warrior values associated with Northern and Germanic deities, and this often (although not necessarily[104]) results in anti-Semitic and white-supremacist *Blut und Boden* ("Blood and Soil") ideologies.[105] A third and final key component of contemporary far-right esotericism consists in widespread *conspiracy fantasies* about the pernicious influence of sinister powers and secret organizations that are seeking to control the world or already *are* in control, from Freemasons, Jesuits, or Illuminati to Occultists, Satanists, or Jews, not to mention shape-shifting reptiles from other dimensions.[106] A popular new term in the contemporary context is CONSPIRITUALITY.[107] As the very distinction between fiction and fact is called into question by a new "post-truth" reality (or irreality) of "alternative facts" and deep-fake technologies, where it would seem that "nothing is true while everything is possible,"[108] we seem to be entering a new world of "fantastic realism"[109] that provides militant far-right activists with unheard-of possibilities for political manipulation and subversive propaganda.

Finally, the politics of *ANTI*-ESOTERICISM is itself a political topic and one that brings us full circle to what the field is all about. I have been arguing throughout this book that our perception of "esotericism" as a distinct field with some immutable "essence" is the artificial imaginal product of an internal-Eurocentric polemical discourse that developed historically from late antiquity to the present, took shape decisively under the impact of Protestantism and the Enlightenment, and remains central to official "Western" cultural identities. In contemporary intellectual discourse and the commercial media, this anti-esoteric discourse may lead to default political suspicions about esotericism as in some sense dangerous to liberal democracy, morality, and reason.

Historically and conceptually, the influential "Critical Theory" of the Frankfurt School has been the chief conduit and source of intellectual support for such popular types of anti-esoteric discourse, which remain very much alive especially in the German-speaking world.[110] This is not just a question of the occasional disparaging remark about occultism as "the metaphysics of dunces."[111] More important is the prevalence of vague insinuations about anti-Semitic subtexts or a subterranean connection that supposedly exists between "esotericism" and "fascism" in general, or as such.[112] Such associations between generic concepts depend on the mental *reification of complex historical formations*[113] that causes them to appear in our imagination as universal or archetypal "phenomena" with an inherent force or dynamic of their own.[114] Precisely because this reification of "-isms" comes so naturally to the human mind, it can have dangerous political consequences in the real world and may end up harming innocent people—it leads us to reduce enormously complicated historical developments, not to mention the specific beliefs and practices of individuals or groups, to abstract phenomenological generalizations and typological simplifications that are perfectly suited for ideological warfare.[115] This is a key reason for my insistence on "empirical" specificity and bottom-up historiography. Always begin by paying full attention to what is actually there, rather than with the theoretical concepts and imaginal formations that may already be present in your own mind.

Yet the core problem with Frankfurt School perspectives is even more fundamental. As pointed out by Adorno himself, we are dealing with a principled rejection of the very project of empirical and historical scholarship in the field of esotericism. Referring to Kant's (presumed) refutation of Swedenborg's "superstition," Adorno complained in his inimitable style that

> Many empiricists . . . are not nearly so determined anymore about taking a stand against superstition [*Aberglaube*]. Even with respect to it [i.e. superstition], they would tend to withdraw to the neutral position of a nonconceptual scholarly practice of mere observation. Occult facts, too, could be approached with a wait-and-see attitude of unprejudiced observation [*abwartend, beobachtend, vorurteilslos*]. One renounces one's right to sharply dismiss the swindle from one's doorstep [the

swindle, that is, which consists in the idea] that that which, by one's own judgment, transgresses the boundaries of any possible sense experience should be made into an object of such experience. One keeps an open mind, even when faced with delusional madness [*Wahn*]. There is such a thing as a false lack of prejudice, an amputation of thought [*Abschneiden des Gedankens*] that unwittingly [*besinnungslos*] surrenders itself to the isolated materials of knowledge.[116]

To be sure, Adorno's critique was directed at the somewhat easy target of a naïve quasi-positivist empiricism that disregards Kant's central concept of "constitutive subjectivity," not to mention the key importance of subjective prejudice (*Vorurteil*) to textual hermeneutics and historical research.[117] But Adorno's position is just as incompatible with post-Kantian and hermeneutically more sophisticated understandings of modern empirical and historical research. The point of his argument is that we do not need an academic study of esotericism at all, because the only relevant conclusion of any such research is already known in advance—it's all *Wahn*, delusional nonsense! This theoretical axiom implies that the very idea of studying esotericism seriously and nonjudgmentally, out of genuine interest in learning more about its ideas or practices and their history, must be dismissed not just as naïve and suspicious but as politically dangerous. Scholars are expected to *fight* "the enemies of reason" instead of taking their ideas seriously or (heaven forbid!) engaging them in dialogue. By now, it should be evident that this entire line of argumentation is just another variation on the standard internal-Eurocentric attitude towards "superstition" or "the occult" that became dominant since the Enlightenment[118] — the very attitude *against which*, as far as I'm concerned, the modern study of esotericism has been establishing itself since the 1990s.

In this regard, I see no possible room for compromise. Scholars of esotericism have not just an intellectual but an ethical and even a political duty to insist on fair, critical, empirical, historical, bottom-up research, and this means that they must steer away from easy generalizations and ideological condemnations a priori, whether inspired by political or other concerns. Investigation comes first, judgments come later—that is how research is supposed to work. As far as I am concerned, instead of starting on a note of suspicion and hostility, we need to cultivate more generous attitudes of charity, open-mindedness, and genuine curiosity about the weird and wonderful world of esoteric practices and beliefs. No matter how critical one may be about certain specific forms of esotericism, there is no basis for dismissing the entire field out of hand as mere delusional madness, as if academics were some kind of police force charged with a holy mission to fight the irrational.[119] As for Adorno's "amputation of thinking," I would rather think of reattaching some limbs that should never have been amputated!

9 The Global Importance of Esotericism

> There are these two young fish swimming along and they happen to meet an older fish swimming the other way, who nods at them and says, "Morning boys. How's the water?"
> And the two young fish swim on for a bit, and then eventually one of them looks over at the other and goes, "What the hell is water?"
>
> (David Foster Wallace, *This is Water*)[1]

In his luminous commencement speech at Kenyon College in 2005, the American writer David Foster Wallace (1962–2008) followed up on these well-known opening sentences to explain the point. "The most obvious, ubiquitous, important realities," he said, "are often the ones that are hardest to see and talk about."[2] I believe that this simple but profound insight holds the key to what the study of esotericism in Western culture is ultimately all about. On the following pages, it will be my point of departure for explaining why precisely a field that has so often been perceived as "marginal" to more important topics of research is actually of *central* importance, not just for scholars or insiders but for the humanities more generally and even for society at large. At a first and most obvious descriptive level, as we have seen, the study of esotericism (always, of course, in the sense of *esotericism*$_1$) is concerned with the scholarly task of paying attention to a wide range of historical traditions, ideas, practices, or beliefs that used to be neglected but deserve to be taken seriously. At a second and deeper, more analytical level, I have argued that its concern is with understanding *and* correcting the deep discursive patterns of Internal Eurocentrism that caused this entire field to be rejected, marginalized, and discredited by the dominant intellectual and academic elites since the eighteenth century—a legacy that continues to shape many of our default assumptions about what is important and what is not, what deserves our attention and what doesn't, or simply what is good and what is bad. But at a third and even deeper level, in this final chapter, I want to call attention to the fundamental problem of *normativity* as such. It would be very shallow to think that modern esotericism research is just about studying neglected but interesting topics while complaining all the time how badly they used to be treated by academics! My narrative about "the rejection of rejected knowledge" is not a victim narrative.[3] On the contrary, it is inspired by an active emancipatory agenda of questioning deep normativities and exposing hidden cultural assumptions about what is "normal" and therefore acceptable and what is not. I will refer to this critical perspective as *counter-normativity*.

In the next two sections, I first turn to the key topic of Eurocentrism, in the context of current debates in the field about esotericism and "the West." I will try to explain why I believe that a correct understanding of esotericism as "rejected knowledge" (for this concept has often been misunderstood) is uniquely important, not just to the field itself but to a global decolonial agenda that resists the imperialist project of imposing Western normative frameworks on non-Western peoples and cultures—not to mention the suppression and even extermination of anything, and anyone, that stands in the way of such agendas. Against this background, I will then zoom in on the concept of counter-normativity, to show the deeper emancipatory potential of esotericism research as I see it. I will argue that the project of restoring rejected knowledge to a status of acceptable knowledge intersects with a broader agenda of questioning our very assumptions about normality as such. Finally, I will explain why I see the study of esotericism as deeply relevant and important, not just intrinsically, and not just for strictly scholarly reasons, but also in view of the enormous challenges that we are facing in our current cultural moment marked by rapidly accumulating social, (geo)political, and environmental crises.

The Externalization of Internal Eurocentrism

In 2010, the Swiss intellectual historian and scholar of religion Urs App published a truly groundbreaking study, based upon a wealth of previously unexplored sources in multiple languages. In the preface to this book, *The Birth of Orientalism*, he stated provocatively that, contrary to common assumptions, "the role of colonialism . . . in the birth of Orientalism dwindles to insignificance compared to the role of religion."[4] App's point was to call attention to the deeper historical backgrounds of the well-known Orientalist discourse that became dominant in the nineteenth century.

> The birth of modern Orientalism was a not a Caesarian section performed by colonialist doctors at the beginning of the nineteenth century when Europe's imperialist powers began to dominate large swaths of Asia. Rather, it was the result of a long process that around the turn of the eighteenth century produced a paradigm change. [It came out of] a centuries-long, gradual broadening of perspectives beyond the sphere circumscribed by Abrahamic religions and the Bible. As in all discoveries, the familiar determined to a large extent the appearance of the new. But Europe's Bible-based worldview with its creation, paradise, fall, deluge, monotheist orthodoxy, and satanic idolatry—the mirror in which Asian religions appeared—was also gradually changing.[5]

At the heart of this change was the loss of biblical authority, resulting finally in "a new Orientalism liberated from the shackles of theology and biblical studies," a context from which Christianity itself came to be perceived as "a relatively insignificant and young local religion based on local varieties of solar myth."[6]

App demonstrated that countless European sources about Asian religions, from early modernity through the eighteenth and into the nineteenth century, were based on the analytical distinction between "esoteric" and "exoteric" forms of religion.[7] This was not a simple matter of terminological imperialism (the one-sided imposition of Western theoretical concepts on non-Western religions or cultures), for the "esoteric distinction" was clearly endorsed and actively promoted by Japanese, Chinese, or Indian authors and traditional sources. This is obviously a fact of great importance to the global history of religions and perfectly congenial to what I have referred to as *esotericism*$_2$. The central role that the "esoteric distinction" has played in early modern intellectual discourse about religion on a global scale can itself be studied historically, as shown by App's exemplary work. Furthermore, contemporary scholars may be inspired to follow the lead of their early modern ancestors, in adopting this particular distinction not just as a topic to be studied historically but also as an analytical instrument. If they do, the result is a global comparative project of research focused on "the dialectics of secrecy concerned with the social regulation or negotiation of access to specific forms of knowledge."[8]

Taking his cue from App's work, Julian Strube has recently been promoting a global *esotericism*$_2$ project along these lines, grounded in the "esoteric distinction" as "a structure in cross-cultural interpretation" that can be traced through the entire period of European colonialism from the fifteenth through the nineteenth and into the twentieth century.[9] But while this is a perfectly valid and obviously interesting enterprise, the primary sources explored by App and Strube do *not* tell us just about an interest in distinguishing between "esoteric" teachings for an initiated elite and "exoteric" doctrines for the people at large. In abundant detail, they document the utter dominance of a deeply Eurocentric discourse premised on Christian superiority, grounded precisely in the Western construction of "rejected knowledge" as a polemical category of radical otherness. One excellent example, among many others discussed by App and Strube, would be the Jesuit missionary João Rodrigues (1561–1633), who became "the best foreign speaker, reader, and writer of Japanese in the Jesuit mission" and also mastered classical Chinese. He spent his entire adult life in East Asia and is considered "by far the most knowledgeable Westerner of his time about the religions of Japan and China."[10] Therefore one might think he was in a particularly good position to understand and possibly even somewhat appreciate Japanese and Chinese religions on their own terms.

But such expectations would be disappointed, for indeed "the familiar determined to a large extent the appearance of the new."[11] During his sixty-five years of studying Confucianism, Daoism, and Buddhism, Rodrigues never came to see anything else in these religions than the standard types of pagan idolatry and demon worship that Christians had been rejecting and suppressing in European culture since the fourth century CE. Against the background of biblical historiographies, he was even convinced that they had all come originally from Chaldea, Persia, or Egypt, the traditional fountainheads or "seed pods" from whence the horrific "genealogy of darkness" had been spreading its "pestilent dogmas" according to standard European scholarship on traditional Platonic-Orientalist foundations.[12] Confucianism was a "diabolical and intrinsically atheistic" sect that had come from Babylonia and believed the world was eternal (i.e., rejected the doctrine of *creatio ex nihilo*);[13] Daoism was in reality "the sect of the Magicians and Persian evil wizards . . . a branch of the ancient Zoroaster"; and Buddhism, identified as "the sect of the ancient Indian gymnosophists," professed "a part of the doctrine of the Egyptians."[14] But their ultimate roots went back all the way to antediluvian times. Encouraged by the devil, "the wicked sons of Cain" had been "the first idolaters in the world and inventors of the magical arts." Noah's evil son Ham "was much given to this magical and judicial art [of astrology], which he learnt from Cain's descendants before the Flood... and from him they spread throughout the world, as many grave authors have noted."[15]

All of this belongs to the standard polemical repertoire of a Western Platonic Orientalism-in-reverse.[16] As abundantly demonstrated by the primary sources that App has studied and made available, this basic pattern of analysis reigned supreme in early modern depictions of Asian religions. They were dominated entirely by countless attempts to distinguish between a "secret doctrine" of pure monotheism and the idolatrous "exoteric" mass superstitions of popular religion.[17] It is therefore not sufficient to just state that early modern encounters between Western and non-Western religions and cultures were dominated by practices of comparison grounded in the "esoteric distinction," if this means ignoring the actual *content* of what "esoteric" and "exoteric" meant respectively for the colonizers and the colonized. We must pay attention to how comparative practices were serving the operations of power, by drawing a normative distinction between "good" monotheistic religion and the "bad" idolatrous practices of pagan superstition. The key point is that insofar as non-Western religions could be seen as containing a secret monotheist creed, this would make it possible for Christian missionaries to eventually bring them into the fold, by convincing the indigenous elites that their own true doctrine did not differ essentially from that of the Christians (the exact same strategy, by the way, that Pico della Mirandola had already been using in his attempt to convert the Jews). For instance, the Jesuit priest Matteo Ricci (1552–1610) relied on the Ficinian *prisca theologia* model in his Chinese catechism *Tianzhu shiyi* ("The True Meaning of the Lord of Heaven").[18] The actual result was

> a *praeparatio evangelica*: a way to entice the rationalist upper crust of Chinese society and to refute the "superstitious" and "foreign" forms of Chinese religion (such as Daoism and Buddhism) by logical argument while interpreting "original" Confucianism as a kind of Old Testament to Christianity.[19]

By the sharpest possible contrast, the "primitive idolatries" and "magical superstitions" typical of popular "exoteric" religion would simply need to be suppressed and exterminated by a combination of education and brute force, following the basic model of how the European elites were used to dealing with paganism and heresy in their own backyard.[20] For instance, the Lutheran missionary Bartholomäus Ziegenbalg (1682–1719) explained the difference between true knowledge (Sanskrit *jñāna*) and ignorance (*ajñāna*), to his Tamil readers, in terms of the classic theological concept of idolatrous worship linked to the Fall of Man and the redemption from sin by Jesus Christ:

> *Aññanam* (*ajñāna*, ignorance) came into this world through the cunning of Picācu (*piśāca*, ghost, goblin) and man's offense. . . . *ajñāna* is present when, instead of the true God, only his creatures are worshipped. Only the *manuṣa-avatāram* (*manuṣāvatāra*, human manifestation) of Christ could bring true *mōṭcam* (*mokṣa*, liberation) and conclusively exterminate *ajñāna*.[21]

The point is perfectly simple, but I believe its implications are enormous. The standard discursive patterns that were originally developed by Christians to demonize "pagan idolatry," and were then transformed by Enlightenment thinkers into a polemical narrative directed against "magic and superstition," provided missionaries and intellectuals with their basic template for discrediting and ultimately destroying non-Christian religious practices across the world. This is true not just for Asia but also for other parts of the world such as Africa and Latin America.[22]

In sum, the Eurocentric narrative of Western superiority that informed the global missionary and colonial enterprise is a straightforward external projection of the original *internal*-Eurocentric narrative of "rejected knowledge" that lies at the heart of our modern perception of "esotericism" as a distinct field. Now that Europe's "Inner Demons" seemed to be receding before the advancing Light of Reason, Western intellectuals, theologians, missionaries, philosophers, explorers, conquerors, or colonial administrators saw themselves faced with the further task of exterminating any remaining vestiges of "pagan superstition" and "demonic idolatry" that might still be lurking in the rest of the world.

Extermination

We have seen in Chapter 3 that Christoph August Heumann, a key figure in the Enlightenment discourse of "rejected knowledge," was of the opinion that all those "superstitious idiocies" promoted as ancient wisdom should be dumped into "the sea of oblivion" to be forgotten forever. As far as he was concerned, they belonged in "no better library."[23] This was a secular-academic parallel to the missionary opinion that those idolatrous cults of the heathen peoples should be "exterminated rather than studied."[24] We have no cause to be naïve about the real-life implications of such messages of destruction. The metaphorical gesture of dumping rejected knowledge into a conceptual "wastebasket" means, quite literally, that ancient sources (manuscripts or books) dealing with such stuff do not deserve to be preserved and certainly have no place in academic libraries or scholarly discussions.[25] What defines the content of a dustbin is precisely the fact that it's perfectly worthless and will be disposed of. Since the discourse of "rejected knowledge" refers to the actual beliefs and activities of real human beings in the real world, it should be evident that there's nothing harmless or innocent about such opinions and recommendations. Rejecting knowledge means rejecting people to whom such knowledge is important in their lives.[26]

At the very heart of the medieval and early modern campaign of eradicating "superstition" from European Christendom lies the biblical prohibition of IDOLATRY.[27] This was the ultimate and unforgivable sin, the "thick wall" that had always "separated the non-pagans from pagans,"[28] and it is utterly central not just to Christian but even to modern and secular concepts of what "magic" is all about.[29] Idolatry had to be exterminated at all costs, and the most effective way of doing so was by exterminating the idolaters. In Europe and America, the campaign to exorcize Europe from its "Inner Demons" led to a massive collective mania known as the witchcraft persecutions. Reaching its peak during the period 1560–1640, all in all it lasted almost three centuries. It claimed the lives of countless innocent people who were tortured and hanged or burned at the stake on suspicion of magical practice, idolatry, and the worship of demons.[30] Meanwhile, perfectly similar atrocities on a massive scale were rampant throughout the colonies, as shown in horrific detail by Bartolomé de las Casas in his famous *Short Account of the Destruction of the Indies* (1552).[31] Always and everywhere, on both sides of the Atlantic and in all the colonies worldwide, we keep seeing one and the same thing: *Civitas Dei contra Paganos*, "The City of God," engaged in its total war "against the Pagans," whose unforgivable sin was defined as idolatry.[32] Significantly, the "magical" and "superstitious" practices of native Peruvians or Mexicans were described specifically *not* as rival forms of religion but as apostasy and heresy—an intentional refusal to accept the message of Christ. The penalty was death.[33] As formulated by Ildikó Kristóf, we are dealing with "a dark, satanic interpretation of the religion(s) of the Native American people," a global intercultural "demon show" based on "the *diabolic representation of the Other*."[34]

The extermination of idolaters was intimately linked to their dehumanization.[35] In the early modern European context, it was common routine to depict witches or magicians as monstrous adversaries, whose condition of being possessed by demonic entities effectively erased their humanity and turned them into instruments of inhuman powers.[36] Unless they could be exorcized, such beings had to be killed. The dehumanization of idolaters was even easier in the colonies, where the very humanity of the native populations could be called into question or even flatly denied. As formulated by De las Casas's adversary Juan Ginés de Sepúlveda,

> Now compare with these Spaniards' intelligence, ingenuity, magnanimity, temperance, humanity, and religion those lesser humans [*homunculi*] among whom you will scarcely find any vestiges of humanity, who not only have no learning but do not even use or know writing [etc.]. . . . Therefore we know that they are – and certainly were before the arrival of the Spaniards – such lesser humans [*homunculi*] in mind and manners, so barbarous, so uncultivated, so inhuman. And yet we haven't even mentioned their impious religion and wicked sacrifices. . . . [T]hose people most especially abuse their faculties for the contempt of God who worship demons in place of God or who live a life that is at variance with divine and natural laws. . . . Therefore Augustine concludes that all heretics and all impious people and idol-worshippers possess their resources unjustly—that is, they may be justly deprived of them by the Catholics and the pious.[37]

According to standard Christian interpretations, idolatry and superstition were actually inspired by *real* demons, and this interpretation was strongly supported by leading scientists during this period.[38] They feared that if such malevolent powers or occult forces would vanish from the world, spiritual entities like angels or God himself would become obsolete as well. They were correct, for that is precisely what happened due to the new spirit of Enlightenment rationalism, which dismissed the Christian belief in demons as mere ignorance and folly.[39] The salutary effect was that it undermined the theoretical rationale for persecuting witches. But while people might no longer be tortured and killed on suspicion of *crimen magiae*, the deeper patterns of systemic denigration and dehumanization did not vanish. In fact, the ever-increasing emphasis on "reason and science" as essential to "(Western) civilization" and societal progress *implied* that "irrational superstition" be promoted as the core defining essence of "backward" "primitive" cultures. That such occult beliefs remained popular among European and American citizens was certainly a matter of serious concern but could always be explained in terms of stupidity or lack of education. This was different beyond the geographical borders of the "civilized world." Here it seemed to be a matter not of yet unenlightened *individuals* but of *entire populations* whose very capacity of rational judgment was seen as questionable at best.[40]

To just quote a particularly famous example, in his notorious poem "The White Man's Burden" (1899), Rudyard Kipling exhorted the United States to take up their sacred mission of civilizing the world by seizing control of the Philippines. He referred to its inhabitants as "Your new-caught, sullen peoples, / Half devil and half child," who have been perverted by "sloth and heathen folly."[41] These standard pagan-heresiological stereotypes, combined with no less standard Orientalist tropes ("sullenness," "sloth"), were placed in a sharply racialized contrast with the "White Man" and his superior civilization. This kind of thinking was of key importance to the new theories of anthropological evolution that dominated the perception of non-Western "natives" in intellectual and popular consciousness during the second half of the nineteenth century. As formulated by George W. Stocking in his standard work on Victorian anthropology, "savages were not just morally relinquent and spiritually deluded, but racially incapable."[42] This attitude was not limited to the British Empire. For instance, see these shocking lines penned by the influential German philosopher Eduard Hartmann (1842–1906):

> No power on earth is able to stop the extermination of inferior human races [*Menschenracen*]. . . . Just as one doesn't do any favor to a dog whose tail must be cut by cutting it off gradually inch by inch, neither is it an expression of human compassion [*Menschlichkeit*] to artificially prolong the death struggle of savages who are on the verge of extinction. Once having understood the natural law of anthropological development, the true philanthropist can only wish for the acceleration of these final convulsions, and labor for that end. Among the best measures is to support the Missions, which (by a truly divine irony of the unconscious) have done more for this purpose of nature [*Naturzweck*] than all the direct works of destruction [*Vernichtungsarbeiten*] undertaken by the white race [*der weissen Race*] against the savages. The more rapidly we pursue the extermination [*Ausrottung*] of such peoples of nature [*Naturvölker*] that are wholly incapable of competing with the white race, and the sooner the entire earth will be occupied entirely by the most highly-developed races so far, the faster we will see the battle between the different branches *inside* the most highstanding race being kindled in admirable dimensions [*in grossartigen Dimensionen entbrennen*].[43]

Similar warrants for genocide may be found in many other authors of the period. For instance, Herbert Spencer (1820–1903) was a famous intellectual who coined the expression "survival of the fittest" and was nominated for the Nobel prize shortly before his death (he did not get it though). Even prior to the emergence of social Darwinism, he wrote that evolution was now "clearing the earth of inferior races of men," and this process had to be welcomed and actively promoted: "The forces which are working out the great scheme of perfect happiness, taking no account of incidental suffering, exterminate such sections of mankind as stand in their way, with the same sternness that they exterminate beasts of prey and herds of useless ruminants. Be he human being, or be he brute, the hindrance must be got rid of."[44] Such opinions were not controversial at the time but perfectly common and widely accepted. My point is that they all relied on deeply ingrained stereotypes of non-Western peoples as not just racially inferior but also genetically predisposed to irrational superstitions such as magic and idolatry.

Therefore the Enlightenment assault on "rejected knowledge" resulted not just in a widespread academic culture of *docta ignorantia* ("learned ignorance")[45] about major dimensions of Western culture, as I have been arguing throughout this book. It also served the agendas of Western imperialism and white supremacy in the age of global colonialism. It is essential to be attentive to the *longue durée*, from late antiquity to modernity. Christians had always seen the extermination of pagan idolatry, first in Europe and then in the rest of the world, as essential to God's providential plan for humanity. The same project was pursued by their secular successors, except that now they were thinking not in terms of divine but of *natural* laws that were governing the course of human evolution. There is no radical break but rather a strong continuity between earlier concepts of divine providence and such later beliefs in spiritual evolution along broadly Hegelian lines. The genocidal implications are perfectly obvious already in Hegel's deliberate use of sacrificial imagery, as part of his famous concept of *die List der Vernunft*, "the cunning of Reason." For instance, the entire earth is depicted as a sacrificial "altar" and world history as a "slaughter-bench [*Schlachtbank*] . . . on which the happiness of peoples, the wisdom of states and the virtue of individuals are being sacrificed" to the supreme idea of Absolute Freedom.[46] Authors such as von Hartmann or Spencer could think of themselves as *Geschäftsführer des Geistes* ("Business Managers of the Spirit")[47] charged with the task of promoting this unpleasant but necessary slaughter of the innocents, all in the interest of promoting human progress. Summing up, from the Christian assault on pagan idolatry to the evolutionists' assault on primitive cultures, the bottom line remained the same. Superior powers were at work in history to promote the Greater Good. They did not just permit but actively *demanded* the Lesser Evil of extermination.

Counter-normativity

If such ideas were perfectly normal in mainstream European and American culture during the age of modernity/coloniality,[48] clearly that is very good reason to be suspicious of the HIDDEN NORMATIVITIES that inform traditional Eurocentric understandings of what Western culture is all about. The central argument of this book is that if we are serious about *rejecting the rejection of rejected knowledge*, we must say goodbye to conventional ideologies of "the West," for the simple reason that the latter's core identity was built on the very rejection of rejected knowledge. Rejecting the rejection of rejected knowledge means recovering all those sources or ideas and practices that used to be dismissed by the academy. However, the project goes further than a strictly historiographical exercise. It also means restoring their *legitimacy* as equal conversation partners whose voices and opinions have the right to be taken seriously on their own terms.[49] If the standards of Enlightenment rationality by which they were excluded from the conversation are in fact ideologies built on normative polemics that are themselves historically contingent, as I have been arguing throughout this book, then their foundational assumptions are not exempt from having their own legitimacy questioned in turn. But how should we imagine such a nonhegemonic conversation between Enlightenment rationality and *das Andere der Vernunft*,[50] given the fact that our normal criteria of critical scholarship and reasonable debate come from those very same traditions whose normative foundations are being called into question? This brings me to the agenda of COUNTER-NORMATIVITY, a new concept that I introduce at this occasion and that should not be confused with *anti*-normativity or deviance.[51]

So far, my focus has been on the relatively straightforward (dare I say "exoteric"?) phenomenon of discursive battles between orthodoxies and heterodoxies about what is ultimately real and true. These polemical arguments and apologetic counterarguments are perfectly *explicit* and out in the open, which means that they can be readily studied in the primary sources by standard historical methods. But on a deeper level of hermeneutic analysis (dare I call it "esoteric"?), the construction of rejected knowledge is based on *hidden normativities*—the tacit application of a norm or standard of normality that seldom needs to explain or defend its *bona fides* because it is taken for granted as self-evident and mostly escapes our conscious awareness. The power of hidden normativities lies precisely in the fact that their presence goes undetected so that they stay exempt from being challenged directly.

Against this background, *counter-normativity* can be defined as the project of demonstrating that what is commonly experienced as "normal" (and gets presented to us as such) may in fact be the reflection of a hidden normative standard that should be critically examined and not just taken for granted.[52] The concern is with questioning deep normativities and exposing hidden assumptions about what we take to be "obviously" real and true.[53] I know of no better formulation than the passage by Rainer Maria Rilke with which I opened this book. The early Christian author Tertullian once remarked, perhaps too optimistically, that *Quod tanto impendio absconditur, etiam solummodo demonstrare, destruere est*, "merely demonstrating that which is concealed so carefully means destroying it."[54] This, too, goes to the essence of counter-normativity as a critical project. By revealing how that which we take to be *normal* is actually based on a normative choice, we destroy the tyrannical power of habituation and win back our liberty to consider different choices.[55]

But what exactly is meant by "normality," and what is its relation to "normativity"? As pointed out by George Canguilhem in a classic study, "the normal" is actually "*the effect* obtained by the execution of the normative project, it is the norm exhibited in the fact."[56] This technical but crucial point is easily missed, because it seems so logical to assume that normality comes first and abnormality second, as the deviation from a norm that must therefore already exist. That same logic serves precisely to confirm the normative message that those who resist the norm must be condemned as "abnormal." But Canguilhem explains that, contrary to what we think, "a norm cannot be original" but is always imposed a posteriori. "It is the historical anteriority of the future abnormal which gives rise to a normative intention."[57] This is why any norm that we tend to take for granted as "obvious" or "natural" (an instance of normality) is actually always "a value disguised as a fact."[58] On this basis, normativity can be defined as "the system through which norms, normalization and the normative are naturalized and made to seem ideal."[59]

The act of imposing a new norm, a new standard of normality, serves to discredit and eventually erase an anterior reality. It colonizes our conscious awareness and banishes other conceptualizations from our view, suggesting that what is different must be wrong. The new normativity "becomes synonymous with the real by obstructing possible alternatives."[60] Under such conditions—and this point is absolutely essential, as will be seen—the suppressed may only ever return to our conscious awareness in the form of what Erik Davis calls ONTOLOGICAL WEIRDNESS.[61] I want to flag this concept for special attention. It is actually significant, and not just of anecdotal interest, that scholars of esotericism so often refer to their field, colloquially and in a playful spirit, as *the weird stuff*. The weird or uncanny (das *Unheimliche* in German) is precisely that which we find hardest to understand, or even just look at and recognize, because we struggle to find any place for it in our normative assumptions about truth and reality.[62] By definition, it is the presence of something that should not be present, the impossible appearing in its very impossibility. In short, the weird is defined precisely by the fact that it's *not normal*. Because it doesn't fit our standards of normality,[63] it threatens our most elementary assumptions about reality and truth, about "how the world works," and may even cause us to question our own sanity. Therefore we naturally defend ourselves against its presence, by means of standard escape mechanisms such as denying, forgetting, ignoring, excluding, suppressing, ridiculing, or rationalizing. These psychological responses all have the same basic function: to reassure us that everything is alright, that the world is reliable, that we're not crazy.

Counter-normality

Ontological weirdness is defined precisely by the fact that it *troubles* our sense of normality. Yet it can do so in many ways, as will be seen, along a very wide spectrum that runs from the utterly shocking to the mildly disturbing or even the pleasurably surprising (or surprisingly pleasurable).[64] As we move away from the former into the direction of the latter, we actually distance ourselves from weirdness in a strong sense to encounter more subtle experiential phenomena that usually go by other names. For this reason, I propose to speak of COUNTER-NORMALITY as a more neutral umbrella term that covers the entire spectrum. Thus we end up with a pair of two complementary technical terms.

Counter-normativity as a critical project questions the process of normalization itself (the imposition of a normative standard that ends up concealing its own presence), while counter-normality refers to the troubling effects of that process (the appearance of phenomena that in some sense are "not normal").

Counter-normality in its weirdest and most radically shocking form is typically referred to as *paranormal* (literally "beside" or "contrary to" the normal). In a series of brilliant and passionate books, the American academic Jeffrey J. Kripal has argued that these deeply troubling manifestations of THE IMPOSSIBLE are perfectly central not just to European and American popular culture but even to the history of religion in general and its "esoteric" traditions more in particular.[65] As regards the weird and occult dimensions of the modern and contemporary imagination, I find this thesis compelling and of major importance to the study of esotericism. Along with Erik Davis's work, it has been a key source of inspiration while I was working out the theoretical argument presented on these pages. Yet I can follow Kripal only up to a point. From a broader perspective of historical research and comparative religion (keeping in mind that in cultures where nothing is held to be impossible, the impossible itself is strictly impossible![66]), I am wary of the risk of overdetermination by American popular culture as the implicit prototypical standard of what "the weird stuff" is all about.[67]

In other words, it is tempting for contemporary scholars to define "weirdness" or "the impossible" in general terms as whatever reminds you of the paranormal and the occult as depicted in "monster magazines, exploitation movies, novelty items, UFO pamphlets, tattoo art, and comic books" such as *Weird Science, Weird Chills, Weird Fantasy*, or *Adventures into Weird World*.[68] Such a focus may work reasonably well as long as we stay with modern and contemporary popular culture, especially in America, but becomes a problem if it leads us to project our own models of paranormal weirdness onto other cultures and historical periods, as a kind of hermeneutic master key to religion and culture. I am pushing back here against a notorious fallacy known as present-centered historiography, or PRESENTISM. It is defined by scholarly procedures that, intentionally or not, privilege our contemporary prejudices as a normative prototypical standard for studying and understanding the past (or, by extension, other cultures).[69] As for Kripal himself, to be sure, his thinking is quite a bit too sophisticated and profoundly hermeneutic to support crudely literalist anachronisms or ethnocentric projections to the effect that "the mystics were really psychics!" or "magicians had superpowers!" Yet I'm not so sure whether more casual and superficial readers will manage to avoid such simplifications, or care to try. For my part, rather than trying to *identify* the unknown (in past or other cultures) in terms of something we already know, my approach is precisely to let it *defamiliarize* the all-too-familiar.

More fundamentally, a focus on the paranormal as the true heart of "impossible" weirdness could easily blind us to the presence of counter-normality in its more subtle manifestations. By calling them more "subtle," I do *not* mean that these are in any way less impressive or less powerful (on the contrary, we know that they may completely change a person's life),[70] but that they challenge normality in a different way that is concerned less with facts than with interpretations. Many *qualitative* phenomena that occur in human experience do not *directly* violate our core assumptions about what is real and true, in a kind of in-your-face manner, but destabilize them more mildly and indirectly. They do so by the simple fact that we do not know "where to put them." At some level, we are aware of having no place for them in our standard normative accounts of how the world works, or of what we're supposed to find important. Among the many examples that could be mentioned are visions or voices, altered states or experiences of possession, lucid dreams or "weird" synchronicities, unitive experiences, intuitions or premonitions, a sense of invisible presences or inner guidance, including an experience of direct "channeled" inspiration resulting in poetry or music, encounters with demons or angels or alien entities, experiences of bliss or ecstatic transport, for instance while making love or running a marathon or listening to music, and so on and so forth.

Such experiences inhabit a liminal place between the possible and impossible, for although we know that they occur, our normative culture gives us the message that they are not really what they seem. And so we fall back on the usual defense mechanisms, just as we do with the paranormal. Perhaps it's something I ate. Some wires must have gotten double-crossed in my brain. Yeah, it happened..., but what can I say? I was definitely tired, I did feel a bit strange. Better ignore it—it was nothing, really. Oh, well, I'll admit it, I was impressed, but now that the memory is fading I wonder what it was really all about. Was it really such a big deal? It could not really be what it seemed, could it? Surely there's some rational explanation. In any case, better not to mention that stuff to my boss. Or even to my friends—they might think I'm crazy. And so on and so forth.[71] My point is that there's a difference between spectacular "paranormal" events that directly violate our commonsense beliefs about physical reality, for instance, Kripal's example of watching a honey jar teleport across your kitchen in broad daylight, and more subtle personal experiences such as hearing a voice in your head that gives you warnings or advice.[72] Skeptics will say about the former that they are simply impossible. About the latter, they will say rather that certain *explanations* are impossible. Yet what they all have in common is that *such things are not supposed to happen.* They are not normal.

Again, counter-normativity must not be confused with anti-normativity. It's not about subverting established norms in order to push our own normative preferences, whatever those may be, or gaining some kind of subcultural satisfaction from "being on the right side" and seeing things better than others do. It's about questioning the very dynamics of normalization, not just in others but in ourselves as well, and being sensitive to its hidden ways of operating. This implies a certain humility on the part of scholars, who are human beings like everybody else and whose normative convictions are no less biased and historically contingent than those of the persons they study. Our inescapable *situatedness* as mortal beings with inherently limited horizons means that any attempt at truly understanding, or even just perceiving, what is strange and unfamiliar requires a genuine dialogue between our own particular prejudices and those of the persons or sources we study.[73] There is no escape from this hermeneutical circle, nor should there be, because it's the very condition that allows us to understand anything at all. Without it, we would be blind. This also means that there's no such thing as a transcendent position of *un*situatedness, some kind of scholarly *gnōsis* that allows us to finally see things "as they really are."[74]

Precisely for this reason, counter-normativity as a critical project must insist on STAYING WITH THE TROUBLE.[75] If esotericism is about "the weird stuff," this implies more than just studying the historical archives of rejected knowledge from a position of comfortable academic distance, or trying to neutralize the counter-normal by means of normative explanations that just serve to confirm the rule of normality.[76] Staying with the trouble of counter-normality requires a willingness, first of all, to *listen* and *observe*—that is, to sit patiently with whatever is there, no matter how uncomfortable we may find it, instead of rushing in with our normative judgments and cherished opinions about what's true and real or valid and right. This is what I mean by an empirical bottom-up approach to research, as opposed to top-down procedures, such as Adorno's and many others', that begin by placing their own theories in the driver's seat and thus allow them to dominate the conversation (or lack of it). This has nothing to do with a "rejection of theory"[77] but refers to the elementary scholarly practice of *respecting the autonomy of our sources* by listening and trying to understand what they might have to tell us.[78] Arguably the biggest problem in the study of esotericism (and more generally in the humanities), at least in my opinion, lies in the fact that academics are often so obsessed with their own theories and normative assumptions that they proceed by forcing the materials they study to fit their favorite theoretical frameworks, rather than allowing those frameworks to be troubled by the materials.

This is a very basic issue that goes to the heart of what counter-normativity is all about. Consider this passage by Carl Gustav Jung, about the traumatic conflict between his own cherished theoretical convictions as an early-twentieth century psychologist and the weird counter-normal experiences that began overwhelming him in 1913 and eventually led to the *Red Book*:

> At the time, I was still wholly under the spell of the Spirit of this Time and thought differently about the human soul. I thought and spoke much about the soul, I knew many learned words about her, I have judged her and made an object of science out of her. It did not occur to me that my soul cannot be the object of my judgment and knowledge: much more is my judgment and knowledge the object of my soul.[79]

As a whole, Jung's *Red Book* exemplifies perfectly what I mean by "staying with the trouble" of counter-normality. In this particular case, we are dealing with an extreme conflict between psychological theory and personal experience (literally between "psycho-logy," an academic "*discourse* about the soul," and the presumed *object* of that discourse),[80] but the same dynamic governs the relation between historians and their sources. Hermetic scholarship is a particularly good example of how academics usually respond to counter-normality. Immediately when the Hermetica were placed on the agenda of scholarly research (with a study by Richard Reitzenstein published in 1904), they became the arena for an academic culture war between philhellenic and neoromantic ideologies over the very nature of Western culture and its relation to the Orient.[81] These theoretical frameworks were based on the fears and obsessions of turn-of-the-century intellectuals about the future of the West and had nothing to do with the actual contents of the Hermetica. Nevertheless, their impact was utterly decisive with regard to how the sources were being read or even *why* they were being read. Because they determined what scholars saw as important and dictated the questions they asked, they also determined what could be neglected and which questions would never be asked.[82]

The chief victim of all these misinterpretations was precisely the dimension of counter-normality, the profound weirdness that lies at the heart of the entire Hermetic literature.[83] Perhaps nothing illustrates the point more clearly than the bizarre detail that *precisely* the most central passage in the central treatise on Hermetic rebirth (itself the central spiritual event of the Hermetic *paideia*) was printed deliberately in small type by Walter Scott, in his influential edition. These were just "silly" passages "lacking in good sense and taste," he explained, so that by removing these "excrescences," the text would be "less unworthy [sic!] to take its place among the other *Hermetica*."[84] As always, the devil is in the details, in this case an editorial decision that deeply affects the text but very easily escapes our attention. We might want to dismiss such an example as utterly extreme and therefore exceptional, but I believe that this would be just another subtle defensive mechanism to avoid staying with the trouble. We are not any better than Scott. None of us is immune to the temptation of relying on our own particular theories and normative convictions as the uniquely privileged vantage point for interpreting what is different and strange. That obviously includes the author of these lines. The trouble of counter-normality is precisely the trouble that we need, if we wish to avoid the traps of normalization and make further progress in understanding.

The Greater Relevance of Esotericism

The world is a very strange place, in which "there are things going on whose nature *no one* understands."[85] This is true. It is an empirical fact and not just a private opinion. But the same world is also dominated by powerful discourses, embodied in powerful institutions, that serve to normalize our perceptions of what is possible and what should be dismissed as impossible. They are part of a grand narrative about "modernity and globalization" that presents itself as a history of social progress rooted in early modern Europe (notably the Reformation, the Scientific Revolution, the Enlightenment, and the French Revolution), the emancipation of "Man" from the orders of nature and divinity, the emergence of capitalism and the nation state, an increasing rationalization of the life-world accompanied by pressures toward universalization and individualization, a triumph of freedom and human rights, global neoliberalism as the necessary consequence both of liberalism and capitalism, and a disenchanted metaphysics that sees the world as made up of things and beings that can be known for what they are and can therefore be controlled by means of calculation. Such is the power of this narrative and its institutional manifestations that it impresses itself on our imagination as an unavoidable historical destiny, by what has been called "the Giddens Effect" (referring to the sociologist Anthony Giddens): *from now on, it's modernity all the way down, everywhere, until the end of times.*[86]

Counter-normativity means opposing the claims to self-evident normality that gives power to this grand narrative, by revealing the deep normative choices on which it actually rests. In contrast to anti-normativity, it is not based on an attitude of simple rejection but insists on deep historical and critical analysis, informed by a conviction that nothing is beyond discussion and there are always alternatives to any belief or ideological claim. Methodologically, counter-normativity begins not with abstract theorization but with an empirical and historical demonstration of *how much has been left out of the story,* as though it never existed, and how much has been distorted almost beyond recognition, as though it *should* not exist. Again, this has nothing to do with a "rejection of theory." It is a simple matter of prioritizing historical and empirical evidence as the most effective way to challenge the power of dominant narratives. To put it very bluntly, most of our standard ideas about Western culture are demonstrably false. They will have to be abandoned to make place for better ideas, based on correct and more adequate knowledge. What is presented to us as normal is in fact a selective account based on normative choices and ideological filters. Just like Herbert Spencer did (in the very same book that contains his genocidal statements about the evolutionary force of sheer necessity), the intimidating voice of the Giddens Effect tells us that There Is No Alternative.[87] But the voice of counter-normativity whispers back: "no, that's not true, there are always alternatives, *it could all be different.*" Once upon a time, it reminds us, the world was incredibly different from how it is now. Reality *is* incredibly different in the very present, as we discover by paying attention to the presence of the counter-normal. And in the future, undoubtedly, it will again be extremely different from anything that we are currently even able to imagine. It is irrational, and a failure of imagination, to think that whereas we are currently living in a reality that would certainly have been beyond the wildest dreams of our ancestors, *we* are blessed with unique capacities of prescience about what will be coming after us.[88]

This brings me to the deep emancipatory potential of esotericism research. Most of this book has been devoted to a project of rejecting the rejection of rejected knowledge, in the precise sense of restoring its academic legitimacy as a perfectly normal field of study. But important as it may be, does this mean that the agenda is merely one of academic *normalization*? No, for that would mean accepting the hidden normativities and ideological choices that caused the field to be rejected in the first place.[89] In this regard, I believe we must differentiate between two antithetical understandings of the Enlightenment project, including its later transformations in dominant "modernization and globalization" narratives. I will refer to them as ENLIGHTENMENT$_1$ and ENLIGHTENMENT$_2$. To begin with the latter, Enlightenment$_2$ (or if you will, "Bad Enlightenment") is based on a dogmatic ideology of reason and science, to the exclusion of everything else, tending ultimately toward the classic positivist doctrine that the exclusive source of reliable knowledge consists of nothing but normal sensory experience interpreted through reason and logic. This perspective defines its very identity in terms of the rejection of rejected knowledge. By sharp contrast, Enlightenment$_1$ ("Good Enlightenment") insists on respect for empirical evidence no matter where it may lead, a rejection of ideological prejudice of any kind, unrestricted freedom of inquiry, openness to all perspectives and all possible outcomes, and confidence in the emancipatory power of critical discussion and argumentation.[90] Therefore it cannot possibly accept the rejection of rejected knowledge. On the contrary, it must insist on studying its materials carefully and critically, just like everything else. It will be evident where my allegiance lies. I consider it not just legitimate but critically important to criticize the logic of *Enlightenment*$_2$ from the perspective of *Enlightenment*$_1$.

Therefore I make no excuse for my conviction that the study of esotericism has a social and political relevance that goes further than that of a strictly academic program. In this regard, I see its mission as similar to other emancipatory projects in the humanities. For instance, it is not enough to restore the voices and activities of women to standard historical narratives while ignoring the hidden operation of a masculine standard by which it used to be "normal" to write the history of humanity as the "History of Man." Likewise, it is not enough to restore people of color to those same historical narratives while ignoring the effects of whiteness as a hidden normative standard of "humanity" as such.[91] By exactly the same logic, it is not enough to restore the history of rejected knowledge to our standard accounts of Western culture while ignoring the hidden normativities that inform the internal Eurocentric narrative and cause it to be experienced as perfectly normal.

The Western academy is based on normative standards of reason and science that, as everybody knows, are very deeply entangled with the grand narrative of "modernity and globalization" with which I opened this final section. Just a few decades ago, it might still have been possible to believe in its ultimately benevolent nature and its grand promises of social progress. But as I am writing these lines in the summer of 2024, I would find it inexcusable to just keep beating that drum, as though we can still ignore the realities it has actually created and keeps supporting. The deep normative ideologies that inform our current normality of modernization and globalization have brought us to a point of "polycrisis" (environmental, social, mental, political, cultural, and academic as well)[92] that compels us to ask ourselves seriously *what went wrong*, why it went wrong, where and when it happened, and what would be needed to at least make a start with moving into a better direction. I obviously do not have the recipe for solving the world's problems. But I do suggest that part of the puzzle consists in reconsidering our standard ways of distinguishing between rejected and acceptable knowledge.

The conflict between two interpretations of the Enlightenment project (the anti-dogmatic *Enlightenment*$_1$ interpretation and its dogmatic *Enlightenment*$_2$ counterpart) has always been there. Yet for a very long time, it was possible for academics to close their eyes to the latter while betting on the former to prevail. This allowed them to think of themselves as part of an educational institution that, for all its weaknesses and limitations, was devoted to positive emancipatory values such as critical thinking, historical awareness, education as the continuing self-cultivation of responsible citizens (*Bildung*), the pursuit of understanding for the sake of understanding itself, the fight against prejudice, the promotion of tolerance and social progress, and the pursuit of truth. These are all typical *Enlightenment*$_1$ values, consistent with an open pluralistic perspective on the search for knowledge and understanding. For countless academics in the humanities, myself included, they remain essential to what our work is all about. But the sad truth is that over the past few decades, for precise reasons that are well known to specialists, the institutions in which we must function have abandoned these key emancipatory values in favor of a modus operandi driven entirely by a doctrine of universal marketization.[93]

As this particular normative standard imposes itself as the new academic normality (as always, by making its hidden normativities appear as self-evident truths), this inevitably results in new realms of counter-normality. As "rational" quantification and calculability becomes the norm of a universal economy driven by nothing but technology and profit, anything *qualitative* and incalculable becomes counter-normal by definition.[94] It can no longer exist. I have noticed again and again that, for countless people who make their living in a business world of finance and technology, there is actually something faintly *weird* about those people (scholars or students in the humanities) who spend their days and are even being paid for studying something spooky, something faintly spectral, concerned with things that evidently cannot be measured and controlled. QUALITY and *QUALIA* are the new impossibles. We do not know "where to put them,"[95] because there actually *is* no place for them in the normative structures of the scientific, technical, and social-economic order that we have been creating together over the past few decades. Again, we are faced here with the basic dynamics of dehumanization, the standard prerequisite for extermination (hence the progressive marginalization of the humanities in institutions supposedly devoted to higher learning). Almost everything that human beings experience as meaningful in their lives is actually qualitative, not quantifiable; but those dimensions are being pushed toward the margins of the dominant culture, where they come to inhabit a liminal realm halfway between existence and nonexistence. Very much like the realm of the occult.

In my opinion, academics in the humanities have an urgent responsibility to fight back against these developments. Therefore, rejecting the rejection of rejected knowledge means more than just creating new academic programs where esotericism can be studied as a normal topic. At least as important is the question of *how* it is studied, under which conditions, and from which perspectives. If the objective is merely one of normalization, in an academic context that is in the process of losing touch with anything qualitative, the successful establishment of esotericism as an "accepted" field of research will be no more than a Pyrrhic victory, because precisely that which makes it important will fade into insignificance or vanish altogether. On the contrary, we have excellent reasons to reject the normative standards *themselves* by which the field used to be rejected, and that still determine what we are being taught on a daily basis to consider normal. The current reign of normality has caused far too much destruction. It exterminates far too much that deserves to be cherished and protected. It is doing far too much damage to human beings and the natural world. Having lost much of its traditional aura of benevolent authority and moral purpose, it is relying ever more openly on sheer violence and coercion, while repeating the standard message of intimidation that There Is No Alternative.

Of course there are alternatives. There always are. Counter-normativity as a critical method explores them historically and empirically, calling our attention to everything that has been pushed into the liminal spaces of counter-normality. The project is defined by its insistence on *staying with the trouble*. This requires cultivating a daily habit of looking wherever we are not supposed to look, paying attention precisely to that which we are being told is not worth our attention, and questioning what we are usually taking for granted. It means insisting on our right to decide for ourselves what we find important, what we consider to be worth taking seriously, instead of letting the surrounding culture make that decision for us. This requires a certain amount of confidence, even courage, and quite a bit of counter-normative skill. Every student or scholar in the field of esotericism has experienced the less-than-subtle pressure of normalization—somebody asks you at a party "so what are you doing in your daily life?," and you feel embarrassed because it sounds silly to just answer "I study esotericism." You may know for yourself that there's nothing silly about it, but how do you explain it so that this person will understand what you mean? In a way, this brings us full circle, to the first pages of my first chapter. I pointed out there that all available terms, beginning with "esotericism" itself, have the effect of making the field and those who study it look a bit unrespectable and, well, weird.

I hope to have made clear why this phenomenon is not incidental but critically important and in fact unavoidable. It reveals the trouble. If esotericism as a field of study would ever become normal, there would no longer be a field of study recognizable as esotericism, because the rejected knowledge it studies would have become acceptable knowledge. By the same token, it would lose its key emancipatory function, that of challenging the rule of normality. Until such time, we need to keep whispering the message of counter-normality.

It could all be different
It already is different
Just look at what's there

Notes

Introduction

1 Rilke, *Die Aufzeichnungen des Malte Laurids Brigge*, 468–470 (abridged; translation WJH). Brigge's journal begins on December 4, 1875, in his room at Rue Toullier.

2 Magnússon, *Dichtung als Erfahrungsmetaphysik*.

3 This is a deliberate nod of appreciation to the original pioneer of esotericism research, Antoine Faivre, to whose memory this book is dedicated: see his two great volumes *Accès de l'ésotérisme occidental* and the shorter English version *Access to Western Esotericism*.

4 E.g., Bruce Lincoln's excellent "Theses on Method," here especially nrs. 2 and 3 (*Gods and Demons*, 1). For the deep dialectics involved, see also, e.g., Scholem, "A Birthday Letter" (used for the motto above Chapter 7).

5 Mann, *Joseph und seine Brüder II*, 689.

6 I am happy to support the founding ethos of the famous Esalen Center in Big Sur, California, which has been a source of inspiration. See the webpage "No One Captures the Flag: Ben Tauber on Embracing a Founding Ethos of Esalen" (https://www.esalen.org).

7 For Faivre's life and career see Hanegraaff with Brach and Pasi, "Antoine Faivre (1934–2021)."

Chapter 1

1 Eco, *Foucault's Pendulum*, 285.

2 Another category could be "spirituality." This term is becoming more current in scholarly discourse and could be understood as covering those types of "religion" that are more concerned with *individual experiential practice* than with social formations or organizations defined by normative doctrines or standard ceremonial practices (Streib & Hood, "'Spirituality'"; Hanegraaff, "Imagining the Future Study"; idem, *Hermetic Spirituality*, 19–22; and below, Chapter 7, pp. 165–169).

3 Hanegraaff, "Esotericism"; idem, *Esotericism and the Academy*, 334–339; Neugebauer-Wölk, "Der Esoteriker und die Esoterik"; eadem, "Historische Esoterikforschung." Aristotle used the word "exoteric" (*exōterikos*) but opposed it to "acroamatic" (from *akroama*, oral instruction). The adjective "esoteric" was introduced around 166 CE by the satirical author Lucian of Samosata, *Vitarum Rustio* 26. See Riffard, *L'ésotérisme*, 65–71.

4 See Chapter 3, pp. 88–99.

5 For the deeper philosophical issues that are at stake here, see below, pp. 17–21 (section "The Discursive Turn").
6 Faivre, "Introduction I," xv–xx; idem, *Access to Western Esotericism*, 10–15.
7 For a bibliographical list of the main contributions until 2012, in chronological order, see Hanegraaff, *Esotericism and the Academy*, 356 note 375. For the period after 2012, we could add, e.g., Asprem, "Beyond the West"; Asprem & Davidsen, "Editor's Introduction"; Crockford & Asprem, "Ethnographies of the Esoteric"; Okropiridze, "Interpretation Reconsidered"; Engler & Gardiner, "(Re)defining Esotericism" (with many responses in the same special issue).
8 Luhrmann, *Of Two Minds*, 41.
9 See quotation by Plotinus in Chapter 7, p. 152. For a good discussion, see Otto, *Magie*, 349–356. The importance of Stoicism to esotericism has not received enough attention; for an excellent discussion by Earl Fontainelle, see *The Secret History of Western Esotericism Podcast* (SHWEP, www.shwep.net), esp. episode 44, "Esoteric Hermeneutics in Stoicism."
10 Faivre, "Ancient and Medieval Sources."
11 For the backgrounds of these choices in Faivre's intellectual biography, see Hanegraaff with Brach & Pasi, "Antoine Faivre (1934–2021)."
12 Yates, *Giordano Bruno and the Hermetic Tradition*; analysis in Hanegraaff, *Esotericism and the Academy*, 322–334.
13 Webb, *Occult Underground*, Chapter 1.
14 Schwab, *The Oriental Renaissance*; and see discussion in Chapter 7, pp. 156–158.
15 Hanegraaff, *Esotericism and the Academy*, 184–188 (with reference to, e.g., Edward Burnett Tylor's concept of magic and superstition as "survivals," or arguments such as Vickers, "On the Function of Analogy in the Occult").
16 Hanegraaff, "How Magic Survived the Disenchantment of the World." This was also the basic thesis of idem, *New Age Religion* (hence the "mirror of secular thought" mentioned in the subtitle).
17 An excellent example would be Partridge, *Re-Enchantment of the West* (2 vols.); and for a more recent encyclopedic overview see Partridge, *The Occult World*.
18 See, for example, the important collective volume edited by Tiryakian, *On the Margin of the Visible* (especially the contributions by Tiryakian, "Toward the Sociology," and Truzzi, "Definitions and Dimensions"). For a critical reassessment, see Asprem, "On the Social Organization," in an important recent volume edited by Hedenborg White and Rudbøg, *Esotericism and Deviance*.
19 For instance Hanegraaff, *New Age Religion*; Owen, *Place of Enchantment*; Treitel, *A Science for the Soul*; Pasi, "Modernity of Occultism."
20 A few pioneering discussions of this phenomenon are Possamai, *Handbook of Hyper-Real Religions*; Cusack, *Invented Religions*; Davidsen, "Fiction and Religion." For metamodernism (and metamodernity?) as a next stage after postmodernity, see Josephson Storm, *Metamodernism*.
21 E.g., Kripal, *Mutants & Mystics*.
22 Davis, *High Weirdness*. See further discussion in Chapter 9, pp. 200–203.
23 Braudel, "La longue durée."

24 For instance von Stuckrad, *Western Esotericism*; Wolfson, *Rending the Veil*; or Urban, *Secrecy*.

25 Goodrick-Clarke, *The Western Esoteric Traditions*, 12–13 (bracketed sentence inserted by me).

26 Hanegraaff, *Esotericism and the Academy*, 126–127, 149, 295–314.

27 Mircea Eliade, arguably the most influential religionist scholar, insisted on referring to his field as *history of religions* (see, e.g., the journal of that name, founded by him in 1961).

28 Eranos religionism was inspired by the hope that, in the study of myths or symbols, humans might find themselves "addressed" or "captured" (*interpellé, ergriffen*) by a numinous otherworldly reality or presence (Hanegraaff, "Generous Hermeneutics," 60–64).

29 Schuon, *Transcendent Unity of Religions*.

30 On the key principle of "methodological agnosticism" concerning any meta-empirical realities that are claimed to exist, see Hanegraaff, "Empirical Method." For the stronger version of a radical agnosticism in the context of a philosophy of radical empiricism, see idem, *Hermetic Spirituality*, 3–5; idem, "Subtle Energies" (and see pp. 257–258 note 85).

31 Von Stuckrad, *Locations of Knowledge*, x–xi; cf. idem, *Western Esotericism*, 10 ("it is often better to talk about *the esoteric* than about *esotericism*"). Writing between 2005 and 2010, von Stuckrad must have been thinking especially of Faivre's concept of esotericism as a "form of thought" and Goodrick-Clarke's *The Western Esoteric Traditions* (see my comparison of these approaches in Hanegraaff, "Textbooks and Introductions").

32 Von Stuckrad, *Locations of Knowledge*, 67.

33 Like the present volume, but by a different route, von Stuckrad's project aspires to deconstruct the traditional master narrative of a "monolithic Christian occident": see, e.g., Kippenberg, Rüpke, & von Stuckrad, *Europäische Religionsgeschichte* (2 vols.); and the *Journal of Religion in Europe* founded by the same authors. For a more detailed analysis of von Stuckrad's perspective and its implications, see Hanegraaff, *Esotericism and the Academy*, 361–367, here 365; and idem, "Textbooks and Introductions," 180–183.

34 E.g., Strube, "Emergence of 'Esoteric'"; idem, "Esotericism between Europe and East Asia"; idem, "Religious Comparativism." See discussion in Chapter 9, pp. 192–195.

35 Urban, "Torment of Secrecy," 210; and see Urban's recent monograph *Secrecy*.

36 The well-known prevalence of authoritarian claims to discursive hegemony and exclusive validity is a particularly troublesome aspect of the post-structuralist-deconstructionist milieus referred to as "Critique," "Theory," or "Critical Theory." For an excellent analysis by an insider, see Felski, *Limits of Critique*, 147–150 ("Critique does not tolerate rivals"). For a both precise and elegant response to various approaches that are "driven by an impulse to discursive domination," see Engler & Gardiner, "Definition as Situated Interpretational Vector," 280–282, here 281. I fully embrace their call for "a framework for collaborative exploration" and "a space for dialogue." If the meaning of meaning is understood in a context of meaning anti-realism (see below, note 46), as they write, "there is no possibility of a single, hegemonic truth; the search for meaning begins with a radical plurality of voices, and it proceeds on the assumption that we share enough with others to begin the process of making sense of each other" (ibid., 288).

37 Urban, *Secrets of the Kingdom*.

38 Schilbrack, "A Metaphysics," 88–90.

39 E.g., Gorski, "What is Critical Realism?," 661; for the study of religion, see Schilbrack, "A Metaphysics."

40 E.g., Iggers, *Historiography*, 118–133, esp. 118–121; Appleby, Hunt & Jacob, *Telling the Truth about History*, 223–231; Toews, "Intellectual History after the Linguistic Turn," esp. 901–902; Fulbrook, *Historical Theory*, 28–30 and *passim*. For the strictly historiographical debate, see, e.g., the famous controversy between Carlo Ginzburg and Hayden White: Can historians state that the holocaust actually took place, or are we dealing just with the relative "effectiveness" of various holocaust discourses? (Ginzburg, "Just One Witness," here 93).

41 See Watts & Mosurinjohn about the strictly parallel debate in the study of religion, about "whether we, as critical scholars of religion, should focus our energies on mapping the discursive battles over the uses of *religion*, or instead study the cultural structures, collective practices, and social performances that the term *religion* is used to refer to" ("Can Critical Religion Play by Its Own Rules?," 15).

42 Medin & Ortony, "Psychological Essentialism," 184. Psychological essentialism is usefully described here as "a psychologically plausible analog of the logically implausible doctrine of metaphysical essentialism" (ibid., 183). On the metaphysics implied in any linguistic statement that "x *is* y," see the excellent analysis in Steiner, *Martin Heidegger*, 19–72.

43 Asprem and Strube claim incorrectly that I think of "Western" esotericism as some kind of "cultural essence" or "phenomenon" that could then be "diffused" to other parts of the world (see pp. 240–241 note 52). Like some other colleagues, they seem to assume that "studying esotericism," in my understanding, implies a quasi-essentialist project of "demonstrating that x or y is esoteric." Thus Dimitry Okropiridze claims that my work is based on "a thesis of ontological access ('we know esotericism to be x' / 'we know esotericism to be constituted of x, y, z')" ("Interpretation Reconsidered," 224, see also 220, 227, 233). This is an unfortunate misinterpretation. If I insist that historians must do their best to "listen" to what the sources have to tell (Hanegraaff, "Power of Ideas," 255, quoted by Okropiridze, o.c., 220), this does not imply that I expect them to tell us "what esotericism *is*." All they can ever tell us is what historical actor x or y *thinks* it is. Anti-essentialism is a constant in all my work, from "On the Construction of "Esoteric Traditions'" (1998), 11 and *passim*, up to *Esotericism and the Academy* (2012), 3, 363 note 399, 368–369, 377, or "The Power of Ideas" (2013), 258–259, 268 with note 32, 270.

44 Admittedly, this misleading formulation still occurred in the first edition of this book, as it did in the work of my "discursive" critics (e.g., von Stuckrad, *Western Esotericism*, 1; Bergunder, "What is Esotericism?").

45 For readers who would like to connect the dots, my philosophical argument can be reconstructed notably from Hanegraaff, *Esotericism and the Academy*, 361–367; idem, "Power of Ideas," 253–255; idem, "Reconstructing 'Religion'," 578–581; idem, "Religion and the Historical Imagination"; idem, "Imagining the Future Study"; idem, *Hermetic Spirituality*, 348–351, 363–368; idem, "Provincializing American Theory," esp. 510; idem, "Subtle Energies"; idem, "Hermes, Hermeneutics & the Humanities," and Hanegraaff & Mukhopadhyay, "Translating Esotericism."

46 My argument here is consistent with critical realism (note 39) *and* with what Engler and Gardiner call *meaning antirealism* ("[Re]defining Esotericism," 154; and see the important

second response in their "Definition as Situated Interpretational Vector," 284–286). As they point out against several critics, meaning anti-realism should *not* be confused with some form of ontological anti-realism: "meaning is not a function of relations between words and the things they represent or refer to . . . it is just a label for what we end up with as we interpret. . . . In sum, the meaning of a word is not given by what it refers to . . .; it is given only by the myriad overlapping ways in which people share its use" ("Definition as Situated Interpretational Vector," 285). Crucially, this means that "Reference is determined by meaning, not the other way around. . . . *What it is* that our words refer to is not fixed by some sort of mysterious glue between word and object; it reflects how we understand the word" (ibid., 286).

47 Hanegraaff, *Hermetic Spirituality*, esp. 313–317 and 324 note 67. Words without discourse (such as words in a language we do not know) are obviously meaningless as well.

48 Hanegraaff, "Reconstructing 'Religion'," 578–581.

49 Castoriadis, *Imaginary Institution of Society*, 127; see also his key text "Discovery of the Imagination" and the broader argument in Hanegraaff, *Hermetic Spirituality*, 366–368.

50 Here I agree with Harari, *Sapiens*, 30–36, 122–133, 200–201, 406.

51 For the etymological connection between mediation and meaning, see Hanegraaff, *Hermetic Spirituality*, 314 note 22. To prevent new misunderstandings, this argument has nothing to do with Faivre's concept of "imagination/mediation," which is based on a metaphysical-spiritual worldview that comes from Corbin and that I do not share.

52 Hanegraaff & Mukhopadhyay, "Translating Esotericism," 9: "what happens in any act of translation always involves a *transfer* of meaning across a discontinuous gap. . . . This very fact of discontinuity is not just what makes translation *necessary* (because it implies the need for some meaning to be carried across from one language to another) but also what makes translation *possible* (because if there is nothing but continuity, it is impossible for anything to get carried across from anywhere to anywhere else)."

53 My allusion is to Gadamer's famous formulation *Being that can be understood is language* (*Hermeneutik I*, 478; on frequent misinterpretations, see Hanegraaff, *Hermetic Spirituality*, 1 note 1). Therefore, with reference to the previous note, any "mediation" between language and nondiscursive reality implies both discontinuity *and* continuity. As for being that cannot be understood but only experienced, think of Wittgenstein's thesis that what cannot be spoken *shows* itself (*Tractatus* 6.522; but I consider it strangely inconsistent that "that which shows itself" but cannot be spoken would nevertheless be *identified* by Wittgenstein as "the mystical").

54 Knausgård, *A Man in Love*, 144–145; cf. idem, *A Death in the Family*, 241–250. For an interesting analysis of Knausgård's views on post-structuralism and writing, see Magnússon, "Aesthetics of Epiphany."

55 Again, see Engler & Gardiner (above, note 46): "Reference is determined by meaning, not the other way around."

56 Please note what this literally means [*sic!*]: "we try to say (or write) *what we mediate*." This demonstrates the inherent paradoxality of meaning. We can only use mediators to express what goes beyond mediation and can therefore never be said directly or conclusively.

57 Hanegraaff, *Esotericism and the Academy*, 152, 377–379; idem, "Unnecessity of Definition." The ideal of an "anti-eclectic historiography" of Western culture would imply that the con-

tents of its reservoir of "rejected knowledge" will no longer be rejected but will be reintegrated into "normality" so that we no longer need a separate field. I will come back to this in Chapter 9.

58 In terms of a helpful discussion by Bergunder ("What is Religion?," 252 [section 1.2]), I have always adhered to the *second* of his three approaches to definition, at least as far as the study of *esotericism* is concerned. Hence my refusal to provide a definition (see pp. 22–23 and 214 note 60). Bergunder dismisses this second approach as "of course . . . intellectually unsatisfactory" because an academic discipline must be able to define its object. This may be true, but the point is precisely that "the study of esotericism" should not, in my opinion, be seen as an "academic discipline" (such as, e.g., historiography, musicology, semiotics, etc.). I see it simply as the study of *a field* consisting of topics that are set apart for pragmatic reasons (discussed in the following section) and can be approached from a great variety of academic disciplines (NB. As regards the study of *religion*, I see the situation as different and more complicated: I define it not as an object or field but as the "pre-comparative *tertium*" in comparative research under conditions of coloniality; see Hanegraaff, "Reconstructing 'Religion'").

59 Hanegraaff, "Esotericism and Democracy."

60 Contrary to what some of my critics have assumed, this is not an implicit definition of "esotericism." E.g., Engler & Gardiner confuse my reference to "a general label [etc.]" with a definition ("[Re]Defining Esotericism," 11; on what I mean by a label, see Hanegraaff, "Esotericism and Democracy"). If I refer to "esotericism" as rejected knowledge, this does not mean that rejected knowledge = "esotericism" (if I refer to cats as animals, this does not mean either that animals are cats!; Hanegraaff, "Unnecessity of Definition").

61 I hold that a strict theoretical definition of "esotericism" is neither possible nor needed. For a more extensive argumentation, see Hanegraaff, *Esotericism and the Academy*, 368–379; idem, "Unnecessity of Definition"; cf. Pasi, "we do not need a definition but a description" ("Where Is History?," 241).

62 Faivre, "Philosophie de la nature," 92–93. For the essential passage in English see Hanegraaff, *Esotericism and the Academy*, 346; and discussion in Hanegraaff with Brach & Pasi, "Antoine Faivre (1934–2021)," 186–188.

63 Hanegraaff, "Introduction" to *DGWE*, xii. For further backgrounds, see Hanegraaff with Brach & Pasi, "Antoine Faivre (1934–2021)," 195 note 84.

64 The *DGWE* is now seen as the first volume in an ongoing project referred to as the "Brill Esotericism Reference Library" (BERL) that intends to cover previously neglected or unexplored dimensions of the field (see Appendix 2).

65 On the ESSWE's website www.esswe.org, see notably the Israeli Network for the Academic Study of Western Esotericism (INASWE), the Judaism and Western Esotericism Network (JUWE, on Facebook), and the European Network for the Study of Islam and Esotericism (ENSIE).

66 See notably Pasi, "Oriental Kabbalah and the Parting of East and West"; Granholm, "Locating the West"; Asprem, "Beyond the West"; Hanegraaff, "Globalization of Esotericism"; Roukema & Kilner-Johnson, "Editorial: Time to Drop the 'Western'"; and several contributions to Asprem & Strube, *New Approaches*.

67 Asprem & Strube, "Esotericism's Expanding Horizon," esp. 2–8; Strube, "Towards the Study" (repeated in slightly different formulations in a whole series of later publications, e.g., *Global Tantra*, 28); Asprem & Strube, "Afterword"; Finley, Gray & Page, "Africana Esoteric Studies," 165 and *passim.*

68 Personally, I never insisted on the adjective but often dispensed with it, even in several book titles, where the adjective is attached not to "esotericism" but to "culture." That the adjective "Western" might be useful for reasons of historical *method* but does no significant *theoretical* work was one of my central points in Hanegraaff, "Globalization of Esotericism," and stands in stark contrast with Asprem & Strube's thesis that "the pre-theoretical baggage of the adjective Western is . . . exceptionally heavy" ("Esotericism's Expanding Horizon," 4 with note 1, responding to my claim that this burden is "in fact quite light": Hanegraaff, "Globalization of Esotericism," 82–83). My point is that the adjective "Western" *as such* does no heavy lifting of any theoretical kind; it only gets to do so, or seems to do so, in terms of *specific* interpretations, theoretical frameworks, and political agendas that scholars or the wider public may choose to attach to the adjective (in other words, the signifier "West[ern]" is no exception to the core Saussurean insight that no intrinsic connection exists between signifier and signified).

69 For all these developments, see Hanegraaff, *Esotericism and the Academy*, and summary version in Chapter 3 of this book.

70 As regards the contested concept of "paganism," I find myself convinced by the argument of Cameron, *Last Pagans of Rome*, 14–32.

71 By *internal Eurocentrism* (the topic of Chapter 3) I therefore mean a narrow ideological view of what is held to be "central" to European identity, i.e., notably Greek rationalism and so-called "Judeo-Christian" monotheism, while defining everything else as "marginal" to that identity. This notion of an "internal Eurocentrism" is implicit in much of my work at least since Hanegraaff, "Forbidden Knowledge" (2005) and *Esotericism and the Academy* (2012), but I coined it explicitly in a public lecture in 2022 (Hanegraaff, "Esotericism and Democracy"). For an interesting parallel, see the title of Norman Cohn's classic *Europe's Inner Demons* (1975), which describes the European witch hunts and their historical antecedents in terms of Christian attempts at internal "purification" by means of collective exorcism.

72 Justine Bakker seems to consider this agenda too "optimistic" ("Hidden Presence," 494), but I would argue that we have no choice. Deeply embedded distortions cannot be corrected otherwise than by a truly "radical" reconstruction, in the literal sense of going to the root (*radix*) of the problem. In response to Bakker's argument that the adjective in "Western Esotericism" is a "metalanguage for white" ("Hidden Presence," 484–485; cf. similar claims about "Western" as presumably a signifier of whiteness in Finley, Gray & Page, "Africana Esoteric Studies," 165, 182–183), I would argue that the racist denigration and dehumanization of non-white peoples in terms of a normative standard of whiteness is most probably a *secondary* interpretation, built on the historically older and conceptually prior template of internal Eurocentrism (for such an order of development, see, e.g., the documentation in Hughes, *Versions of Blackness*, vii–xxviii and *passim*). Christian Europe's demonized and denigrated Others were originally the "pagan idolaters." Eventually, the metaphorical "darkness" of idolatrous magic would make it easy to denigrate the "darkness" of the "savages'" bodies and presumably their minds (e.g., Conrad, *Heart of Dark-*

ness) by contrasting it with the "light" of civilization brought by white Europeans (see further discussion in Chapter 9, pp. 195–198).

73 Frankopan, *Silk Roads*, xiv: "the axis on which the world spun."

74 For a short outline of the basic argument, see Hanegraaff, *Hermetic Spirituality*, 360–364, with reference especially to Bulliet, *The Case for Islamo-Christian Civilization*; Fowden, *Empire to Commonwealth*; idem, *Before and After Muḥammad*; and Melvin-Koushki, "*Taḥqīq* vs. *Taqlīd*" ("Helleno-Islamo-Judeo-Christian" culture resp. "the Hellenic-Abrahamic synthesis," which I would refer to rather as a continuously evolving Hellenic-Abrahamic *dialectics* that never results in a stable synthesis). With "not as a preparation for Christianity but on its own terms," I mean to reject the deeply problematic Christianity-centered notion of a "Judeo-Christian" culture (Hanegraaff, *Hermetic Spirituality*, 362 with note 36). Concerning my concept of "paganism," see note 70 (Cameron).

75 It should be self-evident (although earlier generations had trouble admitting it) that "Western culture," far from being an isolated or self-contained entity, has always been in fruitful contact and interaction with non-Western cultures (e.g., McEvilley, *Shape of Ancient Thought*).

76 For the time being, the problematic concept of "mysticism" (rather than "esotericism") remains dominant in Jewish studies (see the critical discussion in Huss, *Mystifying Kabbalah*). For attempts at discussing "kabbalah" as a discourse across the boundaries between Judaism and Christianity, see, e.g., Kilcher, *Sprachtheorie der Kabbala*.

77 E.g., Saif, "What Is Islamic Esotericism?"; Sedgwick, "Islamic and Western Esotericism." For critical objections, see, e.g., Gardiner, "Translating Esotericism: Arabic"; Melvin-Koushki, "Translating Esotericism: Early Modern Persian." In placing all their cards on the *ẓāhir/bāṭin* distinction, many participants in this debate seem to be indebted either to an "inner traditions" model or to some form of *esotericism*$_2$. For critique of this implicit focus, which goes at the expense of an *esotericism*$_1$ approach, see Engler & Gardiner, "(Re)Defining Esotericism," 196; Hanegraaff, "Unnecessity of Definition"; Melvin-Koushki, "Definition as (De) colonial Weapon," 233–234; and below, Chapter 9 pp. 193–194. As for the idea of building an entire field on just the term "esoteric(ism)," see Asprem & Strube, "Afterword," 247; critical response in Hanegraaff, "Here, There & Everywhere."

78 For authors and titles, see Chapter 2, pp. 43–49 ("What is Islamic Esotericism").

79 Hanegraaff, "Occult/Occultism," 887–888.

80 There is, however, some good scholarship on specific dimensions, e.g., Magdalino & Mavroudi, *Occult Sciences in Byzantium*; Seng, *Platonismus und Esoterik*.

81 Schäfer, "'Adversus cabbalam'," 204.

82 Hanegraaff & Mukhopadhyay, "Translating Esotericism"; Gaitanidis & Klautau, "(Re)defining Esotericism"; and many contributions to the special issue "Translating Esotericism," in *Correspondences* 11:1 (2023).

83 Otto, "Discourse Theory Trumps Discourse Theory," 239 (surely Otto's intention was to write "Arabic and/or Hebrew" resp. "Islamic and/or Jewish").

84 As regards the Islamic occult sciences, Melvin-Koushki speaks of "many hundred of thousands" of unread manuscripts ("Introduction," 295) to which must be added that many collections are uncatalogued or currently not accessible for political reasons ("Is [Islamic] Occult Science Science?," 314).

Chapter 2

1 Foucault, "Nietzsche, la généalogie, l'histoire," 158.

2 Hadot, *What Is Ancient Philosophy?*

3 The concept of "Platonic Orientalism" was introduced in 2001 by John Walbridge, *Wisdom of the Mystic East*, x, 2–3, 8–12. This terminology is independent of the famous polemics against "Orientalism" associated with the work of Edward Said.

4 Comprehensive discussion in Hanegraaff, *Hermetic Spirituality*. "Hermetism" refers to the original Hermetic literature and its later reception history, whereas "Hermeticism" refers to a broader and more vaguely defined field that, among other things, also includes alchemy (Faivre, "Questions of Terminology," 4, 9; Goodrick-Clarke, "Hermeticism and Hermetic Societies").

5 Currently the most reliable standard edition is the French series in five volumes published by Les Belles Lettres in Paris under the title *Hermes Trismégiste* (vols. 1–2 edited by A.D. Nock and A.-J. Festugière; vols. 3–4 by Festugière; and vol. 5 by Jean-Pierre Mahé). Most English translations (notably the extremely problematic one by Walter Scott) are less than ideal; but Johannes of Stobi's collection is available in an excellent modern translation by M. David Litwa (*Hermetica II*). A groundbreaking new edition and translation of the *Corpus Hermeticum* is forthcoming from Christian Wildberg.

6 For reliable editions and translations see Meyer, *Nag Hammadi Scriptures*; Layton, *Gnostic Scriptures.*

7 The game-changing publications in this regard were Williams, *Rethinking "Gnosticism"*, and King, *What Is Gnosticism?* Short discussions of the basic problematics in Hanegraaff, *Hermetic Spirituality*, 85–86, 353–354; Burns, "Gnosticism, Gnostics, and Gnosis."

8 English translation in Majercik, *Chaldean Oracles.*

9 Jamblique [Iamblichus], *Réponse à Porphyre* (much to be preferred over the older English translation). Discussion of theurgy in Hanegraaff, *Hermetic Spirituality*, 101–118; and see now especially Shaw, *Hellenic Tantra.*

10 The standard abbreviation PGM stands for *Papyri Graecae Magicae*; but the English edition by Betz, *Greek Magical Papyri*, includes the Demotic materials as well. A superior new edition and translation is now in production by Faraone & Torallas Tovar (eds.), *Greek and Egyptian Magical Formularies.* About one-sixth of the Coptic texts are available in Meyer & Smith, *Ancient Christian Magic*; for ongoing research, see the online "Coptic Magical Papyri" website and database https://www.coptic-magic.phil.uni-wuerzburg.de, and Dosoo & Preininger, *Papyri Copticae Magicae*, vol. 1. For a useful overview of the Theban "Magical" library and the history of its discovery, see Dosoo, "History of the Theban Magical Library."

11 Dosoo, "Rituals of Apparition."

12 PGM IV 475–829 (the title is not original but comes from the first modern scholar of this text, Albrecht Dieterich). The current standard edition is Betz, *"Mithras Liturgy,"* and a new edition by Faraone & Toralles Tovar is forthcoming (see above). Discussion in Hanegraaff, *Hermetic Spirituality*, 35–42.

13 Noll, *Jung Cult*, 181–184; Hanegraaff, *New Age Religion*, 505–508 with note 429.

14 Dosoo, “Rituals of Apparition,” 48–55.

15 As far as European languages are concerned, the term “occult sciences” seems to have originated in the sixteenth century with Blaise de Vigenère (1523–1596; “des occultes & secretes sciences, ensevelies pour le present,” *Traicté des chiffres*, 18v). The original concept of a unified *philosophia occulta* comes from Cornelius Agrippa (1486–1535). Discussion in Hanegraaff, *Esotericism and the Academy*, 182–191. On the one hand, this terminology has been criticized with strong arguments by major scholars such as William R. Newman and Lawrence M. Principe; but on the other hand, it is central to important new scholarship, notably in the study of Islamic esotericism (e.g., Saif, Leoni, Melvin-Koushki, & Yahya, *Islamicate Occult Sciences*). In the latter context, “occult sciences” is used as translation of the Arabic standard terminology *ʿulūm khafiyya*, followed later by *ʿulūm al-gharība* for “disciplines that are unusual or difficult,” or “sciences of the weird,” including various mathematical sciences (Melvin-Koushki, “Translating Esotericism: Early Modern Persian,” 104–108).

16 For detailed overviews, see, e.g., Graf, *Magic in the Ancient World*; Bohak, *Ancient Jewish Magic*; Harari, *Jewish Magic*; Copenhaver, *Magic in Western Culture*. For many primary sources in English, see, e.g., Luck, *Arcana Mundi*; and Copenhaver, *Book of Magic*. As regards Jewish magic in later periods, the so-called “practical kabbalah” (*kabbalah ma’asit*) remains un underexplored topic, for which we look forward to a forthcoming PhD dissertation by John MacMurphy.

17 In terms of Bernd-Christian Otto’s key distinction between a polemical *Ausgrenzungsdiskurs* and a self-referential *Aufwertungsdiskurs* (see p. 236 note 10), it is relevant to note that the rough Arabic equivalent *siḥr* is just as problematic, in a similar way. It became an umbrella term for polemicists but was never used as a self-identification by practitioners, though many valorized it as a standard natural science in its own right (Melvin-Koushki, “Powers of One”).

18 See Chapter 6, pp. 134–136. For a particularly incisive modern discussion, see Otto, *Magie*; and for a shorter synthesis, see Hanegraaff, “Magic.”

19 E.g., Clark, *Thinking with Demons*. Overviews in, e.g., Kieckhefer, *Magic in the Middle Ages*; Flint, *Rise of Magic*; Fanger & Klaassen, “Magic III: Middle Ages”; Brach, “Magic IV: Renaissance-17th Century.”

20 Fanger, “Medieval Ritual Magic”; eadem, *Rewriting Magic*.

21 Pingree, “Hellenophilia versus the History of Science,” 560; Thorndike, “True Place of Astrology in the History of Science,” 276.

22 Von Stuckrad, *Das Ringen um die Astrologie*.

23 Melvin-Koushki, “Early Modern Islamicate Empire”; Zarakol, *Before the West*.

24 The best general introduction is Principe, *Secrets of Alchemy*.

25 Hanegraaff, *Hermetic Spirituality*, 77–99.

26 Concerning the controversial topic of Jewish alchemy, see Scholem, *Alchemy and Kabbalah*. The large monograph by Patai, *The Jewish Alchemists*, has been heavily criticized (Freudenthal, Review of Patai; Langermann, Review of Patai).

27 Zuber, *Spiritual Alchemy*.

28 Newman & Principe, “Alchemy vs. Chemistry.”

29 Principe, *Aspiring Adept*; Westfall, *Never at Rest.*

30 See the so-called "New Historiography of Alchemy," represented notably by Lawrence M. Principe and William R. Newman (Principe, *Aspiring Adept*; Newman, *Gehennical Fire*; Newman & Principe, *Alchemy Tried in the Fire*; and many other publications by these authors).

31 On the pivotal role of Mary Anne South (known as Mrs. Atwood), see Zuber, *Spiritual Alchemy*; Hanegraaff, "A Suggestive Inquiry into Hermetic Rebirth."

32 Zuber, *Spiritual Alchemy*, 6.

33 Comprehensive overview and descriptions of textual contents in Schäfer, *Origins of Jewish Mysticism.* For an analysis that emphasizes the dimensions of experiential practice (which are played down by Schäfer), see Davila, *Descenders to the Chariot*; idem, *Hekhalot Literature in Translation.*

34 Schäfer, *Origins of Jewish Mysticism*, 180–185.

35 On the "magical" dimensions during this early period, exemplified by the so-called *Sar-Torah* texts in the Hekhalot literature, see Swartz, *Scholastic Magic.*

36 The concept of *unio liturgica* (as an alternative to *unio mystica*) comes from Schäfer, *Hidden and Manifest God*, 165; Schäfer, *Origins of Jewish Mysticism*, 92, 96, 153, 281, 341, 349.

37 Hayman, *Sefer Yeṣira*; Weiss, *Sefer Yeṣirah and Its Contexts.*

38 Anonymous, *Book of Bahir.*

39 For the visual culture of *ilanot*, see the impressive, abundantly illustrated standard work by Chajes, *Kabbalistic Tree.*

40 Scholem, *Kabbalah*; Garb, *A History of Kabbalah.*

41 On the authorship of the Zoharic literature, see Green, *Guide to the Zohar*, 162–168; Abrams, *Kabbalistic Manuscripts and Textual Theory*, 224–428.

42 For the *Zohar* in English translation, see the multivolume Pritzker edition published by Stanford University Press. There is an enormous amount of scholarship devoted to the *Zohar*. For the reception history, see Huss, *Zohar: Reception and Impact.* For special attention to the experiential dimensions, see Hellner-Eshed, *A River Flows from Eden.*

43 Zohar II, 99a-b; in Scholem, *On the Kabbalah and Its Symbolism*, 55–56. On the levels of Torah exegesis alluded to in this passage, see McAuliffe, Walfish & Goering, *With Reverence for the Word.*

44 Idel, *Mystical Experience of Abraham Abulafia*; idem, *Studies in Ecstatic Kabbalah*; idem, *Language, Torah, and Hermeneutics*; idem, *Abraham Abulafia's Esotericism*; Wolfson, *Abraham Abulafia*; Hames, *Like Angels.*

45 *Shaare Tsedek*; see the long translated passage in Scholem, *Major Trends*, 146–155.

46 Ibid.; and Idel, *The Mystical Experience of Abraham Abulafia*, 13–52; Arzi & Idel, *Kabbalah.*

47 On Luria and his "kabbalistic fellowship," with discussion of all these dimensions, see Fine, *Physician of the Soul.* On these unique practices and related kabbalistic meditations, see MacMurphy, "Are Kabbalistic Meditations All about Ecstasy?"

48 Scholem, *Sabbatai Sevi*; Goldish, *Sabbatean Prophets*; Baer, "Dönme."

49 Idel, *Hasidism.*

50 Garb, *Shamanic Trance in Modern Kabbalah.*

51 Giller, *Shalom Shar'abi.*

52 See Chapter 1, p. 28.
53 Huss, "Ask No Questions."
54 Meir, *Kabbalistic Circles in Jerusalem.*
55 Wolfson, *Open Secret.*
56 Huss, Pasi & von Stuckrad, *Kabbalah and Modernity*; Huss, *Kabbalah and Contemporary Spiritual Revival*; Chajes & Huss, *The Cosmic Movement.*
57 Myers, *Kabbalah and the Spiritual Quest.*
58 On the synthetic function of Islamic culture in systematizing, consolidating, and ultimately becoming the culmination of all these currents from late antiquity, see Fowden, *Before and after Muḥammad.*
59 Melvin-Koushki, "Early Modern Islamicate Empire."
60 The indispensable study, on which I rely in what follows, is Amir-Moezzi, *Divine Guide.*
61 On the central importance of *ʿaql*, see Amir-Moezzi, *Divine Guide*, 6–13.
62 However, see also the Arabic discourse on *ghayb* ("the unseen realm"): Sedgwick, "Islamic and Western Esotericism," 279–281.
63 Asatryan & Burns, "Is Ghulāt Religion Islamic Gnosticism?"
64 The indispensable study is Daftary, *The Ismāʿīlīs* (with an overview of basic Ismāʿīli teachings on pp. 128–136).
65 Here I rely on the excellent historical overview by Knysh, *Islamic Mysticism* (see also his later, more theory-driven volume *Sufism*). An older but still very readable discussion that puts extra emphasis on Sufi poetry is Schimmel, *Mystical Dimensions of Islam.*
66 Discussion in Hanegraaff, *Hermetic Spirituality*, 338–341.
67 Schimmel, *Mystical Dimensions*, 42–47, here 43.
68 Knysh, *Islamic Mysticism*, 52–56, here 54.
69 Ibid., 102–115.
70 Ibid., 140–149.
71 Al-Khalili, *House of Wisdom.*
72 Gutas, *Greek Thought, Arabic Culture*; Adamson & Taylor, *The Cambridge Companion to Arabic Philosophy*; Melvin-Koushki & Gardiner, *Islamicate Occultism*; El-Bizri & Orthmann, *Occult Sciences in Pre-Modern Islamic Cultures*; Brentjes, *Routledge Handbook on the Sciences in Islamicate Societies*; Saif, Leoni, Melvin-Koushki & Yahya, *Islamicate Occult Sciences.*
73 Saif, "Preliminary Study of the Pseudo-Aristotelian Hermetica."
74 For the Hermetic materials, the standard treatment is van Bladel, *Arabic Hermes.*
75 Saif, *Arabic Influences*; eadem, "From *Ġāyat al-ḥakīm* to *Šams al-maʿārif*"; Travaglia, *Magic, Causality and Intentionality* (about al-Kindī). The Latin *Picatrix* is available in an English translation (Attrell & Porreca, *Picatrix*), and a translation of the Arabic original by Liana Saif is forthcoming.
76 Melvin-Koushki, personal communication; Walbridge, *Leaven of the Ancients*; idem, *Wisdom of the Mystic East.* Suhrawardī's *Ḥilmat al-ishrāq* is available in an English translation by John Walbridge & Hossein Ziai (*Suhrawardī: The Philosophy of Illumination*).
77 For Ibn ʿArabī's life, see Addas, *Quest for the Red Sulphur.*
78 Melvin-Koushki, "Translating Esotericism: Early Modern Persian," 110–111.

79 There is no complete translation in English; a translation of selected parts was published under direction of Michel Chodkiewicz (Ibn al ʿArabi, *Meccan Revelations*).

80 Corbin, "*Mundus Imaginalis*"; cf. idem, *Spiritual Body and Celestial Earth*, 135–143 (in connection with a series of other texts by Muslim authors).

81 In this regard, see the discussion of "esotericist reading communities" in Gardiner, "Esotericism in a Manuscript Culture."

82 Gardiner, "Diagrams and Visionary Experience"; idem, "Esotericism in a Manuscript Culture."

83 Ibid.

84 Melvin-Koushki, "An Islamic Scientific Revolution?"

85 Melvin-Koushki, "Is (Islamic) Occult Science Science?," here 311–316; idem, "Better than Sufi Sex."

86 Binbaş, *Intellectual Networks in Timurid Iran*, 106–113; Melvin-Koushki, "New Brethren of Purity."

87 See list of names in Melvin-Koushki, "Introduction," 289–290.

88 Melvin-Koushki, "Ibn Turka" (in EI3); idem, *Occult Philosophers and Philosopher Kings*; idem, "Occult Ecumenism."

89 Melvin-Koushki, "How to Rule the World."

90 Melvin-Koushki, "Is (Islamic) Occult Science Science?," 316.

91 Melvin-Koushki, "Mīr Dāmād's *On Doffing*."

92 Morgan, "Spokesman of the Unseen World."

93 Doostdar, *Iranian Metaphysicals*.

94 Sedgwick, *Western Sufism*.

95 Piraino, *Sufism in Europe*, 94–152.

96 Ibid., 153–215.

97 Piraino, "Between Real and Virtual Communities."

98 Piraino, *Sufism in Europe*, 216–281.

99 Ibid., 282–332; idem, "Esotericisation and De-Esotericisation of Sufism."

100 Surprisingly, there is no comprehensive, up-to-date overview of Renaissance esotericism. Frances Yates's famous bestseller *Giordano Bruno and the Hermetic Tradition* is thoroughly inspiring but outdated and misleading in many respects (Hanegraaff, *Esotericism and the Academy*, 322–334). D. P. Walker's *Spiritual and Demonic Magic* has aged better but still belongs to a bygone era of scholarship. Ioan P. Couliano's *Eros and Magic in the Renaissance* is fascinating but also highly idiosyncratic in its approach. For more recent historical overviews (although even these already date from twenty years ago), see the lengthy entries on "Hermes Trismegistus," "Hermetic Literature," "Hermetism," and "Hermeticism and Hermetic Societies" in Hanegraaff, *Dictionary*.

101 Hasse, *Success and Suppression*; Melvin-Koushki, "*Taḥqīq* vs. *Taqlīd*."

102 Siniossoglou, *Radical Platonism in Byzantium*; Hanegraaff, *Esotericism and the Academy*, 28–41.

103 For an in-depth discussion of the council and the role of Plethon, see now Neugebauer-Wölk, *Kosmologische Religiosität*.

104 Stausberg, *Faszination Zarathushtra*. On Plethon's likely encounters with the New Brethren of Purity see Siniossoglou, "Sect and Utopia in Shifting Empires."

105 English translation (Sears Jayne): Ficino, *Commentary on Plato's Symposium on Love*.

106 Standard edition and translation (Michael J. B. Allen and James Hankins): Ficino, *Platonic Theology* (seven volumes).

107 Under its original title, *Liber de Potestate et Sapientia Dei, Pimander* ("Book on the Power and Wisdom of God, Pimander"), this key edition is available in an affordable facsimile edition. For the problematic transmission of Hermetic treatises by medieval Byzantine scribes, see Hanegraaff, *Hermetic Spirituality*, 123–132.

108 Hanegraaff, "How Hermetic was Renaissance Hermetism?" For an impressive illustrated overview of all these editions, see Gentile & Gilly, *Marsilio Ficino and the Return of Hermes Trismegistus*.

109 Ficino, *Three Books on Life* (ed. Kaske & Clark).

110 Hanegraaff & Bouthoorn, *Lodovico Lazzarelli (1447–1500)* (with editions and English translations of all the relevant sources).

111 Complete edition with translation and commentary in Farmer, *Syncretism in the West*.

112 Especially after the Second World War (with an extremely influential volume *The Renaissance Philosophy of Man* (1948) and later translations by Paul J. W. Miller and colleagues (1965)), generations of students were introduced to Pico's *Oratio* as the ultimate manifesto of modern Humanism and the "dignity of man," suggestive of modern democratic values and human rights. In fact, the contents of Pico's speech are much more traditionally Christian than has been commonly believed (see Copenhaver, *Magic and the Dignity of Man*, and Copenhaver's new edition and translation: Gianfancesco Pico della Mirandola, *Life of Giovanni Pico della Mirandola* & Giovanni Pico della Mirandola, *Oration*). On the other hand, due to Copenhaver's rather traditional view of the Hermetica as tending toward "gnostic" world-denial, he misses the remarkable impact of Hermetic world-*affirmation* on Pico's Oratio. I hope to discuss this point in a future publication.

113 Brach, "Number Symbolism"; idem, "Mathematical Esotericism."

114 The popular paperback translation (Martin and Sarah Goodman) *On the Art of the Kabbalah* (1983) is unfortunately far from reliable. The standard edition of Reuchlin's two main works is in German: Reuchlin, *Sämtliche Werke* (ed. Ehlers, Roloff & Schäfer) I,1 *De verbo mirifico / Das wundertätige Wort* and 1,2 *De arte cabalistica libri tres / Die Kabbalistik*. For Reuchlin's life and his defense of Jewish traditions against the anti-Judaism of his time, see Posset, *Johannes Reuchlin*.

115 François Secret's classic *Les Kabbalistes chrétiens de la Renaissance* (1964; new ed. 1984) has unfortunately never been translated. In the absence of comprehensive histories in English, a useful resource is Dan, *Christian Kabbalah*.

116 Petry, *Gender, Kabbalah and the Reformation*; Kuntz, *Guillaume Postel*. Specifically for the symbolism of numbers, see Postel (Brach, ed.), *Des admirables secrets*.

117 Coudert, *Impact of the Kabbalah in the Seventeenth Century*. For primary sources, see, e.g., Spector, *Francis Mercury van Helmont's Sketch of Christian Kabbalism*; or van Helmont, *Alphabet of Nature*.

118 New English translation by Eric Purdue: Agrippa, *Three Books of Occult Philosophy*.

119 Van der Poel, *Cornelius Agrippa.*

120 On Agrippa's Lazzarellian Hermetism as the key to his worldview, see Hanegraaff, "Better than Magic."

121 Among the many biographies and books devoted to Dee and Kelley, see in particular Clulee, *John Dee's Natural Philosophy*; Szönyi, *John Dee's Occultism*; and Harkness, *John Dee's Conversations with Angels.*

122 Asprem, *Arguing with Angels.* The records of these angelic conversations are now available in annotated facsimile editions: see Casaubon, *True and Faithful Relation*; Klein, *Complete Mystical Records of Dr. John Dee.*

123 For Khunrath and his work, see the definitive four-volume study by Forshaw, *The Mage's Images*; an English translation of the *Amphitheatrum* is forthcoming from the same author as well.

124 Specifically about Copernicanism, see Bruno, *Ash Wednesday Supper* (Hilary Gatti, transl.).

125 Bruno, *On the Heroic Frenzies* (Ingrid Rowland, transl.).

126 Bruno, *Expulsion of the Triumphant Beast* (Arthur D. Imerti, transl.).

127 English translation in Bruno, *Cause, Principle and Unity; and Essays on Magic.*

128 The scholarly literature on Bruno is very extensive. For a reliable biography and scholarly overviews in English, see Rowland, *Giordano Bruno*; and Gatti (ed.), *Giordano Bruno.* On Bruno and mnemonics, see the old classic by Yates, *Art of Memory.*

129 For another, less famous case, see the burning of Quirinus Kuhlmann (a follower of Jacob Böhme, see below) in Moscow, 1689: Collis, *Petrine Instauration*, 1–5.

130 Among the many biographies of Paracelsus in English, I would recommend Weeks, *Paracelsus*; and Webster, *Paracelsus.* It is unfortunate that Alexandre Koyré's brilliant short synthesis of Paracelsus in his *Mystiques, spirituels, alchimistes* has never been translated. Paracelsus's difficult German is a challenge for translators, but see the short selection of fragments in Goodrick-Clarke, *Paracelsus*; and the excellent edition of some important texts translated by Andrew Weeks in *Paracelsus . . . Essential Theoretical Writings* and by Andrew Weeks and Didier Kahn in *Paracelsus . . . Cosmological and Metereological Writings.* Allen G. Debus has traced the international history of Paracelsian "chemical philosophy" in several important monographs.

131 Gilly, "'Theophrastia Sancta'." For Weigel, see Weeks, *Valentin Weigel*; and for English translations, see Weeks's collection *Valentin Weigel: Selected Spiritual Writings.*

132 General overview in Faivre, "The Theosophical Current." For Böhme's life and work, see Weeks, *Boehme*; and Hessayon & Apetrei (eds.), *An Introduction to Jacob Boehme.* For a short synthesis of Böhme's essential worldview, see Hanegraaff, "Jacob Boehme." Excellent English translations of some major works now exist thanks to the labors of Andrew Weeks: see Boehme, *Aurora*; idem, *De Tribus Principiis.*

133 For this entire lineage, see Zuber, *Spiritual Alchemy.*

134 Faivre, "Sensuous Relation" (with English translation of some key passages).

135 Zuber, *Spiritual Alchemy*, 142–159.

136 *The Works of Jacob Behmen* (ed. William Law; 4 volumes; Freher's images toward the end of vols. 3 and 4).

137 For this aspect, see especially Gibbons, *Gender in Mystical and Occult Thought* (focused entirely, in spite of the title, on Christian-Theosophical circles in England).

138 Temme, *Krise der Leiblichkeit.*

139 The only discussion of Oetinger in English is Hanegraaff, *Swedenborg, Oetinger, Kant*, 67–85; for more about *Geistleiblichkeit*, see Deghaye, *La naissance de Dieu* and "Jacob Boehme and his Followers." Oetinger's most important works are the Christian-kabbalistic *Lehrtafel der Prinzessin Antonia* ("Princess Antonia's Educational Tableau"; 1763), *Biblisches und Emblematisches Wörterbuch* ("Biblical and Emblematic Dictionary"; 1776), and *Die Metaphysic in Connexion mit der Chemie* ("Metaphysics in Connection with Chemistry"; 1771). Sadly, none of Oetinger's writings has been translated into English.

140 The best-known book about Saint-Martin in English was written by the occultist amateur historian Arthur Edward Waite, titled *The Unknown Philosopher*; for a reliable modern monograph, see Jacques-Lefèvre, *Louis-Claude de Saint-Martin.* For von Baader, most important are the many studies by Antoine Faivre published in his major monographs, e.g., *Accès* (1996), vol. 1, 138–177, 244–337; vol. 2, 220–240. Von Baader's collective works are available in German: *Sämmtliche Werke* (16 vols.).

141 The indispensable classic remains Viatte, *Les sources occultes du Romantisme* (2 vols.); for the wider context and more titles, see Hanegraaff, *Esotericism and the Academy*, 335–338 (with reference to Eliade, "Occultism and Freemasonry").

142 The three manifestoes are published as Andreae, *Fama Fraternitatis—Confessio Fraternitatis—Chymische Hochzeit* (Richard van Dülmen, ed.). English translation of the first two manifestoes in Yates, *Rosicrucian Enlightenment* (an influential but problematic study that must be read with great caution), 235–260; for the third one, see Anonymous, *Chemical Wedding* (transl. Joscelyn Godwin). For general discussions, see, e.g., Edighoffer, *Les Rose-Croix*; and Bibliotheca Philosophica Hermetica, *Rosenkreuz als europäisches Phänomen.* An overview in English for general readers is McIntosh, *The Rosicrucians.*

143 For Maier, see Tilton, *Quest for the Phoenix.* An old study of Fludd in English is Craven, *Dr. Robert Fludd*; a modern one in German is Rösche, *Robert Fludd.*

144 Fludd's imagery is published separately in Godwin, *Robert Fludd*; and for a similar separate edition of Maier's Emblems, Fugues, and Epigrams, see Maier, *Atalanta Fugiens* (ed. Godwin).

145 See Geffarth, *Religion und arkane Hierarchie*; and for an English study, see McIntosh, *Rose Cross and the Age of Reason.*

146 A useful overview in German is Lamprecht, *Neue Rosenkreuzer.* Shorter overviews in English are Edighoffer, "Rosicrucianism II" and Introvigne, "Rosicrucianism III."

147 For the backgrounds and early history of Freemasonry, see Stevenson, *Origins of Freemasonry*; and for a general introduction to the English development, see Hamill, *The Craft.* A short synthetic discussion of Freemasonry and the notion of intiatic traditions can be found in Hanegraaff, *Esotericism and the Academy*, 207–218. On Freemasonry in America, see Bullock, *Revolutionary Brotherhood.*

148 Next to Viatte, *Les sources occultes du Romantisme* (already mentioned above), indispensable standard works are Le Forestier, *La Franc-Maçonnerie Templière et Occultiste* (2 vols.) and *La Franc-Maçonnerie occultiste.* For the key personality of Willermoz, see Joly, *Un mystique Lyon-*

nais. For modern scholarship in these domains, see many publications by Antoine Faivre; and for an encyclopedic overview in German, see Frick, *Die Erleuchteten.* Unfortunately, there is not much reliable scholarship in English. Harvey's *Beyond Enlightenment* is full of errors and omissions; a more reliable discussion is Collis & Bayer, *Initiating the Millennium.*

149 Faivre, *De Londres à Saint-Pétersbourg.* The expression "man of desire" comes from Saint-Martin (who had been a member of the Elus Coëns) and refers to the desire for spiritual illumination.

150 Dachez, *Histoire illustrée du Rite Écossais Rectifié.*

151 See Neugebauer-Wölk, "Illuminaten."

152 Eco, *Foucault's Pendulum* (unfortunately, the English translation is a fast commercial product that cuts many corners and neglects Eco's many subtle hints and references); Brown's mega bestseller *The Da Vinci Code* is based on a popular pseudo-historical narrative (which has spawned an entire literature of its own) about the supposed "mystery of Rennes-le-Château" outlined, e.g., in Baigent, Leigh & Lincoln, *Holy Blood.*

153 Barruel, *Mémoires*; Robison, *Proofs of a Conspiracy.*

154 Rogalla von Bieberstein, *Mythos von der Verschwörung*; Pierre-André Taguieff, *La foire aux illuminés* (repetitive but full of precious information). For a succinct historical overview in English, see Oberhauser, "Freemasons, Illuminati and Jews."

155 Introvigne, *Satanism*, 158–226.

156 The indispensable standard work is Kreis, *Quis ut Deus?*

157 Cohn, *Warrant for Genocide*; Taguieff, *Hitler, les Protocoles.*

158 Hanegraaff, *Esotericism and the Academy*, 218–256.

159 Asprem, *Problem of Disenchantment*; Josephson Storm, *Myth of Disenchantment.* On the relation between Enlightenment and esotericism, see the excellent trilogy of collective volumes in German edited by Monica Neubauer-Wölk and collaborators as *Aufklärung und Esoterik* (1999; 2008; 2013).

160 Lamm, *Emanuel Swedenborg*; Benz, *Emanuel* Swedenborg; Hanegraaff, *Swedenborg, Oetinger, Kant*; Stengel, *Aufklärung bis zum Himmel.* For Swedenborg's wider cultural influences, see, e.g., Larsen, Larsen, Lawrence, & Woofenden, *Emanuel Swedenborg*; Rose, Shotwell, & Bertucci, *Scribe of Heaven.* Swedenborg's writings are available in excellent English translations (the "New Century Edition") published by the American Swedenborg Foundation.

161 Crabtree, *From Mesmer to Freud*; Gauld, *History of Hypnotism*; Meheust, *Somnambulisme et médiumnité* (2 vols.); Winter, *Mesmerized.* For the development of modern psychology and psychiatry out of somnambulism, see Ellenberger, *Discovery of the Unconscious.*

162 A good standard history is Oppenheim, *The Other World.* For the American context, see, e.g., Moore, *In Search of White Crows*; Gutierrez, *Plato's Ghost.* For France, see Monroe, *Laboratories of Faith.* For Germany, see Sawicki, *Leben mit den Toten.*

163 Ellenberger, *Discovery of the Unconscious*; Hanegraaff, *Esotericism and the Academy*, 260–295.

164 See critical analysis in Hanegraaff, "Imagining the Unconscious."

165 For the lineage that leads from somnambulism to New Thought, see, e.g., Fuller, *Mesmerism and the American Cure of Souls*; and for the broader phenomenon of American "Meta-

physical Religion," see Albanese, *Republic of Mind and Spirit*. For the "creating our own reality" concept, see Hanegraaff, *New Age Religion*, 229–245. As for the popular contemporary doctrine of "manifestation," see Rhonda Byrne's mega bestseller *The Secret* (2006).

166 E.g., Faivre & Zimmermann, *Epochen der Naturmystik*; Zimmermann, *Das Weltbild des jungen Goethe*; Faivre, *Philosophie de la nature*; Hanegraaff, "Romanticism and the Esoteric Connection."

167 Hanegraaff, "Imagining the Unconscious," 566.

168 Hanegraaff, *Swedenborg, Oetinger, Kant*, 87–114. See, e.g., Goethe's *Faust* (*Die Geisterwelt ist nicht verschlossen; Dein Sinn ist zu, dein Herz ist todt!*: "the world of spirits is not closed; it's your sense that is shut; it's your heart that is dead!"); or Schelling's *Clara*.

169 Kerner, *Seherin von Prevorst*. Discussion in Hanegraaff, "A Woman Alone"; idem, "Versuch über Friederike Hauffe" (2 parts); idem, "Carl August von Eschenmayer and the Somnambulic Soul." Kerner's writings are just the tip of a very large iceberg: there is a stunning number of nowadays forgotten books, pamphlets, and specialized popular journals devoted entirely to the meticulous description of innumerable somnambulic cases. Kerner himself edited two such periodicals, *Blätter aus Prevorst* and *Magikon*, but there were many others.

170 Still the most reliable historical overview, although very difficult to read, is Laurant, *L'ésotérisme chrétien*.

171 Unfortunately, the best scholarship is usually not in English. The well-known old study by James Webb, *Occult Underground*, may still be the most readable general overview in English even today. For Eliphas Lévi and his political-occultist contexts, the standard reference is now Strube, *Sozialismus, Katholizismus und Okkultismus*. Lévi's occultist works are conveniently published together in a recent edition titled *Secrets de la magie*; instead of the unreliable old translation by A.E. Waite, see the recent one by John Michael Greer and Mark Anthony Mikituk (2017).

172 See below, Chapter 8, pp. 175, 178, 180–181. As a first introduction, see the popular overview by Churton, *Occult Paris*.

173 Introvigne, "Martinism: Second Period."

174 McCalla, "Fabre d'Olivet."

175 Laurant, "Saint-Yves d'Alveydre."

176 Chaitow, *Son of Prometheus*.

177 Toth, "Gnostic Church."

178 See, e.g., Faxneld, *Satanic Feminism*.

179 The two indispensable standard works are Introvigne, *Satanism*; and van Luijk, *Children of Lucifer*. For an extremely useful reader of primary sources, see Faxneld & Nilsson, *Satanism*.

180 Guénon, *L'erreur spirite*; idem, *Le Théosophisme*.

181 See notably Guénon, *Introduction générale*; idem, *La crise du monde moderne*; idem, *Le règne de la quantité et les signes des temps*.

182 Olesen, "Perennial Solidarity of the East."

183 The standard refence on this topic (obviously with much attention to Guénon) is now Sedgwick, *Traditionalism*.

184 Evola's deep involvement in Italian fascism and German National-Socialism is carefully documented in Hansen (ps. of Hans Thomas Hakl), "Introduction: Julius Evola's Political Endeavors" (and for further updates based on later research, see Baroni, "Philosophical Gold," 45–47). For Evola's virulent anti-Semitism (which was not just "spiritual," as often argued by his apologists), see Lloyd Thomas, *Julius Evola e la tentazione razzista*. We are anticipating a major critical study on Evola, esotericism, and politics by Peter Staudenmaier. Meanwhile, see the careful analyses in Sedgwick, *Traditionalism* (above).

185 Houman, *From the* Philosophia Perennis *to American Perennialism.*

186 Pasi, "Modernity of Occultism."

187 Godwin, *Theosophical Enlightenment.*

188 For Blavatsky's biography, see Keller & Sharandak, *Madame Blavatsky* (unfortunately not yet available in English).

189 Britten is now widely seen as the real author; but note that she attributed both volumes to a mysterious "Chevalier Louis de B—," who claimed that the book was not fictional but based entirely on fact. Discussion in Hanegraaff, "Western Esotericism and the Orient in the First Theosophical Society," 38–46.

190 For the story of these key volumes by Britten and Blavatsky and the "Western" focus of early Theosophy combined with its Orientalist perspectives, see Hanegraaff, "Western Esotericism and the Orient in the First Theosophical Society"; idem, "The Theosophical Imagination."

191 For the development of Theosophy in the context of Bengal, see Strube, *Global Tantra*; Mukhopadhyay, "Occult World of Bengalis." Two modern collectives volumes about Theosophy East and West are Rudbøg & Reenberg Sand, *Imagining the East*; and Krämer & Strube, *Theosophy Across Boundaries.*

192 See Nethercot, *First Five Lives of Annie Besant*; idem, *Last Four Lives of Annie Besant*; Tillett, *The Elder Brother*; Mühlematter, *Accelerating Human Evolution.*

193 For Anthroposophy with a focus on its Theosophical backgrounds, the standard work is Zander, *Anthroposophie in Deutschland.* For the German Idealist backgrounds, see the many extensive introductions by Christian Clement in the multivolume critical edition of Steiner, *Schriften.*

194 Deveney, *Paschal Beverly Randolph.*

195 The standard history is Howe, *Magicians of the Golden Dawn.*

196 Greer, *Women of the Golden Dawn.*

197 Pasi, "Oriental Kabbalah and the Parting of East and West."

198 On the many Crowley biographies, see overview by Pasi, "Never-endingly Told Story." For a solid volume of scholarship, see Bogdan & Starr, *Aleister Crowley and Western Esotericism.*

199 Asprem, *Problem of Disenchantment*; Josephson Storm, *Myth of Disenchantment.*

200 For a now classic analysis, see Luhrmann, *Persuasions of the Witch's Craft.*

201 Moore, *Gurdjieff*; Webb, *Harmonious Circle.* Special issues have been devoted to Gurdjieff in *Aries* 20:1 (2020) and *Correspondences* 8:2 (2020).

202 Kaplan & Lööw, *The Cultic Milieu* (with a reprint of Colin Campbell's classic 1972 essay "The Cult, the Cultic Milieu and Secularization"); Partridge, "Occulture is Ordinary"; and for an encyclopedic overview, see Partridge, *Re-Enchantment of the West* (2 vols.).

203 Horkheimer & Adorno, *Dialectics of Enlightenment*, 94–136.

204 Hanegraaff, *New Age Religion*, 94–110, 331–361; Sutcliffe, *Children of the New Age*; idem, "Origins of 'New Age' Religion."

205 An early anthropological classic is Festinger, Riecken & Schachter, *When Prophecy Fails.* The phenomenon of UFO religions is now an entire research field in its own right (see, e.g., Lewis, *The Gods Have Landed*; Partridge, *UFO Religions*). For the importance of UFOs in major black esoteric traditions such as the Nation of Islam, see, e.g., Finley, "Mathematical Theology," and idem, *In and Out of This World.*

206 For a strongly engaged discussion of key figures such as Charles Fort and Jacques Vallee, see Kripal, *Authors of the Impossible.* For an important structural analysis of esoteric myth and symbolism in famous American superhero comics, see idem, *Mutants and Mystics.*

207 Renard, "Le mouvement *Planète*"; Eliade, "Cultural Fashions," 8–9; Karbovnik, "L'échec d'une 'religion' New Age." *Planète*'s parallel publishing ventures were *Pianeta* (Italy), *Planeta* (Argentinia), *Horizonte* (Spain), *Planet* (Germany), and *Bres* (the Netherlands).

208 Karbovnik, "L'ésotérisme grand public."

209 Baigent, Leigh & Lincoln, *Holy Blood*; Brown, *Da Vinci Code.*

210 For the historical origins of the Atlantis/Lemuria/Mu myth in late-nineteenth-century speculative historiography and occultism, see Sprague de Camp, *Lost Continents.* On the history of Lemuria in the Orientalist/Colonialist imagination East and West, see Ramaswany, *Lost Land of Lemuria.* The theme remains extremely popular today, as seen notably by the bestselling books by Graham Hancock and his 2022 Netflix documentary *Ancient Apocalypse.*

211 For a still indispensable historicization of "The Modern Mythology of Nazi Occultism," see Goodrick-Clarke, *Occult Roots of Nazism*, 217–225. To a disturbing extent, this mythology keeps influencing even some modern historians who write books on Nazism for the general public, such as Kurlander, *Hitler's Monsters* (see Strube, Review of Kurlander; Kingsepp, "Scholarship as Simulacrum").

212 Title of Pauwels & Bergier, *Le matin des magiciens*, Part Three. On the importance of this theme to their oeuvre, see Mette & Karbovnik, "La condition surhumaine." For a recent exploration of "the superhuman" indebted to the same traditions in American popular culture (superhero comics, UFOs, the paranormal, "the unexplained") but without any overt references to Pauwels & Bergier or the *Planète* tradition, see Kripal, *Superhumanities.*

213 For general discussions, see Butter & Knight, *Routledge Handbook of Conspiracy Theories.* For special attention to esotericism in this context, see, e.g., Taguieff, *La foire aux Illuminés*; Dyrendal, Robertson & Asprem, *Handbook of Conspiracy Theory*; Piraino, Pasi & Asprem, *Religious Dimensions of Conspiracy Theories.*

214 Adler, *Drawing down the Moon*; Hutton, *Triumph of the Moon*; Luhrmann, *Persuasions of the Witch's Craft*; Clifton & Harvey, *Paganism Reader.*

215 Gardell, *Gods of the Blood.*

216 Johnston & Aloi, *New Generation Witches*; Berger & Ezzy, *Teenage Witches*; Boorstein, "From Spellcasting to Podcasting."

217 Lucas, "Summit Lighthouse"; Whitsel, *The Church Universal and Triumphant*; Prophet, *Prophet's Daughter.*

218 Refslund Christensen, "Scientology"; Lewis, *Scientology*; Urban, *The Church of Scientology*; Westbrook, *Among the Scientologists.*

219 Introvigne, "Rosicrucianism III"; Lamprecht, *Neue Rosenkreuzer.*

220 Cusack, *Invented Religions*; many contributions to Possamai, *Handbook of Hyper-Real Religions*; Greer, "Angel-Headed Hipsters"; idem, "The Psychedelic Church Movement"; Davis, *High Weirdness.*

221 Williams, "Hakim Bey and Ontological Anarchism"; Greer, "Hakim Bey" (and see his chapter on Hakim Bey in "Angel-Headed Hipsters").

222 Urban, *Magia Sexualis*, 222–54. The foundational title of chaos magic was Carroll, *Liber Null & Psychonaut.*

223 The basic primary source is Breyer P-Orridge, *Thee Psychick Bible.*

224 Dowling, *Aquarian Gospel of Jesus the Christ*; Notovich, *La vie inconnue de Jésus Christ.* On these and many other similar texts, see Goodspeed, *Modern Apocrypha.*

225 Knight, *Five Percenters*, 19.

226 Ibid., 21–28.

227 Fard Muhammad, *Supreme Wisdom Lessons*, 14–15; summary in Urban, *Secrecy*, 111–113. See also Knight, "'I am Sorry, Mr. White Man'"; idem, *Supreme Wisdom Lessons.*

228 Malcolm X's post-*hajj* letter: Knight, *Five Percenters*, 44.

229 Fard Muhammad, *Supreme Wisdom Lessons*, 26–27.

230 For an excellent detailed history, see Knight, *Five Percenters.*

231 Urban, *Secrecy*, 130; Knight, *Five Percenters*, 55.

232 Urban, *Secrecy*, 117. For a nuanced analysis, see Knight, *Five Percenters*, 5 and *passim.*

233 Knight, *Five Percenters*, 49–54.

234 Urban, *Secrecy*, 120 (referring to Umberto Eco).

235 Discussion in Urban, *Secrecy*, 122–130.

236 On this "New Age *sensu lato*," as distinct from the original "New Age *sensu stricto*," see Hanegraaff, *New Age Religion.*

237 Hanegraaff, *New Age Religion*, 62–76.

238 Hutton, *Shamans*; Znamenski, *Beauty of the Primitive.*

239 Eliade, *Shamanism.*

240 Castaneda, *Teachings of Don Juan.*

241 Harner, *Way of the Shaman.*

242 Grof, *Beyond the Brain.*

243 McKenna, *True Hallucinations*; Pinchbeck, *2012.*

244 Dobkin de Rios & Rumrrill, *Hallucinogenic Tea*; Labate & Jungaberle, *Internationalization of Ayahuasca*; Labate & Cavnar, *Ayahuasca Shamanism.*

245 E.g., Sylvan, *Trance Formation*; Hanegraaff, "Entheogenic Esotericism." On the role of "entheogenic" or psychoactive substances in modern and contemporary esotericism, see the fascinating study by Partridge, *High Culture.*

246 Braden et al., *Mysteries of 2012*; Hanegraaff, "'And End History. And go to the Stars'."

247 Zuboff, *The Age of Surveillance Capitalism.*

248 Sedgwick, *Traditionalism*; and idem, *Key Thinkers of the Radical Right.*

249 The term was coined by Victoria Nelson, *Secret Life of Puppets*; see also her *Gothica.*

Chapter 3

1 Michel de Montaigne, *Essays* 23.
2 Hammer & von Stuckrad, "Introduction."
3 Hanegraaff, "Religion and the Historical Imagination."
4 For this important concept, see Assmann, *Moses the Egyptian.*
5 This chapter relies on the book-length exposition in Hanegraaff, *Esotericism and the Academy*.
6 Of central importance in this regard is the "coloniality of knowledge" concept pioneered by Aníbal Quiano ("Coloniality and Modernity/Rationality"). See, e.g., Mignolo, *Darker Side of Western Modernity*, 18 *et passim*. With reference to a critique by Asprem, "Rejected Knowledge Reconsidered," 130–131, I argue that we *are* in fact dealing with what he calls "a persistent structural injustice at the heart of 'Western culture'." As further explained in Chapter 9, pp. 192–198, I see this as the chief internal-European precedent and intellectual template of "legitimation" for the eventual injustices of colonial domination (cf. pp. 215–216 notes 71–72).
7 Concerning my terminological choice for the "paganism" rubric, p. 215 note 70.
8 Halbertal & Margalit, *Idolatry*, 237.
9 Tertullian, *De praescriptione haereticorum* 7.9.
10 Droge, *Homer or Moses?*
11 Origen, *Contra Celsum* 5.33, 8.2.
12 Eusebius, *Praep. Evang.* I.2.4 (Droge, *Homer or Moses?*, 175).
13 See above, Chapter 2, p. 32 with note 3.
14 Augustine, *Retractationes* I.1.2.3.
15 Augustine, *De Civitate Dei* VIII.5.9. Augustine did, however, reject Hermes Trismegistus as an idolater (ibid., VIII.2.3-4).
16 King, *What is Gnosticism?*, 29–30.
17 As demonstrated in detail by King, *What Is Gnosticism?*
18 Weyer, *De praestigiis daemonum* II.3.
19 Hanegraaff, *Esotericism and the Academy*, 83–86.
20 George of Trebizond, *Comparatio philosophorum Platonis et Aristotelis* (responding to Plethon); see Hanegraaff, *Esotericism and the Academy*, 78–79.
21 Pattison, *Isaac Casaubon*, 322.
22 The indispensable study is available only in German: Lehmann-Brauns, *Weisheit in der Weltgeschichte*. For a complete version of the argument in this section, see Hanegraaff, *Esotericism and the Academy*, Chapter Two.
23 May, *Creatio ex Nihilo*.
24 Colberg, *Platonisch-Hermetisches Christenthum*, vol. 1.5.
25 Ibid., vol. 1.116.
26 Arnold, *Historie und Beschreibung*, 15–16 (chapt. 1.19).
27 Albrecht, *Eklektik*.
28 Daniel Georg Morhof (1639–1691) was a well-known scholar, known best for his encyclopedic *Polyhistor* (1688–1707). For these and similar books as early modern repositories of

traditional information about "barbarian philosophy," cf. Hanegraaff, *Esotericism and the Academy*, 101 with note 86.

29 Heumann, "Von denen Kennzeichen der falschen und unächten Philosophie," 209–211. Julian Strube wants to see this passage as evidence for the new interest of European scholars for Oriental religions such as Brahmanism or the Chinese *I Ching*, and for Persian, Arabic, and Asian languages such as Sanskrit ("Emergence of 'Esoteric'," 362). On the contrary, far from wishing to support new research programs focused on Oriental languages and traditions, Heumann was simply quoting the old Platonic-Orientalist tropes of "barbarian philosophy" in order to *dismiss* "idolatry" from the domain of serious scholarship as "superstitious nonsense." What Strube presents as early modern evidence for a genuine interest in non-Western "esotericism" actually exemplifies Western agendas, in the colonial era, of erasing "superstition" from Europe and the rest of the world! On this important point, see also Chapter 9, pp. 193–198.

30 Voltaire, *Treatise on Tolerance and Other Writings*, 83; idem, *Dictionnaire philosophique*, 394, 396.

31 Subtitle of Gay, *The Enlightenment: An Interpretation*, vol. 2: *The Rise of Modern Paganism.*

32 Hanegraaff, *Esotericism and the Academy*, 260–277.

33 Hanegraaff, *New Age Religion*, 302–330.

34 Hanegraaff, *Esotericism and the Academy*, 277–295.

35 Hakl, *Eranos*; Hanegraaff, "Generous Hermeneutics."

36 Eliade, *Myth of Eternal Return*, Chapter 4.

37 Hanegraaff with Brach and Pasi, "Antoine Faivre (1934–2021)."

38 Hanegraaff, *Esotericism and the Academy*, 377–378.

Chapter 4

1 Clement of Alexandria, *Excerpta ex Theodoto*, 78.

2 Salinger, "Teddy," 138.

3 For an excellent analysis, see Loy, *Nonduality*.

4 For this critique of Kashmir Śaivism directed at Advaita Vedānta, see Dyczkowski, *Doctrine of Vibration*, 36–38; Hanegraaff, *Hermetic Spirituality*, 359 note 27; and cf. idem, "A Poem" (Parmenides).

5 Anonymus, *A Course in Miracles*; Hanegraaff, *New Age Religion*, 37–38, 115–116.

6 Hanegraaff, *New Age Religion*, 128–132.

7 CH I 3–8. Discussion in Hanegraaff, *Hermetic Spirituality*, 163–167, 359–360.

8 Hanegraaff, *Hermetic Spirituality*, 99–118 (with reference to Plato, *Symp* 206e on p. 106), 187–194; Shaw, *Hellenic Tantra.*

9 Plato, *Rep.* 514a–520a.

10 Van Rijckenborgh and De Petri, *De Chinese Gnosis*, 140–141.

11 I put "gnostic" between quotation marks because this concept of "gnosticism" is no longer supported by modern research (see Chapter 2, p. 33–34).

12 The classic description of this perspective is Jonas, *The Gnostic Religion*; but see discussion in Hanegraaff, *Hermetic Spirituality*, 353–354.

13 *Manichaean Psalms of Thomas* 8.

14 E.g., Stoyanov, *The Other God*.

15 Bogdan, "Explaining the Murder-Suicides of the Order of the Solar Temple"; Introvigne, "Ordeal by Fire"; Zeller, "Euphemization of Violence."

16 Lovejoy, *Great Chain of Being*, 315.

17 This concept of the "alien God" was popularized by von Harnack, *Marcion* (see the subtle of his book). Partly in the wake of Nietzsche's "death of God," it became a kind of intellectual obsession for many scholars of esoteric traditions before and shortly after the Second World War, notably André-Jean Festugière and Hans Jonas (Hanegraaff, *Hermetic Spirituality*, 317 with note 30, 353).

18 For the centrality of the *pēgē* to the Hermetica, see Hanegraaff, *Hermetic Spirituality*, esp. 54–58 and 264–307.

19 Concerning my choice for the word "imaginal": in this context, the concept of "creative imagination" does not mean that the universe is just an illusion or fantasy. On the contrary, imagination is understood as an *active* force of manifestation through which God literally "imagines the world into existence" (see discussion in Hanegraaff, *Hermetic Spirituality*, 231 with note 39).

20 Pico della Mirandola, *Oration* 6 (Copenhaver ed., 82–84).

21 Plato, *Phaedrus* 246a–257b.

22 Copenhaver points out that the title *De hominis dignitate* does not come from Pico but was added by Jerome Emser in 1504 ("Introduction," xxxvi–xxxvii); yet Emser's title is remarkably appropriate given the actual concept of human dignity that Pico adopted from the Hermetic *Asclepius* (Hanegraaff, "Hermetic Freedom and Human Dignity").

23 Pope, *An Essay on Man* I: 3–18.

24 Ficino, *Three Books on Life* (Kaske & Clarke, eds.), 236–393.

25 On the problematics of "mysticism" as a scholarly category see, e.g., Schmidt, "Making of Modern 'Mysticism'"; for the Jewish context, see Huss, *Mystifying Kabbalah*.

26 *Ascl.* 23–24, 37–38. Discussion in Hanegraaff, *Hermetic Spirituality*, 61–72.

27 Augustine, *De Civitate Dei* 8.

28 E.g., Weil-Parot, "Astral Magic and Intellectual Changes."

29 Hanegraaff, "Better than Magic."

30 Hanegraaff, *New Age Religion*, 203–255, esp. 229–245.

31 Kripal, *Mutants and Mystics*; idem, *The Superhumanities*.

32 CH XI 20–22.

33 Versluis, *American Transcendentalism and Asian Religions*; for the Hermetic connection, including Bucke, see Hanegraaff, *Hermetic Spirituality*, 254–255.

34 E.g., Lazier, *God Interrupted*; on this shift away from existential pessimism after the Second World War, see Hanegraaff, *Hermetic Spirituality*, 354–358.

35 On Esalen as the center of this "Human Potential Movement," see Anderson, *Upstart Spring*; Kripal, *Esalen*.

36 Hanegraaff, "Roberts, Dorothy Jane."

37 Baur, *Epochen der kirchlichen Geschichtsschreibung*, 40.

38 For the sexual dimension see Principe, "Revealing Analogies"; Gibbons, *Gender in Mystical and Occult Thought.*

39 Oetinger, *Biblisches und emblematisches Wörterbuch*, vol. 1, 223.

40 E.g., Kilcher & Theisohn, *Enzyklopädik der Esoterik.*

41 For instance Baur, *Die christliche Gnosis*; Benz, *Schellings theologische Geistesahnen*; Zimmermann, *Das Weltbild des jungen Goethe*; Faivre & Zimmermann, *Epochen der Naturmystik*; Faivre, *Philosophie de la nature*; Magee, *Hegel and the Hermetic Tradition.*

42 Hanegraaff, *New Age Religion*, 462–482; and see Chapter 7, pp. 159–162.

43 Hanegraaff, *New Age Religion*, 482–513; and see Chapter 7, pp. 162–165.

44 Hanegraaff, *Esotericism and the Academy*, 266–277.

45 Ibid., 277–295.

46 Jung, *The Black Books* (7 vols.); idem, *The Red Book.* Discussion in Baier, "Das Rote Buch"; Hanegraaff, "The Great War of the Soul."

Chapter 5

1 Crowley, *The Solitudes*, 219 (cf. 104–105).

2 Von Stuckrad, *Locations of Knowledge*, 60–61.

3 Plutarch, "Isis and Osiris" 9 (354c): "In Saïs, the statue of Athena, whom they believe to be Isis, bore the inscription 'I am all that has been, and is, and shall be, and no mortal has yet uncovered my robe'."

4 Plato, *Phaedrus* 249d; *Symposium* 211d-212a (Hanegraaff, *Hermetic Spirituality*, 190–194).

5 On the foundational concept of the three "transcendentals" (Beauty, Goodness, Truth), see Hanegraaff, *Hermetic Spirituality*, 187–194 (and consult the Index under "Goodness-Beauty-Truth").

6 For such conceptions of an ultimate One beyond Being, "the *Nous* of the luminous *Nous*," the ultimate Good, or Source (*pēgē*), see Hanegraaff, *Hermetic Spirituality*, 266–271.

7 I am aware of the standard counterargument that, e.g., states of mystical unity experienced in deep meditation can be checked "independently" by practicing meditation. For instance, in a well-known older study, Frits Staal argued that mysticism can be studied scientifically by learning how to induce mystical experiences (Staal, *Exploring Mysticism*). But the argument is flawed. First of all, even *if* we assume that the researcher succeeds in having a "mystical" experience, he will still be in no better position than any traditional "mystic" in trying to communicate the ineffable by means of discursive language. He will meet the same language barrier that has traditionally frustrated all attempts to discover the "true" nature of mysticism. In Staal's case, the implicit assumption is that mystical talk about "ineffability" is just a reflection of nonscientific obscurantism or irrationalism. However, if the scientist would be able to describe his particular experience in precise discursive language, "mystics" would have perfectly good reasons to respond that, therefore, whatever experience he had cannot have been a "mystical" one! To refute that argument, Staal would have to solve the formidable (and, as far as I can tell, unsurmountable) prob-

lem of how to verify *independently* that an independent researcher's experience X, induced for scientific reasons, will actually be the same as the "mystic"'s experience Y, induced for spiritual reasons.

8 The triad comes from the title of a Dutch volume published in 1988 (Quispel, *Gnosis: De derde component*). This does not mean that I adopt some kind of Jungian-Quispelian religionism, as assumed incorrectly by Burns ("Gnosticism, Gnostics, and Gnosis," 17–21; see my response in *Hermetic Spirituality*, 86 note 33) and Robertson (*Gnosticism and the History of Religions*, 123–136; including a suspicion of "essentialism" on which see Chapter 1, pp. 19–20). For my refutation of Quispel's approach, see Hanegraaff, "Reason, Faith, and Gnosis," esp. 138; for the story of my personal relation to Quispel, whose approach I rejected already during my years as a student, see Hanegraaff, "The Third Kind."

9 CH IX 10. Note that I interpret *alētheia* as "what is real" (in line with Litwa, *Hermetica II*, 30 note 1; Hanegraaff, *Hermetic Spirituality*, 201 note 57): in a Hermetic context, ultimate truth and ultimate reality are one and the same. The final sentence is ambiguous (see remarks in Hanegraaff, "Altered States of Knowledge," 134 note 16); in my understanding, whether or not we insert the word *ou* (not), the intention is that *logos* can get you all the way to the very edge of what is ultimately real, while only *nous* can take the extra step of attaining reality itself.

10 E.g., Stengel, *Aufklärung bis zum Himmel.*

11 Van der Poel, *Cornelius Agrippa.*

12 Hanegraaff, *New Age Religion*, 62–76, 113–181.

13 For rare exceptions, see Fowden, *Egyptian Hermes*, 105–114; Faivre, "Le terme et la notion de 'gnose'" ; Hanegraaff, "Gnosis." My monograph *Hermetic Spirituality* is an attempt to fill the lacuna by deep exploration of a central tradition that was all about attaining *gnōsis.*

14 Festugière, *La révélation d'Hermès Trismégiste*, vol. 4, 267; Fowden, *Egyptian Hermes*, 215.

15 NH VI^{6} 57:31-58:7. Discussion in Hanegraaff, *Hermetic Spirituality*, 298–301.

16 Walbridge, *Leaven of the Ancients*; Hanegraaff, *Hermetic Spirituality*, 335–341.

17 Suhrawardī, *Ḥikmat al-ishrāq* II.2.165-166 (Suhrawardī, *Philosophy of Illumination*, 107–108).

18 CH X 5–6.

19 Pfister, "Ekstase"; and see now the exhaustive study by Ustinova, *Divine Mania.*

20 Detailed analysis of these successive stages in Hanegraaff, *Hermetic Spirituality*, 145–307.

21 For my take on "mysticism," see Hanegraaff, "Teaching Experiential Dimensions," 154–158; and for a historicization of the concept, see Schmidt, "Making of Modern 'Mysticism'." For "Magic," see Chapter 6, pp. 134–136; and Hanegraaff, "Magic." For "Shamanism," see, e.g., Flaherty, *Shamanism and the Eighteenth Century*; Hutton, *Shamans*; Znamenski, *Beauty of the Primitive.*

22 Barušs, *Alterations of Consciousness.* See also the fascinating two-volume collection by Cardeña & Winkelman, *Altering Consciousness.*

23 The classic reference is Tart, *Altered States of Consciousness.*

24 Ludwig, "Altered States of Consciousness."

25 As regards sensory deprivation, see the exemplary study by Ustinova, *Caves and the Ancient Greek Mind*; for sensory overload, one could think of countless types of group ritual, for

instance, Bahian Candomblé (e.g., van de Port, *Ecstatic Encounters*) or contemporary rave culture (Sylvan, *Trance Formation*). Next to states of hypoalertness such as common day-dreaming (and indeed, dreaming itself), an excellent example of hyperalertness in esoteric contexts would by the ecstatic kabbalah of Abraham Abulafia (Idel, *Mystical Experience of Abraham Abulafia*, 13–52; and Scholem, *Major Trends*, 146–155).

26 The importance of trauma has been emphasized particularly by Kripal, e.g., *Authors of the Impossible*.

27 The classic statement comes from William James in *The Varieties of Religious Experience*: "Our normal waking consciousness, rational consciousness as we call it, is but one special type of consciousness, whilst all about it, parted from it by the filmiest of screens, there lie potential forms of consciousness entirely different. We may go through life without suspecting their existence; but apply the requisite stimulus, and at a touch they are there in all their completeness."

28 By contrast, the traditional perspective is exemplified, e.g., by Festugière's insistence on Hermetic accounts as "historical fictions," with the argument that "for us, moderns, it is evident that the Hellenistic stories of revelation contain absolutely no foundation of truth" and the accounts of ecstasies or celestial ascents "[do] not concern a real fact but a psychological phenomenon" (*La révélation*, vol. 1, 309; criticized in Hanegraaff, *Hermetic Spirituality*, 36 with note 52).

29 Geertz, "Religion as a Cultural System."

30 Plato, *Phaedrus* 249d.

31 Hanegraaff, "Platonic Frenzies in Marsilio Ficino"; idem, "Under the Mantle of Love."

32 Hanegraaff, "How Hermetic Was Renaissance Hermetism?"

33 Böhme, *Morgen-Röte im Aufgangk*, ch. 19 (van Ingen ed., 336).

34 For explicit attention to the nature of Swedenborg's altered states, see Benz, *Emanuel Swedenborg*.

35 Hanegraaff, "Magnetic Gnosis" (including the perception of somnambulists as "information machines").

36 Baier, *Meditation und Moderne*.

37 E.g., Asprem, *Problem of Disenchantment* (esp. Part Three, "Esoteric Epistemologies"); Hanegraaff, "The Theosophical Imagination."

38 Hanegraaff, *Hermetic Spirituality*, 3 with note 6; idem, "Subtle Energies."

39 Again, see von Stuckrad, *Locations of Knowledge*, 60–61.

40 For a classic formulation, see Max Weber's discussion of science as based on the principle of disenchantment, in the specific sense of certainty or firm belief that no "mysterious incalculable forces" exist in the world so that ultimately it should be possible to attain perfect or definitive knowledge about reality by means of "technical instruments and calculation" (Weber, *Wissenschaft als Beruf*, 9; cf. Hanegraaff, *Esotericism and the Academy*, 253; Asprem, *Problem of Disenchantment*, 17–49). On why the concept of state-specific knowledge undermine Weber's concept, see Hanegraaff, "Subtle Energies."

41 Next to comprehensive theological systems as developed for instance by scholastic authors such as Thomas Aquinas, "modern forms of occultism such as Theosophy and Anthroposophy or its countless 'New Age' derivations are profoundly *explanatory* systems of thought.

They promise to explain exactly, often in meticulous detail, how everything works at all levels of reality, both visible and invisible" (Hanegraaff, "Generous Hermeneutics," 73).

42 The foundational reference here is Gadamer, *Hermeneutik I* (*Wahrheit und Methode*: "Truth and Method"). For the relevance of Gadamerian hermeneutics to the Hermetica, see Hanegraaff, *Hermetic Spirituality*, 132–138, 342–351.

43 As shown in exemplary fashion by the impressive oeuvre of Elliot Wolfson (e.g., *Through a Speculum that Shines*, or *Language, Eros, Being*), this might be applied not just to kabbalistic hermeneutics of scripture but also to further scholarly hermeneutics of kabbalistic hermeneutics itself, which might again be subjected to a further hermeneutics (as, e.g., in Kripal, *Road of Excess*, 258–298), and so on *ad infinitum*.

44 E.g., Kilcher, *Sprachtheorie der Kabbala*.

45 The following paragraph is based on Bernd-Christian Otto's innovative "CAS-E" program "Alternative Rationalities and Esoteric Practices from a Global Perspective" (University of Erlangen, Germany). For discussion, see various contribution to the special issue devoted to CAS-E by *Method & Theories in the Study of Religion* 37 (2025).

46 Here I follow Otto, "Introduction."

47 Hanegraaff, *Hermetic Spirituality*, 220–307.

Chapter 6

1 van de Port, *Ecstatic Encounters*, 11.

2 *Dhikr* recitation: evocative descriptions in Piraino, *Sufism in Europe*. Pilgrimage: Greer & Oing, *Kumano Kodo*. Ayahuasca drinking: e.g., Blainey, *Christ Returns from the Jungle*. Ceremonial sex: Urban, *Magia Sexualis*. Harming enemies: e.g., Hutin, *Casting Spells*. Qdrops: Argentino, "Qvangelism." Psytrance festivals: Sylvan, *Trance Formation*.

3 E.g., Smith, *Drudgery Divine*, 1–35; idem, *To Take Place*, 96–117.

4 This hiatus is now being addressed by Bernd-Christian Otto's innovative CAS-E project (see p. 236 note 45) and the Research Network for the Study of Esoteric Practices (RENSEP; see Appendix 2).

5 E.g., Crockford & Asprem, "Ethnographies of the Esoteric."

6 For a longer discussion see Hanegraaff, "Magic." The most detailed and, in my opinion, conclusive argument can be found in Otto, *Magie*, 1–132.

7 Hanegraaff, *Esotericism and the Academy*, 164–77.

8 Medin & Ortony, "Psychological Essentialism"; see Chapter 1, p. 20.

9 For the basic argument, see Hanegraaff, "Reconstructing 'Religion'."

10 For these two complementary discourses of polemical exclusion (*Ausgrenzungsdiskurs*) and self-referential acceptance (*Aufwertungsdiskurs*), see Otto, *Magie*. A brief summary in English can be found in Hanegraaff, Review of Otto, 115–16.

11 E.g., Kieckhefer, *Magic in the Middle Ages*, 56–94.

12 E.g., Ogden, "Binding Spells."

13 E.g., Faraone, *Ancient Greek Love Magic*.

14 Hanegraaff, *Hermetic Spirituality*, 154–155, 244–253.
15 William Ernest Henley, "Invictus" (famously quoted by Nelson Mandela).
16 See, e.g., the contributions by Frank Klaassen, Claire Fanger, and Michael Camille, in Fanger, *Conjuring Spirits*; and Fanger, *Rewriting Magic*.
17 Kieckhefer, *Magic in the Middle Ages*, 151–175.
18 Clucas, "John Dee's Angelic Conversations."
19 Charmasson, "Divinatory Arts."
20 Godwin, *Theosophical Enlightenment*, 169–186.
21 See p. 152.
22 Diacceto, *De Pulchro* (*Opera Omnia*, 45–46), here quoted in the translation by Walker, *Spiritual and Demonic Magic*, 32–33.
23 Yates, *Art of Memory*.
24 E.g., Owen, *Place of Enchantment*, 1, 156–157, and *passim*.
25 Luhrmann, *Persuasions of the Witch's Craft*, 191–202.
26 Corbin, "*Mundus Imaginalis*"; and for Faivre, see Chapter 1, pp. 10–11.
27 Analysis in Hanegraaff, "The Theosophical Imagination."
28 Kerner, *Seherin von Prevorst* (discussion in Hanegraaff, "A Woman Alone").
29 Ellenberger, *Discovery of the Unconscious*.
30 Hanegraaff, *New Age Religion*, 496–513; idem, *Esotericism and the Academy*, 260–295.
31 Gibbons, *Gender in Mystical and Occult Thought*; Faivre, "Sensuous Relation"; Zuber, *Spiritual Alchemy*.
32 Hanegraaff, *New Age Religion*, 462–482, and Chapter 7, pp. 159–162.
33 Iamblichus, *Réponse à Porphyre* ("De Mysteriis"), 12; Hanegraaff, *Hermetic Spirituality*, 106–118; Shaw, *Hellenic Tantra*.
34 E.g., Fanger, "Medieval Ritual Magic."
35 E.g., Brann, *Trithemius and Magical Theology*; Harkness, *John Dee's Conversations with Angels*.
36 Benz, *Emanuel Swedenborg*, 151–200, 275–325.
37 Randolph, *Dealings with the Dead*, 151; Deveney, *Paschal Beverly Randolph*, 104.
38 Griscom, *Ecstasy Is a New Frequency*, 82; Hanegraaff, *New Age Religion*, 197–202.
39 Ridall, *Channeling*, 9.
40 Davidsen, "Fiction-Based Religion."
41 Hanegraaff, "Entheogenic Esotericism."
42 Hanegraaff, "Teaching Experiential Dimensions," 154–158.
43 Of course, the reference is to Faivre's influential definition (Chapter 1, pp. 10–11).
44 E.g., Shantz, *Paul in Ecstasy*, 79–87 (with primary reference to the work of Eugene D'Aquili and Andrew Newberg).
45 CH I 4, 6–7; Hanegraaff, *Hermetic Spirituality*, 163–167, 318–321.
46 CH XIII 11, 13; Hanegraaff, *Hermetic Spirituality*, 150–154.
47 Bucke, *Cosmic Consciousness*, 2; Hanegraaff, *Hermetic Spirituality*, 254–255.
48 Houston, *The Possible Human*, 186. Remarkably similar descriptions of spiritual "openings," all occurring suddenly and apparently spontaneously, can be found in many other authors,

for instance, the British poet and Zen Buddhist Henry Shukman (*One Blade of Grass*, 46–47) or the American New Testament scholar Dale C. Allison (Kripal, *Superhumanities*, 158–159).

49 Joly, *Un mystique Lyonnais*. For some other examples, see, e.g., Faivre, *Kirchberger*; idem, *De Londres à Saint-Petersbourg* (Carl Friedrich Tieman).

Chapter 7

1 Scholem, "A Birthday Letter," 216 (*Gewiss, Geschichte mag im Grunde ein Schein sein, aber ein Schein, ohne den in der Zeit keine Einsicht in das Wesen möglich ist*).

2 See the "inner traditions" perspective discussed in Chapter 1 (pp. 15–17) and its close relation to the "religionism" associated with the Eranos tradition (discussed in Chapter 3, pp. 97–98, and Chapter 7, 148–151) as well as the closely related phenomenon of perennialism or Traditionalism. Perhaps the most influential representative of such approaches in recent research is the American scholar Arthur Versluis.

3 Hanegraaff, "Here, There & Everywhere." Present-centeredness (also known as presentism) must not be confused with the *perspectivism* expounded for instance in a classic article by Foucault, "Nietzsche, la généalogie, l'histoire." My own argument is grounded in Gadamerian hermeneutics and takes for granted that there is no such thing as "the view from nowhere," because any historical project is always *situated* (see Haraway, "Situated Knowledges"). The historian's personal patterns of "prejudice" (*Vorurteil, Vormeinung, Vorverständnis*) are essential to the hermeneutic encounter without which no historical research of any kind would even be possible; but it only works if the sources are allowed to "talk back" (Hanegraaff, *Hermetic Spirituality*, 132–138; idem, "Hermes, Hermeneutics & the Humanities"). I will return to these issues in Chapter 9, in the context of my argument for counter-normativity and counter-normality.

4 Obviously, the reference is to Antoine Faivre's influential definition of "esotericism" (see Chapter 1, pp. 10–11), which I see as actually the reverse mirror image of a historically specific *Enlightenment* "form of thought" (Hanegraaff, "Globalization of Esotericism," 77–80).

5 I do not claim that these terms are equivalent but would see them as different ways of capturing what is going on in an extremely complicated series of interwoven historical events. For my basic take on *Modernization*, see Hanegraaff, "Protecting the Sacred after (Post)Modernity." In my study *New Age Religion*, I used the term *Secularization* resp. the emergence of *Secular Thought*. As for the "problem" (rather than the "process") of *Disenchantment*, I basically follow Asprem, *Problem of Disenchantment*. My general argument in this chapter is modeled roughly on Chapter Fifteen of *New Age Religion*, 411–513, but with the addition of the "religious supermarket" as a fifth element.

6 Likewise, in the field of contemporary esotericism, we find elaborate spiritual worldviews defended with reference to quantum mechanics and other scientific theories. See, e.g., Hammer, *Claiming Knowledge*, 201–330; Hanegraaff, *New Age Religion*, 62–76.

7 For the notion of the "intellectual sacrifice," see Weber, *Wissenschaft als Beruf*, 1–23; and analysis in Asprem, *Problem of Disenchantment* (consult the Index).

8 On these developments in the context of Protestant anti-apologeticism, see Hanegraaff, *Esotericism and the Academy*, 101–127, e.g., 103 with note 96 and 121–122 with note 161, referring throughout to the crucial analysis by Lehmann-Brauns, *Weisheit in der Weltgeschichte*.

9 Casaubon, *De rebus sacris et ecclesiasticis exercitationes XVI*. For all the relevant evidence, including Casaubon's predecessors, see Mulsow, *Das Ende des Hermetismus*; English summary of the book's argument in Hanegraaff, *Review of Mulsow*.

10 For a brilliant analysis of Nietzsche's view of history, see Foucault, "Nietzsche, la généalogie, l'histoire."

11 Hanegraaff, *Esotericism and the Academy*, 302–308.

12 Among many examples of this key sentiment, see, e.g., the most famous line in James Joyce's *Ulysses*, "History is a nightmare from which I am trying to awake" (cf. Jehl, "The 'Nightmare of History'") or, closer to esotericism, Terence McKenna's apocalyptic desire to "end history" and "go to the stars" (Hanegraaff, "'And End History. And go to the Stars'"). For Corbin's desperate battle against historicity and time, see Hanegraaff, "Henry Corbin as Knight of the Temple."

13 Hanegraaff, "Generous Hermeneutics," 60–64 (with special reference to Paul Ricoeur).

14 It is precisely for this reason that Corbin kept insisting so strongly that anything of true spiritual importance can only lie "outside the process of becoming, outside historical causality and the norms of chronology, of filiations whose justification depends on archives and legal documents" (Corbin, "L'*Imago Templi*," 290, and many similar statements throughout this long article; see analysis in Hanegraaff, "Henry Corbin as Knight of the Temple").

15 Hanegraaff, *Hermetic Spirituality*, 3–5 (methodological agnosticism).

16 Above, Chapter 1, pp. 16–17.

17 See motto above Chapter 2.

18 See my reflections on this point in Hanegraaff, "A Woman Alone," 218–219, 246–247.

19 I mean this as a playful nod to the world-renowned Bibliotheca Philosophica Hermetica in Amsterdam (created by the businessman Joost Ritman), which nowadays calls itself The Embassy of the Free Mind (https://embassyofthefreemind.com/nl/). My other reference is, of course, to Immanuel Kant's famous dictum *Sapere aude* (orig. Horace, *First Book of Letters*; Kant, "What Is Enlightenment?").

20 The reference is to Josephson Storm, *Metamodernism*.

21 Plotinus, *Ennead* IV.4.32; cf. IV.4.41-42 (for the Stoic background, see reference to Earl Fontainelle on p. 210 note 9).

22 Hanegraaff, *Esotericism and the Academy*, 189–191 with note 139; 294–295.

23 E.g., Garin, *Medioevo e Rinascimento*, 154; Foucault, *Les mots et les choses*, chapter 2 ("la prose du monde," "the prose of the world").

24 E.g., Vickers, "On the Function of Analogy in the Occult."

25 Kaske & Clark, "Introduction," 48–53.

26 Travaglia, *Magic, Causality and Intentionality*.

27 Ficino, *De Vita* III.3.31-33 (Kaske & Clark, ed., 256–257).

28 Weber, *Wissenschaft als Beruf*, 9; see p. 235 note 40.

29 Hanegraaff, *Swedenborg, Oetinger, Kant*. On kabbalistic interpretations of Swedenborg, see idem, "Swedenborg, the Jews, and Jewish Traditions." For very similar conclusions, see the large study by Stengel, *Aufklärung bis zum Himmel*.

30 Luhrmann, *Persuasions of the Witch's Craft*, 274–282.

31 Kant, *Träume eines Geistersehers*; discussion in Hanegraaff, *Swedenborg, Oetinger, Kant*, 87–107.

32 Hutchison, "What Happened to Occult Qualities in the Scientific Revolution?"

33 Asprem, *Problem of Disenchantment*, 208–225; idem, "Pondering Imponderables."

34 E.g., Gauld, *Founders of Psychical Research*; Oppenheim, *The Other World*; Asprem, *Problem of Disenchantment*, 287–412.

35 E.g., Watts, "Morphic Fields and Extended Mind."

36 Jung & Pauli, *The Interpretation of Nature and the Psyche*.

37 Hanegraaff, *New Age Religion*, 62–70. For an excellent recent example by an academic scholar of religion, see Kripal, *The Flip*.

38 Again, the reference is to Asprem's discussion (based on Max Weber) in *Problem of Disenchantment*.

39 Halbfass, *India and Europe*, 5, 18, 20

40 Ibid., 30–31.

41 See further discussion below, Chapter 9, pp. 192–198.

42 Schwab, *The Oriental Renaissance*. See also Maillard, *L'Inde vue d'Europe*.

43 Ibid., 6.

44 E.g., Sharpe, *Comparative Religion*; Kippenberg, *Discovering Religious History*; Turner, *Philology*; Pollock, Elman & Chang, *World Philology*.

45 Godwin, *Theosophical Enlightenment*, Chapters 1–4.

46 Ibid., 266.

47 Said, *Orientalism*.

48 E.g., Campbell, *Ancient Wisdom Revived*.

49 Hanegraaff, "Western Esotericism and the Orient in the First Theosophical Society"; and on Blavatsky's referential corpus, see idem, "The Theosophical Imagination," 7–11. For the *non*-Jewish understanding of kabbalah among occultists *and* established scholars prior to the pioneering work of Gershom Scholem, idem, "Beginnings of Occultist Kabbalah."

50 Many instructive examples in Strube, *Global Tantra*; Mukhopadhyay, "Occult World of Bengalis." For parallel cases from Mexico and Peru, see Bernand & Gruzinski, *De l'idolâtrie*, 122–145 (Garcilaso de la Vega, Fernando de Alva Ixtilxochitl).

51 Excellent discussion in Cantú, "'Don't Take Any Wooden Nickels'."

52 Hanegraaff, "Western Esotericism and the Orient in the First Theosophical Society," 30–31 ("the lines of influence went in both directions"). This article appeared in a collective volume coedited by Strube, who discussed previous drafts with me and therefore knew it well. This makes it hard to understand that, in a whole series of later publications, he makes claims to the effect that I promote a pernicious "export model" of esotericism based on the unilateral "diffusion" of some immutable "esoteric essence" to "passive recipients" deprived of agency (e.g., Asprem & Strube, "Esotericism's Expanding Horizon," 3–4; Strube, "Theosophy, Race," 1185–1186; idem "Religious Comparativism," 3–4; "Towards the Study," 52;

idem, *Global Tantra*, 3, 28). Whoever may have been promoting such ideas, I'm not one of them. On the contrary, I obviously agree with Strube's many statements to the effect that, for instance, "Theosophical debates about Tantra and yoga were *not* shaped by a unidirectional interpretation of Westerners or an 'import' of Western esotericism, but through complex exchanges with Indian and other Asian actors" (*Global Tantra*, 7).

53 Rudbøg & Reenberg Sand, *Imagining the East*; Krämer & Strube, *Theosophy across Boundaries*. On the key topic of karma and reincarnation, see Hanegraaff, *New Age Religion*, 283–290; Chajes, *Recycled Lives*.

54 De Michelis, *History of Modern Yoga*; Urban, *Tantra*; Strube, *Global Tantra*.

55 Versluis, *American Transcendentalism and Asian Religions*.

56 Albanese, *Republic of Mind and Spirit*.

57 See the pioneering volume by Finley, Guillory & Page, *Esotericism in African American Religious Experience*. I am personally not familiar with modern research that might exist about the reverse impact of esoteric traditions of Western provenance on modern and contemporary Africa.

58 Also by myself, see Hanegraaff, *Western Esotericism*, 131 (corrected in idem, "Globalization of Esotericism," 61 note 21; as acknowledge by Finley, Gray, & Page, "Africana Esoteric Studies," 164).

59 Bakker, "Esotericism, that's for White Folks, Right?"; eadem, "Race and (the Study of) Esotericism"; eadem, "Hidden Presence." There is no basis for the strange suspicions expressed by Finley, Gray, & Page, to the effect that the modern study of "Western" esotericism "through intellectual hegemony and its disciplinary methodologies . . . marginalizes AES [Africana Esoteric Studies]" ("Africana Esoteric Studies," 184 and *passim*). On the contrary, this AES project was welcomed from the beginning (the foundational volume *Esotericism in African American Religious Experience* was published in Brill's Aries Book Series), and I'm not aware of any attempts at "marginalization" in the context of the ESSWE or anywhere else.

60 E.g., Albanese, *Nature Religion in America*; Hutton, *Shamans*; Znamenski, *Beauty of the Primitive*.

61 Hanegraaff, "Entheogenic Esotericism."

62 For the crucial topic of translation in a global perspective on esotericism, see Hanegraaff & Mukhopadhyay, "Translating Esotericism."

63 King, *Orientalism and Religion*.

64 Kripal, *Mutants & Mystics*, 31–69.

65 This mythology goes back to Blavatsky's *Secret Doctrine* (vol. 2, 374, 549–553, 618) and especially Alice Bailey's *Initiation: Human and Solar*. For a useful insider's discussion, see Richmond, "The Pleiades."

66 See pp. 113–114.

67 Lovejoy, *Great Chain of Being*, 244 (emphasis added).

68 For instance, see the opening illustration to Bonnet, *Oeuvres d'histoire naturelle et de philosophie* 4:1, 1.

69 Conner, *Cosmic Optimism*.

70 It is notoriously difficult to translate this German terminology into English. For Hegel, *die Vernunft* (commonly translated into English as "reason") did not mean our common concept

of instrumental rationality but was closer to the Greek notion of *nous* (e.g., Hegel, *Vorlesungen über die Philosophie der Geschichte*, 51, 57). *Der Weltgeist* translates most easily into "the World Spirit," but "World Mind" or "World Intellect" is arguably closer to what is meant by *Geist*.

71 Nietzsche's chilling vision of "the last man" appears in *Also Sprach Zarathustra* I.5 (1883). During the high period of neoliberal globalization, the political scientist Francis Fukuyama published his bestselling volume *The End of History and the Last Man* (1992); and we also find it in modern literature, e.g., Houellebecq, *Possibility of an Island*.

72 A vision of spiritual evolution toward a "supermind" is central to Sri Aurobindo's "integral yoga" (Heehs, *Lives of Sri Aurobindo*). The idea of a "new man" or "superhuman" appears prominently in the third part of Pauwels's and Bergier's mega bestseller *Le matin des magiciens* (The Morning of the Magicians, 1960). Quite similarly, the hopeful vision of a "super-humanity" (with explicit reference to Nietzsche) is at the heart of many recent publications by Jeffrey J. Kripal, from *Mutants & Mystics* to *The Superhumanities*.

73 Hanegraaff, *Esotericism and the Academy*, 266–277.

74 Hanegraaff, "The Theosophical Imagination," 9–10 (with reference to William Emmette Coleman).

75 The most comprehensive historical overview is Zander, *Geschichte der Seelenwanderung in Europa*. For Plato, see the vision of Er attached to his Republic; for the Jewish kabbalah, see the chapter on *Gilgul* in Scholem, *On the Mystical Shape of the Godhead*; for the Christian kabbalah see Coudert, *Impact of the Kabbalah*.

76 Hanegraaff, *New Age Religion*, 470–482; Chajes, *Recycled Lives*.

77 Hanegraaff, "Roberts, Dorothy Jane."

78 See above, pp. 32–33; detailed analysis in Hanegraaff, *Hermetic Spirituality*.

79 MacDonald, *History of the Concept of Mind* (2 vols.). The idea that the soul has vanished under the impact of secularization (e.g., Feld, *Das Ende des Seelenglaubens*) is based precisely on the standard neglect of "esoteric" traditions in modern and contemporary culture and severely underestimates the human capacity of innovation and creative reinterpretation. For a history of how belief in the soul may have largely vanished from academic science and the humanities *but* is actually omnipresent in contemporary culture, see von Stuckrad, *A Cultural History of the Soul*.

80 See, e.g., the contemporary debate between philosophers of consciousness such as Daniel Dennett (representing a strict monistic materialism; e.g., Dennett, *Consciousness Explained*) and David Chalmers (representing the ultimately dualistic concept that consciousness cannot be strictly explained in material terms; e.g., Chalmers, *The Conscious Mind*).

81 Feuerbach, *Das Wesen des Christentums*.

82 For an interesting analysis informed by gnosticism and modern esotericism, see Kripal, *The Serpent's Gift*, 59–89 (reviewed in Hanegraaff, "Leaving the Garden").

83 This famous trope of three "masters of suspicion" and their hermeneutical project of "unmasking" pious illusions was introduced in 1975 by Paul Ricoeur, *De l'interprétation* (translated into English as *Freud and Philosophy*, in 1970; discussion in Hanegraaff, "Generous Hermeneutics").

84 Kerner, *Seherin von Prevorst*, 220–249, esp. 227–228 (Solar Circle, Soul-Circle). Discussion in Hanegraaff, "Magnetic Gnosis."

85 Flournoy, *From India to the Planet Mars*.

86 Kripal, *Authors of the Impossible*, 1–35.

87 Jung, *Red Book*, 282–293; discussion in Hanegraaff, "Great War of the Soul," 117–118.

88 Pasi, "Varieties of Magical Experience," 143–160.

89 Hanegraaff, "Fiction in the Desert of the Real."

90 E.g., Alan Moore's splendid *Promethea* comics cycle (1999–2005) is based explicitly on the key doctrine that "there is no difference between fiction and reality" (Hanegraaff, "Alan Moore's *Promethea*").

91 The concept of the "cultic milieu" was introduced in a famous article by Campbell, "The Cultic Milieu" (1972); see also the reprint and additional discussions in Kaplan & Lööw, *The Cultic Milieu*. Discussion in relation to esotericism in Hanegraaff, *New Age Religion*, 14–18.

92 Campbell, "The Cultic Milieu," 121–122.

93 Geertz, "Religion as a Cultural System." For the complete argument, see Hanegraaff, "Defining Religion in Spite of History"; idem, "New Age Spiritualities as Secular Religion"; idem, "Reconstructing 'Religion'."

94 Durkheim, *Elementary Forms*, 43–44.

95 Berger, *The Heretical Imperative*.

Chapter 8

1 Moore, *Promethea* # 31.

2 "There are dragons here." For this analogy with premodern maps, see discussion in Hanegraaff, *Esotericism and the Academy*, 1–4.

3 Hanegraaff, "Reconstructing 'Religion'."

4 For an extremely representative example, see the violent clash between the founder of modern "history of science" George Sarton and the pioneer of pre- and early modern history of science Lynn Thorndike, the author of an eight-volume standard work *History of Magic and Experimental Science*. What happened between these two scholars, and why it was bound to happen, can be read in Hanegraaff, *Esotericism and the Academy*, 317–323.

5 For the key importance of the seventeenth- and eighteenth-century principle of historiographical *eclecticism*, see Chapter 3, pp. 93–96; and Hanegraaff, *Esotericism and the Academy*, 128–152. In the sharpest possible contrast, I advocate an *anti-eclectic historiography* (ibid., 377–378).

6 See in particular the self-described "New Historiography of Alchemy" (e.g., Principe, "Reflections," and many later publications by Lawrence M. Principe and William R. Newman). There have been very similar developments in the history of astrology, "magic," and science.

7 For a further development of this metaphor, with esotericism as "the mushrooms of history" (as opposed to the official "cucumbers" in an artificial greenhouse environment), see my personal reminiscences in Hanegraaff, "Will-Erich Peuckert and the Light of Nature."

8 Melvin-Koushki, "New Brethren of Purity."

9 Cavendish, *Man, Myth & Magic* (orig. 1970; revised new editions in 1985 and 1995).

10 Grillot de Givry, *Pictorial Anthology*; idem, *Illustrated Anthology* (original French edition *Le musée des Sorciers*, 1929).

11 Gettings, *The Occult in Art.*

12 Klossowski de Rola, *The Golden Game.*

13 Roob, *Alchemy & Mysticism*; Forshaw, *Occult.*

14 Obrist, *Les débuts* (important also because Obrist was among the very first modern scholars to challenge C. G. Jung's approach to alchemical symbolism).

15 Van Lennep, *Alchimie.*

16 De Jong, *Michael Maier's Atalanta Fugiens.*

17 Forshaw, *The Mage's Images* (4 vols.).

18 www.alchemywebsite.com

19 Van den Doel, *Ficino and Fantasy.*

20 Betz, *Licht vom unerschaffenen Lichte*; Oetinger, *Die Lehrtafel.*

21 Blake, *The Complete Illuminated Books*; von Meurs, "William Blake and his Gnostic Myths."

22 For rich pictorial documentation, see Larsen, Larsen, Lawrence & Woofenden, *Emanuel Swedenborg.*

23 See Chapter 4, p. 113.

24 Nelson, *Gothica.*

25 Eco, *Interpretation and Overinterpretation*; and see Eco's famous novels, which can be seen as fictional parallels to his theoretical work, notably *Foucault's Pendulum* and *The Prague Cemetery*. Surprisingly, Eco's emphasis on semiotics and hermeneutics in conspirational thinking still tends to be neglected by specialists. For rare exceptions, see Leone, Madisson, & Ventsel, "Semiotic Approaches"; Leone, "Double Debunking."

26 E.g., Bauduin, *Surrealism and the Occult.*

27 Alleau (see notably his *Aspects de l'alchimie traditionnelle*) is a neglected key figure who would deserve a major study. For a good historical overview in English of this modern alchemical tradition, see Caron, "Alchemy V."

28 Tuchman, *The Spiritual in Art.* See also the enormous catalog *Okkultismus und Avantgarde* published ten years later (based on an exhibition at the Shirn Kunsthalle in Frankfurt).

29 [Diverse authors], *Luigi Pericle.*

30 Kandinsky, *On the Spiritual in Art*; Malewitsch, *Suprematismus* (see, e.g., discussion in Fischer, "Geheimlehren und modern Kunst," 367–370).

31 Grant & Pasi, "Works of Art without Parallel in the World"; Pasi, "The Art of Esoteric Posthumousness." Houghton describes her spiritualist séances (1870–1881) in Houghton, *Evenings at Home.*

32 Bashkoff, *Hilma af Klint: Paintings for the Future*; Almqvist, *Hilma af Klint: The Complete Catalogue Raisonné* (7 vols.); Voss, *Hilma af Klint*; Pasi, "Hilma af Klint, Western Esotericism." Painting mediums produced figurative art as well, for instance, the Dutch psychic

and author Jozef Rulof (1898–1952): see Anonymus, *Het schilderend mediumschap van Jozef Rulof.*

33 Drayer, *Nicholas & Helena Roerich*; Ratcliffe, *Ithell Colquhoun*; Hale, *Ithell Colquhoun*; Aberth, *Leonora Carrington*; Kissane, *Leonora Carrington*; Hanegraaff, "A Visual World"; Chadwick, *Women Artists and the Surrealist Movement*; van Raay et al., *Surreal Friends*; Luidinga, *Johfra*; Grey, *Transfigurations*; Grey and Grey, *Net of Being.*

34 Marco Pasi, Keynote lecture at the 8th biannual conference of the European Society for the Study of Western Esotericism (ESSWE), Cork, Ireland, 2022.

35 See, e.g., the representative catalog of the 2008 exhibition at the Centre Pompidou, *Traces du sacré.*

36 In a response to my 2013 "Guide for the Perplexed," Christine Ferguson has challenged what she calls "the myth of critical silence." She argues that "the occult" actually *did* receive plenty of attention in scholarship on the modernist canon since the 1950s ("Beyond Belief," 207–212), while also criticizing recent studies in esotericism for what she sees as an undue belief in authorial intention (ibid., 212–215). A first problem I see with this argument is that most of the scholarship she mentions is focused quite narrowly on Symbolism and Victorian literature in English, with a very strong preference for W. B. Yeats, to the exclusion of earlier periods and other languages. A second problem is that most of this scholarship (which certainly attempted to break with earlier dismissals of "the occult," as Ferguson correctly notes) tended to approach esotericism not historically but *typologically,* usually based on outdated essentialist assumptions about occultism as an inherently anti-modern "flight from reason," whereas modern scholarship stresses precisely the *modernity* of occultism (e.g., Godwin, *Theosophical Enlightenment*; Owen, *Place of Enchantment*; Pasi, "Modernity of Occultism"). A final problem is that Ferguson sets up a straw man in accusing modern "literary esotericism studies" of attempts to impose one particular kind of scholarship as "canonical" while minimizing, marginalizing, discrediting, or discarding "postmodern" critical theories. I see no basis for such complaints. To the best of my knowledge, the field has always been open to all critical methods or theoretical perspectives.

37 Ferguson, "Beyond Belief," 211.

38 Surette, *Birth of Modernism*, x.

39 Colonna, *Hypnerotomachia Poliphili*; Godwin, *Pagan Dream*, 21–37.

40 For a longer list of titles see Faivre, *Western Esotericism*, 51.

41 Schuler, *Alchemical Poetry 1575–1700.*

42 Bila, *La croyance à la magie*; Thalmann, *Der Trivialroman* (badly written but very well documented, and a major influence on Thomas Mann's *Zauberberg*; see Hanegraaff, "Ironic Esotericism"); Faivre, *L'ésotérisme au XVIIIe siècle*, 187–190; idem, "Genèse d'un genre narratif"; Vernière, "Un aspect de l'irrationnel."

43 De Villars, *Comte de Gabalis* (Didier Kahn ed., 2010). Hanegraaff, *Esotericism and the Academy*, 222–230, with note 259 for the secondary literature.

44 Anonymus [Emma Hardinge Britten], *Ghost Land*; summary and discussion in Hanegraaff, "Western Esotericism and the Orient in the First Theosophical Society," 42–46.

45 On the importance of Bulwer-Lytton, see especially Godwin, *Theosophical Enlightenment.*

46 But Huysmans is just the tip of a much larger literary iceberg, as shown in impressive detail by Faxneld, *Satanic Feminism.*

47 Binder, *Gustav Meyrink*; Harmsen, *Der magische Schriftsteller.*

48 Magus, *Rider Haggard and the Imperial Occult.*

49 Surette, *Birth of Modernism*

50 See the splendid deep analysis in Magnússon, *Dichtung als Erfahrungsmetaphysik.*

51 Roukema, *Esotericism and Narrative.*

52 E.g., Pasi, "The Influence of Aleister Crowley on Fernando Pessoa's Esoteric Writings" (and see the long list of references in his note 4).

53 E.g., Cowan, "Devils in the Ink"; idem, "What Most People Would Call Evil."

54 Hanegraaff, "Ironic Esotericism."

55 Crowley, *The Solitudes*; idem, *Love and Sleep*; idem, *Daemonomania*; idem, *Endless Things.* Analysis in Hanegraaff, "Heroic Martyr and Prophet of Hermetic Renovation." See also Crowley's early classic *Little, Big.*

56 Cavalier, *Les Ogres du Gange*; *Les Loups de Berlin*; *Les Anges de Palerme*; *La Dame de Toscane.*

57 [South a.k.a. Atwood], *A Suggestive Inquiry into the Hermetic Mystery.* Analysis in Hanegraaff, "A Suggestive Inquiry into Hermetic Rebirth."

58 Hanegraaff, *Hermetic Spirituality*, 288–297.

59 Godwin, "Revival of Speculative Music"; see also Godwin's anthology *Music, Mysticism and Magic.*

60 See for instance Walker, *Music, Spirit and Language in the Renaissance*; Tomlinson, *Music in Renaissance Magic*; Wuidar, *Music and Esotericism*; Gouk, *Music, Science and Natural Magic*; de Jong, "Music I"; Teeuwen, "Music II"; Gouk, "Music III"; Godwin, "Music IV"; Roth and George, *Explorations in Music and Esotericism.*

61 Godwin, "Music IV," 816.

62 The indispensable study is Godwin, *Music and the Occult.*

63 All recorded by Reinbert de Leeuw in 2011 (KTC 1427, *Uspud*, 2 CDs; www.etcetera-records.com).

64 Stolzenberg, "Esoterik in der Musik der Moderne"; Aniello, "Musica pietrificata."

65 Hanegraaff, "The Unspeakable and the Law"; Gratzer, *Zur "wunderlichen Mystik" Alban Bergs*; Johnson, *Webern and the Transformation of Nature.*

66 See Schönberg's opera *Moses und Aron* (premiere 1957).

67 Stockhausen, *Texte zur Musik*, vols. 4 and 6.

68 Bauermeister, *Ich hänge im Triolengitter*; Kurtz, *Stockhausen*; Maconie, *Other Planets.*

69 Godwin, "Stockhausen's *Donnerstag aus Licht* and Gnosticism."

70 Hanegraaff, "Transitioning to the Cosmos" (*Trans-States* https://www.youtube.com/watch?v=1HVe-4SBOZs; written version forthcoming); Ulrich, *Stockhausens Zyklus Licht.*

71 See however Partridge, *Re-Enchantment of the West*, vol. 1, 143–184; idem, "The Occult and Popular Music"; Greer, "Angel-Headed Hipsters"; Granholm, "Ritual Black Magic"; idem, "Popular Music and the Occult"; idem, "Why all that Satanist Stuff in Heavy Metal?"; Introvigne, *Satanism*, 462–505.

72 Partridge, "Esoterrorism and the Wrecking of Civilization"; Breyer P-Orridge, *Thee Psychick Bible*; eadem, *Sacred Intent.*

73 E.g., Sylvan, *Trance Formation.*

74 Partridge, "Occulture Is Ordinary."

75 Carrette and King, *Selling Spirituality.*

76 Of course, my reference is to a famous chapter in Horkheimer and Adorno, *Dialectic of Enlightenment.*

77 As for the deep ironies of how this logic works, see the honest admissions of a pioneer critic of corporate "branding," Naomi Klein, *Doppelganger*, 46–67 (author of the 1999 bestseller *No Logo*).

78 On the dialectics of authenticity and fakery in American popular culture, see, e.g., Chidester, *Authentic Fakes.*

79 The most important organizations remain CESNUR Center for Studies on New Religions, www.cesnur.org; and INFORM https://inform.ac (see Appendix 2).

80 There are many good overviews. For instance, see various contributions to Lewis, *Oxford Handbook of New Religious Movements*; or Melton, "The Modern Anti-Cult Movement in Historical Perspective." The comparatively recent distinction between anti-cult and counter-cult organizations comes from Introvigne, "The Secular Anti-Cult and the Religious Counter-Cult Movement."

81 Introvigne, "Ordeal by Fire"; Lewis, "Solar Temple 'Transits'"; Chryssides, "'Come On Up'...." For many excellent discussions of fact and fiction in this domain, see Lewis & Aagaard Petersen, *Controversial New Religions*; Lewis, *Violence and New Religious Movements.*

82 For the basic argument, published in an important volume about the definition of religion, see Introvigne, "Religion as Claim."

83 E.g., Anthony & Robbins, "Conversion and 'Brainwashing'"; Shupe, "Deprogramming Violence."

84 A now classic example is the deeply problematic French government report on NRMs (1995): Gest & Guyard, *Les sectes en France.* For critical responses by many experts, see the volume edited by Introvigne & Melton, *Pour en finir avec les sectes.* Concerning the more recent controversies around the Romanian Movement for Spiritual Integration into the Absolute (MISA), see Introvigne, *Sacred Eroticism.*

85 See for instance Dybdal Pedersen, "Second Golden Age of Theosophy in Denmark."

86 Luhrmann, *Persuasions of the Witch's Craft*; Brown, *The Channeling Zone*; Crockford, *Ripples of the Universe.*

87 See notably Susannah Crockford and Egil Asprem's edited special issue "Ethnographies of the Esoteric," in *Correspondences* 6:1 (2018).

88 A pioneering study in this regard was Bednarowski, *New Religions and the Theological Imagination.*

89 This is a reference to the descriptive definition proposed by the Quality Assurance Agency for Higher Education in the United Kingdom (2000), quoted by Adrian Leftwich, "Thinking Politically," 20. Leftwich deconstructs this attempt at creating an "official" definition of politics (along with many other proposed definitions) by claiming, in a rather obviously

circular argument, that definitions of politics are "themselves, in a manner of speaking, political processes."

90 Melvin-Koushki, "Early Modern Islamicate Empire"; idem, "The Occult Court."

91 Rees, "Ficino's Advice to Princes"; Rummel, *The Case against Johann Reuchlin*; Posset, *Johann Reuchlin*; Hanegraaff, *Esotericism and the Academy*, 68–73 (Steuco); Woolley, *The Queen's Conjuror*, 97–114; Yates, *Rosicrucian Enlightenment* (deeply contested, as mentioned above); Rogalla von Bieberstein, *Mythos von der Verschwörung*; Roy-Di Piazza, "Enslaved by African Angels"; Argentino, "Qvangelicalism."

92 Strube, *Sozialismus, Katholizismus und Okkultismus*; idem, "Socialist Religion."

93 E.g., Josephson Storm, *Myth of Disenchantment*, 226–236 (Walter Benjamin); Martin, *Migration of Metaphysics* (Adorno and Scholem); Kadarkay, *Georg Lukács* (information about his interest in kabbalah and other esoteric traditions scattered through the book). The relevance of esotericism to Ernst Bloch (e.g., *Erbschaft dieser Zeit*) has not received the attention it deserves, but this will hopefully change with the forthcoming PhD dissertation by Mikheil Kakabadze (Stockholm University).

94 E.g., Pasi, "Modernity of Occultism"; Braude, *Radical Spirits*; Dixon, *Divine Feminine*; Green, *Mountain of Truth*; Owen, *Place of Enchantment*; Treitel, *A Science for the Soul*; Faxneld, *Satanic Feminism*; Hedenborg White, *The Eloquent Blood*.

95 Ransom, *Short History of the Theosophical Society*, 545–553, here 549. Especially in Germany, H.P. Blavatsky's theory of "root races" is often conflated or confused with the virulently racist and anti-Semitic far-right Ariosophy of Lanz von Liebenfels (1874–1954; see Goodrick-Clarke, *Occult Roots of Nazism*), resulting in widespread misperceptions of Blavatsky's Theosophy as a conservative or reactionary "right-wing" movement. Such interpretations neglect the fact that racial theories, far from being an esoteric specialty, were more or less omnipresent during the later nineteenth century (see, e.g., the cases of Eduard Hartmann and Herbert Spencer, Chapter 9, pp. 197–198). For an excellent discussion in German that corrects such mistakes, see Stottmeister, *Der George-Kreis und die Theosophie*, esp. 344–371, about Blavatsky's "race-theoretical anti-racism." But of course, individual esotericists and occultists could be just as susceptible to racial prejudice as anyone else, sometimes resulting in theories or statements that make for painful reading today. On the well-known example of Rudolf Steiner's Anthroposophy, see the exemplary analyses in Staudenmaier, *Between Occultism and Nazism*.

96 Dixon, *Divine Feminine*; Rudbøg & Reenberg Sand, *Imagining the East*; Krämer & Strube, *Theosophy across Boundaries*; Strube, *Global Tantra*; Mukhopadhyay, "Occult World of Bengalis."

97 Sellars, "Hakim Bey."

98 See Chapter 2, p. 74.

99 Hanegraaff, "Generous Hermeneutics" (with reference to such influential critical analyses as Holz, "ERANOS," and Wasserstrom, *Religion after Religion*). As demonstrated by the famous case of Thomas Mann's *Betrachtungen eines Unpolitischen*, often the claim of being "non-political" reflects a politically conservative perspective. An excellent example would be the young Mircea Eliade, who wanted to "make Romania great again" but was thinking

of his far-right nationalist engagement as "spiritual" and "messianic" (Lincoln, *Secrets, Lies, and Consequences*, 8–34).

100 Hanegraaff, "Great War of the Soul."

101 Interestingly, in spite of enormous differences in their understanding of esotericism, this was also the message of Pauwels' & Bergier's seminal 1960 bestseller *Le matin des magiciens*. The first part was dominated by the mythology of ancient wisdom and "vanished civilizations," while the third part focused on a future "superhumanity." In between the remote past and the remote future, modernity was depicted as a period of stagnation, of which the very recent past had been dominated by a "demonic" alternate reality known as Nazism.

102 See the subtitle of Sedgwick, *Traditionalism*.

103 For a very instructive introduction see Sedgwick, *Key Thinkers of the Radical Right*. Regarding the wider anti-modern milieus of Roman Traditionalism, see Giudice, *Occult Imperium*.

104 As a counterexample from a well-known scholar of esotericism, see McIntosh, *Beyond the North Wind*.

105 Gardell, *Gods of the Blood* (discussing such American traditions as Odinism, Wotansvolk, Asatrú, and Occult National Socialism). For a good impression of this type of paganism, see, e.g., the journal *Tyr* (published in four large volumes between 2002 and 2014).

106 Here the most influential author is David Icke, whose esoteric roots are in the Theosophically oriented New Age and channeling culture of the 1970s and 1980s. Among many titles, see especially his *. . . And the Truth Shall Set You Free* (1995), *The Biggest Secret* (1999), and *The David Icke Guide to Global Conspiracy* (2007).

107 Introduced by Ward & Voas, "Emergence of Conspirituality."

108 On the pioneering importance of Putin's Russia in this regard, see Pomerantsev, *Nothing Is True and Everything Is Possible*.

109 My reference is, again, to Pauwels & Bergier, *Le matin des magiciens*.

110 Hanegraaff, *Esotericism and the Academy*, 312–314; idem, "Textbooks and Introductions," 193–195 (critical review of Hartmut Zinser). Many representative examples, with helpful translations from German sources, can be found in Hakl, "'Occultism is the Metaphysics of Dunces'." I disagree with Asprem's claim that this is just a "compilation of ludicrous statements" (Review of Versluis, 249–250); on the contrary, they document the remarkably pervasive impact of Frankfurt School stereotypes on public and academic discourse in the German-speaking world.

111 Nr. 6 in Adorno's "Theses against Occultism" in his *Minima Moralia*. Discussion in Kilcher, "Is Occultism a Product of Capitalism?"

112 Hanegraaff, "Rejected Knowledge . . .," 148 (with references); Kilcher, "Is Occultism a Product of Capitalism?, 171, 175–176; Strube, "Doesn't Occultism lead straight to Fascism?" (all in Hanegraaff, Forshaw & Pasi, *Hermes Explains*).

113 I adopt this concept from Pasi, "Where Is History?," 241.

114 For the underlying process of psychological essentialism, see Chapter 1, p. 20 and p. 212 note 42. For the reification of imaginal formations, see Hanegraaff, "Reconstructing 'Religion'," 578–581. For the trash genre of populist alarmism about "esotericism" based on the same phenomenon, a contemporary parallel to early modern anti-witchcraft pamphlets, see, e.g., Caberta, *Schwarzbuch Esoterik*; Lamberty & Nocun, *Gefährlicher Glaube*.

115 A few older cases (Eric Voegelin, Carl Raschke) are discussed in Hanegraaff, "On the Construction," 28–40. Another famous example, always based on the same phenomenon of mental reification, would be Gershom Scholem's reference to gnosticism as "metaphysical antisemitism" (Wasserstrom, *Religion after Religion*, 178–179 and 326 notes 45–46). For an apt and humorous deconstruction of such generalizations, see Culiano, "The Gnostic Revenge," 290.

116 Adorno, "Meinung Wahn Gesellschaft," 123. Adorno's argument is based on the standard misreading of *Träume eines Geistersehers* shared by all Kant specialists of his generation (discussion in Hanegraaff, "Swedenborg aus der Sicht von Kant"). Note that his formulation "by one's own judgment" (orig. *dem eigenen Sinn nach*) is a key component of Enlightenment eclectic method (Chapter 3, p. 93).

117 I am obviously referring to the central importance of *Vorurteil* in Gadamerian hermeneutics (Gadamer, *Hermeneutik I*, 194, 202, 221, and esp. 270–281; discussion in Hanegraaff, *Hermetic Spirituality*, 132–138; idem, "Hermes, Hermeneutics & the Humanities"). Adorno's focus on a naïve empiricism that disregards the "constitutive subjectivity" at the heart of Kant's transcendental idealism is made explicit on the same page from which I took the quotation.

118 In terms of Horkheimer & Adorno's famous *Dialektik der Aufklärung*, I would argue that Adorno's argument about superstition demonstrates precisely how easily the project of Enlightenment gets perverted so that what should have been a force of liberation becomes one of authoritarianism and totalitarianism. In this regard, see my distinction between two types of Enlightenment (Chapter 9, pp. 205–206).

119 For a typical example close to Adorno's mentality (his debt to psychoanalysis is well known), see Jung's famous anecdote about Sigmund Freud's view of psychoanalysis as a "bulwark" that must be erected to stem "the dark tide of occultism" (*die schwarze Schlammflut . . . des Okkultismus*) (*Erinnerungen, Träume, Gedanken*, 171).

Chapter 9

1 Wallace, *This is Water*, 3–4.

2 Ibid., 8.

3 Hanegraaff, "Rejected Knowledge . . . So you mean that Esotericists are the Losers of History?"

4 App, *Birth of Orientalism*, xi.

5 Ibid., xiii. On what makes the book so innovative, see ibid., xvi: "It is the fate of pioneering studies to burden the reader with such 'unknowns' and much detail that may at first sight seem peripheral and inconsequential. This was also the case, for example, with studies on the role of clandestine literature in the formation of the age of Enlightenment. However, such studies not only put the spotlight on many seminal texts and personages but demonstrated that they formed the pillars on which the Enlightenment was erected." Many of the materials on which App's argument is based were translated by him for the first time, from a variety of languages (ibid., xvii).

6 Ibid.

7 App, *Birth of Orientalism*, 2–3 and *passim*.

8 See p. 19.

9 Strube, "Esotericism between Europe and East Asia."

10 App, *Birth of Orientalism*, 23.

11 Ibid., xiii (quoted in main text, above). On this key fallacy in historical or cultural comparativism, see Hanegraaff, *Hermetic Spirituality*, 8–9 with note 18 (referring to Jonathan Z. Smith), 137–138.

12 For the horror-inspiring imagery of a "seed pod" (also a "Platonic egg") as the demonic origin of a heretical "genealogy of darkness," see Hanegraaff, *Esotericism and the Academy*, 86, 88–89, 111, 148. Pestilence etc.: App, *Birth of Orientalism*, 122, 145, 155 (referring to Kircher, *China Illustrata* [1667] and Martini, *Novus Atlas Sinensis* [1655]).

13 Rodriguez to the Jesuit General, January 22, 1616. Transl. in Cooper, "Rodrigues in China," 277, 311–312 ("They teach everlasting matter, or chaos, and . . . they believe the universe to contain nothing but one substance"; on the key importance of this point, see Hanegraaff, *Esotericism and the Academy*, 105–107, 117, 119, 134, 137, 142, 156, 370).

14 Rodrigues to the Jesuit General, February 5, 1633 (Cooper, "Rodrigues in China," 238; App, *Birth of Orientalism*, 25–26; Strube, "Esotericism between Europe and East Asia," 14–15).

15 [Rodrigues], *João Rodrigues's Account*, 378; App, *Birth of Orientalism*, 27.

16 On the characteristic reversal of Platonic Orientalist genealogies of wisdom into genealogies of darkness based on a concept of degeneration due to demonic infiltration, see Hanegraaff, *Esotericism and the Academy*, 73, 86–89, 148.

17 Unfortunately, App's study has no subject index, but the term "superstition" appears in his book aaproximately seventy times and "idolatry" almost ninety times.

18 Ricci, *True Meaning* (Lancashire & Hu Kuo-chen, transl.).

19 App, *Birth of Orientalism*, 22. Colonialized elites could, of course, use European models to argue for the superiority of their own traditions. For instance, see raja Krishnachandra's evident appropriation of standard Platonic-Orientalist narratives (Strube, "Emergence of 'Esoteric'," 355–357) or Ixtlilxóchitl's references to "divine Plato" and so on (Bernand & Gruzinski, *De l'idolâtrie*, 136).

20 Strube provides many instances of this anti-idolatry discourse in his instructive study of modern Indian tantra discourses but pays it no further attention. For my part, referring, e.g., to his discussion of Shashadhar Tarkachuramani's Spiritual Science, I would attach much greater importance to the significant fact that "the term 'idolatry' had been introduced by the English, and English-educated Bengalis created an equivalent (*pauttalikatā*)" (Strube, *Global Tantra*, 204; for the relevance of "idolatry" to the "esoteric distinction" see also 47, 63–64, 83, 86, 129, 173, 176, 181, 240). This introduction of "idolatry" as a new term in colonial contexts, which was then appropriated by the indigenous elites, who even went so far as to invent a new word for it, exemplifies precisely what I mean by terminological imperialism.

21 App, *Birth of Orientalism*, 94–95; referring to Jeyaraj, *Bartholomäus Ziegenbalgs "Genealogie der malabarischen Götter"*, 311–312 (the bracketed words are Sanskrit equivalents of the Tamil terms).

22 E.g., Johnson, "Idolatrous Cultures"; Bernand & Gruzinski, *De l'idolâtrie*; Chidester, *Savage Systems* (see critical discussion in Hanegraaff, "Reconstructing 'Religion'," 593); Kristóf,

"The Uses of Demonology"; eadem, "Missionaries, Monsters, and the Demon Show." For the analytical relevance of "religion" as the "pre-comparative *tertium*" in this context, see Hanegraaff, "Reconstructing 'Religion'."

23 Chapter 3, p. 94.

24 App, *Birth of Orientalism*, 16. See the straight parallel with Adorno's perspective, criticized in the previous chapter, pp. 188–189.

25 Hanegraaff, "*Ad Loca Secretiora*."

26 Bakker, "Hidden Presence," 488–493.

27 Detailed analysis in Hanegraaff, *Esotericism and the Academy*, 156–164. The indispensable standard work is Harmening, *Superstitio*.

28 Halbertal & Margalit, *Idolatry*, 237; and see the by now classic discussion in Assmann, *Moses the Egyptian*, 1–22; idem, *Mosaische Unterscheidung*. For further elaboration, see Hanegraaff, "Trouble with Images," and idem, "Idolatry."

29 For the largely forgotten centrality of "idolatry" to the extremely influential theories of Edward B. Tylor and James G. Frazer, see Hanegraaff, "Emergence of the Academic Science of Magic."

30 Cohn, *Europe's Inner Demons*, 225–255; Levack, *Witch Hunt*; Roper, *Witch Craze*; Hutton, *The Witch*, 180–184.

31 De las Casas, *Short Account*; Clayton, *Bartolomé de las Casas*. For the ongoing "normality" of such practices in colonial contexts far into the twentieth century, see, e.g., Michel Taussig's shocking evocation of the "death space" of random torture and murder in the Amazonian Putumayo region during the rubber boom (*Shamanism, Colonialism, and the Wild Man*, 3–135).

32 The reference is obviously to Augustine, *De Civitate Dei*, including the important polemics against Hermetic idolatry in Book Eight (discussion in Hanegraaff, "Hermetism"). For the case of South Africa (with critical reference to Chidester, *Savage Systems*), see Hanegraaff, "Reconstructing 'Religion'," 592–595.

33 Bernand & Gruzinski, *De l'idolâtrie*, 146–194. For the definition of indigenous religion as apostasy and heresy grounded in the sin of idolatry, see, e.g., the canon *De Haereticis* of the 3rd Mexican Council (1585) (ibid., 156 and cf. López-Cano, Berumen, & Hernández, "El Tercer Concilio Provincial Mexicano," 46: "The eradication of idolatry and superstitions among all the Indians" and "the destruction of 'idols' and temples" should be pursued with "great rigor and powerful punishments").

34 Kristóf, "Missionaries, Monsters, and the Demon Show," 42 (emphasis in original).

35 For my language of "extermination" (cf. Bernand & Gruzinski's parallel "extirpation"), see the classic indictment by Lindqvist, "'Exterminate all the Brutes'."

36 E.g., Clark, *Thinking with Demons*, 369–370; Stephens, *Demon Lovers*, 279–287. Even more important than textual depictions is the abundant visual imagery of demonic monstrosity: see, e.g., Kristóf, "Missionaries," and several other contributions to the collective volume by Kérchy & Zittlau, *Exploring* (referring to "Freak Shows" and "Enfreakment").

37 Sepúlveda, *Democrates secundus* (ca. 1544), quoted according to the new critical edition by Glanville, Lupher, & Feile Tomes, *Sepúlveda on the Spanish Invasion of the Americas*, 111, 182, 152. It is unclear to me why *inhumani* should be rendered as "uncivilized."

38 See Chapter 7, p. 153: contrary to what is commonly assumed, leading scientists (e.g., Joseph Glanvill, Henry More, Thomas Willis, George Sinclair, or Robert Boyle) "went out of their way to insist on the reality of witchcraft and the importance of demonic activity in the natural world," while the most skeptical treatments of witchcraft were "steeped in theological, rather than natural scientific orthodoxies" (see the authoritative discussion in Clark, *Thinking with Demons*, 294–311, here 296).

39 Of central importance in this regard was Balthasar Bekker's international bestseller *De Betoverde Weereld* ("The World Enchanted," 1691–1693); see discussion in Israel, *Radical Enlightenment*, 375–405.

40 On the denial of "natural reason" to colonialized people, leading to their routine depiction as "irrational" or "subrational" and therefore similar to animals, see, e.g., Wynter, "Unsettling the Coloniality."

41 Kipling, "The White Man's Burden."

42 Stocking, *Victorian Anthropology*, 237; see also idem, *Race, Culture and evolution.*

43 Von Hartmann, *Philosophie des Unbewussten*, vol. 2, 331–332. Hartmann evidently means to say that all non-white races should be exterminated as quickly as possible so that the further evolution of humanity can concentrate its energies on the various branches of the white race battling it out among one another.

44 Spencer, *Social Statics*, 416. Such opinions could find support in Darwin himself, whose biological evolutionism was indebted to social evolutionism (rather than the other way around, as often assumed) and who wrote for instance that "At some future period, not very distant as measured in centuries, the civilised races will almost certainly exterminate, and replace, the savage races throughout the world" (Stocking, "The Dark-Skinned Savage," 113–115). Stocking points out that Spencer's *Principles of Sociology* (orig. 1876) "largely structured the thinking of the two generations of social scientists before about 1920" (ibid., 117), in support of "a raciocultural hierarchy in terms of which civilized men . . . were large-brained white men, and only large-brained white men . . . were fully civilized" (ibid., 122; cf. 128).

45 The reference is to a famous volume by Nicholas Cusanus, *De Docta Ignorantia* (1440).

46 Hegel, *Vorlesungen über die Philosophie der Geschichte*, 62, 64, 78. I deliberately speak of "*spiritual* evolution," with reference to Hegel's concept of *Geist* (confusingly combined by him with *Vernunft*).

47 Ibid., 76.

48 I am impressed by the argument of the so-called MC collective (to which I will return) that modernity and coloniality are two sides of the same coin. For the basic argument, see Escobar, "Worlds and Knowledges Otherwise."

49 This further agenda is relevant to Asprem's distinction between what he calls the "strict" and the "inflated" version of my rejected knowledge model ("Rejected Knowledge Reconsidered"). While the adjective "inflated" is inherently pejorative and unfit for academic discourse, it is correct that I defend my model not just in a *sensu stricto* but also in a *sensu lato* version that, unfortunately, bears little resemblance to how it gets presented in Asprem's chapter.

50 Böhme & Böhme, *Das Andere der Vernunft* (roughly translatable as "Rationality's Other").

51 *Anti*-normativity could be defined as opposition to a normative standard that is experienced as restrictive or oppressive, typically resulting in gestures of rebellion or transgression that may themselves become attractive as a form of (sub)cultural capital. By this dynamic, esotericism or occultism as "rejected knowledge" may be embraced by oppositional subcultures (Kaplan & Lööw, *Cultic Milieu*) or individual consumers on the spiritual market (Frank, *Conquest of Cool*) as signifying dissent and independence from the mainstream. The importance of this topic in the study of esotericism is demonstrated by an excellent recent volume; Hedenborg White & Rudbøg, *Esotericism and Deviance*.

52 While the term "anti-normativity" is somewhat common, especially in the context of queer theory (McCann & Monaghan, *Queer Theory Now*, 14–16), "counter-normativity" has hardly been theorized (ibid., see Index under Normativity) and occurs just rarely in other academic contexts (e.g., Sepielli, "Quietism and Counter-Normativity"). Clearly, my argument resonates with the core program of queer theory understood in a broad sense (e.g., the questioning of masculinity as the implicit normative standard by which women are reduced to subordinate status, of heteronormativity as the implicit sexual standard by which other sexual orientations are dismissed as deviant, or of whiteness as the implicit norm even of what it means to be human at all). It might seem paradoxical but is psychologically predictable that queerness often gets "deployed as an identity label" (Johnston, "Disrupting Sanctified Deviance," 80), i.e., interpreted in terms of *anti*- rather than counter-normativity (McCann & Monaghan, *Queer Theory Now*, 11–16). I wish to thank the organizers of the sessions on "Normativity" at the ESSWE9 conference in Malmö (2023), which gave me the idea of theorizing "counter-normativity." To my knowledge, the only passing mention of this term in an esotericism context occurs in an episode of Earl Fontainelle's excellent SHWEP podcast (see Appendix 2).

53 Lincoln, "Theses on Method," nr. 10 (*Gods and Demons*, 2).

54 Tertullian, *Adversus Valentinianos* III.5. I also used this as the motto for my introduction to *Esotericism and the Academy*.

55 See the quotation by Montaigne above Chapter 3.

56 Canguilhem, *The Normal and the Pathological*, 243 (emphasis added).

57 Ibid.

58 Cryle & Stephens, *Normality*, 6 (with reference to Carter, *Heart of Whiteness*, 4); and see ibid. 5: "being taken for granted came precisely to be one of the key features of the normal" (referring to the remarkably short history of "normality" and "the normal," a word that does not appear in English prior to 1848 and was still described as "new in the language" by the end of the nineteenth century": ibid., 3–4).

59 McCann & Monaghan, *Queer Theory Now*, 13.

60 Mignolo, *Darker Side of the Renaissance*, 5. My previous sentences are deliberate paraphrases of Mignolo's formulations on this page, reflecting the close convergence of my argument with the core perspective of the MC collective (see above, p. 253 note 48).

61 Davis, *High Weirdness*, 8–17, esp. 9–11: next to "aesthetic weirdness" or "the weird as a space of deviancy," Davis argues, "the third and most substantial sense of the weird is *ontological*." I'm indebted to Davis's discussion but have a somewhat different way of slicing the cake. Davis sees "the uncanny" as concerned with psychological (especially psychoanalytic) expla-

nations and is concerned to keep it at some distance from "the weird" as exemplified by American popular culture (ibid., 15). By contrast, I understand the weird and the uncanny as entirely equivalent; psychoanalytic interpretations I see as secondary attempts to normalize the weirdness of the uncanny by means of rationalization; and I resist an overdetermination of weirdness by the paranormal American style (for both points, see text).

62 I find it significant that Sigmund Freud, in his famous essay "Das Unheimliche" (where he also coined the term "the return of the repressed," *die Wiederkehr des Verdrängten*, to which I allude in my text), discusses the uncanny precisely with reference to the eeriness of puppets or dolls, i.e., the sense that materials objects might in fact be animated, with the concomitant fear that living beings might therefore *not* have a soul (Freud's reference here is to Jentsch, "Zur Psychologie des Unheimlichen," 197). I interpret these fears *historically*, as a direct reflection of the idolatry concept that, as I emphasize in this book, lies at the heart of the European construction of rejected knowledge.

63 Hence the language of "misfits." See, e.g., Rudbøg, "'The Judges'," 83–84, 101 (with reference to Washington, *Madame Blavatsky's Baboon: A History of the Mystics, Mediums, and Misfits who brought Spiritualism to America*); Davis, *High Weirdness*, 16; Godwin, "Afterword."

64 Without further insisting on it here, I find it significant that in classical music, precisely the skillful deviation from a normative standard (i.e., by using tones that are dissonant in relation to the diatonic scale) is the key to musical effect. Not by any coincidence, when the counter-normal appears in any context, we typically experience it as a "dissonance." On a nearly metaphysical level, we might also think of the profoundly "weird" phenomenon known as the Pythagorean comma (the point being that nature would seem to resist perfect regularity and require some measure of deviation from the norm).

65 Kripal, *Authors of the Impossible*; idem, *Mutants and Mystics*; idem, *The Superhumanities*; idem, *How to Think Impossibly*. See also Strieber & Kripal, *The Super Natural*; and the "Archives of the Impossible" housed at Rice University, Houston.

66 I find it relevant that Kripal comes from a background of Catholicism (*Roads*, 87–97, 147–155, and *passim*; *Secret Body*, 21–55) that accepts the possibility of miracles. To say that miracles could be real is another way of saying that the impossible is possible (and therefore not the impossible). Seen from this perspective (see, e.g., *Superhumanities*, 139–152), Kripal's argument seems to be directed precisely against the profoundly disenchanting impact of Protestantism and the Enlightenment. For a strictly parallel struggle for clarification about "the occult" as the possibility of the impossible, see the fictional biography of Pierce Moffett (likewise raised as an American Catholic) in John Crowley's *Aegypt* novels.

67 See discussion of prototypes in Chapter 1, pp. 9–10.

68 Davis, *High Weirdness*, 15.

69 The classic reference is Butterfield, *Whig Interpretation of History*. Today, the type of historiography that used to be known as "whig(gish) history" is usually referred to as *present-centeredness* or *presentism*. As formulated by Ashplant & Wilson, it is based on the "anachronistic error . . . that the historian, in seeking to study, reconstruct and write about the past, is constrained by necessarily starting from the perceptual and conceptual categories of the present" ("Present-Centred History," 253; see also Wilson & Ashplant, "Whig History"). In George Stocking's formulation ("On the Limits," 3), presentism

attempts "to understands the past for the sake of the present," whereas historiography proper attempts "to understand the past for the sake of the past." Of course, the point is *not* that it would be illegitimate to learn lessons for the present from studying the past! The point is that for any such lesson to make any sense, it will have to be based on a somewhat adequate understanding of the past *on its own terms* and not just of the projection of our own categories onto that past. It should be obvious that any attempt to understand the past "on its own terms" is a *hermeneutic* act in the classic Gadamerian sense (see below, note 74, 76). This excludes both a naïve Rankean-positivist concept of writing down *wie es eigentlich gewesen* ("how it truly was") *and* a radical presentism as recently promoted, e.g., by Michael Bergunder ("Umkämpfte Historisierung," 66–69; Hanegraaff, "Here, There & Everywhere") but implies an intermediary position of *perspectivism* that allows historians to engage their sources in dialogue (Hanegraaff, "Hermes, Hermeneutics & the Humanities").

70 As regards such life-changing cases of counter-normality, I am thinking for instance of the Kālī experience recounted by Kripal, *Roads*, 199–206; Dale C. Allison's experience of divine presence when "the stars came down" as he was sixteen years old, quoted in Kripal, *Superhumanities*, 158–159; Jean Houston's unitive experience quoted in Chapter 6, p. 144; or Henry Shukman's "opening" described in his Zen memoir *One Blade of Grass*, 46–47.

71 A key reference for counter-normality would be Rainer Maria Rilke's oeuvre, with whom I began this book, as is evident from the impressive analyses by Magnússon, *Dichtung als Erfahrungsmetaphysik*, e.g., 298–323 and *passim*. For our common resistance against "staying with the trouble" of counter-normality, see ibid., 315 and 340 (the "Christine episode" in *Notebooks of Malte Laurids Brigge* and Rilke's insistence in *Letter to a Young Poet* on having the courage to stay with "the strangest, most wondrous, and most unexplainable that may appear to us," rather than giving in to *die tägliche Abwehr*, i.e., our "daily resistance").

72 Honey jar: see a paranormal event reported by Dale C. Allison, in Kripal, *Superhumanities*, 157. Voice in the head: the most famous example would be Socrates's *daimonion*, but the hearing of voices is in fact an excellent example of counter-normality in contemporary society (e.g., Blackman, *Hearing Voices*)

73 Haraway, "Situated Knowledges."

74 This general perspective on interpretation finds strong support in Gadamerian hermeneutics (Gadamer, *Hermeneutik I*). My book *Hermetic Spirituality* is an attempt to exemplify it in practice, by applying it to the study of the Hermetica. On the all-important difference between hermeneutic understanding and *gnōsis*, see ibid., 345.

75 This is of course a nod to Haraway, *Staying with the Trouble*; cf. Johnston, "Disrupting Sanctified Deviance," 71.

76 My advocacy of counter-normativity is informed by a firm Gadamerian commitment to the classic *Erklären-Verstehen* distinction. While I fully support the importance and legitimacy of scholarly projects focused on scientific explanation of whatever *can* be explained, I am deeply skeptical of the totalizing claim that absolute knowledge ever could or should be achieved by means of "explaining" human culture in terms of quantifiable material processes, as in the classic Weberian ideal of science (see Chapter 5, pp. 129–130 with p. 235 note 40; cf. Hanegraaff, "Subtle Energies")."

77 Asprem, "Rejected Knowledge Reconsidered," 143. Asprem is "puzzled" by what he perceives as a "peculiarity" in some of my recent work but ignores my arguments in the sources he quotes (Hanegraaff, *Esotericism and the Academy*, 366–367; idem, "Power of Ideas," 266–267). He also avoids the key example of Zeno's paradox that I used in both publications to explain my point (as I did again in "Provincializing American Theory," 510–511). Far from just a recent "peculiarity," empiricism has been a constant in my work since the mid-1990s (Hanegraaff, "Empirical Method").

78 I have been surprised by the almost allergic reaction to my simple statement that historians can "listen to the sources" (discussion in Hanegraaff, "Hermes, Hermeneutics & the Humanities"). I would consider it self-evident that "listening" (as opposed to "hearing") is a profoundly hermeneutic process that both involves *and* requires the subjectivities of the listener. If we can't listen to others, we are left with nothing but the echoes of our own voices (Hanegraaff, "Teaching Experiential Dimension," 167; cf. Grondin, "Universality of Hermeneutic Understanding," 29).

79 Jung, *Red Book*, 232.

80 Note that the very identification of this object as "soul" is a theoretical act. What makes the *Red Book* so impressive is the extreme extent to which Jung was willing, or able, to relinquish control and allow the flow of experience to dissolve his theory-driven "judgment and knowledge." The obvious price to pay was enormous fear, especially the fear of going mad; see discussion in Hanegraaff, "Great War of the Soul."

81 Hanegraaff, "Out of Egypt"; for the larger story, see idem, *Hermetic Spirituality*.

82 Along perfectly similar lines, the deep Christian commitments of major scholars caused them to impose biblical models on the Hermetic literature, as a normative framework for interpreting texts from pagan Egypt that had nothing to do with the bible. Again, this was not just an additional frame but one that utterly dominated academic perceptions of the Hermetica as a whole (Hanegraaff, *Hermetic Spirituality*, 170–179, 283–284; e.g., Mahé's acceptance of CH I as the account of a Fall determined his interpretation of CH XIII as concerned with correcting that Fall).

83 Ibid., 138–144 ("Weirdness at the Center"). Of course, I anticipate the objection (since it is perfectly predictable) that this claim about the Hermetic literature is just my own particular interpretation, a mere projection of my own prejudices. I respond that the proof of the pudding is in the eating. Critics are invited to read *Hermetic Spirituality and the Historical Imagination* and decide for themselves in how far I have succeeded in my attempt to listen to the sources by engaging them in dialogue and allowing them to challenge the theoretical frameworks that previous scholars have imposed on them.

84 Scott, *Hermetica* I, 242–245; II, 385 (Hanegraaff, *Hermetic Spirituality*, 248 note 101).

85 Godwin, "Afterword," 424–425. After thirty years, I see no reason to abandon the basic argument for "radical" agnosticism and empiricism that I made in Hanegraaff, "Empirical Method," 107–108: "[I]f we are radically honest, we must admit that none of us has a clue about what is *really* going on around us (and especially *how*, and for what reasons, it is going on).... [T]o admit the grave inadequacies in our knowledge and understanding of 'reality' is more scientific than to fool ourselves about them." Likewise, I reaffirm my statements about the profoundly "therapeutic" effect of dismantling the discursive power of the "Grand

Polemical Narrative" (i.e., of Internal Eurocentrism) as formulated in Hanegraaff, "Forbidden Knowledge," 249–251, with note 67.

86 In broad terms, my summary here is indebted to Escobar, "World and Knowledges Otherwise," 181–183 (italicized sentence on p. 183). Among the major references are Jürgen Habermas, *Der philosophische Diskurs der Moderne*; Weber, *Wissenschaft als Beruf*; and Giddens, *Consequences of Modernity.*

87 Spencer, *Social Statics*, 42, 307. The There Is No Alternative (TINA) slogan was famously used by Margaret Thatcher to claim that neoliberal market capitalism is the only possible option. Again, see the disturbing analysis by Krastev & Holmes of what happens when any particular ideology, no matter how well intended, claims that "There Is No Other Way" (*The Light That Failed*, here 5, and *passim*).

88 On the emancipatory importance of our ignorance about the future, see, e.g., Solnit, *Hope in the Dark.*

89 As already noted in note 49, Asprem perceives correctly that my work is based on a stricter and a broader agenda, the second of which could be called "emancipatory"; but he misunderstands it as inspired by an apologetic project of "defending esotericism" against "anti-esotericism" ("Rejected Knowledge Reconsidered," 137). Asprem's personal commitment to a scientific naturalism congenial to "methodological atheism" (*Problem of Disenchantment*, 85–86 note 118) may help explain his evident irritation about what he calls "simplified, partisan, and even soft conspirational explanations" directed against "polemically charged simplifications such as 'reductionism,' 'materialism,' and more recently 'postmodernism'" (ibid.). In actual fact, all my work is based consistently on an empirical and radically historical approach grounded in hermeneutics and methodological agnosticism. I would argue that Asprem's scientific naturalism must be seen as just another worldview, based ultimately on a metaphysical a priori, not as an inherently superior scientific perspective whose normative foundations are beyond critique (Hanegraaff, "Historical Approaches to Contemporary Esotericism").

90 Hanegraaff, "Rejected Knowledge . . .," 149. In terms of the analysis by Krastev & Holmes, this precise opposition lies at the core of what has happened to liberal democracy over the past couple of decades: "It is a story, among others things, of liberalism abandoning pluralism for hegemony" (*The Light That Failed*, 6).

91 As regards both gender and race, there might be no better illustration than the case of two terracotta images of "the average American boy and girl" that were proudly displayed at the New York World's Fair in 1939. Although obviously white, their bodies were said to represent an average based on the measurements of 15,000 American women and several million soldiers and young men in the Ivy League, and therefore their names were Normman and Norma! (Carter, *Heart of Whiteness*, 1–41).

92 Tooze, "Welcome to the World of Polycrisis." With "mental," I mean to refer to the crisis of mental health especially among younger generations since the 2010s (e.g., Haidt, *The Anxious Generation*).

93 For my understanding of neoliberalism as a historically contingent ideology that succeeded in establishing itself as the new normality, I have profited in particular from Harvey, *Brief History of Neoliberalism*; Jones, *Masters of the Universe*; Slobodian, *Globalists*; Hertz, *Silent*

Takeover; Brown, *Undoing the Demos*; Steger & Roy, *Neoliberalism*; and Zuboff, *The Age of Surveillance Capitalism*. For a particularly clear summary, see Monbiot, "Neoliberalism." There is now a large literature about the destructive effects of neoliberal marketization not just on the foundations of liberal democracy but also on the universities as institutions for higher learning. An excellent early analysis (written during the time of transition, when the earlier model was still present but was beginning to get eroded) remains Readings, *The University in Ruins*; a more recent discussion is Nussbaum, *Not For Profit*. To get an idea of the extreme "Western-centrist" narrative of history that informs orthodox neoliberalism, see, e.g., Rougier, *The Genius of the West* (with a preface by Friedrich Hayek).

94 This is a very close parallel to how the project of disenchantment, as explained in a classic argument by Max *Weber* (*Wissenschaft als Beruf*), required the disappearance of "mysterious, incalculable forces." See brief discussion in Chapters 5, pp. 129–130 and 7, pp. 154–155. Detailed discussion in Asprem, *Problem of Disenchantment*; Hanegraaff, *Esotericism and the Academy*, 252–255; idem, "Subtle Energies."

95 As admitted, with disarming honesty, by Daniel Dennett, *Sweet Dreams*, 79: "Yes, it is indeed difficult to deny that there are qualia. I've been working on the task for years, with scant progress!" For documentation of that ongoing struggle, see, e.g., *Consciousness Explained*, esp. 368–411 ("Qualia Disqualified") or Dennett's much earlier *Content and Consciousness*, e.g., 159 ("somehow insusceptible to analysis and explanation within the physical sciences").

Appendix 1

Glossary of Technical Terms

Agnosticism In the context of this book, this term has two dimensions.

Methodological agnosticism assumes that the existence or nonexistence of divine, spiritual, or sacred realities is beyond empirical verification or falsification by scholarly methods. This is not some mild form of atheism or an expression of polite indifference ("who cares?") but a true admission that *we honestly do not know*. Is it possible that angels exists? Yes, it is possible. Are there scholarly methods for finding out whether they actually do exist? No, there aren't. Therefore the question remains open. Discussion: Chapter 1, pp. 16–17 with p. 211 note 40. Source: Hanegraaff, "Empirical Method," 100–108 (referring to the work of Jan Platvoet; but the argument could ultimately be traced to Immanuel Kant on the limits of human reason).

Radical Agnosticism takes the philosophical (metaphysical) consequences of methodological agnosticism to its ultimate conclusion by acknowledging our incapacity as human beings to "radically" (from *radix*, root, i.e., in terms of its ultimate roots or foundations) understand the ultimate nature of the reality in which we find ourselves. In my understanding, radical agnosticism is closely connected with a Gadamerian approach to the humanities as concerned with hermeneutics rather than explanation. Discussion: Hanegraaff, *Hermetic Spirituality*, 4–5 with notes 7–8.

Alchemical Paradigm In the context of this book, the term refers to a structural paradigm that emerged in German culture during the sixteenth century and emphasizes linear temporality, dynamic organic processes such as generation and birth, and personal experience (in contrast to the Platonic Paradigm, see below). Discussion: Chapter 4, pp. 110–114. Source: Hanegraaff, *Esotericism and the Academy*, 191–194.

Anti-Apologeticism An influential school of German Protestant historians of philosophy and theological polemicists (notably Jacob Thomasius, Ehregott Daniel Colberg, Christoph August Heumann, and Jacob Brucker) who were active during the seventeenth and eighteenth centuries. They held the Patristic Apologists responsible for a pernicious "Hellenization of Christianity" that, by giving legitimacy to Platonic Orientalism, had allowed the history of philosophy to be infected by pagan errors. Anti-Apologeticism became the key theoretical foundation of the Enlightenment campaign against Rejected Knowledge. Discussion: Chapter 3, pp. 88–90. Source: Lehmann-Brauns, *Weisheit in der Weltgeschichte*, 7, 16, 23, 26, and *passim*. Applied to esotericism: Hanegraaff, *Esotericism and the Academy*, esp. 101–152.

Anti-Eclectic Historiography The rejection of Eclectic Historiography as a methodological principle in the study of history. Discussion: Chapter 3, p. 99 and 213–214 note 57. Source: Hanegraaff, *Esotericism and the Academy*, 152, 197, 377–378.

Counter-Normality The phenomenon that, as a result of the imposition of a normative standard that ends up concealing its own presence by appearing as normal, certain dimensions of human experience come to be experienced as "not normal." Discussion and source: Chapter 9, pp. 200–204.

Counter-Normativity The project of demonstrating that what is commonly experienced as "normal" (and gets presented to us as such) may in fact be the reflection of a hidden normative standard that should be critically examined and not just taken for granted. Discussion and source: Chapter 9, pp. 198–200.

Discursive Turn An important trend in the humanities that developed in the wake of post-structuralism, including the study of religion and esotericism. It is defined by an assumption that discourse is the central or even the exclusive dimension that can or must be studied in history and human culture. Discussion: Chapter 1, pp. 17–21. Source: a convenient reference is von Stuckrad, "Discursive Study of Religion" (although he does not speak literally of a "discursive turn," this is clearly intended, given the references on p. 255 to several previous "turns").

Eclectic Historiography A methodological approach to the history of philosophy (and, by extension, to historiography generally) that became dominant since the eighteenth century. As an alternative to the traditional method of *philosophia sectaria*, this *philosophia eclectica* was based on the principle that historians of philosophy do not need to cover all traditions that have developed over the history of thought but must use their *own* faculty of rational judgment to separate the "wheat" of what they consider true philosophy from the "chaff" of what could be discarded as pseudo-philosophy. Discussion: Chapter 3, pp. 93–96. The sources of eclecticism go back at least to the eighteenth century, but a standard overview is Albrecht, *Eklektik*.

Empiricism In the context of this book, the term refers to an approach to the study of esotericism (and of religion more generally) that is neither religionist nor reductionist but takes an intermediary position that prioritizes "bottom-up" historical and empirical research, on a basis of methodological agnosticism as regards ultimate realities. I would argue that a philosophical interpretation in terms of radical agnosticism (see above) implies a *radical empiricism* as well. Source: Hanegraaff, "Empirical Method," 100–108; and idem, *Hermetic Spirituality*, 4–5.

Esotericism A noun that appeared for the first time in German in 1792 (*Esoterik*), after which it was translated into French (*l'ésotérisme*) in 1828 and in English (*esotericism*) in 1883. Only the adjective "esoteric" can be traced back to late antiquity (Lucien of Samosata, second century CE). In modern academic vocabulary, the noun and/or adjective are generally used in two different ways that should not be confused. In this book, I introduce the convention of distinguishing them as follows:

Esotericism$_1$ A collection of historical traditions, ideas, practices, or social formations that are grouped together because they are considered to have certain things in common.

Esotericism$_2$ The dialectics of secrecy concerned with the social regulation or negotiation of access to specific forms of knowledge.
Discussion and source: Chapter 1, pp. 18–19.

Internal Eurocentrism A polemical/apologetic discourse (or set of discourses) concerned with stipulating what should be considered "central" to European identity, notably an idealization of Greek rationalism and a presumed "Judeo-Christian" (but not Islamic) monotheism. To the extent that something is seen as falling short of this normative standard, it becomes "marginal" to that identity, notably "pagan" traditions associated with, e.g., "idolatry," "magic," or "superstition" (but also Islam). I argue in this book that during the age of colonialism and imperialism, Internal Eurocentrism became the basic template that allowed Western intellectuals to justify the suppression and extermination of "pagan idolatry" and "superstition" in the rest of the world. Discussion: Chapter 1, p. 25 with 215 note 71, Chapter 3 (*passim*), Chapter 9, pp. 192–198. Source (of the concept, but not yet the term): Hanegraaff, *Esotericism and the Academy*.

Mnemohistory History as remembered in the collective imagination, regardless of what actually happened in the past. Discussion: Chapter 3, pp. 80–81. Source: Jan Assmann, *Moses the Egyptian*, 6–22 (but see also earlier discussion in German: *Das kulturelle Gedächtnis*).

Mnemohistoriography The project of writing the history of how the past has been remembered or imagined over time. Discussion: Chapter 3, p. 80. Source: Hanegraaff, *Esotericism and the Academy*, 375–376.

Philhellenism An intellectual school that dominated classical studies during the nineteenth century. Philhellenists believed that the true identity of Europe was based on the "superior" civilization of the ancient Greeks, usually seen in combination with a "superior" biblical morality as understood from a predominantly Protestant perspective. Informed by a much longer history of internal Eurocentrism, the implication was that "barbarian" traditions "from the Orient" (including Egypt) had always posed an external threat to Western civilization, and their "irrational superstitions" deserved no intellectual or religious legitimacy. Discussion: Chapter 1, pp. 26–27, Chapter 3, p. 99. Source: Suzanne Marchand, *Down from Olympus* and "From Liberalism to Neoromanticism." Applied to esotericism: Hanegraaff, *Hermetic Spirituality*, 360–362 and "Out of Egypt."

Philosophia perennis The belief in one single tradition of supreme and eternal wisdom that has always been available throughout the history of humanity. Discussion: Chapter 3, pp. 84–85. Source: Agostino Steuco, *De perenni philosophia* (1540).

Platonic Orientalism The belief that Platonism is essentially a spiritual wisdom tradition whose core doctrines did not originate with Socrates and Plato in Athens but came from Oriental sources and authorities (notably the Persian or Chaldaean Zoroaster, the Egyptian Hermes Trismegistus, or the Hebrew Moses). Not to be confused with Orientalism as famously understood by Edward Said. Discussion: Chapter 2, p. 32 and Chapter 3, pp. 82–83. Source: John Walbridge, *Wisdom of the Mystic East*. Applied to esotericism: Hanegraaff, *Esotericism and the Academy*, 12–17.

Platonic Paradigm In the context of this book, the term refers to a structural paradigm that informs the Platonic-Christian worldview as seen from predominantly Roman-Catholic perspectives during the Italian Renaissance. In contrast to the Alchemical Paradigm, it emphasizes spatial harmony and the traditional authority of "ancient" or "eternal" sources of wisdom. Discussion: Chapter 4, pp. 105–110. Source: Hanegraaff, *Esotericism and the Academy*, 191–194.

Prisca theologia The belief in an ancient and original theology or wisdom tradition. In contrast to Philosophia perennis, the assumption is that the supreme divine knowledge of ancient wisdom has declined or been corrupted and largely forgotten over time and must therefore be recovered and restored. Discussion: Chapter 3, pp. 84–85. Source: various works by Ficino (see Hanegraaff, *Esotericism and the Academy*, 7 note 7).

Reified Imaginal Formations Generic concepts such as "religion" or "esotericism" (but also, e.g., "the economy") strictly exist only in our common discourse and our collective imagination. However, the human mind tends to *reify* discursive and imaginal formations so that they seem to exist in the world "out there" (e.g., "there *is* such a thing as religion"). Discussion: Chapter 1, p. 20. Source: Hanegraaff, "Reconstructing 'Religion' from the Bottom Up," 578–581.

Rejected Knowledge In this book, the term covers all those traditions, ideas, or practices in Western culture that were rejected as illegitimate or nonsensical by Enlightenment intellectuals. Based on the anti-apologetic argument against "pagan superstitions" (itself the culmination of a long history of internal-Eurocentric identity formation), and following the principles of an Eclectic Historiography on rationalist foundations, all these materials should be dumped into the "sea of oblivion." On these same foundations, in the wake of the Enlightenment, similar traditions, ideas, or practices should be exterminated in the rest of the world, as part of a global "civilizing" process based on an ideology of Western superiority. Two common misunderstandings about Rejected Knowledge should be avoided. Firstly: that specific traditions (e.g., astrology or alchemy) were rejected by the Enlightenment does not imply that they were *always* rejected during earlier periods of history. Often the opposite is true. Secondly: "rejected knowledge" is not intended as a *definition* of "esotericism." The statement "esotericism is rejected knowledge" could be seen as similar to the statement "cats are animals," which doesn't imply that "animals are cats." Discussion: Chapter 1, pp. 21–23. Source: the term seems to have been introduced by James Webb, *Occult Underground*, 191 (but see further discussion in Asprem, "On the Social Organization"). My understanding of Rejected Knowledge as developed in *Esotericism and the Academy* rests on foundations that are different from Webb's.

Religionism An influential approach to the academic study of religion defined by the paradoxical claim that a correct approach to the "*history* of religions" (as exemplified, e.g., by Mircea Eliade) must accept the presence—and not just *belief* in the presence—of a *non*-historical (i.e., spiritual, atemporal, perennial) dimension that defines the true nature of "religion" or "the sacred" as a phenomenon sui generis. This technical meaning of "religionism" is often misunderstood. Contrary to common assumptions, a rejection of religionism does *not* imply a "reductionist" doctrine to the effect that no spiritual dimension exists. It only means that such a spiritual dimension, if it were to exist, would be beyond the reach of scholarly and historical methods by definition (see Methodological Agnosticism). In this book, I embrace an empirical-historical perspective that is neither religionist nor reductionist. Discussion: Chapter 1, pp. 15–17. Source: Hanegraaff, *Esotericism and the Academy*, esp. 127 with note 174, 149–150, 295-314, 357–358 (and idem, "Empirical Method," 100–108).

Spirituality In this book, the term is used to emphasize those dimensions of "religion" that are focused on individual experience and praxis rather than on social organizations or collective doctrines. Discussion and source: Hanegraaff, *Hermetic Spirituality*, 19–22.

Western Culture This book as a whole intends to present a program of discarding outdated concepts of "Western culture" based on (internal-)Eurocentric normative prejudice, so as to make room for a more comprehensive and historically more adequate understanding of the Greater West. Discussion: Chapter 1, pp. 23–29.

Appendix 2

Sources and Resources

Newcomers to the study of esotericism may easily get lost in the dense forests of academic literature. They may also find it hard to tell reliable sources apart from the doubtful products of (crypto-)esoteric apologetics or dilletante scholarship. The situation is not made easier by the fact that mediocre publications may come from the pen of established academics, whereas excellent research is sometimes produced by authors without university credentials. Scholarship of superior quality may well be hidden away in specialized periodicals that are known only to experts and do not appear in the lists of peer-reviewed journals. In this field, articles that appear in major scholarly media are not always more reliable than those that do not; and monographs published by university presses are not necessarily better than books that appear with obscure publishers, sometimes connected to specific esoteric organizations.

Partly this situation is typical of a young field of study; but partly it reflects some peculiarities unique to the domain of esotericism as such. The traditional status of esotericism or the occult as "rejected knowledge" has given rise to a kind of parallel universe of amateur scholarship, part of which is bad but some of which is actually very good. Some of the best publications may be hard or even impossible to find in standard university libraries, as opposed to private libraries or archives. Some of the best collections were created by devoted connoisseurs, who do not necessarily make their treasures available to scholars, or have the means to do so. The rise of the internet has made it easier to publish materials online that would have been inaccessible in the past; but as in so many other fields, it has also created a lot of confusion about what to take seriously and what not. Although there are no shortcuts or easy solutions, below I provide some information about useful sources and resources that can help you gain entrance to the modern study of esotericism.

Organizations

- By far the most important professional organization in the study of esotericism is the *European Society for the Study of Western Esotericism* (ESSWE; www.esswe.org). Membership is open to academics, students, and nonacademic individuals with a serious interest in the field. The ESSWE was founded in 2005 and has been organizing biannual conferences all over Europe: Tübingen, Germany (2006), Strasbourg, France (2009), Szeged, Hungary (2011), Gothenburg, Sweden (2013), Riga, Latvia (2015), Erfurt, Germany (2017), Amsterdam, the Netherlands (2019), Cork, Ireland (2022, delayed because of the pandemic), Malmö, Sweden (2023), and Vilnius, Lithuania (2025). Interested outsiders are welcome to attend these conferences for a modest fee. The ESSWE also has a wide range of associated regional and thematic networks (accessible through the website) that organize activities of their own, including workshops and conferences.

- The French organization *Politica Hermetica* (https://politicahermetica.wordpress.com) organizes annual conferences and runs an important journal under the same name. In spite of the title, the focus is on all aspects of esotericism and not just on politics.
- Another important organization focused on the medieval period is the *Societas Magica* (https://societasmagica.org). It organizes annual conferences in Kalamazoo and publishes a newsletter.
- A new organization with much potential is the Research Network for the Study of Esoteric Practices (www.rensep.org), whose mission is "to promote and advance the interdisciplinary and comparative study of esoteric practices from a global perspective."
- The Center for Studies on New Religions (CESNUR) organizes annual conferences and has a website (www.cesnur.org) with incredibly large archives of scholarly information on New Religious Movements, including those that fall under the "esoteric" rubric.
- Esotericism is also well represented at conferences organized by several international organizations in the study of religion, notably the International Association for the History of Religions (IAHR; www.iahr.dk), the European Association for the Study of Religions (EASR; www.easr.eu), and the American Academy of Religion (AAR; www.aarweb.org).

Libraries

- The most famous scholarly library in the field, particularly for the period prior to the nineteenth century, is the *Bibliotheca Philosophica Hermetica* in Amsterdam. Today, its unique collections are housed partly in the *Embassy of the Free Mind* (www.embassyofthefreemind.com) and partly in the Allard Pierson Museum of the University of Amsterdam (https://allardpierson.nl/en/), both located at walking distance from one another in the old center of Amsterdam.
- An extremely important collection created by a private collector (Hans Thomas Hakl) is known as the *Octagon Library*. While not yet accessible at the time of writing, it is destined to become part of the *Fondazione Cini* at the Island of San Giorgo Maggiore in Venice, Italy.

- Two other famous collections with great relevance to the history of esotericism are the library of the Warburg Institute in London (www.warburg.sas.ac.uk) and the Manly P. Hall Archive owned by the Philosophical Research Society in Los Angeles (www.manlyphall.org).
- Next to publicly accessible collections housed by academic institutions, some excellent libraries are owned by esoteric or affiliated organizations such as Freemasonry or the Theosophical Society. While some may restrict access only to members, others are open to general visitors.

University Programs

- The first academic chair devoted to the study of esotericism was created in 1965 at the *École Pratique des Hautes Études* (Sorbonne) in Paris and offers weekly seminars.
- The second chair was created in 1999 at the University of Amsterdam. It is part of the Centre for History of Hermetic Philosophy and Related Currents (HHP; www.amsterdamhermetica.nl). Its five-person staff covers the history of esotericism in Late Antiquity, the Middle Ages, Early Modernity, and Modernity. It is currently the only program in the world to offer a complete program of undergraduate and graduate courses.
- In the United States, Rice University (Houston, Texas; https://www.rice.edu) offers a certificate in *Gnosticism, Esotericism, and Mysticism* (GEM).
- The University of South Carolina (USA) in collaboration with the University of Exeter (UK) recently launched an innovative masters program focused on the Occult Sciences in Islamicate cultures.
- Next to specialized programs, courses in esotericism are being offered with increasing frequency at many other universities in Europe (most notably in Sweden, e.g., Stockholm and Gothenborg) and the United States.

Dictionary Project

- The logical starting point for finding reliable information and bibliographical references is the 1,200-page *Dictionary of Gnosis and Western Esotericism* (DGWE) edited by Wouter J. Hanegraaff in collaboration with Antoine Faivre, Roelof van den Broek, and Jean-Pierre Brach (Brill: Leiden/Boston 2005; also available in an online edition).
- As the field developed rapidly into new directions after 2005, Brill publishers decided to create a broader dictionary concept known as the "Brill Esotericism Reference Library" (BERL; see https:/brill.com/display/serial/BERL), in order to provide room for additional volumes focused on dimensions not yet covered by the original DGWE.

- The first addition to the DGWE was a large dictionary focused on *Western Esotericism in Scandinavia*, edited by Henrik Bogdan and Olav Hammer (2016).
- A *Dictionary of Contemporary Esotericism* edited by Egil Asprem is announced as forthcoming, with many dictionary entries already available as prepublications at https://contern.org.
- Further volumes will hopefully be published in the future for such fields as esotericism in Middle and Eastern Europe, Jewish Esotericism, or Islamic Esotericism.

Academic Journals

- Since 2001, Brill publishes the flagship peer-reviewed academic journal *Aries: Journal for the Study of Western Esotericism* (www.brill.nl/aries).
- The second major peer-reviewed academic journal *Correspondences* was launched in 2013 and is available in open access: see https://correspondencesjournal.com.
- Since 2024, a brand-new peer-reviewed online journal, *Praxis-Knowledge*, focuses on the study of esoteric practices. See https://rensep.org/praxis-knowledge/
- Note that the early predecessor of *Aries* (*ARIES* first series, published by La Table d'Emeraude in Paris from 1985 until 1999) is available online on the ESSWE website (search under Publications/Journal).
- Another important resource is the journal *Magic, Religion & Witchcraft*, published by Penn Press since 2006 (https://muse.jhu.edu/journal/387).
- Two important older journals are the French *Politica Hermetica* (since 1987) and the now-defunct online journal *Esoterica* (1999–2007; still accessible at https://esoteric.msu.edu).
- As the study of esotericism became more prominent during the 2010s, further series with a strong focus on esotericism have started to appear in recent years, such as *La Rosa di Paracelso* (since 2017: see www.larosadiparacelso.com) and *Religiographies* (since 2022; see https://www.cini.it/pubblicazioni/religiographies). Other journals with considerable significance for the study of esotericism are *Ambix* (published by the Society for the History of Alchemy and Chemistry, www.ambix.org) and *Magic, Ritual & Witchcraft* (www.pennpress.org).

Academic Monograph Series

- Since 2006, Brill publishes an important series of scholarly monographs and collective volumes known as the *Aries Book Series* (www. brill.nl/publications/aries-book-series), consisting of thirty-three volumes at the time of writing.
- Since 2016, Oxford University Press has a similar specialized series restricted to monographs, the *Oxford Studies in Western Esotericism* (see under https://global.oup.com/academic).

- Furthermore, *Palgrave Studies in New Religions and Alternative Spiritualities* (https://link.springer.com/series/14608) is devoted increasingly to topics in the field.
- Since 1993, State University of New York Press publishes the SUNY series in Western Esoteric Traditions (https://sunypress.edu/Series/S/SUNY-series-in-Western-Esoteric-Traditions).
- Outside these specialized series as well, monographs on esoteric themes have become common with all major academic publishers. A particularly good example is the *Magic in History* book series published by Penn State University Press.

Podcasts and YouTube Channels

- Earl Fontainelle's brilliant *Secret History of Western Esotericism Podcast* (SHWEP; https://shwep.net) is devoted to the ambitious attempt of exploring the entire history of esotericism from its beginnings to the present. The podcast is of excellent quality and slowly works its way forward in time, from the Presocratics to the present. It includes many guest interviews with major specialists. The parallel Oddcast series consists of interviews with scholars about all aspects of esotericism from antiquity to the present. Next to a large majority of freely available episodes, members-only episodes delve more deeply into the topics under discussion.
- Another valuable educational resource is Justin's Sledge's YouTube channel *Esoterica* (www.youtube.com/@TheEsotericaChannel). Professionally presented, and hosted by a very knowledgeable scholar, this channel casts its net widely while focusing especially on the history of the occult sciences.
- Focusing on a somewhat younger and hipper audience, Angela Puca's delightful channel *Angela's Symposium* (https://www.youtube.com/@drangelapuca) is an excellent demonstration of how to break the barrier between academics and insiders/practitioners by showing the "academic fun" of studying esotericism.

Bibliography

Aberth, Susan L., *Leonora Carrington: Surrealism, Alchemy and Art*, Lund Humphries: Aldershot / Burlington 2004.

Abrams, Daniel, *Kabbalistic Manuscripts and Textual Theory: Methodologies of Textual Scholarship and Editorial Practice in the Study of Jewish Mysticism*, Cherub Press: Los Angeles 2010.

Adamson, Peter & Richard C. Taylor (eds.), *The Cambridge Companion to Arabic Philosophy*, Cambridge University Press: Cambridge 2005.

Addas, Claude, *Quest for the Red Sulphur: The Life of Ibn ʿArabi*, The Islamic Text Society: Cambridge 1993.

Adler, Margot, *Drawing Down the Moon: Witches, Druids, Goddess-Worshippers, and Other Pagans in America Today*, 2nd ed., Beacon Press: Boston 1986.

Adorno, Theodor W., "Meinung Wahn Gesellschaft," in: *Bemerkungen zu* The Autoritarian Personality *und weitere Texte* (Eva-Maria Ziege, ed.), Suhrkamp: Berlin 2019, 109–131.

Agrippa, Heinrich Cornelius, *Three Books of Occult Philosophy* (Eric Purdue, translation), Inner Traditions: Rochester 2021.

Albanese, Catherine, *Nature Religion in America: From the Algonkian Indians to the New Age*, The University of Chicago Press: Chicago / London 1990.

Albanese, Catherine, *A Republic of Mind and Spirit: A Cultural History of American Metaphysical Religion*, Yale University Press: New Haven / London 2007.

Albrecht, Michael, *Eklektik: Eine Begriffsgeschichte mit Hinweisen auf die Philosophie- und Wissenschaftsgeschichte*, frommann-holzboog: Stuttgart / Bad Cannstatt 1994.

Al-Khalili, Jim, *The House of Wisdom: How Arabic Science Saved Ancient Knowledge and Gave Us the Renaissance*, Penguin: London 2010.

Alleau, René, *Aspects de l'alchimie traditionnelle*, Les Editions de Minuit: Paris 1953.

Almqvist, Kurt (ed.), *Hilma af Klint: The Complete Catalogue Raisonné*, 7 vols., Thames & Hudson: New York 2021.

Amir-Moezzi, Mohammad Ali, *The Divine Guide in Early Shiism: The Sources of Esotericism in Islam*, State University of New York Press: Albany 1994.

Anderson, Walter Truett, *The Upstart Spring: Esalen and the Human Potential Movement. The First Twenty Years*, Authors Guild Backinprint 2004.

Andreae, Johann Valentin, *Fama Fraternitatis / Confessio Fraternitatis / Chymische Hochzeit: Christiani Rosenkreutz. Anno 1459* (Richard van Dülmen, ed.), Calwer: Stuttgart 1973.

Aniello, Barbara, "Musica pietrificata, sculture sonore: Aleksandr Skrjabin tra estasi e teosofia," in: Wuidar, *Music and Esotericism*, 295–328.

Anonymus, *A Course in Miracles: The Text, Workbook for Students and Manual for Teachers* (1975), Arkana: London 1985.

Anonymus, *The Chemical Wedding of Christian Rosenkreutz* (Joscelyn Godwin, translation), Phanes Press: Grand Rapids 1991.

Anonymus, *Het schilderend mediumschap van Jozef Rulof*, Wayti Press: Apeldoorn 2002.

Anonymus, *The Book of Bahir: Flavius Mithridates' Latin Translation, the Hebrew Text and an English Version* (Saverio Campanini, ed.), Nino Aragno: Torino 2005.

Anonymus, *Traces du sacré*, Centre Pompidou: Paris 2008.

Anonymus [Anna Hardinge Britten], *Ghost Land; or Researches into the Mysteries of Occultism. Illustrated in a Series of Autobiographical Sketches*, Published for the Editor: Boston 1876.

Anthony, Dick & Thomas Robbins, "Conversion and 'Brainwashing' in New Religious Movements," in: Lewis, *Oxford Handbook of New Religious Movements*, 243–297.

App, Urs, *The Birth of Orientalism*, University of Pennsylvania Press: Philadelphia / Oxford 2010.

Appleby, Joyce, Lynn Hunt & Margaret Jacob, *Telling the Truth about History*, Norton & Co.: New York / London 1994.

Argentino, Marc-André, "Qvangelism: QAnon as a Hyper-Real Religion," in: Piraino, Pasi & Asprem, *Religious Dimensions of Conspiracy Theories*, 257–279.

Arnold, Gottfried, *Unparteyische Kirchen- und Ketzer-Historie, vom Anfang des Neuen Testaments biß auf das Jahr Christi 1688*, 2 vols., Thomas Fritsch: Frankfurt a.M. 1699–1700.

Arnold, Gottfried, *Historie und Beschreibung der Mystischen Theologie, oder geheimen Gottes Gelehrtheit, wie auch derer alten und neuen Mysticorum*, Thomas Fritsch: Frankfurt 1703.

Arzi, Shahar & Moshe Idel, *Kabbalah: A Neurocognitive Approach to Mystical Experience*, Yale University Press: New Haven 2015.

Asatryan, Mushegh & Dylan M. Burns, "Is Ghulāt Religion Islamic Gnosticism? Religious Transmissions in Late Antiquity," in: Mohammad Ali Amir-Moezzi (ed.), *L'ésotérisme shi'ite: Ses racines et ses prolongements / Shi'i Esotericism: Its Roots and Developments*, Brepols: Turnhout 2016, 55–86.

Ashplant, T. G. & Adrian Wilson, "Present-Centred History and the Problem of Historical Knowledge," *The Historical Journal* 31:2 (1988), 253–274.

Asprem, Egil, "Pondering Imponderables: Occultism in the Mirror of Late Classical Physics," *Aries* 11:2 (2011), 129–165.

Asprem, Egil, *Arguing with Angels: Enochian Magic & Modern Occulture*, State University of New York Press: Albany 2012.

Asprem, Egil, "Beyond the West: Towards a New Comparativism in the Study of Esotericism," *Correspondences* 2:1 (2014), 3–33.

Asprem, Egil, *The Problem of Disenchantment: Scientific Naturalism and Esoteric Discourse 1900-1939*, Brill: Leiden / Boston 2014 (State University of New York Press: Albany 2018).

Asprem, Egil, Review of Arthur Versluis, Lee Irwin & Melina Phillips, *Esotericism, Religion, and Politics*, *Aries* 14 (2014), 247–274.

Asprem, Egil, "Rejected Knowledge Reconsidered: Some Methodological Notes on Esotericism and Marginality," in: Asprem & Strube, *New Approaches*, 127–146.

Asprem, Egil, "On the Social Organization of Rejected Knowledge: Reassessing the Sociology of the Occult," in: Hedenborg White & Rudbøg, *Esotericism and Deviance*, 21–57.

Asprem, Egil & Markus Altena Davidsen, "Editors' Introduction: What Cognitive Science Offers the Study of Esotericism," *Aries* 17 (2017), 1–15.

Asprem, Egil & Kennet Granholm (eds.), *Contemporary Esotericism*, Equinox: Sheffield / Bristol 2013.

Asprem, Egil & Julian Strube, "Afterword: Outlines of a New Roadmap," in: Asprem & Strube, *New Approaches*, 241–251.

Asprem, Egil & Julian Strube, “Esotericism’s Expanding Horizon: Why This Book Came to Be,” in: Asprem & Strube, *New Approaches*, 1–19.

Asprem, Egil & Julian Strube (eds.), *New Approaches to the Study of Esotericism*, Brill: Leiden / Boston 2021.

Assmann, Jan, *Moses the Egyptian: The Memory of Egypt in Western Monotheism*, Harvard University Press: Cambridge, MA / London 1997.

Assmann, Jan, *Die Mosaische Unterscheidung, oder der Preis des Monotheismus*, Carl Hanser Verlag: Munich / Vienna 2003.

Assmann, Jan, *Religio Duplex: Ägyptische Mysterien und Europäische Aufklärung*, Insel Verlag: Berlin 2010.

Attrell, Dan & David Porreca, *Picatrix: A Medieval Treatise on Astral Magic*, The Pennsylvania State University Press: University Park 2019.

Baader, Franz von, *Sämmtliche Werke* (Franz Hoffmann, ed.), 16 vols., Herrmann Bethmann: Leipzig 1851–1860.

Baer, Marc D., “Dönme,” in: *Encyclopedia of Islam 3*, Brill: Leiden / Boston (forthcoming; online version).

Baier, Karl, *Meditation und Moderne: Zur Genese eines Kernbereichs moderner Spiritualität in der Wechselwirkung zwischen Westeuropa, Nordamerika und Asien*, 2 vols., Königshausen & Neumann: Würzburg 2009.

Baier, Karl, “Das Rote Buch im Kontext Europäischer Spiritualitätsgeschichte,” *Recherches Germaniques*, hors série 8 (2011), 13–40.

Baigent, Michael, Richard Leigh & Henry Lincoln, *The Holy Blood and the Holy Grail*, Arrow: London 1997.

Bailey, Alice A., *Initiation: Human and Solar*, Lucis Publishing Company: New York 1977.

Bakker, Justine, “Esotericism, that’s for White Folks, Right?,” in: Hanegraaff, Forshaw & Pasi, *Hermes Explains*, 21–28.

Bakker, Justine, “Hidden Presence: Race and / in the History, Construct, and Study of Western Esotericism,” *Religion* 50:4 (2020), 479–503.

Bakker, Justine, “Race and (the Study of) Esotericism,” in: Asprem & Strube, *New Approaches*, 147–167.

Baroni, Francesco, “The Philosophical Gold of Perennialism: Hans Thomas Hakl, Julius Evola and the Italian Esoteric Milieus,” *Religiographies* 2:1 (2023), 39–58.

Barruel, Augustin, *Mémoires pour servir à l’histoire du Jacobinisme* (1798), Théodore Pitrat: Lyon 1818–1819.

Baruŝs, Imants, *Alterations of Consciousness: An Empirical Analysis for Social Scientists*, American Psychological Association: Washington 2003.

Bashkoff, Tracey (ed.), *Hilma af Klint: Paintings for the Future*, Guggenheim Museum: New York 2018.

Bauduin, Tessel M., *Surrealism and the Occult: Occultism and Western Esotericism in the Work and Movement of André Breton*, Amsterdam University Press 2014.

Bauermeister, Mary, *Ich hänge im Triolengitter: Mein Leben mit Karlheinz Stockhausen*, Elke Heidenreich bei C. Bertelsmann: Munich 2011.

Baur, Ferdinand Christian, *Die christliche Gnosis oder die christliche Religions-Philosophie in ihrer geschichtlichen Entwiklung*, C.F. Osiander: Tübingen 1835.

Baur, Ferdinand Christian, *Die Epochen der kirchlichen Geschichtsschreibung* (1852), Georg Olms: Hildesheim 1962.

Bednarowski, Mary Farrell, *New Religions and the Theological Imagination in America*, Indiana University Press: Bloomington / Indianapolis 1989.

Bekker, Balthasar, *De Betoverde Weereld* (1691–1694), Marinus de Vries: Deventer 1739.

Benz, Ernst, *Schellings Theologische Geistesahnen*, Franz Steiner: Wiesbaden 1955.

Benz, Ernst, *Emanuel Swedenborg: Visionary Savant in the Age of Reason*, Swedenborg Foundation: West Chester 2002.

Berger, Peter L., *The Heretical Imperative: Contemporary Possibilities of Religious Affirmation*, Anchor Press / Doubleday: New York 1980.

Berger, Helen & Douglas Ezzy, *Teenage Witches: Magical Youth and the Search for the Self*, Rutgers University Press: New Brunswick 2007.

Bergunder, Michael, "What is Esotericism? Cultural Studies Approaches and the Problems of Definition in Religious Studies," *Method & Theory in the Study of Religion* 22 (2010), 9–36.

Bergunder, Michael, "What is Religion? The Unexplained Subject Matter of Religious Studies," *Method & Theory in the Study of Religion* 26 (2014), 246–286.

Bergunder, Michael, "Umkämpfte Historisierung: Die Zwillingsgeburt von 'Religion' und 'Esoterik' in der zweiten Hälfte des 19. Jahrhunderts und das Programm einer globalen Religionsgeschichte," in: Klaus Hock (ed.), *Wissen um Religion: Erkenntnis – Interesse. Epistemologie und Episteme in Religionswissenschaft und Interkultureller Theologie*, Evangelische Verlagsanstalt: Leipzig 2020, 47–131.

Bernand, Carmen & Serge Gruzinski, *De l'idolâtrie: Une archéologie des sciences religieuses*, Éditions du Seuil: Paris 1988.

Betz, Hans Dieter, *The "Mithras Liturgy": Text, Translation, and Commentary*, Mohr Siebeck: Tübingen 2003.

Betz, Hans Dieter (ed.), *The Greek Magical Papyri in Translation, Including the Demotic Spells*, The University of Chicago Press: Chicago / London 1986.

Betz, Otto, *Licht vom unerschaffenen Lichte: Die kabbalistische Lehrtafel der Prinzessin Antonia in Bad Teinach*, Sternberg: Metzingen 2000.

Bibliotheca Philosophica Hermetica (ed.), *Rosenkreuz als europäisches Phänomen im 17. Jahrhundert*, In de Pelikaan: Amsterdam 2002.

Bila, Constantin, *La croyance à la magie au XVIIIe siècle en France dans les contes, romans & traités*, J. Gamber: Paris 1925.

Binbaş, Ilker Evrim, *Intellectual Networks in Timurid Iran: Sharaf al-Dīn ʿAlī Yazdī and the Islamicate Republic of Letters*, Cambridge University Press: Cambridge 2016.

Binder, Hartmut, *Gustav Meyrink: Ein Leben im Bann der Magie*, Vitalis: Prague 2009.

Blackman, Lisa, *Hearing Voices: Embodiment and Experience*, Free Association Books: London / New York 2001.

Bladel, Kevin van, *The Arabic Hermes: From Pagan Sage to Prophet of Science*, Oxford University Press: Oxford 2009.

Blainey, Marc G., *Christ Returns from the Jungle: Ayahuasca Religion as Mystical Healing*, State University of New York Press: Albany 2021.

Blake, William, *The Complete Illuminated Books*, Thames & Hudson: London 2000.

Blavatsky, Helena P., *The Secret Doctrine: The Synthesis of Science, Religion, and Philosophy*, 2 vols., The Theosophical Publishing Company: London 1888.

Bloch, Ernst, *Erbschaft dieser Zeit*, Suhrkamp: Frankfurt a.M. 1985.

Boehme, Jacob, *The Works of Jacob Behmen, the Teutonic Philosopher* (William Law, ed.), 4 vols., M. Richardson: London 1764–1772–1781.

Boehme, Jacob, *Aurora (Morgen Röte im auffgang, 1612) and Fundamental Report (Gründlicher Bericht, Mysterium Pansophicum, 1620)* (Andrew Weeks, translation & commentary), Brill: Leiden / Boston 2013.

Boehme, Jacob, *De Tribus Principiis, oder Beschreibung der Drey Principien Göttliches Wesens (Of the Three Principles of Divine Being, 1619)* (Andrew Weeks, translation & commentary), Brill: Leiden / Boston 2019.

Bogdan, Henrik, "Explaining the Murder-Suicides of the Order of the Solar Temple: A Survey of Hypotheses," in: Lewis, *Violence*, 133–145.

Bogdan, Henrik & Olav Hammer (eds.), *Western Esotericism in Scandinavia*, Brill: Leiden / Boston 2016.

Bogdan, Henrik & Martin P. Starr (eds.), *Aleister Crowley and Western Esotericism*, Oxford University Press: Oxford / New York 2012.

Bohak, Gideon, *Ancient Jewish Magic: A History*, Cambridge University Press: Cambridge 2008.

Böhme, Hartmut & Gernot Böhme, *Das Andere der Vernunft: Zur Entwicklung von Rationalitätsstrukturen am Beispiel Kants*, Suhrkamp: Frankfurt a.M. 1983.

Böhme, Jacob, *Morgen-Röte im Aufgank*, in: Ferdinand van Ingen (ed.), *Jacob Böhme: Werke*, Deutscher Klassiker Verlag: Frankfurt a.M. 1997.

Bonnet, Charles, *Oeuvres d'histoire naturelle et de philosophie*, Samuel Fauche: Neuchâtel 1779.

Boorstein, Michelle, "From Spellcasting to Podcasting: Inside the Life of a Teenage Witch," *The Washington Post*, October 28, 2021.

Brach, Jean-Pierre, "Magic IV: Renaissance-17th Century," in: Hanegraaff, *Dictionary*, 731–738.

Brach, Jean-Pierre, "Number Symbolism," in: Hanegraaff, *Dictionary*, 874–883.

Brach, Jean-Pierre, "Mathematical Esotericism: Some Perspectives on Renaissance Arithmology," in: Hanegraaff & Pijnenburg, *Hermes in the Academy*, 75–89.

Braden, Gregg et al., *The Mysteries of 2012: Predictions, Prophecies & Possibilities*, Sounds True: Boulder 2007.

Brann, Noel L., *Trithemius and Magical Theology: A Chapter in the Controversy over Occult Studies in Early Modern Europe*, State University of New York Press: Albany 1999.

Braude, Ann, *Radical Spirits: Spiritualism and Women's Rights in Nineteenth-Century America*, Indiana University Press: Bloomington 2001.

Braudel, Fernand, "La longue durée," *Annales* 13:4 (1958), 725–753.

Brentjes, Sonja (ed.), *Routledge Handbook on the Sciences in Islamicate Societies: Practices from the 2nd/8th to the 13th/19th Centuries*, Routledge: London / New York 2023.

Breyer P-Orridge, Genesis, *Thee Psychick Bible: The Apocryphal Scriptures ov Genesis Breyer P-Orridge and Thee Third Mind ov Thee Temple ov Psychick Youth*, Feral House: Port Townsend 1994.

Breyer P-Orridge, Genesis, *Sacred Intent: Conversations with Carl Abrahamsson 1986-2019*, Trapart Books: Vimmerby 2020.

Broek, Roelof van den & Wouter J. Hanegraaff (eds.), *Gnosis and Hermeticism from Antiquity to Modern Times*, State University of New York Press: Albany 1998.

Brown, Dan, *The Da Vinci Code*, Doubleday: New York 2003.

Brown, Wendy, *Undoing the Demos: Neoliberalism's Stealth Revolution*, Zone Books: New York 2015

Brown, Michael F., *The Channeling Zone: American Spirituality in an Anxious Age*, Harvard University Press: Cambridge, MA / London 1997.

Bruno, Giordano, *The Expulsion of the Triumphant Beast* (Arthur D. Imerti, translation), University of Nebraska: Lincoln / London 1964.

Bruno, Giordano, *Cause, Principle and Unity; and Essays on Magic*, Cambridge University Press: Cambridge 1998.

Bruno, Giordano, *On the Heroic Frenzies* (Ingrid D. Rowland, translation), University of Toronto Press: Toronto / Buffalo / London 2013.

Bruno, Giordano, *The Ash Wednesday Supper* (Hilary Gatti, translation), University of Toronto Press: Toronto / Buffalo / London 2018.

Bucke, Richard Maurice, *Cosmic Consciousness: A Study in the Evolution of the Human Mind* (1901), Innes & Sons: Philadelphia 1905.

Bulliet, Richard W., *The Case for Islamo-Christian Civilization*, Columbia University Press: New York 2004.

Bullock, Steven C., *Revolutionary Brotherhood: Freemasonry and the Transformation of the American Social Order, 1730-1840*, University of North Carolina Press: Chapel Hill / London 1996.

Burns, Dylan M., "Gnosticism, Gnostics, and Gnosis," in: Trompf, *Gnostic World*, 9–25.

Butter, Michael & Peter Knight (eds.), *Routledge Handbook of Conspiracy Theories*, Routledge: London / New York 2020.

Butterfield, Herbert, *The Whig Interpretation of History*, W.W. Norton & Company: New York 1965.

Byrne, Rhonda, *The Secret*, Simon & Schuster: New York 2006.

Caberta, Ursula, *Schwarzbuch Esoterik*, Gütersloher Verlagshaus: Gütersloh 2010.

Cameron, Alan, *The Last Pagans of Rome*, Oxford University Press: Oxford 2011.

Campbell, Bruce F., *Ancient Wisdom Revived: A History of the Theosophical Movement*, University of California Press: Berkeley / Los Angeles / London 1980.

Campbell, Colin, "The Cult, the Cultic Milieu and Secularization," *A Sociological Yearbook of Religion in Britain* 5 (1972), 119–136.

Canguilhem, Georges, *The Normal and the Pathological*, Zone Books: New York 1991.

Cantú, Keith, "'Don't Take Any Wooden Nickels': Western Esotericism, Yoga, and the Discourse of Authenticity," in: Asprem & Strube, *New Approaches*, 109–126.

Cardeña, Etzel & Michael Winkelman (eds.), *Altering Consciousness: Multidisciplinary Perspectives*, 2 vols., Praeger: Santa Barbara / Denver / Oxford 2011.

Caron, Richard, "Alchemy V," in: Hanegraaff, *Dictionary*, 50–58.

Caron, Richard, Joscelyn Godwin, Wouter J. Hanegraaff & Jean-Louis Vieillard-Baron (eds.), *Ésotérisme, gnoses & imaginaire symbolique: Mélanges offerts à Antoine Faivre*, Peeters: Louvain 2001.

Carrette, Jeremy & Richard King, *Selling Spirituality: The Silent Takeover of Religion*, Routledge: London / New York 2005.

Carroll, Peter J., *Liber Null & Psychonaut: An Introduction to Chaos Magic*, Weiser: Boston / York Beach 1987.

Carter, Julian B., *The Heart of Whiteness: Normal Sexuality and Race in America, 1880-1940*, Duke University Press: Durham 2007.

Casas, Bartolomé de las, *A Short Account of the Destruction of the Indies*, Penguin: London 1992.

Casaubon, Meric, *A True and Faithful Relation of What Passed for Many Years between Dr. John Dee and Some Spirits*, Magical Childe Publishing: New York 1993.

Cassirer, Ernst, Paul Oskar Kristeller & John Herman Randall (eds.), *The Renaissance Philosophy of Man*, The University of Chicago Press: Chicago & London 1948.
Castaneda, Carlos, *The Teachings of Don Juan: A Yaqui Way of Knowledge*, University of California Press: Berkeley 1968
Castoriadis, Cornelius, *The Imaginary Institution of Society*, Polity Press: Cambridge / Malden 1987.
Castoriadis, Cornelius, "The Discovery of the Imagination," in: *World in Fragments: Writings on Politics, Society, Psychoanalysis and the Imagination*, Stanford University Press: Redwood City 1997, 213–245.
Cavalier, Philippe, *Les Loups de Berlin*, Éditions Anne Carrière: Paris 2005.
Cavalier, Philippe, *Les Ogres du Gange*, Éditions Anne Carrière: Paris 2005.
Cavalier, Philippe, *Les Anges de Palerme*, Éditions Anne Carrière: Paris 2006.
Cavalier, Philippe, *La Dame de Toscane*, Éditions Anne Carrière: Paris 2008.
Cavendish, Richard (ed.), *Man, Myth & Magic: The Illustrated Encyclopedia of Mythology, Religion and the Unknown*, Marshall Cavendish: New York / London / Toronto / Sydney 1995.
Chadwich, Whitney, *Women Artists and the Surrealist Movement*, Thames and Hudson: New York 1985.
Chaitow, Sasha, *Son of Prometheus: The Life and Work of Joséphin Péladan*, Theion: Munich 2022.
Chajes, J.H., *The Kabbalistic Tree*, The Pennsylvania State University Press: University Park 2022.
Chajes, Julie, *Recycled Lives: A History of Reincarnation in Blavatsky's Theosophy*, Oxford University Press: Oxford 2019.
Chajes, Julie & Boaz Huss (eds.), *The Cosmic Movement: Sources, Contexts, Impact*, Ben-Gurion University of the Negev Press: Beer Sheva 2020.
Chalmers, David J., *The Conscious Mind: In Search of a Fundamental Theory*, Oxford University Press: New York / Oxford 1996.
Charmasson, Thérèse, "Divinatory Arts," in: Hanegraaff, *Dictionary*, 313–319.
Chidester, David, *Savage Systems: Colonialism and Comparative Religion in Southern Africa*, University Press of Virginia: Charlottesville 1996.
Chidester, David, *Authentic Fakes: Religion and American Popular Culture*, University of California Press: Berkey / Los Angeles / London 2005.
Chryssides, George D., "'Come On Up, and I Will Show Thee': Heaven's Gate as a Postmodern Group," in: Lewis & Petersen, *Controversial New Religions*, 353–370.
Churton, Tobias, *Occult Paris: The Lost Magic of the Belle Époque*, Inner Traditions: Rochester / Toronto 2016.
Clark, Stuart, *Thinking with Demons: The Idea of Witchcraft in Early Modern Europe*, Oxford University Press: Oxford 1997.
Clayton, Lawrence A., *Bartolomé de las Casas: A Biography*, Cambridge University Press: Cambridge 2012.
Clifton, Chas & Graham Harvey (eds.), *The Paganism Reader*, Routledge: London / New York 2004.
Clucas, Stephen, "John Dee's Angelic Conversations and the *Ars Notoria*: Renaissance Magic and Mediaeval Theurgy" (2006), in: *Magic, Memory and Natural Philosophy in the Sixteenth and Seventeenth Centuries*, Ashgate Variorum: Farnham / Burlington 2011 (I).
Clulee, Nicholas H., *John Dee's Natural Philosophy: Between Science and Religion*, Routledge: London / New York 1988.
Cohn, Norman, *Europe's Inner Demons*, Paladin: Herts 1975.

Cohn, Norman, *Warrant for Genocide: The Myth of the Jewish World Conspiracy and the Protocols of the Elders of Zion* (1967), Serif: London 2005.

Colberg, Ehre Gott Daniel, *Das Platonisch-Hermetisches Christenthum, Begreiffend Die Historische Erzehlung vom Ursprung und vielerley Secten der heutigen Fanatischen Theologie, unterm Namen der Paracelsisten, Weigelianer, Rosencreuzer, Quäcker, Böhmisten, Wiedertäuffer, Bourignisten, Labadisten, und Quietisten*, 2 vols., Moritz Georg Weidmann: Frankfurt / Leipzig 1690–1691.

Collis, Robert, *The Petrine Instauration: Religion, Esotericism and Science at the Court of Peter the Great, 1689-1725*, Brill: Leiden / Boston 2012.

Collis, Robert & Natalie Bayer, *Initiating the Millennium: The Avignon Society and Illuminism in Europe*, Oxford University Press: Oxford 2020.

Colonna, Francesco, *Hypnerotomachia Poliphili: The Strife of Love in a Dream*, Thames & Hudson: London 1999.

Conner, Frederick William, *Cosmic Optimism: A Study of the Interpretation of Evolution by American Poets from Emerson to Robinson*, University of Florida Press: Gainesville 1949.

Conrad, Joseph, *Heart of Darkness, with The Congo Diary*, Penguin: London 1995.

Cooper, Michael, "Rodrigues in China; The Letters of João Rodrigues, 1611-1633," in: Tadao Doi, *Kokugoshi e no michi*, vol. 2, Sanshodo: Tokyo 1981, 355–231.

Copenhaver, Brian P., *The Book of Magic: From Antiquity to the Enlightenment*, Penguin: London 2015.

Copenhaver, Brian P., *Magic in Western Culture: From Antiquity to the Enlightenment*, Cambridge University Press: Cambridge 2015.

Copenhaver, Brian P., *Magic and the Dignity of Man: Pico della Mirandola and His* Oration *in Modern Memory*, The Belknap Press of Harvard University Press: Cambridge, MA / London 2019.

Copenhaver, Brian P., "Introduction," in: Pico della Mirandola & Pico della Mirandola, *Life … / Oration*, vii–lxxxvii.

Corbin, Henry, *Spiritual Body and Celestial Earth: From Mazdean Iran to Shī'ite Iran*, I.B. Tauris & Co.: London 1976.

Corbin, Henry, "L'*Imago Templi* face aux normes profanes," in: *Temple et contemplation: Essais sur l'Islam Iranien*, Flammarion: Paris 1980, 285–422.

Corbin, Henry, "*Mundus Imaginalis*, or the Imaginary and the Imaginal," *Spring* (1972), 1–19; new translation by Leonard Fox in Corbin, *Swedenborg and Esoteric Islam*, Swedenborg Foundation: West Chester 1995, 1–33.

Coudert, Allison P., *The Impact of the Kabbalah in the Seventeenth Century: The Life and Thought of Francis Mercury van Helmont (1614-1698)*, Brill: Leiden / Boston / Cologne 1999.

Couliano, Ioan P., *Eros and Magic in the Renaissance*, The University of Chicago Press: Chicago / London 1987.

Cowan, Tommy P., "What Most People Would Call Evil: The Archontic Spirituality of William S. Burroughs," *La Rosa di Paracelso* 2:1–2 (2018), 83–122.

Cowan, Tommy P., "Devils in the Ink: William Burroughs, Brion Gysin, and Geometry as a Method for Accessing Intermediary Beings," *Aries* 19 (2019), 167–211.

Crabtree, Adam, *From Mesmer to Freud: Magnetic Sleep and the Roots of Psychological Healing*, Yale University Press: New Haven / London 1993.

Craven, J.B., *Dr. Robert Fludd (Robertus de Fluctibus), the English Rosicrucian: Life and Writings*, W. Peace: Kirkwall 1902.

Crockford, Susannah, *Ripples of the Universe: Spirituality in Sedona, Arizona*, The University of Chicago Press: Chicago / London 2021.

Crockford, Susannah & Egil Asprem, "Ethnographies of the Esoteric: Introducing Anthropological Methods and Theories to the Study of Contemporary Esotericism," *Correspondences* 6:1 (2018), 1–23.

Crowley, John, *The Solitudes: Aegypt Book One*, The Overlook Press: Woodstock & New York 1987.

Crowley, John, *Love and Sleep: Aegypt Book Two*, The Overlook Press: Woodstock & New York 1994.

Crowley, John, *Daemonomania: Aegypt Book Three*, The Overlook Press: Woodstock & New York 2000.

Crowley, John, *Little, Big* (1981), Harper Perennial: New York / London / Toronto / Sydney 2002.

Crowley, John, *Endless Things: A Part of Aegypt*, The Overlook Press: Woodstock & New York 2007.

Cryle, Peter & Elizabeth Stephens, *Normality: A Critical Genealogy*, The University of Chicago Press: Chicago / London 2017.

Culianu, Ioan P., "The Gnostic Revenge: Gnosticism and Romantic Literature," in: Jacob Taubes (ed.), *Religionstheorie und Politische Theologie*, vol. 2: *Gnosis und Politik*, Wilhelm Fink/ Ferdinand Schöningh 1984, 290–306.

Cusack, Carole M., *Invented Religions: Imagination, Fiction and Faith*, Ashgate: Farnham / Burlington 2010.

Dachez, Roger, *Histoire illustrée du Rite Écossais Rectifié*, Dervy: Paris 2021.

Daftary, Farhad, *The Ismāʿīlīs: Their History and Doctrines*, Cambridge University Press: Cambridge 2007.

Dan, Joseph, *The Christian Kabbalah: Jewish Mystical Books and their Christian Interpreters*, Harvard College Library: Cambridge, MA 1997.

Davidsen, Markus Altena, "Fiction-Based Religion: Conceptualising a New Category against History-Based Religion and Fandom," *Culture and Religion* 14:4 (2013), 378–395.

Davidsen, Markus Altena, "Fiction and Religion: How Narratives about the Supernatural inspire Religious Belief. Introducing the Thematic Issue," *Religion* 46:4 (2016), 489–499.

Davila, James R., *Descenders of the Chariot: The People behind the Hekhalot Literature*, Brill: Leiden / Boston / Cologne 2001.

Davila, James R., *Hekhalot Literature in Translation: Major Texts of Merkavah Mysticism*, Brill: Leiden / Boston 2013.

Davis, Erik, *High Weirdness: Drugs, Esoterica, and Visionary Experience in the Seventies*, Strange Attractor Press / The MIT Press: London / Cambridge, MA 2019.

Deghaye, Pierre, *La naissance de Dieu, ou la doctrine de Jacob Boehme*, Albin Michel: Paris 1985.

Deghaye, Pierre, "Jacob Boehme and his Followers," in: Faivre & Needleman, *Modern Esoteric Spirituality*, 210–247.

Dennett, Daniel C., *Content and Consciousness*, Routledge: London / New York 1969.

Dennett, Daniel C., *Consciousness Explained*, Penguin: London 1991.

Dennett, Daniel C., *Sweet Dreams: Philosophical Obstacles to a Science of Consciousness*, The MIT Press: Cambridge, MA / London 2005.

Deveney, John Patrick, *Paschal Beverly Randolph: A Nineteenth-Century Black American Spiritualist, Rosicrucian, and Sex-Magician*, State University of New York Press: Albany 1997.

[Diverse authors], *Okkultismus und Avantgarde: Von Munch bis Mondrian 1900-1915*, Schirn Kunsthalle: Frankfurt 1995.

[Diverse authors], *Luigi Pericle: A Rediscovery*, Estorick Collection of Modern Italian Art / Archivio Luigi Pericle: n.p. 2022.

Dixon, Joy, *Divine Feminine: Theosophy and Feminism in England*, The Johns Hopkins University Press: Baltimore / London 2001.

Dobkin de Rios, Marlene & Roger Rumrrill, *A Hallucinogenic Tea, Laced with Controversy: Ayahusca in the Amazon and the United States*, Praeger: Westport / London 2008.

Doel, Marieke J.E. van den, *Ficino and Fantasy: Imagination in Renaissance Art and Theory from Botticelli to Michelangelo*, Brill: Leiden / Boston 2022.

Doering-Manteuffel, Sabine, *Das Okkulte: Eine Erfolgsgeschichte im Schatten der Aufklärung. Von Gutenberg bis zum World Wide Web*, Siedler Verlag: Munich 2008.

Doostdar, Alireza, *The Iranian Metaphysicals: Explorations in Science, Islam, and the Uncanny*, Princeton University Press: Princeton 2018.

Dosoo, Korshi, "Rituals of Apparition in the Theban Magical Library," Ph.D. Dissertation, Macquarie University: Sydney 2014.

Dosoo, Korshi, "A History of the Theban Magical Library," *Bulletin of the American Society of Papyrologists* 53 (2016), 251–274.

Dosoo, Korshi & Markéta Preininger (eds.), *Papyri Copticae Magicae: Coptic Magical Texts, vol. 1: Formularies*, De Gruyter: Berlin / Boston 2023.

Dowling, Levi H., *The Aquarian Gospel of Jesus the Christ: The Philosophic and Practical Basis of the Religion of the Aquarian Age of the World and of The Church Universal*, E.S. Dowling: Los Angeles 1911.

Drayer, Ruth A., *Nicholas & Helena Roerich: The Spiritual Journey of Two Great Artists and Peacemakers*, Quest Books: Wheaton / Chennai 2005.

Droge, Arthur J., *Homer or Moses? Early Christian Interpretations of the History of Culture*, J.C.B. Mohr (Paul Siebeck): Tübingen 1989.

Durkheim, Emile, *The Elementary Forms of Religious Life*, The Free Press: New York 1995.

Dybdal Pedersen, René, "The Second Golden Age of Theosophy in Denmark: An Existential 'Template' for Late Modernity," *Aries* 9:2 (2009), 233–262.

Dyczkowski, Mark S.G., *The Doctrine of Vibration: An Analysis of the Doctrines and Practices of Kashmir Shaivism*, Motilal Banarsidass: Delhi 1989.

Dyrendal, Asbjørn, David G. Robertson & Egil Asprem (eds.), *Handbook of Conspiracy Theory and Contemporary Religion*, Brill: Leiden / Boston 2018.

Eco, Umberto, *Interpretation and Overinterpretation*, Cambridge University Press: Cambridge 1992.

Eco, Umberto, *Foucault's Pendulum*, Vintage: London 2001.

Eco, Umberto, *The Prague Cemetery*, Houghton Mifflin Harcourt / Harvill Secker: Boston / London 2011.

Edighoffer, Roland, *Les Rose-Croix et la crise de la conscience européenne au XVIIe siècle*, Dervy: Paris 1998.

Edighoffer, Roland, "Rosicrucianism II: 18th Century," in: Hanegraaff, *Dictionary*, 1014–1017.

El-Bizri, Nader & Eva Orthmann (eds.), *Occult Sciences in Premodern Islamic Culture*, Orient-Institut Beirut: Beirut 2017.

Eliade, Mircea, *The Myth of the Eternal Return; or, Cosmos and History*, Princeton University Press: Princeton 1954.

Eliade, Mircea, *Shamanism: Archaic Techniques of Ecstasy*, Arkana: London 1964.

Eliade, Mircea, "Occultism and Freemasonry in Eighteenth-Century Europe" (review of René le Forestier, *La Franc-Maçonnerie Templière et Occultiste aux XVIIIe et XIXe siècles*), *History of Religions* 13:1 (1973), 89–91.

Eliade, Mircea, "Cultural Fashions and History of Religions," in: *Occultism, Witchcraft, and Cultural Fashions: Essays in Comparative Religions*, The University of Chicago Press: Chicago / London 1976, 1–17.

Ellenberger, Henri F., *The Discovery of the Unconscious: The History and Evolution of Dynamic Psychiatry*, Basic Books: n.p. 1970.

Engler, Steven & Mark Q. Gardiner, "(Re)defining Esotericism: Fluid Definitions, Property Clusters and the Cross-Cultural Debate," *Aries* 24:2 (2024), 151–207.

Engler, Steven & Mark Q. Gardiner, "Definition as Situated Interpretational Vector: Response to Commentaries," *Aries* 24:2 (2024), 277–290.

Escobar, Arturo, "Worlds and Knowledges Otherwise: The Latin American Modernity/ Coloniality Research Program," *Cultural Studies* 21:2–3 (2007), 179–210.

Faivre, Antoine, *Kirchberger et l'Illuminisme du dix-huitième siècle*, Martinus Nijhoff: The Hague 1966.

Faivre, Antoine, *L'ésotérisme au XVIIIe siècle en France et Allemagne*, La Table d'Émeraude / Seghers: Paris 1973.

Faivre, Antoine, "Philosophie de la nature et naturalisme scientiste," *Cahiers de l'Université Saint Jean de Jérusalem 1: Sciences Traditionnelles et Sciences Profanes*, André Bonne: Paris 1975, 91–110.

Faivre, Antoine, "Genèse d'un genre narratif, le fantastique (essai de périodisation)," in: *La littérature fantastique* (Cahiers de l'Hermétisme), Albin Michel: Paris 1991, 15–43.

Faivre, Antoine, "Introduction I," in: Faivre & Needleman, *Modern Esoteric Spirituality*, xv–xx.

Faivre, Antoine, "Ancient and Medieval Sources of Modern Esoteric Movements," in: Faivre & Needleman, *Modern Esoteric Spirituality*, 1–70.

Faivre, Antoine, *Access to Western Esotericism*, State University of New York Press: Albany 1994.

Faivre, Antoine, *Accès de l'ésotérisme occidental*, revised and expanded ed., 2 vols., Gallimard: Paris 1996.

Faivre, Antoine, *Philosophie de la Nature: Physique sacrée et théosophie XVIIIe-XIXe siècles*, Albin Michel: Paris 1996.

Faivre, Antoine, "Questions of Terminology proper to the Study of Esoteric Currents in Modern and Contemporary Europe," in: Faivre & Hanegraaff, *Western Esotericism and the Science of Religion*, 1–10.

Faivre, Antoine, "The Theosophical Current: A Periodization," in: *Theosophy, Imagination, Tradition*, State University of New York Press: Albany 2000, 3–48.

Faivre, Antoine, "Sensuous Relation with Sophia in Christian Theosophy," in: Hanegraaff & Kripal, *Hidden Intercourse*, 281–307.

Faivre, Antoine, "Le terme et la notion de 'gnose' dans les courants ésotériques occidentaux modernes," in: Jean-Pierre Mahé, Paul-Hubert Poirièr & Madeleine Scopello (eds.), *Les textes de Nag Hammadi: Histoire des Religions, Approches contemporaines*, AIBI / Diffusion De Boccard: Paris 2010, 87–112.

Faivre, Antoine, *Western Esotericism: A Concise History*, State University of New York Press: Albany 2010.

Faivre, Antoine, *De Londres à Saint-Pétersbourg: Carl Friedrich Tieman (1743-1802) aux carrefours des courants illuministes et maçonniques*, Archè: Milan 2018.

Faivre, Antoine & Rolf Christian Zimmermann (eds.), *Epochen der Naturmystik: Hermetische Tradition im wissenschaftlichen Fortschritt*, Erich Schmidt: Berlin 1979.

Faivre, Antoine & Jacob Needleman (eds.), *Modern Esoteric Spirituality*, Crossroad: New York 1992.

Faivre, Antoine & Wouter J. Hanegraaff (eds.), *Western Esotericism and the Science of Religion*, Peeters: Louvain 1998.

Fanger, Claire, "Medieval Ritual Magic: What It Is and Why We Need to Know More About It," in: Fanger, *Conjuring Spirits*, vii–xviii.

Fanger, Claire, *Rewriting Magic: An Exegesis of the Visionary Autobiography of a Fourteenth-Century French Monk*, The Pennsylvania State University Press: University Park 2015.

Fanger, Claire (ed.), *Conjuring Spirits: Texts and Traditions of Medieval Ritual Magic*, Sutton: Phoenix Mill 1998.

Fanger, Claire & Frank Klaassen, "Magic III: Middle Ages," in: Hanegraaff et al., *Dictionary*, 724–731.

Faraone, Christopher A., *Ancient Greek Love Magic*, Harvard University Press: Cambridge, MA / London 1999.

Faraone, Christopher A. & Sofía Torallas Tovar (eds.), *Greek and Egyptian Magical Formularies: Text and Translation*, vol. 1, California Classical Studies: Berkeley 2022 (more volumes forthcoming).

Farmer, S.A., *Syncretism in the West: Pico's 900 Theses (1486). The Evolution of Traditional Religious and Philosophical Systems*, Medieval & Renaissance Texts & Studies: Tempe 1998.

Faxneld, Per, *Satanic Feminism: Lucifer as the Liberator of Woman in Nineteenth-Century Culture*, Oxford University Press: Oxford 2017.

Faxneld, Per & Johan Nilsson (eds.), *Satanism: A Reader*, Oxford University Press: Oxford 2023.

Feld, Helmut, *Das Ende des Seelenglaubens: Vom antiken Orient bis zur Spätmoderne*, Lit: Berlin 2013.

Felski, Rita, *The Limits of Critique*, The University of Chicago Press: Chicago / London 2015.

Ferguson, Christine, "Beyond Belief: Literature, Esotericism Studies, and the Challenges of Biographical Reading in Arthur Conan Doyle's *The Land of Mist*," *Aries* 22 (2022), 205–230.

Festinger, Leon, Henry W. Riecken & Stanley Schachter, *When Prophecy Fails*, University of Minnesota Press: Minneapolis 1956.

Festugière, André-Jean, *La révélation d'Hermès Trismégiste*, 4 vols., Les Belles Lettres: Paris 1942–1954.

Festugière, André-Jean, *Hermès Trismégiste*, vols. 3–5 (1954), Les Belles Lettres: Paris 2002 / 2019.

Feuerbach, Ludwig, *Das Wesen des Christentums*, Reclam: Stuttgart 1969.

Ficino, Marsilio, *Commentary on Plato's Symposium On Love*, Spring Publications: Woodstock 1985.

Ficino, Marsilio, *Three Books on Life: A Critical Edition and Translation with Introduction and Notes* (Carol V. Kaske & John R. Clark, ed. & translation), Medieval & Renaissance Texts & Studies: Binghamton, New York 1989.

[Ficino, Marsilio, translation], *Mercurii Trismegisti Liber de Potestate et Sapientia Dei: Pimander*, Facs. Reprint, Studio per Edizioni Scelte: Florence 1989.

Ficino, Marsilio, *Platonic Theology*, 7 vols., The I Tatti Renaissance Library / Harvard University Press: Cambridge, MA / London 2004.

Fine, Lawrence, *Physician of the Soul, Healer of the Cosmos: Isaac Luria and His Kabbalistic Fellowship*, Stanford University Press: Redwood City 2003.

Finley, Stephen C., "Mathematical Theology: Numerology in the Religious Thought of Tynnetta Muhammad and Louis Farrakhan," in: Finley, Guillory & Page, *Esotericism in African American Religious Experience*, 123–137.

Finley, Stephen C., Biko Mandela Gray & Hugh R. Page Jr., "Africana Esoteric Studies and Western Intellectual Hegemony: A Continuing Conversation with Western Esotericism," *History of Religions* 60:3 (2021), 163–187.

Finley, Stephen C., *In and Out of this World: Material and Extraterrestrial Bodies in the Nation of Islam*, Duke University Press: Durham 2022.

Finley, Stephen C., Margarita Simon Guillory & Hugh R. Page Jr. (eds.), *Esotericism in African American Religious Experience: "There is a Mystery"*, Brill: Leiden / Boston 2015.

Fischer, Friedhelm Wilhelm, "Geheimlehren und moderne Kunst," in: Roger Bauer *et alii*, *Fin de Siècle: Zu Literatur und Kunst der Jahrhundertwende*, Vittorio Klostermann: Frankfurt a.M. 1977, 344–377.

Flaherty, Gloria, *Shamanism and the Eighteenth Century*, Princeton University Press: Princeton 1992.

Flint, Valerie I.J., *The Rise of Magic in Early Medieval Europe*, Princeton University Press: Princeton 1991.

Flournoy, Théodore, *From India to the Planet Mars: A Case of Multiple Personality with Imaginary Languages* (Sonu Shamdasani, ed.), Princeton University Press: Princeton 1994

Forestier, René le, *La Franc-Maçonnerie occultiste au XVIIIe siècle & L'ordre des Élus Coens* (1928), La Table d'Émeraude: Paris 1987.

Forestier, René le, *La Franc-Maçonnerie templière et occultiste aux XVIIIe et XIXe siècles* (Antoine Faivre, ed.), 2 vols., La Table d'Émeraude: Paris 1987.

Forshaw, Peter J., *Occult: Decoding the Visual Culture of Mysticism, Magic and Divination*, Thames & Hudson: London 2024.

Forshaw, Peter J., *The Mage's Images: Heinrich Khunrath in his Oratory and Laboratory*, 4 vols., Brill: Leiden / Boston 2025.

Foucault, Michel, *Les mots et les choses: Une archéologie des sciences humaines*, Gallimard: Paris 1966.

Foucault, Michel, "Nietzsche, la généalogie, l'histoire," in: *Hommage à Jean Hyppolite*, Presses Universitaires de France: Paris 1971, 145–172.

Fowden, Garth, *The Egyptian Hermes: A Historical Approach to the Late Pagan Mind*, Princeton University Press: Princeton 1986.

Fowden, Garth, *Empire to Commonwealth: Consequences of Monotheism in Late Antiquity*, Princeton University Press: Princeton 1993.

Fowden, Garth, *Before and After Muḥammad: The First Millennium Refocused*, Princeton University Press: Princeton / Oxford 2014.

Frank, Thomas, *The Conquest of Cool: Business Culture, Counterculture, and the Rise of Hip Consumerism*, The University of Chicago Press: Chicago / London 1997.

Frankopan, Peter, *The Silk Roads: A New History of the World*, Bloomsbury: London 2015.

Freud, Sigmund, "Das Unheimliche," *Imago* 5/6 (1919), 297–324.

Freudenthal, Gad, Review of Patai, *The Jewish Alchemists*, *Isis* 86:2 (1995), 318–319.

Frick, Karl R.H., *Die Erleuchteten: Gnostisch-theosophische und alchemistisch-rosenkreuzerische Geheimgesellschaften bis zum Ende des 18. Jahrhunderts: Ein Beitrag zur Geistesgeschichte der Neuzeit*, Akademische Druck- und Verlagsanstalt: Graz 1973.

Fukuyama, Francis, *The End of History and the Last Man*, Free Press: New York 1992.

Fulbrook, Mary, *Historical Theory*, Routledge: London / New York 2002.
Fuller, Robert C., *Mesmerism and the American Cure of Souls*, University of Pennsylvania Press: Philadelphia 1982.
Gadamer, Hans-Georg, *Hermeneutik I: Wahrheit und Methode. Grundzüge einer philosophischen Hermeneutik*, J.C.B. Mohr (Paul Siebeck): München 1986.
Gaitanidis, Ioannis & Orion Klautau, "(Re)defining Esotericism: A Response from Two Scholars in Japan," *Aries* 24:2 (2024), 223–226.
Garb, Jonathan, *Shamanic Trance in Modern Kabbalah*, The University of Chicago Press: Chicago / London 2011.
Garb, Jonathan, *A History of Kabbalah: From the Early Modern Period to the Present Day*, Cambridge University Press: Cambridge 2020.
Gardell, Mattias, *Gods of the Blood: The Pagan Revival and White Separatism*, Duke University Press: Durham 2003.
Gardiner, Noah, "Esotericism in a Manuscript Culture: Aḥmad al-Būnī and his Readers through the Mamlūk Period," Ph.D. Dissertation, University of Michigan 2014.
Gardiner, Noah, "Diagrams and Visionary Experience in al-Būnī's *Laṭāʾif al-ishārāt fī al-ḥurūf al-ʿulwīyat*," in: Giovanni Maria Martini (ed.), *Visualizing Sufism: Studies on Graphic Representations in Sufi Literature (13th to 16th Century)*, Brill: Leiden / Boston 2023, 16–50.
Gardiner, Noah, "Translating Esotericism: Arabic," *Correspondences* 11:1 (2023), 31–41.
Garin, Eugenio, *Medioevo e Rinascimento: Studi e ricerche*, Gius. Laterza & Figli: Bari 1954.
Gatti, Hilary, *Essays on Giordano Bruno*, Princeton University Press: Princeton / Oxford 2011.
Gauld, Alan, *The Founders of Psychical Research*, Schocken: New York 1968.
Gauld, Alan, *A History of Hypnotism*, Cambridge University Press: Cambridge 1992.
Gay, Peter, *The Enlightenment: An Interpretation*, vol. 2: *The Rise of Modern Paganism*, W.W. Norton & Company: New York / London 1966.
Geertz, Clifford, "Religion as a Cultural System," in: Michael Banton (ed.), *Anthropological Approaches to the Study of Religion*, Tavistock: London 1966, 1–46.
Geffarth, Renko, *Religion und arkane Hierarchie: Der Orden der Gold- und Rosenkreuzer als Geheime Kirche im 18. Jahrhundert*, Brill: Leiden / Boston 2007.
Gentile, Sebastiano & Carlos Gilly (eds.), *Marsilio Ficino and the Return of Hermes Trismegistus / Marsilio Ficino et il ritorno di Ermete Trismegisto*, Centro Di: Florence 1999.
Gest, Alain & Jacques Guyard, *Les sectes en France* (Assemblée Nationale, Rapport no. 2468), Automédon: Paris 1995.
Gettings, Fred, *The Occult in Art*, Rizzoli: New York 1979.
Gibbons, B.J., *Gender in Mystical and Occult Thought: Behmenism and its Development in England*, Cambridge University Press: Cambridge 1996.
Giddens, Antony, *The Consequences of Modernity*, Polity Press: Cambridge 1990.
Giller, Pinchas, *Shalom Shar'abi and the Kabbalists of Beit El*, Oxford University Press: Oxford 2008.
Gilly, Carlos, "'*Theophrastia Sancta*': Paracelsianism as a Religion, in Conflict with the Established Churches," in: Ole Peter Grell (ed.), *Paracelsus: The Man and his Reputation, his Ideas and their Transformation*, Brill: Leiden / Boston / Cologne 1998, 151–185.
Ginzburg, Carlo, "Just One Witness: The Extermination of the Jews and the Principle of Reality," in: Saul Friedländer (ed.), *Probing the Limits of Representation: Nazism and the "Final Solution,"* Harvard University Press 1992; repr. in Ginzburg, *Threads and Traces: True False Fictive*, University of California Press: Berkeley / Los Angeles / London 2012, 165–179.

Giudice, Christian, *Occult Imperium: Arturo Reghini, Roman Traditionalism, and the Anti-Modern Reaction in Fascist Italy*, Oxford University Press: Oxford 2022.

Glanville, Luke, David Lupher & Maya Feile Tomes (eds.), *Sepúlveda on the Spanish Invasion of the Americas: Defending Empire, Debating Las Casas*, Oxford University Press: Oxford 2023.

Godwin, Joscelyn, "The Revival of Speculative Music," *Musical Quarterly* 68 (1982), 373–389.

Godwin, Joscelyn, *Robert Fludd: Hermetic Philosopher and Surveyor of Two Worlds*, Phanes Press: Grand Rapids 1991.

Godwin, Joscelyn, *The Theosophical Enlightenment*, State University of New York Press: Albany 1994.

Godwin, Joscelyn, *Music and the Occult: French Musical Philosophies, 1750-1950*, University of Rochester Press: Rochester 1996.

Godwin, Joscelyn, "Stockhausen's *Donnerstag aus Licht* and Gnosticism," in: van den Broek & Hanegraaff, *Gnosis and Hermeticism*, 347–358.

Godwin, Joscelyn, *The Pagan Dream of the Renaissance*, Thames & Hudson: London 2002.

Godwin, Joscelyn, "Music IV: 18th Century to the Present," in: Hanegraaff, *Dictionary*, 815–818.

Godwin, Joscelyn, "Afterword: Rejected Knowledge as a Liberal Art," in: Hedenborg White & Rudbøg, *Esotericism and Deviance*, 419–433.

Godwin, Joscelyn (ed.), *Music, Mysticism and Magic: A Sourcebook*, Arkana: New York / London 1986.

Goldish, Matt, *The Sabbatean Prophets*, Harvard University Press: Cambridge, MA / London 2004.

Goodrick-Clarke, Nicholas, *The Occult Roots of Nazism: Secret Aryan Cults and their Influence on Nazi Ideology* (1985), I.B. Tauris: London / New York 1992.

Goodrick-Clarke, Nicholas, *Paracelsus: Essential Readings*, North Atlantic Books: Berkeley 1999.

Goodrick-Clarke, Nicholas, "Hermeticism and Hermetic Societies," in: Hanegraaff, *Dictionary*, 550–558.

Goodrick-Clarke, Nicholas, *The Western Esoteric Traditions: A Historical Introduction*, Oxford University Press: Oxford 2008.

Goodspeed, Edgar J., *Modern Apocrypha*, The Beacon Press: Boston 1956.

Gorski, Philip S., "What is Critical Realism? And Why Should You Care?," *Contemporary Sociology* 42:5 (2013), 658–670.

Gouk, Penelope, *Music, Science and Natural Magic in Seventeenth-Century England*, Yale University Press: New Haven / London 1999.

Gouk, Penelope, "Music III: Renaissance," in: Hanegraaff, *Dictionary*, 812–815.

Graf, Fritz, *Magic in the Ancient World*, Harvard University Press: Cambridge, MA / London 1997.

Granholm, Kennet, "Locating the West: Problematizing the *Western* in Western Esotericism and Occultism," in: Henrik Bogdan & Gordan Djurdjevic (eds.), *Occultism in a Global Perspective*, Acumen: Durham 2013, 17–36.

Granholm, Kennet, "Ritual Black Metal: Popular Music as Occult Mediation and Practice," *Correspondences* 1:1 (2013), 5–33.

Granholm, Kennet, "Popular Music and the Occult," in: Christopher Partridge & Marcus Moberg (eds.), *The Bloomsbury Handbook of Religion and Popular Music*, Bloomsbury: London etc. 2019, 198–209.

Granholm, Kennet, "Why all that Satanist Stuff in Heavy Metal?," in: Hanegraaff, Forshaw & Pasi, *Hermes Explains*, 120–126.

Grant, S. & M. Pasi, "'Works of Art without Parallel in the World': Georgiana Houghton's Spirit Drawings," in: Ernst Vegelin van Claerbergen & Barnaby Wright (eds.), *Georgiana Houghton: Spirit Drawings*, The Courtauld Gallery: London 2016, 9–23.

Gratzer, Wolfgang, *Zur "wunderlichen Mystik" Alban Bergs: Eine Studie*, Böhlau: Vienna / Cologne / Weimar 1993.

Green, Arthur, *A Guide to the Zohar*, Stanford University Press: Redwood City 2004.

Green, Martin, *Mountain of Truth: The Counterculture Begins. Ascona 1900-1920*, Tufts University / University Press of New England: Hanover / London 1986.

Greer, J. Christian, "Hakim Bey," in: Partridge, *The Occult World*, 424–426.

Greer, J. Christian, "Angel-Headed Hipsters: Psychedelic Militancy in Nineteenth-Eighties North America," Ph.D. Dissertation, University of Amsterdam 2020.

Greer, J. Christian, "The Psychedelic Church Movement," in: Egil Asprem (ed.), *Dictionary of Contemporary Esotericism*, Brill: Leiden / Oxford forthcoming (pre-print: https://contern.files.wordpress.com)

Greer, J. Christian & Michelle K. Oing, *Kumano Kodo: Pilgrimage to Powerspots*, OSGH Press: San Francisco 2022.

Greer, Mary K., *Women of the Golden Dawn: Rebels and Priestesses*, Park Street Press: Rochester 1995.

Grey, Alex, *Transfigurations*, Inner Traditions: Rochester 2001.

Grey, Alex & Allyson Grey, *Net of Being*, Inner Traditions: Rochester / Toronto 2012.

Grillot de Givry, Émile-Jules, *Le musée des Sorciers: Mages et Alchimistes*, Librairie de France: Paris 1929.

Grillot de Givry, Émile-Jules, *A Pictorial Anthology of Witchcraft, Magic & Alchemy*, University Books: Chicago / New York 1958.

Grillot de Givry, Émile-Jules, *Illustrated Anthology of Sorcery, Magic and Alchemy*, Causeway Books: New York 1973.

Griscom, Chris, *Ecstasy is a New Frequency: Teachings of the Light Institute*, Simon & Schuster: New York 1987.

Grof, Stanislav, *Beyond the Brain: Birth, Death, and Transcendence in Psychotherapy*, State University of New York Press: Albany 1985.

Grondin, Jean, "The Universality of Hermeneutic Understanding: The Strong, somewhat Metaphysical Conclusion of *Truth and Method*," in: Theodore George & Gert-Jan van der Heijden (eds.), *The Gadamerian Mind*, Routledge: London / New York 2022, 24–36.

Guénon, René, *Introduction générale à l'étude des doctrines hindoues*, Véga: Paris 1921.

Guénon, René, *La crise du monde moderne*, Gallimard: Paris 1927.

Guénon, René, *Le règne de la quantité et les signes des temps*, Gallimard: Paris 1945.

Guénon, René, *Le Théosophisme: Histoire d'une pseudo-religion* (1921), Éditions Traditionnelles: Paris 1986.

Guénon, René, *L'erreur spirite* (1923), Éditions Traditionnelles: Paris 1991.

Gutas, Dimitri, *Greek Thought, Arabic Culture: The Graeco-Arabic Translation Movement in Baghdad and Early 'Abāsid Society (2nd-4th / 8th-10th Centuries)*, Routledge: Abingdon / New York 1998.

Gutierrez, Cathy, *Plato's Ghost: Spiritualism in the American Renaissance*, Oxford University Press: Oxford 2009.

Habermas, Jürgen, *Der philosophische Diskurs der Moderne*, Suhrkamp: Frankfurt a.M. 1985.

Hadot, Pierre, *What is Ancient Philosophy?*, The Belknap Press of Harvard University Press: Cambridge, MA / London 2002.

Haidt, Jonathan, *The Anxious Generation: How the Great Rewiring of Childhood is Causing an Epidemic of Mental Illness*, Allen Lane: London 2024.

Hakl, Hans Thomas, "'Occultism is the Metaphysics of Dunces': The Conflation of Esotericism, Irrationalism, and Fascism in Postwar Germany," in: Arthur Versluis, Lee Irwin & Melinda Phillips (eds.), *Esotericism, Religion, and Politics*, North American Academic Press: Minneapolis 2012, 1–40.

Hakl, Hans Thomas, *Eranos: An Alternative Intellectual History of the Twentieth Century*, Equinox: Sheffield / Bristol 2013.

Halbertal, Moshe & Avishai Margalit, *Idolatry*, Harvard University Press: Cambridge, MA / London 1992.

Halbfass, Wilhelm, *India and Europe: An Essay in Philosophical Understanding*, Motilal Banarsidass Publishers: Delhi 2017.

Hale, Amy, *Ithell Colquhoun: Genius of the Fern Loved Gully*, Strange Attractor Press: London 2020.

Hames, Harvey J., *Like Angels on Jacob's Ladder: Abraham Abulafia, the Franciscans, and Joachimism*, State University of New York Press: Albany 2007.

Hamill, John, *The Craft: A History of English Freemasonry*, Crucible: Wellingborough 1986.

Hammer, Olav, *Claiming Knowledge: Strategies of Epistemology from Theosophy to the New Age*, Brill: Leiden / Boston / Cologne 2001.

Hammer, Olav & Kocku von Stuckrad, "Introduction: Western Esotericism and Polemics," in: Hammer & Von Stuckrad, *Polemical Encounters*, vii–xxii.

Hammer, Olav & Kocku von Stuckrad (eds.), *Polemical Encounters: Esoteric Discourse and Its Others*, Brill: Leiden / Boston 2007.

Hanegraaff, Wouter J., "Empirical Method in the Study of Esotericism," *Method & Theory in the Study of Religion* 7:2 (1995), 99–129.

Hanegraaff, Wouter J., *New Age Religion and Western Culture: Esotericism in the Mirror of Secular Thought*, Brill: Leiden / Boston / Cologne 1996 (State University of York Press: Albany 1998).

Hanegraaff, Wouter J., "The Emergence of the Academic Science of Magic: The Occult Philosophy in Tylor and Frazer," in: Arie L. Molendijk & Peter Pels (eds.), *Religion in the Making: The Emergence of the Sciences of Religion*, Royal E.J. Brill: Leiden / Boston / Cologne 1998, 253–275.

Hanegraaff, Wouter J., "On the Construction of 'Esoteric Traditions'," in: Antoine Faivre & Wouter J. Hanegraaff, *Western Esotericism and the Science of Religion: Selected Papers Presented at the 17th Congress of the International Association for the History of Religions, Mexico City 1995*, Peeters: Louvain 1998, 11–61.

Hanegraaff, Wouter J., "Romanticism and the Esoteric Connection," in: van den Broek & Hanegraaff, *Gnosis and Hermeticism*, 237–268.

Hanegraaff, Wouter J., "Defining Religion in Spite of History," in: Platvoet & Molendijk, *Pragmatics of Defining Religion*, 337–378.

Hanegraaff, Wouter J., "A Woman Alone: The Beatification of Friederike Hauffe *née* Wanner (1801-1829)," in: Anne-Marie Korte (ed.), *Women and Miracle Stories: A Multidisciplinary Exploration*, Royal E.J. Brill: Leiden / Boston / Cologne 2001, 211–247.

Hanegraaff, Wouter J., "Ironic Esotericism: Alchemy and Grail Mythology in Thomas Mann's *Zauberberg*," in: Caron, Godwin, Hanegraaff & Vieillard-Baron, *Ésotérisme, gnoses & imaginaire symbolique*, 575–594.

Hanegraaff, Wouter J., "Versuch über Friederike Hauffe: Zum Verhältnis zwischen Lebensgeschichte und Mythos der 'Seherin von Prevorst'," *Suevica* 8 (1999/2000), 17–38; 9 (2001/2002), 233–276.

Hanegraaff, Wouter J., "How Magic Survived the Disenchantment of the World," *Religion* 33:4 (2003), 357–380.

Hanegraaff, Wouter J., Review of Martin Mulsow (ed.), *Das Ende des Hermetismus, Aries* 4:1 (2004), 108–111.

Hanegraaff, Wouter J., "Forbidden Knowledge: Anti-Esoteric Polemics and Academic Research," *Aries* 5:2 (2005), 225–254.

Hanegraaff, Wouter J., "Idolatry," *Rever: Revista de Estudos da Religião* 5:4 (2005), http://www.pucsp.br/rever/rv4_2005.

Hanegraaff, Wouter J., "Introduction," in: Hanegraaff, *Dictionary*, vii–xiii.

Hanegraaff, Wouter J., "Esotericism," in: Hanegraaff, *Dictionary*, 336–340.

Hanegraaff, Wouter J., "Occult/Occultism," in: Hanegraaff, *Dictionary*, 884–889.

Hanegraaff, Wouter J., "Roberts, Dorothy Jane," in: Hanegraaff, *Dictionary*, 997–1000.

Hanegraaff, Wouter J., "Swedenborg, the Jews, and Jewish Traditions," in: Peter Schäfer & Irina Wandrey (eds.), *Reuchlin und seine Erben*, Thorbecke: Ostfildern 2005, 135–154.

Hanegraaff, Wouter J., "Fiction in the Desert of the Real: Lovecraft's Cthulhu Mythos," *Aries* 7:1 (2007), 85–109.

Hanegraaff, Wouter J., *Swedenborg, Oetinger, Kant: Three Perspectives on the Secrets of Heaven*, The Swedenborg Foundation: West Chester 2007.

Hanegraaff, Wouter J., "The Trouble with Images: Anti-Image Polemics and Western Esotericism," in: Hammer & von Stuckrad, *Polemical Encounters*, 107–136.

Hanegraaff, Wouter J., "Altered States of Knowledge: The Attainment of *Gnōsis* in the Hermetica," *The International Journal of the Platonic Tradition* 2:2 (2008), 128–163.

Hanegraaff, Wouter J., "Leaving the Garden (in Search of Religion): Jeffrey J. Kripal's Vision of a Gnostic Study of Religion" (review article of Jeffrey J. Kripal, *The Serpent's Gift*), *Religion* 38:3 (2008), 259–276.

Hanegraaff, Wouter J., "Reason, Faith, and Gnosis: Potentials and Problematics of a Typological Construct," in: Peter Meusburger, Michael Welker & Edgar Wunder (eds.), *Clashes of Knowledge: Orthodoxies and Heterodoxies in Science and Religion*, Springer Science & Business Media: Dordrecht 2008, 133–144.

Hanegraaff, Wouter J., "Swedenborg aus der Sicht von Kant und der akademischen Kantforschung," in: Friedemann Stengel (ed.), *Kant und Swedenborg: Zugänge zu einem umstrittenen Verhältnis*, Max Niemeyer: Tübingen 2008, 157–172.

Hanegraaff, Wouter J., "Under the Mantle of Love: The Mystical Eroticisms of Marsilio Ficino and Giordano Bruno," in: Hanegraaff & Kripal, *Hidden Intercourse*, 175–207.

Hanegraaff, Wouter J., "Better than Magic: Cornelius Agrippa and Lazzarellian Hermetism," *Magic, Ritual & Witchcraft* 4:1 (2009), 1–25.

Hanegraaff, Wouter J., "Will-Erich Peuckert and the Light of Nature," in: Arthur Versluis, Claire Fanger, Lee Irwin & Melinda Phillips (eds.), *Esotericism, Religion, and Nature*, North American Academic Press: Michigan 2009, 281–305.

Hanegraaff, Wouter J., "'And End History. And go to the Stars': Terence McKenna and 2012," in: Carole M. Cusack & Christopher Hartney (eds.), *Religion and Retributive Logic: Essays in Honour of Professor Garry W. Trompf*, Brill: Leiden / Boston 2010, 291–312.

Hanegraaff, Wouter J., "The Beginnings of Occultist Kabbalah: Adolphe Franck and Eliphas Lévi," in: Huss, Pasi & von Stuckrad, *Kabbalah and Modernity*, 107–128.

Hanegraaff, Wouter J., "Magnetic Gnosis: Somnambulism and the Quest for Absolute Knowledge," in: Andreas B. Kilcher & Philipp Theisohn (eds.), *Die Enzyklopädik der Esoterik: Allwissenheitsmythen und universalwissenschaftliche Modelle in der Esoterik der Neuzeit*, Wilhelm Fink: Paderborn 2010, 259–275.

Hanegraaff, Wouter J., "The Platonic Frenzies in Marsilio Ficino," in: Jitse Dijkstra, Justin Kroesen & Yme Kuiper (eds.), *Myths, Martyrs and Modernity: Studies in the History of Religions in Honour of Jan N. Bremmer*, Brill: Leiden / Boston 2010, 553–567.

Hanegraaff, Wouter J., "The Unspeakable and the Law: Esotericism in Anton Webern and the Second Viennese School," in: Wuidar, *Music and Esotericism*, 329–353.

Hanegraaff, Wouter J., "Teaching Experiential Dimensions of Western Esotericism," in: William B. Parsons (ed.), *Teaching Mysticism*, Oxford University Press: Oxford 2011, 154–169.

Hanegraaff, Wouter J., *Esotericism and the Academy: Rejected Knowledge in Western Culture*, Cambridge University Press: Cambridge 2012.

Hanegraaff, Wouter J., "Imagining the Unconscious," *Intellectual History Review* 22:4 (2012), 563–568.

Hanegraaff, Wouter J., "Entheogenic Esotericism," in: Asprem & Granholm, *Contemporary Esotericism*, 392–409.

Hanegraaff, Wouter J., "Hermetism," in: Karla Pollmann et al. (eds.), *The Oxford Guide to the Historical Reception of Augustine*, Oxford University Press: Oxford 2013, 1135–1139.

Hanegraaff, Wouter J., "The Power of Ideas: Esotericism, Historicism, and the Limits of Discourse," *Religion* 43:2 (2013), 252–273.

Hanegraaff, Wouter J., "Textbooks and Introductions to Western Esotericism," *Religion* 43:2 (2013), 178–200.

Hanegraaff, Wouter J., *Western Esotericism: A Guide for the Perplexed*, Bloomsbury: London 2013.

Hanegraaff, Wouter J., "A Visual World: Leonora Carrington and the Occult," *Abraxas: International Journal of Esoteric Studies* 6 (2014), 101–112.

Hanegraaff, Wouter J., "The Globalization of Esotericism," *Correspondences* 3 (2015), 55–91.

Hanegraaff, Wouter J., "How Hermetic Was Renaissance Hermetism?," *Aries* 15:2 (2015), 179–209.

Hanegraaff, Wouter J., "Jacob Boehme and Christian Theosophy," in: Christopher Partridge (ed.), *The Occult World*, Routledge 2015, 119–127.

Hanegraaff, Wouter J., "*Ad loca secretiora*: Rejected Knowledge and the Future of Libraries," in: Hans Thomas Hakl (ed.), *OCTAGON*, vol. 2 (English): *The Quest for Wholeness mirrored in a Library dedicated to Religious Studies, Philosophy, and Esotericism in Particular*, Scientia Nova: Gaggenau 2016, 25–34.

Hanegraaff, Wouter J., "Alan Moore's *Promethea*: Countercultural Gnosis and the End of the World," *Gnosis: Journal of Gnostic Studies* 1 (2016), 234–258.

Hanegraaff, Wouter J., "Magic," in: Magee, *Cambridge Handbook*, 393–404.

Hanegraaff, Wouter J., "Reconstructing 'Religion' from the Bottom Up," *Numen* 63 (2016), 576–605.

Hanegraaff, Wouter J., "The Great War of the Soul: Divine and Human Madness in Carl Gustav Jung's *Liber Novus*," in: Lutz Greisiger, Alexander van der Haven & Sebastian Schüler (eds.), *Religion und Wahnsinn um 1900: Zwischen Pathologisierung und Selbstermächtigung / Religion and Madness around 1900: Between Pathology and Self-Empowerment*, Würzburg: Ergon Verlag 2017, 101–135.

Hanegraaff, Wouter J., "Religion and the Historical Imagination: Esoteric Tradition as Poetic Invention," in: Christoph Bochinger & Jörg Rüpke (eds.), in cooperation with Elisabeth Begemann, *Dynamics of Religion: Past and Present*, De Gruyter: Berlin 2017, 131–153.
Hanegraaff, Wouter J., "The Theosophical Imagination," *Correspondences* 5 (2017), 3–39.
Hanegraaff, Wouter J., "Rejected Knowledge... So you mean that Esotericists are the Losers of History?," in: Hanegraaff, Forshaw & Pasi, *Hermes Explains*, 145–152.
Hanegraaff, Wouter J., "Imagining the Future Study of Religion and Spirituality," *Religion* 50:1 (2020), 72–82.
Hanegraaff, Wouter J., "The Third Kind: Gilles Quispel and Gnosis," *Creative Reading*, July 11, 2020, www.wouterjhanegraaff.blogspot.com.
Hanegraaff, Wouter J., "Western Esotericism and the Orient in the First Theosophical Society," in: Krämer & Strube, *Theosophy across Boundaries*, 29–64.
Hanegraaff, Wouter J., "Carl August Eschenmayer and the Somnambulic Soul," in: Pokorny & Winter, *Occult Nineteenth Century*, 15–35.
Hanegraaff, Wouter J., "Protecting the Sacred after (Post)Modernity," *Creative Reading*, March 6, 2021. www.wouterjhanegraaff.blogspot.nl.
Hanegraaff, Wouter J., "Esotericism and Democracy: Some Clarifications," *Creative Reading*, October 7, 2022. www.wouterjhanegraaff.blogspot.com.
Hanegraaff, Wouter J., *Hermetic Spirituality and the Historical Imagination: Altered States of Knowledge in Late Antiquity*, Cambridge University Press: Cambridge 2022.
Hanegraaff, Wouter J., with Jean-Pierre Brach & Pasi Marco, "Antoine Faivre (1934-2021): The Insider as Outsider," *Aries* 22:2 (2022), 167–204.
Hanegraaff, Wouter J., "Provincializing American Theory" (response to Joseph Ā. Josephson Storm, *Metamodernism*), *Religious Studies Review* 48:4 (2022), 509–512.
Hanegraaff, Wouter J., "Generous Hermeneutics: Hans Thomas Hakl and Eranos," *Religiographies* 2:1 (2023), 59–75.
Hanegraaff, Wouter J., "A Poem at the Edge of Reality," *Creative Reading*, December 4, 2023. www.wouterjhanegraaff.blogspot.com.
Hanegraaff, Wouter J., "Hermes, Hermeneutics & the Humanities," *Creative Reading*, August 22, 2024. www.wouterjhanegraaff.blogspot.com.
Hanegraaff, Wouter J., "Out of Egypt: Hermetic Theosophy between Reitzenstein and Mead," in: Charles Stang & Jason Ā. Josephson Storm (eds.), *Theosophy and the Study of Religion*, Brill: Leiden / Boston 2024, 83–111.
Hanegraaff, Wouter J., "A Suggestive Inquiry into Hermetic Rebirth: Nondual *Noēsis* and Bodily Fluids in Victorian England," in: Sarah Perez, Bastiaan van Rijn & Jens Schlieter (eds.), *Intentional Transformative Experiences: Theorizing Self-Cultivation in Religion and Esotericism*, De Gruyter: Berlin 2024.
Hanegraaff, Wouter J., "The Unnecessity of Definition," *Aries* 24:2 (2024).
Hanegraaff, Wouter J., "Historical Approaches to Contemporary Esotericism," in: Egil Asprem (ed.), *Dictionary of Contemporary Esotericism*, Brill: Leiden / Boston forthcoming [preprint evailable at https://contern.org (CRESARCH Repository)].
Hanegraaff, Wouter J., "Subtle Energies in Ayahuasca Healing," in: Julian Strube, Marleen Thaler & Dominic Zöhrer (eds.), *Subtle Energies in Therapy, Spirituality, Arts, and Politics*, Brill: Leiden / Boston (forthcoming).
Hanegraaff, Wouter J., "Henry Corbin as Knight of the Temple," in: Hadi Fakhoury (ed.), *New Perspectives on Henry Corbin*, Palgrave MacMillan: Cham 2025.

Hanegraaff, Wouter J., "Here, There & Everywhere: Esoteric Practices and the Global Agenda," *Method & Theory in the Study of Religion* 37 (2025) (forthcoming).

Hanegraaff, Wouter J., "Hermetic Freedom and Human Dignity," in *Eranos Jahrbuch* 76, Daimon Verlag: Einsiedeln 2025.

Hanegraaff, Wouter J., "The Heroic Martyr and Prophet of Hermetic Renovation: Giordano Bruno in John Crowley's *Aegypt*," in: Caroline Van Der Stichele & Jacqueline Borsje (eds.), *Tyrants, Heroes, Prophets, and Martyrs: Shifting Images from the Past to the Present*, Brill: Leiden / Boston 2025.

Hanegraaff, Wouter J. & Ruud M. Bouthoorn, *Lodovico Lazzarelli (1447-1500): The Hermetic Writings and Related Documents*, Arizona Center for Medieval and Renaissance Studies: Tempe 2005.

Hanegraaff, Wouter J. & Mriganka Mukhopadhyay, "Translating Esotericism: Scepticism, Optimism, Agency," *Correspondences* 11:1 (2023), 1–30.

Hanegraaff, Wouter J. (ed.), in collaboration with Antoine Faivre, Roelof van den Broek & Jean-Pierre Brach, *Dictionary of Gnosis and Western Esotericism*, Brill: Leiden / Boston 2005.

Hanegraaff, Wouter J. & Jeffrey J. Kripal (eds.), *Hidden Intercourse: Eros and Sexuality in the History of Western Esotericism*, Brill: Leiden / Boston 2008.

Hanegraaff, Wouter J. & Joyce Pijnenburg (eds.), *Hermes in the Academy: Ten Years' Study of Western Esotericism at the University of Amsterdam*, Amsterdam University Press: Amsterdam 2009.

Hanegraaff, Wouter J., Peter J. Forshaw & Marco Pasi (eds.), *Hermes Explains: Thirty Questions about Western Esotericism*, Amsterdam University Press: Amsterdam 2019.

Hansen, H.T. (= Hans Thomas Hakl), "Julius Evola's Political Endeavors," in: Julius Evola, *Men among the Ruins: Postwar Reflections of a Radical Traditionalist*, Inner Traditions: Rochester 2002, 1–104.

Harari, Yuval, *Jewish Magic before the Rise of Kabbalah*, Wayne State University Press: Detroit 2017.

Harari, Yuval Noah, *Sapiens: A Brief History of Humankind*, Vintage Books: London 2011.

Haraway, Donna, "Situated Knowledges: The Science Question in Feminism and the Privilege of Partial Perspective," *Feminist Studies* 14:3 (1988), 575–599.

Haraway, Donna, *Staying with the Trouble: Making Kin in the Chthulucene*, Duke University Press: Durham / London 2016.

Harkness, Deborah E., *John Dee's Conversations with Angels: Cabala, Alchemy, and the End of Nature*, Cambridge University Press: Cambridge 1999.

Harmening, Dieter, *Superstitio: Überlieferungs- und theoriegeschichtliche Untersuchungen zur kirchlich-theologischen Aberglaubensliteratur des Mittelalters*, Erich Schmidt: Berlin 1979.

Harmsen, Theodor, *Der magische Schriftsteller Gustav Meyrink, seine Freunde und sein Werk*, In de Pelikaan: Amsterdam 2009.

Harnack, Adolf von, *Marcion: Das Evangelium vom fremden Gott: Eine Monographie zur Geschichte der Grundlegung der Katholischen Kirche*, J.C. Hinrichs: Leipzig 1921.

Harner, Michael, *The Way of the Shaman*, 2nd ed., Harper: San Francisco 1990.

Hartmann, Eduard von, *Philosophie des Unbewussten*, Carl Ducker's Verlag: Berlin 1876.

Harvey, David, *A Brief History of Neoliberalism*, Oxford University Press: Oxford 2005.

Harvey, David Allen, *Beyond Enlightenment: Occultism and Politics in Modern France*, Northern Illinois University Press: Dekalb 2005.

Hasse, Dag Nikolaus, *Success and Suppression: Arabic Sciences and Philosophy in the Renaissance*, Harvard University Press: Cambridge, MA / London 2016.

Hayman, P.A., *Sefer Yeṣira*, Mohr-Siebeck: Tübingen 2004.

Hedenborg White, Manon, *The Eloquent Blood: The Goddess Babalon & the Construction of Femininities in Western Esotericism*, Oxford University Press: Oxford 2020.

Hedenborg White, Manon & Tim Rudbøg (eds.), *Esotericism and Deviance*, Brill: Leiden / Boston 2024.

Heehs, Peter, *The Lives of Sri Aurobindo*, Columbia University Press: New York 2008.

Hegel, Georg Wilhelm Friedrich, *Vorlesungen über die Philosophie der Geschichte*, Philipp Reclam: Stuttgart 1961.

Hellner-Eshed, Melila, *A River Flows from Eden: The Language of Mystical Experience in the Zohar*, Stanford University Press: Redwood City 2009.

Helmont, Francis Mercury van, *The Alphabet of Nature* (Allison P. Coudert & Taylor Corse, ed. & translation), Brill: Leiden / Boston 2007.

Hertz, Noreena, *The Silent Takeover: Global Capitalism and the Death of Democracy*, Arrow: London 2001.

Hessayon, Ariel & Sarah Apetrei (eds.), *An Introduction to Jacob Boehme: Four Centuries of Thought and Reception*, Routledge: New York / London 2014.

Heumann, Christoph August, "Von denen Kennzeichen der falschen und unächten Philosophie," *Acta Philosophorum* 2 (1715), 179–236.

Holz, Hans Heinz, "ERANOS: Eine Modern Pseudo-Gnosis," in: Jacob Taubes (ed.), *Religionstheorie und Politische Theologie*, vol. 2: *Gnosis und Politik*, Wilhelm Fink / Ferdinand Schöningh: Paderborn / Munich 1984, 249–263.

Horkheimer, Max & Theodor W. Adorno, *Dialectic of Enlightenment: Philosophical Fragments*, Stanford University Press: Redwood City 2002.

Houellebecq, Michel, *The Possibility of an Island*, Knopf: New York 2005.

Houghton, Georgiana, *Evenings at Home in Spiritual Séance* (Sara William, ed. & introd.), Victorian Secrets: Brighton 2013.

Houman, Setareh, *From the* Philosophia Perennis *to American Perennialism*, Kazi Publications: Chicago n.d.

Houston, Jean, *The Possible Human: A Course in Extending your Physical, Mental, and Creative Abilities*, J.P. Tarcher Inc.: Los Angeles 1982.

Howe, Ellic, *The Magicians of the Golden Dawn: A Documentary History of a Magical Order 1887-1923*, Routledge & Kegan Paul: London 1972.

Hughes, Derek, *Versions of Blackness: Key Texts on Slavery from the Seventeenth Century*, Cambridge University Press: Cambridge 2007.

Huss, Boaz, "Ask No Questions: Gershom Scholem and the Study of Contemporary Jewish Mysticism," *Modern Judaism* 25:2 (2005), 141–158.

Huss, Boaz, *The Zohar: Reception and Impact*, The Littman Library of Jewish Civilization: Oxford / Portland, Oregon 2016.

Huss, Boaz, *Mystifying Kabbalah: Academic Scholarship, National Theology, & New Age Spirituality*, Oxford University Press: Oxford 2020.

Huss, Boaz (ed.), *Kabbalah and Contemporary Spiritual Revival*, Ben-Gurion University of the Negev Press: Beer-Sheva 2011.

Huss, Boaz, Marco Pasi & Kocku von Stuckrad (eds.), *Kabbalah and Modernity: Interpretations, Transformations, Adaptations*, Brill: Leiden / Boston 2010.

Hutchison, Keith, "What happened to Occult Qualities in the Scientific Revolution?," *Isis* 73 (1982), 233–253.

Hutin, Serge, *Casting Spells*, Barrie & Jenkins: London 1978.

Hutton, Ronald, *The Triumph of the Moon: A History of Modern Pagan Witchcraft*, Oxford University Press: Oxford 1999.

Hutton, Ronald, *Shamans: Siberian Spirituality and the Western Imagination*, Hambledon Continuum: London / New York 2001.

Hutton, Ronald, *The Witch: A History of Fear, from Ancient times to the Present*, Yale University Press: New Haven / London 2017.

[Iamblichus], *Réponse à Porphyre* (De Mysteriis) (Henri Dominique Saffrey & Alain-Philippe Segonds, ed. & translation), Les Belles Lettres: Paris 2018.

Ibn al ʿArabi, *The Meccan Revelations* (Michel Chodkiewicz, ed.; William C. Chittick & James W. Morris, translation), 2 vols., Pir Press: New York 2005.

Icke, David, *...And the Truth Shall Set You Free*, Bridge of Love Publications: Scottsdale 1995.

Icke, David, *The Biggest Secret: The Book that will Change the World*, Bridge of Love Publications: Scottsdale 1999.

Icke, David, *The David Icke Guide to the Global Conspiracy (and How to End It)*, David Icke Books: Ryde 2007.

Idel, Moshe, *The Mystical Experience in Abraham Abulafia*, State University of New York Press: Albany 1988.

Idel, Moshe, *Studies in Ecstatic Kabbalah*, State University of New York Press: Albany 1988.

Idel, Moshe, *Language, Torah, and Hermeneutics in Abraham Abulafia*, State University of New York Press: Albany 1989.

Idel, Moshe, *Hasidism: Between Mysticism and Magic*, State University of New York Press: Albany 1995.

Idel, Moshe, *Abraham Abulafia's Esotericism : Secrets and Doubts*, Walter de Gruyter: Berlin 2020.

Iggers, Georg G., *Historiography in the Twentieth Century: From Scientific Objectivity to the Postmodern Challenge*, Wesleyan University Press: Baltimore 2005.

Introvigne, Massimo, "Ordeal by Fire: The Tragedy of the Solar Temple," *Religion* 25:3 (1995), 267–283.

Introvigne, Massimo, "The Secular Anti-Cult and the Religious Counter-Cult Movement: Strange Bedfellows or Future Enemies?," in: Eric Towler (ed.), *New Religions and the New Europe*, Aarhus University Press: Aarhus / Oxford / Oakville 1995, 32–54.

Introvigne, Massimo, "Religion as Claim: Social and Legal Controversies," in: Platvoet & Molendijk, *Pragmatics of Defining Religion*, 41–72.

Introvigne, Massimo, "Martinism: Second Period," in: Hanegraaff, *Dictionary*, 780–783.

Introvigne, Massimo, "Rosicrucianism III: 19th-20th Century," in: Hanegraaff, *Dictionary*, 1018–1020.

Introvigne, Massimo, *Satanism: A Social History*, Brill: Leiden / Boston 2016.

Introvigne, Massimo, *Sacred Eroticism: Tantra and Eros in the Movement for Spiritual Integration into the Absolute (MISA)*, Mimesis International: n.p. 2022.

Introvigne, Massimo & J. Gordon Melton (eds.), *Pour en finir avec les sectes: Le débat sur le rapport de la commission parlementaire*, Dervy: Paris 1996.

Israel, Jonathan I., *Radical Enlightenment: Philosophy and the Making of Modernity 1650-1750*, Oxford University Press: Oxford 2001.

Jacques-Lefèvre, Nicole, *Louis-Claude de Saint-Martin, le philosophe inconnu (1743-1803)*, Dervy: Paris 2003.

Jehl, Roby Evan Record, "The 'Nightmare of History' in James Joyce's *Ulysses*," *Humanities and Social Sciences* 9 (2013), 1–9.

Jentsch, Ernst, "Zur Psychologie des Unheimlichen," *Psychiatrisch-Neurologische Wochenschrift* 22 (1906), 195–205.

Jeyaraj, Daniel, *Bartholomäus Ziegenbalgs "Genealogie der malabarischen Götter"*, Francke: Halle 2003.

Johnson, Carina L., "Idolatrous Cultures and the Practice of Religion," *Journal of the History of Ideas* 67:4 (2006), 597–621.

Johnson, Julian, *Webern and the Transformation of Nature*, Cambridge University Press: Cambridge 1999.

Johnston, Hannah E. & Peg Aloi (eds.), *The New Generation Witches: Teenage Witchcraft in Contemporary Culture*, Ashgate: Aldershot / Burlington 2007.

Johnston, Jay, "Disrupting Sanctified Deviance: The Benefits of Boredom," in: Hedenborg White & Rudbøg, *Esotericism and Deviance*, 70–82.

Joly, Alice, *Un Mystique Lyonnais et les secrets de la Franc-Maçonnerie: Jean-Baptiste Willermoz 1730-1824* (1938), Télètes: Paris n.d.

Jonas, Hans, *The Gnostic Religion: The Message of the Alien God and the Beginnings of Christianity*, Beacon Press: Boston 1958.

Jones, Daniel Stedman, *Masters of the Universe: Hayek, Friedman, and the Birth of Neoliberal Politics*, Princeton University Press: Princeton / Oxford 2012.

Jong, Albert F. de & Mariken Teeuwen, "Music I: Antiquity," in: Hanegraaff, *Dictionary*, 808–810.

Jong, H.M.E. de, *Michael Maier's Atalanta Fugiens: Sources of an Alchemical Book of Emblems*, Nicolas Hays: York Beach, Maine 2002.

Josephson Storm, Jason Ā., *The Myth of Disenchantment: Magic, Modernity, and the Birth of the Human Sciences*, The University of Chicago Press: Chicago / London 2017.

Josephson Storm, Jason Ā., *Metamodernism: The Future of Theory*, The University of Chicago Press: Chicago / London 2021.

Jung, Carl Gustav, *The Red Book: Liber Novus* (Sonu Shamdasani, ed.), W.W. Norton & Co.: New York / London 2009.

Jung, Carl Gustav, *Erinnerungen, Träume, Gedanken* (Aniela Jaffé, ed.), 18th ed., Edition C.G. Jung / Patmos Verlag: Ostfildern 2013.

Jung, Carl Gustav, *The Black Books*, 7 vols. (Sonu Shamdasani, ed.), W.W. Norton & Company: New York / London 2020.

Jung, Carl Gustav & Wolfgang Pauli, *The Interpretation of Nature and the Psyche*, Pantheon Books: New York 1955.

Kadarkay, Arpad, *Georg Lukács: Life, Thought, and Politics*, Basil Blackwell: Cambridge, MA 1991.

Kandinsky, Wassily, *On the Spiritual in Art*, Solomon R. Guggenheim Foundation: New York 1946.

Kant, Immanuel, *Träume eines Geistersehers, erläutert durch Träume der Metaphysik* (1766; Rudolf Malter, ed.), Reclam: Stuttgart 1976.

Kant, Immanuel, "What is Enlightenment?," in: Margaret C. Jacob, *The Enlightenment: A Brief History with Documents*, Bedford / St. Martins: Boston / New York 2001, 202–208.

Kaplan, Jeffrey & Heléne Lööw (eds.), *The Cultic Milieu: Oppositional Subcultures in an Age of Globalization*, Rowman & Littlefield: Walnut Creek / Lanham / New York / Oxford 2002.

Karbovnik, Damien, "L'ésotérisme grand public: Le réalisme fantastique et sa réception. Contribution à une sociohistoire de l'occulture," Ph.D. Thesis, L'Université Paul-Valéry Montpellier 3, 2017.

Karbovnik, Damien, "L'échec d'une 'religion' New Age: L'exemple des Ateliers *Planète*," *Revue de l'histoire des religions* 238 (2021), 515–545.

Kaske, Carol V. & John R. Clark, "Introduction," in: Ficino, *Three Books on Life*, 3–90.

Keller, Ursula & Natalja Sharandak, *Madame Blavatsky: Eine Biographie*, Insel Verlag: Berlin 2013.

Kérchy, Anna & Andreas Zittlau (eds.), *Exploring the Cultural History of Continental European Freak Shows and "Enfreakment*, Cambridge Scholars Publishing: Newcastle upon Tyne 2012.

Kerner, Justinus, *Die Seherin von Prevorst: Eröffnungen über das innere Leben des Menschen und über das Hereinragen einer Geisterwelt in die unsere* (1829), Reclam: Leipzig 1846.

Kieckhefer, Richard, *Magic in the Middle Ages*, Cambridge University Press: Cambridge 1989.

Kilcher, Andreas B., *Die Sprachtheorie der Kabbala als ästhetisches Paradigma: Die Konstruktion einer ästhetischen Kabbala seit der frühen Neuzeit*, J.B. Metzler: Stuttgart / Weimar 1998.

Kilcher, Andreas B., "Is Occultism a Product of Capitalism?," in: Hanegraaff, Forshaw & Pasi, *Hermes Explains*, 168–176.

Kilcher, Andreas B. & Philipp Theisohn (eds.), *Die Enzyklopädie der Esoterik: Allwissenheitsmythen und universalwissenschaftliche Modelle in der Esoterik der Neuzeit*, Wilhelm Fink: München 2010, 259–275.

King, Karen L., *What is Gnosticism?*, The Belknap Press of Harvard University Press: Cambridge, MA / London 2003.

King, Richard, *Orientalism and Religion: Postcolonial Theory, India and "The Mystic East,"* Routledge: London / New York 1999.

Kingsepp, Eva, "Scholarship as Simulacrum: The Case of *Hitler's Monsters*," *Aries* 19 (2019), 265–281.

Kipling, Rudyard, "The White Man's Burden," *The Times*, February 4, 1899 (and many later reprints).

Kippenberg, Hans G., *Discovering Religious History in the Modern Age*, Princeton University Press: Princeton / Oxford 2002.

Kippenberg, Hans G., Jörg Rüpke & Kocku von Stuckrad (eds.), *Europäische Religionsgeschichte: Ein mehrfacher Pluralismus*, 2 vols., Vandenhoeck & Ruprecht: Göttingen 2009.

Kissane, Séan (ed.), *Leonora Carrington*, Irish Museum of Modern Art: Dublin 2013.

Klein, Kevin, *The Complete Mystical Records of Dr. John Dee*, 2 vols., Llewellyn Publications: Woodbury 2017.

Klein, Naomi, *Doppelganger: A Trip into the Mirror World*, Allen Lane / Penguin: London 2023.

Klossowski de Rola, Stanislas, *The Golden Game: Alchemical Engravings of the Seventeenth Century*, Thames and Hudson: London 1988.

Knausgård, Karl Ove, *A Death in the Family* (*My Struggle* 1), Vintage: London 2013.

Knausgård, Karl Ove, *A Man in Love* (*My Struggle* 2), Vintage: London 2013.

Knight, Michael Muhammad, *The Five Percenters: Islam Hiphop and the Gods of New York*, Oneworld: Oxford 2007.

Knight, Michael Muhammad, "'I am Sorry, Mr. White Man, These are Secrets that You are Not Permitted to Learn': The Supreme Wisdom Lessons and Problem Book," *Correspondences* 7:1 (2019), 167–200.

Knight, Michael Muhammad, *The Supreme Wisdom Lessons: A Scripture of American Islam*, Equinox: Sheffield 2024.

Knysh, Alexander, *Islamic Mysticism: A Short History*, Brill: Leiden / Boston / Cologne 2000.

Knysh, Alexander, *Sufism: A New History of Islamic Mysticism*, Princeton University Press: Princeton / Oxford 2017.

Koyré, Alexandre, *Mystiques, spirituels, alchimistes du XVIe siècle allemand*, Gallimard: Paris 1971, 75–129.

Krämer, Hans Martin & Julian Strube (eds.), *Theosophy across Boundaries: Transcultural and Interdisciplinary Perspectives on a Modern Esoteric Movement*, State University of New York Press: Albany 2020.

Krastev, Ivan & Stephen Holmes, *The Light That Failed: A Reckoning*, Penguin: London 2019.

Kreis, Emmanuel, *Quis ut Deus ? Antijudéo-maçonnisme et occultisme en France sous la IIIe République*, 2 vols., Les Belles Lettres: Paris 2017.

Kripal, Jeffrey J., *Roads of Excess, Palaces of Wisdom: Eroticism and Reflexivity in the Study of Mysticism*, The University of Chicago Press: Chicago / London 2001.

Kripal, Jeffrey J., *The Serpent's Gift: Gnostic Reflections on the Study of Religion*, The University of Chicago Press: Chicago / London 2007.

Kripal, Jeffrey J., *Esalen: America and the Religion of No Religion*, The University of Chicago Press: Chicago / London 2007.

Kripal, Jeffrey J., *Authors of the Impossible: The Paranormal and the Sacred*, The University of Chicago Press: Chicago / London 2010.

Kripal, Jeffrey J., *Mutants and Mystics: Science Fiction, Superhero Comics, and the Paranormal*, The University of Chicago Press: Chicago / London 2011.

Kripal, Jeffrey J., *Secret Body: Erotic and Esoteric Currents in the History of Religions*, The University of Chicago Press: Chicago / London 2017.

Kripal, Jeffrey J., *The Flip: Epiphanies of Mind and the Future of Knowledge*, Bellevue Literary Press: New York 2019.

Kripal, Jeffrey J., *The Superhumanities: Historical Precedents, Moral Objections, New Realities*, The University of Chicago Press: Chicago / London 2022.

Kripal, Jeffrey J., *How to Think Impossibly: About Souls, UFOs, Time, Belief, and Everything Else*, The University of Chicago Press: Chicago / London 2024.

Kristóf, Ildikó Sz., "Missionaries, Monsters, and the Demon Show: Diabolized Representations of American Indians in Jesuit Libraries of Seventeenth and Eighteenth Century Upper Hungary," in Kérchy & Zittlau, *Exploring*, 38–73.

Kristóf, Ildikó Sz., "The Uses of Demonology: European Missionaries and Native Americans in the American Southwest (17-18th Centuries)," in: György E. Szönyi & Casaba Maczelka (eds.), *Centers and Peripheries in European Renaissance Culture: Essays by East-Central European Fellows*, JATE Press: Szeged 2012, 161–182.

Kuntz, Marion L., *Guillaume Postel: Prophet of the Restitution of All Things. His Life and Thought.* Martinus Nijhoff: The Hague / Boston / London 1981.

Kurlander, Eric, *Hitler's Monsters: A Supernatural History of the Third Reich*, Yale University Press: New Haven / London 2017.

Kurtz, Michael, *Stockhausen: A Biography*, Faber & Faber: London / Boston 1992.

Labate, Beatriz Caiuby & Clancy Cavnar (eds.), *Ayahuasca Shamanism in the Amazon and Beyond*, Oxford University Press: Oxford 2014.

Labate, Beatriz Caiuby & Henrik Jungaberle (eds.), *The Internationalization of Ayahuasca*, Lit: Vienna / Berlin 2011.

Lamberty, Pia & Katharina Nocun, *Gefährlicher Glaube: Die radikale Gedankenwelt der Esoterik*, Quadriga: Cologne 2022.

Lamm, Martin, *Emanuel Swedenborg: The Development of his Thought*, Swedenborg Foundation Publishers: West Chester 2000.

Lamprecht, Harald, *Neue Rosenkreuzer: Ein Handbuch*, Vandenhoeck & Ruprecht: Göttingen 2004.

Langermann, Y.T., Review of Patai, *The Jewish Alchemists*, *The Journal of the American Oriental Society* 116:4 (1996), 792–793.

Larsen, Robin, Stephen Larsen, James F. Lawrence & William Ross Woofenden (eds.), *Emanuel Swedenborg, a Continuing Vision: A Pictorial Biography & Anthology of Essays & Poetry*, Swedenborg Foundation: New York 1988.

Laurant, Jean-Pierre, *L'ésotérisme chrétien en France au XIXe siècle*, L'Âge d'Homme: Lausanne 1992.

Laurant, Jean-Pierre, "Saint-Yves d'Alveydre, Joseph," in: Hanegraaff, *Dictionary*, 1031–1032.

Layton, Bentley (ed.), *The Gnostic Scriptures: A New Translation with Annotations and Introductions*, Doubleday: New York etc. 1987.

Lazier, Benjamin, *God Interrupted: Heresy and the European Imagination between the World Wars*, Princeton University Press: Princeton 2008.

Leftwich, Adrian, "Thinking Politically: On the Politics of Politics," in: Adrian Leftwich (ed.), *What is Politics? The Activity and its Study*, Polity Press: Cambridge / Malden 2004, 1–22.

Lehmann-Brauns, Sicco, *Weisheit in der Weltgeschichte: Philosophiegeschichte zwischen Barock und Aufklärung*, Max Niemeyer: Tübingen 2004.

Lennep, Jacques van, *Alchimie: Contribution à l'histoire de l'art alchimique*, Crédit Communal: Brussels 1985.

Leone, Massimo, "Double Debunking: Modern Divination and the End of Semiotics," *Chinese Semiotic Studies* 11:4 (2015), 433–477.

Leone, Massimo, Mari-Liis Madisson & Andreas Ventsel, "Semiotic Approaches to Conspiracy Theories," in: Butter & Knight, *Routledge Handbook of Conspiracy Theories*, 43–55.

Levack, Brian P., *The Witch-Hunt in Early Modern Europe*, Routledge: London / New York 2016.

Lévi, Éliphas, *Secrets de la magie: Dogme et rituel de la haute magie / Histoire de la magie / La clef des grands mystères*, Robert Laffont: Paris 2000.

Lévi, Éliphas, *The Doctrine and Ritual of High Magic: A New Translation* (John Michael Greer & Anthony Mikituk, transl.), TarcherPerigee: New York 2017.

Lewis, James R., *The Oxford Handbook of New Religious Movements*, Oxford University Press: Oxford 2004.

Lewis, James R., "The Solar Temple 'Transits': Beyond the Millennialist Hypothesis," in: Lewis & Petersen, *Controversial New Religions*, 295–317.

Lewis, James R., *Scientology*, Oxford University Press: Oxford / New York 2009.

Lewis, James R., *Violence and New Religious Movements*, Oxford University Press: Oxford / New York 2011.

Lewis, James R. (ed.), *The Gods Have Landed: New Religions from Other Worlds*, State University of New York Press: Albany 1995.

Lewis, James R. & Jesper Aagaard Petersen (eds.), *Controversial New Religions*, Oxford University Press: Oxford 2005.

Lincoln, Bruce, *Gods and Demons, Priests and Scholars: Critical Explorations in the History of Religions*, The University of Chicago Press: Chicago / London 2012.

Lincoln, Bruce, *Secrets, Lies, and Consequences: A Great Scholar's Hidden Past and his Protégé's Unsolved Murder*, Oxford University Press: Oxford 2024.

Lindqvist, Sven, "'Exterminate All the Brutes'," in: *Saharan Journey*, Granta: London 1992, 145–333.

Litwa, M. David, *Hermetica II: The Excerpts of Stobaeus, Papyrus Fragments, and Ancient Testimonies in an English Translation with Notes and Introductions*, Cambridge University Press: Cambridge 2018.

Lloyd Thomas, Dana, *Julius Evola e la tentazione razzista: L'inganno del pangermanesimo in Italia*, Sulla rotta del sole, Giordano editore: Mesagne 2006.

López-Cano, María del Pilar Martínez, Elisa Itzel García Berumen & Marcelo Rocío García Harnández, "El Tercer Concilio Provincial Mexicano (1585)," in: María del Pilar Martínez López-Cano & Francisco Javier Cervantes Bello (eds.), *Los concilios provinciales en Nueva España: Reflexiones e influencias*, Universidad Nacional Autónoma de México 2005, 41–70.

Lovejoy, Arthur O., *The Great Chain of Being: A Study of the History of an Idea*, Harvard University Press: Cambridge, MA / London 1964.

Loy, David R., *Nonduality: In Buddhism and Beyond*, Wisdom Publications: Somerville 1988.

Lucas, Philip Charles, "Summit Lighthouse," in: Hanegraaff, *Dictionary*, 1093–1096.

Luck, Georg, *Arcana Mundi: Magic and the Occult in the Greek and Roman World. A Collection of Ancient Texts*, The Johns Hopkins University Press: Baltimore / London 1985; 2nd ed. 2006.

Ludwig, Arnold M., "Altered States of Consciousness," in: Tart, *Altered States of Consciousness*, 11–24.

Luhrmann, Tanya M., *Persuasions of the Witch's Craft: Ritual Magic in Contemporary England*, Harvard University Press: Cambridge, MA 1989.

Luhrmann, Tanya M., *Of Two Minds: An Anthropologist looks at American Psychiatry*, Vintage Books: New York 2000.

Luidinga, Gerrit, *Johfra: Hoogste lichten en diepste schaduwen. Een kunstenaarsleven in woord en beeld 1919-1998*, Kosmos-Z&K: Utrecht / Antwerpen 2001.

Luijk, Ruben van, *Children of Lucifer: The Origins of Modern Religious Satanism*, Oxford University Press: Oxford 2016.

MacDonald, Paul S., *History of the Concept of Mind: Speculations about Soul, Mind and Spirit from Homer to Hume*, Ashgate: Aldershot / Burlington 2003.

MacDonald, Paul S., *History of the Concept of Mind*, vol. 2: *The Heterodox and Occult Tradition*, Ashgate: Aldershot / Burlington 2007.

MacMurphy, John, "Are Kabbalistic Meditations All About Ecstasy?," in: Hanegraaff, Forshaw & Pasi, *Hermes Explains*, 184–190.

Maconie, Robin, *Other Planets: The Complete Works of Karlheinz Stockhausen, 1950-2007*, Rowman & Littlefield: Lanham / Boulder / New York / London 2016.

Magdalino, Paul & Maria Mavroudi (eds.), *The Occult Sciences in Byzantium*, La Pomme d'Or: Geneva 2006.

Magee, Glenn Alexander, *Hegel and the Hermetic Tradition*, Cornell University Press: Ithaca / London 2001.

Magee, Glenn Alexander (ed.), *The Cambridge Handbook of Western Mysticism and Esotericism*, Cambridge University Press: Cambridge 2016.

Magnússon, Gísli, *Dichtung als Erfahrungsmetaphysik: Esoterische und okkultistische Modernität bei R.M. Rilke*, Königshausen & Neumann: Würzburg 2009.

Magnússon, Gísli, "The Aesthetics of Epiphany in Karl Ove Knausgård's *Min kamp*," *Scandinavian Studies* 92:3 (2020), 348–368.

Magus, Simon, *Rider Haggard and the Imperial Occult: Hermetic Discourse and Romantic Contiguity*, Brill: Leiden / Boston 2022.

Mahé, Jean-Pierre, *Hermès Trismégiste*, vol. 5, *Paralipomènes*, Les Belles Lettres: Paris 2019.

Maier, Michael, *Atalanta Fugiens: An Edition of the Emblems, Fugues and Epigrams* (Joscelyn Godwin, translation), Phanes Press: Grand Rapids 1989.

Maillard, Christine, *L'Inde vue d'Europe: Histoire d'une rencontre (1750-1950)*, Albin Michel: Paris 2008.

Majercik, Ruth, *The Chaldean Oracles: Text, Translation, and Commentary*, Brill: Leiden / New York / Copenhagen / Cologne 1989.

Malewitsch, Kasimir, *Suprematismus: Die gegenstandslose Welt*, DuMont: Cologne 1989.

Mann, Thomas, *Joseph und seine Brüder II: Joseph in Ägypten / Joseph der Ernährer* (Grosse Kommentierte Frankfurter Ausgabe 8.1), S. Fischer Verlag: Frankfurt a.M. 2018.

Martins, Ansgar, *The Migration of Metaphysics into the Realm of the Profane: Theodor W. Adorno Reads Gershom Scholem*, Brill: Leiden / Boston 2020.

May, Gerhard, *Creatio ex Nihilo: The Doctrine of "Creation out of Nothing" in Early Christian Thought*, T&T Clark: London / New York 2004.

McAuliffe, Jane Dammen, Barry Dov Walfish & Joseph W. Goering, *With Reverence for the Word: Medieval Scriptural Exegesis in Judaism, Christianity and Islam*, Oxford University Press: Oxford 2003.

McCalla, Arthur, "Fabre d'Olivet, Antoine," in: Hanegraaff, *Dictionary*, 350–354.

McCann, Hannah & Whitney Monaghan, *Queer Theory Now: From Foundations to Futures*, Red Globe Press: London 2020.

McEvilley, Thomas, *The Shape of Ancient Thought: Comparative Studies in Greek and Indian Philosophies*, Allworth Press: New York 2002.

McIntosh, Christopher, *The Rose Cross and the Age of Reason: Eighteenth-Century Rosicrucianism in Central Europe and its Relationship to the Enlightenment*, Brill: Leiden / New York / Cologne 1992.

McIntosh, Christopher, *The Rosicrucians: The History, Mythology, and Rituals of an Esoteric Order*, Samuel Weiser: York Beach 1997.

McIntosh, Christopher, *Beyond the North Wind: The Fall and Rise of the Mystic North*, Samuel Weiser: York Beach 2019.

McKenna, Terence, *True Hallucinations: Being an Account of the Author's Extraordinary Adventures in the Devil's Paradise*, Harper Collins: San Francisco 1993.

Medin, Douglas & Andrew Ortony, "Psychological Essentialism," in: Stella Vosniadou & Andrew Ortony (eds.), *Similarity and Analogical Reasoning*, Cambridge University Press: Cambridge 1989, 179–196.

Meheust, Bertrand, *Somnambulisme et médiumnité*, 2 vols., Institut Synthélabo: Le Plessis-Robinson 1999.

Meir, Jonatan, *Kabbalistic Circles in Jerusalem (1896-1948)*, Brill: Leiden / Boston 2016.

Melton, J. Gordon, "The Modern Anti-Cult Movement in Historical Perspective," in: Kaplan & Lööw, *Cultic Milieu*, 265–289.

Melvin-Koushki, Matthew, "Introduction: De-orienting the Study of Islamicate Occultism," *Arabica* 64 (2017), 287–295.

Melvin-Koushki, Matthew, "Powers of One: The Mathematicalization of the Occult Sciences in the High Persianate Tradition," *Intellectual History of the Islamicate World* 5:1 (2017), 127–199.

Melvin-Koushki, Matthew, "Early Modern Islamicate Empire: New Forms of Religiopolitical Legitimacy," in: Armando Salvatore et al. (eds.), *The Wiley-Blackwell History of Islam*, Wiley-Blackwell: Hoboken 2018, 353–375.

Melvin-Koushki, Matthew, "*Taḥqīq* vs. *Taqlīd* in the Renaissances of Western Early Modernity," *Philological Encounters* 3 (2018), 193–249.

Melvin-Koushki, Matthew, "*How to Rule the World*: Occult-Scientific Manuals of the Early Modern Persian Cosmopolis," *Journal of Persianate Studies* 11:2 (2018), 140–154.

Melvin-Koushki, Matthew, "Better than Sufi Sex: Ibn Turka on the Superiority of Lettrism to Sufism as Model of Occult Islamic Humanism," *La Rosa di Paracelso* 2 (2020), 53–80.

Melvin-Koushki, Matthew, "Is (Islamic) Occult Science Science?," *Theology and Science* 18:2 (2020), 303–324.

Melvin-Koushki, Matthew, "Occult Ecumenism: Mahmūd Dihdār Shīrāzī's *Unveiling Secrets* as Exemplar of Timurid-Safavid Sunni-Shiʿi Science," *Iranian Studies* (2022), 1–31.

Melvin-Koushki, Matthew, "An Islamic Scientific Revolution? Early Modern Occult Science, Cosmic Philology and the Weird," *History of Science* 61:2 (2023), 166–172.

Melvin-Koushki, Matthew, "Translating Esotericism: Early Modern Persian," *Correspondences* 11:1 (2023), 103–112.

Melvin-Koushki, Matthew, "Definition as (De)colonial Weapon: Western Esotericism Meets Islamic Ocultism and Is Weirded Out," *Aries* 24:2 (2024), 231–235.

Melvin-Koushki, Matthew, "The New Brethren of Purity: Ibn Turka and the Renaissance of Pythagoreanism in the Early Modern Persian Cosmopolis," *Intellectual History of the Islamicate World* 13:2 (2025), forthcoming.

Melvin-Koushki, Matthew, "Ibn Turka," in: Kate Fleet et al. (eds.), *Encyclopedia of Islam 3*, Brill: Leiden / Boston (forthcoming).

Melvin-Koushki, Matthew, "Mīr Dāmād's *On Doffing*: Safavid Philosophy, Ritual Magic and Out-of-Body Experience" (forthcoming).

Melvin-Koushki, Matthew, "The Occult Court: ʿAlī Ṣafī's *Boon for the Khan* (1522) as Timurid-Safavid Manual of Boozing and Battling Magic and Marker of Early Modernity" (forthcoming).

Melvin-Koushki, Matthew, *Occult Philosophers and Philosopher Kings in Early Modern Iran: The Life and Legacy of Ibn Turka, Timurid Lettrist* (forthcoming).

Melvin-Koushki, Matthew & Noah Gardiner (eds.), *Islamicate Occultism: New Perspectives*, special issue *Arabica* 64:3–4 (2017).

Mette, Isabelle & Damien Karbovnik, "La condition surhumaine, une réalité fantastique," *Revue de la BNF* 54:1 (2017), 150–159.

Meurs, Jos van, "William Blake and his Gnostic Myths," in: van den Broek & Hanegraaff, *Gnosis and Hermeticism*, 269–309.

Meyer, Marvin W. (ed.), *The Nag Hammadi Scriptures: The Revised and Updated Translation of Sacred Gnostic Texts*, Harper: New York 2007.

Meyer, Marvin W. & Richard Smith (eds.), *Ancient Christian Magic: Coptic Texts of Ritual Power*, Princeton University Press: Princeton 1994.

Michelis, Elisabeth de, *A History of Modern Yoga*, Frances Pinter Publishers: London 2004.

Mignolo, Walter D., *The Darker Side of the Renaissance: Literacy, Territoriality, & Colonization*, The University of Michigan Press: Ann Arbor 2003.

Mignolo, Walter D., *The Darker Side of Western Modernity: Global Futures, Decolonial Options*, Duke University Press: Durham 2011.

Monbiot, George, "Neoliberalism: The Ideology at the Root of All Our Problems," *The Guardian*, April 15, 2016.

Monroe, John Warne, *Laboratories of Faith: Mesmerism, Spiritism, and Occultism in Modern France*, Cornell University Press: Ithaca / London 2008.

Moore, James, *Gurdjieff: A Biography*, Element: Shaftesbury / Melbourne / Boston 1999.

Moore, R. Laurence, *In Search of White Crows: Spiritualism, Parapsychology, and American Culture*, Oxford University Press: New York 1977.

Morgan, Daniel J., "Spokesman of the Unseen World: Shāh Walī Allāh (1703-62), Islamic Reform and Applied Cosmology in Late-Mughal Delhi," Ph.D. Dissertation, The University of Chicago 2021.

Mühlematter, Yves, *Accelerating Human Evolution by Theosophical Initiation: Annie Besant's Pedagogy and the Creation of Benarus Hindu University*, De Gruyter: Oldenbourg 2023.

Mukhopadhyay, Mriganka, "The Occult World of Bengalis," Ph.D. dissertation, University of Amsterdam 2025.

Mulsow, Martin (ed.), *Das Ende des Hermetismus: Historische Kritik und neue Naturphilosophie in der Spätrenaissance. Dokumentation und Analyse der Debattte um die Datierung der hermetischen Schriften von Genebrard bis Casaubon (1567-1614)*, Mohr Siebeck: Tübingen 2002.

Myers, Jody, *Kabbalah and the Spiritual Quest: The Kabbalah Centre in America*, Praeger: Westport / London 2007.

Nelson, Victoria, *The Secret Life of Puppets*, Harvard University Press: Cambridge MA / London 2001.

Nelson, Victoria, *Gothica: Vampire Heroes, Human Gods, and the New Supernatural*, Harvard University Press: Cambridge MA / London 2012.

Nethercot, Arthur H., *The First Five Lives of Annie Besant*, Rupert Hart-Davis: London 1961.

Nethercot, Arthur H., *The Last Four Lives of Annie Besant*, Rupert Hart-Davis: London 1963.

Neugebauer-Wölk, Monika, "Illuminaten," in: Hanegraaff, *Dictionary*, 590–597.

Neugebauer-Wölk, Monika, "Der Esoteriker und die Esoterik: Wie das Esoterische im 18. Jahrhundert zum Begriff wird und seinen Weg in die Moderne findet," *Aries* 10:2 (2010), 217–231.

Neugebauer-Wölk, Monika, "Historische Esoterikforschung, oder: Der länge Weg der Esoterik zur Moderne," in: Neugebauer-Wölk, Geffarth & Meumann, *Aufklärung und Esoterik*, 37–72.

Neugebauer-Wölk, Monika, *Kosmologische Religiosität am Ursprung der Neuzeit, 1400 bis 1450*, Ferdinand Schöningh: Paderborn 2019.

Neugebauer-Wölk, Monika (ed.) with Holger Zaunstöck, *Aufklärung und Esoterik* (Studien zum Achtzehnten Jahrhundert 24), Felix Meiner: Hamburg 1999.

Neugebauer-Wölk, Monika (ed.) with Andre Rudolph, *Aufklärung und Esoterik: Rezeption, Integration, Konfrontation*, Max Niemeyer: Tübingen 2008.

Neugebauer-Wölk, Monika, Renko Geffarth & Markus Meumann (eds.), *Aufklärung und Esoterik: Wege in die Moderne*, De Gruyter: Berlin / Boston 2013.

Newman, William R., *Gehennical Fire: The Lives of George Starkey, an American Alchemist in the Scientific Revolution*, Harvard University Press: Cambridge, MA / London 1994.

Newman, William R. & Lawrence M. Principe, "Alchemy *vs.* Chemistry: The Etymological Origins of a Historiographic Mistake," *Early Science and Medicine* 3 (1998), 32–65.

Newman, William R. & Lawrence M. Principe, *Alchemy Tried in the Fire: Starkey, Boyle, and the Fate of Helmontian Chymistry*, The University of Chicago Press: Chicago / London 2002.

Nock, A.D. & A.-J. Festugière, *Hermès Trismégiste*, vols. 1–2 (1946), Les Belles Lettres: Paris 1991 / 1992.

Noll, Richard, *The Jung Cult: Origins of a Charismatic Movement*, Princeton University Press: Princeton 1994.

Notovich, Nicolas, *La vie inconnue de Jésus Christ*, Paul Ollendorff: Paris 1894.

Nussbaum, Martha, *Not For Profit: Why Democracy Needs the Humanities*, Princeton University Press: Princeton / Oxford 2010.

Oberhauser, Claus, "Freemasons, Illuminati and Jews: Conspiracy Theories and the French Revolution," in: Butter & Knight, *Routledge Handbook of Conspiracy Theories*, 555–568.

Obrist, Barbara, *Les débuts de l'imagerie alchimique (XIVe-XVe siècles)*, Le Sycomore: Paris 1982.

Oetinger, Friedrich Christoph, *Die Metaphysic in Connexion mit der Chemie*, Johann Christoph Messerer: Schwäbisch Hall 1771.

Oetinger, Friedrich Christoph, *Die Lehrtafel der Prinzessin Antonia* (Reinhard Breymayer & Friedrich Häussermann, ed.), 2 vols., Walter de Gruyter: Berlin / New York 1977.

Oetinger, Friedrich Christoph, *Biblisches und Emblematisches Wörterbuch* (Gerhard Schäfer, ed.), 2 vols., Walter de Gruyter: Berlin / New York 1999.

Ogden, Daniel, "Binding Spells: Curse Tablets and Voodoo Dolls in the Greek and Roman Worlds," in: Valerie Flint, Richard Gordon, Georg Luck & Daniel Ogden, *Witchcraft and Magic in Europe: Ancient Greece and Rome*, The Athlone Press: London 1999.

Okropiridze, Dimitry, "Interpretation Reconsidered: The Definitional Progression in the Study of Esotericism as a Case in Point for the Varifocal Theory of Interpretation," in: Asprem & Strube, *New Approaches*, 217–240.

Olesen, Mattias Gori, "The Perennial Solidarity of the East: René Guénon, Sufism and Easternist Anti-Colonialism in Early Twentieth-Century Egypt," *Aries* (2024) (pre-print).

Oppenheim, Janet, *The Other World: Spiritualism and Psychical Research in England, 1850-1914*, Cambridge University Press: Cambridge 1985.

Otto, Bernd-Christian, *Magie: Rezeptions- und diskursgeschichtliche Analysen von der Antike bis zur Neuzeit*, De Gruyter: Berlin / New York 2011.

Otto, Bernd-Christian, "Discourse Theory Trumps Discourse Theory: Wouter Hanegraaff's *Esotericism and the Academy*," *Religion* 43:2 (2013), 231–240.

Otto, Bernd-Christian, "Introduction," *Method & Theory in the Study of Religion* 37 (2025), forthcoming.

Owen, Alex, *The Place of Enchantment: British Occultism and the Culture of the Modern*, University of Chicago Press: Chicago / London 2004.

Paracelsus, *Essential Readings* (Nicholas Goodrick-Clarke, ed.), North Atlantic Books: Berkeley 1999.

Paracelsus, *Essential Theoretical Writings* (Andrew Weeks, translation), Brill: Leiden / Boston 2008.

Paracelsus, *Cosmological and Metereological Writings* (Andrew Weeks & Didier Kahn, edition and translation), Brill: Leiden / Boston 2024.

Partridge, Christopher (ed.), *UFO Religions*, Routledge: London / New York 2003.

Partridge, Christopher, *The Re-Enchantment of the West: Alternative Spiritualities, Sacralization, Popular Culture, and Occulture*, 2 vols., T & T Clark: London / New York 2004 / 2005.

Partridge, Christopher, "Occulture is Ordinary," in: Asprem & Granholm, *Contemporary Esotericism*, 113–133.

Partridge, Christopher, "Esoterrorism and the Wrecking of Civilization: Genesis P-Orridge and the Rise of Industrial Paganism," in: Donna Weston & Andy Bennett (eds.), *Pop Pagans: Paganism and Popular Music*, Acumen: Stocksfield 2014, 189–212.

Partridge, Christopher, "The Occult and Popular Music," in: Partridge, *The Occult World*, 509–530.

Partridge, Christopher (ed.), *The Occult World*, Routledge 2015.

Partridge, Christopher, *High Culture: Drugs, Mysticism & the Pursuit of Transcendence in the Modern World*, Oxford University Press: Oxford 2018.

Pasi, Marco, "The Influence of Aleister Crowley on Fernando Pessoa's Esoteric Writings," in: Caron, Godwin, Hanegraaff & Vieillard-Baron, *Ésotérisme, gnoses & imaginaire symbolique*, 693–711.

Pasi, Marco, "The Neverendingly Told Story: Recent Biographies of Aleister Crowley," *Aries* 3:2 (2003), 224–245.

Pasi, Marco, "The Modernity of Occultism: Reflections on Some Crucial Aspects," in: Hanegraaff & Pijnenburg, *Hermes in the Academy*, 59–74.

Pasi, Marco, "Oriental Kabbalah and the Parting of East and West in the Early Theosophical Society," in: Huss, Pasi & von Stuckrad, *Kabbalah and Modernity*, 151–166.

Pasi, Marco, "Varieties of Magical Experience: Aleister Crowley's Views on Occult Practice," Bogdan & Starr, *Aleister Crowley and Western Esotericism*, 53–87.

Pasi, Marco, "Hilma af Klint, Western Esotericism and the Problem of Modern Artistic Creativity," in: Kurt Almqvist & Louise Belfrage (eds.), *Hilma af Klint: The Art of Seeing the Invisible*, Thames & Hudson: New York 2015, 101–116.

Pasi, Marco, "The Art of Esoteric Posthumousness," in: Pokorny & Winter, *Occult Nineteenth Century*, 159–176.

Pasi, Marco, "Where is History? A Response to '(Re)defining Esotericism'," *Aries* 24:2 (2024), 240–243.

Patai, Raphael, *The Jewish Alchemists: A History and Source Book*, Princeton University Press: Princeton 1994.

Pattison, Mark, *Isaac Casaubon, 1559-1614*, 2nd ed., At the Clarendon Press: Oxford 1892.

Pauwels, Louis & Jacques Bergier, *Le matin des magiciens*, Gallimard: Paris 1960.

Petry, Yvonne, *Gender, Kabbalah and the Reformation: The Mystical Theology of Guillaume Postel (1510-1581)*, Brill: Leiden / Boston 2004.

Pfister, Friedrich, "Ekstase," in: *Reallexikon für Antike und Christentum*, vol. 4, Hiersemann: Stuttgart 1959, 944–987.

Pico della Mirandola, Giovanni, *On the Dignity of Man / On Being and the One / Heptaplus*, Hackett Publishing Company: Indianapolis / Cambridge 1965.

Pico della Mirandola, Gianfrancesco & Pico della Mirandola, Giovanni, *Life of Giovanni Pico della Mirandola / Oration* (Brian P. Copenhaver, ed. & translation), The I Tatti Renaissance Library / Harvard University Press: Cambridge, MA / London 2022.

Pinchbeck, Daniel, *2012: The Return of Quetzalcoatl*, Jeremy Tarcher / Penguin: London 2006.

Pingree, David, "Hellenophilia versus the History of Science," *Isis* 83:4 (1992), 554–563.

Piraino, Francesco, "Between Real and Virtual Communities: Sufism in Western Societies and the Naqshbandi Haqqani Case," *Social Compass* 63:1 (2016), 93–108.

Piraino, Francesco, "Esotericisation and De-esotericisation of Sufism: The Aḥmadiyya-Idrīsiyya Shādhiliyya in Italy," *Correspondences* 7:1 (2019), 239–276.

Piraino, Francesco, *Sufism in Europe: Islam, Esotericism and the New Age*, Edinburgh University Press: Edinburgh 2024.

Piraino, Francesco, Marco Pasi & Egil Asprem (eds.), *Religious Dimensions of Conspiracy Theories: Comparing and Connecting Old and New Trends*, Routledge: London / New York 2023.

Platvoet, Jan G. & Arie L. Molendijk (eds.), *The Pragmatics of Defining Religion: Contexts, Concepts & Contests*, Royal E.J. Brill: Leiden / Boston / Cologne 1999.

Poel, Marc van der, *Cornelius Agrippa, the Humanist Theologian and his Declamations*, Brill: Leiden / New York / Cologne 1997.

Pöhlmann, Matthias, *Rechte Esoterik: Wenn sich alternatives Denken und Extremismus gefährlich vermischen*, Herder: Freiburg / Basel / Vienna 2021.

Pokorny, Lukas & Franz Winter (eds.), *The Occult Nineteenth Century: Roots, Developments, and Impact on the Modern World*, Palgrave MacMillan: Cham 2021.

Pollock, Sheldon, Benjamin A. Elman & Ku-ming Kevin Chang (eds.), *World Philology*, Harvard University Press: Cambridge, MA / London 2015.

Pomerantsev, Peter, *Nothing is True and Everything is Possible: The Surreal Heart of the New Russia*, Public Affairs: New York 2014.

Port, Mattijs van de, *Ecstatic Encounters: Bahian Candomblé and the Quest for the Really Real*, Amsterdam University Press: Amsterdam 2011.

Possamai, Adam (ed.), *Handbook of Hyper-Real Religions*, Brill: Leiden / Boston 2012.

Posset, Franz, *Johann Reuchlin (1455-1522), A Theological Biography*, De Gruyter: Berlin / Boston 2015.

Postel, Guillaume, *Des admirables secrets des nombres platoniciens* (Jean-Pierre Brach, ed.), J. Vrin: Paris 2001.

Principe, Lawrence M., *The Aspiring Adept: Robert Boyle and his Alchemical Quest*, Princeton University Press: Princeton 1998.

Principe, Lawrence M., "Reflections on Newton's Alchemy in Light of the New Historiography of Alchemy," in: James E. Force & Sarah Hutton (eds.), *Newton and Newtonianism: New Studies*, Kluwer: Dordrecht / Boston / London 2004, 205–219.

Principe, Lawrence M., "Revealing Analogies: The Descriptive and Deceptive Roles of Sexuality and Gender in Latin Alchemy," in: Hanegraaff & Kripal, *Hidden Intercourse*, 209–229.

Principe, Lawrence M., *The Secrets of Alchemy*, The University of Chicago Press: Chicago / London 2013.

Prophet, Erin, *Prophet's Daughter: My Life with Elizabeth Clare Prophet inside the Church Universal and Triumphant*, The Lyon's Press: Guilford 2009.

Quiano, Anibal, "Coloniality and Modernity/Rationality." *Cultural Studies* 21:2/3 (2007), 168–178.

Quispel, Gilles (ed.), *Gnosis: De derde component van de Europese cultuurtraditie*, Hes: Utrecht 1988.

Raay, Stefan van, Joanna Moorhead & Tersa Arcq, *Surreal Friends: Leonora Carrington, Remedios Varo and Kati Horna*, Lund Humphries: Farnham / Burlington 2010.

Ramaswamy, Sumathi, *The Lost Land of Lemuria: Fabulous Geographies, Catastrophic Histories*, University of California Press: Berkeley / Los Angeles / London 2004.

Randolph, Paschal Beverly, *Dealings with the Dead: The Human Soul, its Migrations and its Transmigrations*, M.J. Randolph: Utica 1861–1862.

Ransom, Josephine, *A Short History of the Theosophical Society, 1875-1937*, Theosophical Publishing House: Adyar 1938.

Ratcliffe, Eric, *Ithell Colquhoun: Pioneer Surrealist Artists, Occultist, Writer, and Poet,* Mandrake: Oxford 2007.

Readings, Bill, *The University in Ruins,* Harvard University Press: Cambridge, MA / London 1996.

Rees, Valery, "Ficino's Advice to Princes," in: Michael J.B. Allen & Valery Rees (eds.), *Marsilio Ficino: His Theology, his Philosophy, his Legacy,* Brill: Leiden / Boston / Cologne 2002, 339–357.

Refslund Christensen, Dorthe, "Scientology," in: Hanegraaff, *Dictionary,* 1046–1050.

Renard, Jean-Bruno, "Le mouvement *Planète*: Un épisode important de l'histoire culturelle française," *Politica Hermetica* 10 (1996), 152–167.

Reuchlin, Johannes, *On the Art of the Kabbalah / De Arte Cabalistica* (Martin & Sarah Goodman, translation), University of Nebraska Press: Lincoln / London 1983.

Reuchlin, Johannes, *De verbo mirifico / Das wundertätige Wort (1494)* (Widu-Wolfgang Ehlers, Lothar Mundt, Hans-Gert Roloff, Peter Schäfer, ed.; Sämtliche Werke Bd. I.1), frommann-holzboog: Stuttgart / Bad Cannstatt 1996.

Reuchlin, Johannes, *De arte cabalistica libri tres / Die Kabbalistik* (Widu-Wolfgang Ehlers, Lothar Mundt, Hans-Gert Roloff, Peter Schäfer, ed.; Sämtliche Werke Bd. II.1), frommann-holzboog: Stuttgart / Bad Cannstatt 2010.

Ricci, Matteo, *The True Meaning of the Lord of Heaven* (Douglas Lancashire & Peter Hu Kuo-chen, eds.; rev. ed. Thierry Meynard), Institute of Jesuit Sources, Boston College 2016.

Richmond, Maureen Temple, "The Pleiades," *The Esoteric Quarterly,* Summer 2019, 13–29.

Ricoeur, Paul, *De l'interprétation: Essai sur Freud,* Editions du Seuil: Paris 1965.

Ricoeur, Paul, *Freud and Philosophy: An Essay on Interpretation,* Yale University Press: New Haven / London 1970.

Ridall, Kathryn, *Channeling: How to reach out to your Spirit Guides,* Bantam Books: New York 1988.

Riffard, Pierre, *L'ésotérisme,* Robert Laffont: Paris 1990.

Rijckenborgh, Jan van & Catharose de Petri, *De Chinese Gnosis,* Rozekruis Pers: Haarlem 1987.

Rilke, Rainer Maria, "Die Aufzeichnungen des Malte Laurids Brigge," in: *Werke,* vol. 3: *Prosa und Dramen,* Insel Verlag: Frankfurt a.M. / Leipzig 1996, 453–635.

Robertson, David G., *Gnosticism and the History of Religions,* Bloomsbury: London / New York / Oxford / New Delhi / Sydney 2022.

Robison, John, *Proofs of a Conspiracy against all the Religions and Governments of Europe, Carried on in the Secret Meetings of Free Masons, Illuminati, and Reading Societies,* T. Cadell, W. Davies & W. Creech: London 1798.

[Rodrigues, João], *João Rodrigues's Account of Sixteenth-Century Japan* (Michael Cooper, ed.), The Hakluyt Society: London 2001.

Rogalla von Bieberstein, Johannes, *Der Mythos von der Verschwörung: Philosophen, Freimaurer, Juden, Liberale und Sozialisten als Verschwörer gegen die Sozialordnung,* Marix Verlag: Wiesbaden 2008.

Roob, Alexander, *Alchemy & Mysticism,* Taschen: Cologne 1997.

Roper, Lyndal, *Witch Craze: Terror and Fantasy in Baroque Germany,* Yale University Press: New Haven / London 2004.

Rösche, Johannes, *Robert Fludd: Der Versuch einer hermetischen Alternative zur neuzeitlichen Naturwissenschaft,* V & R Unipress: Göttingen 2008.

Rose, Jonathan S., Stuart Shotwell & Mary Lou Bertucci (eds.), *Scribe of Heaven: Swedenborg's Life, Work, and Impact,* Swedenborg Foundation: West Chester 2005.

Roth, Marjorie & Leonard George (eds.), *Explorations in Music and Esotericism*, University of Rochester Press: Rochester 2023.
Rougier, Louis, *The Genius of the West*, Nash Publishing: Los Angeles 1971.
Roukema, Aren, *Esotericism and Narrative: The Occult Fiction of Charles Williams*, Brill: Leiden / Boston 2018.
Roukema, Aren & Allan Kilner-Johnson, "Editorial: Time to Drop the 'Western'," *Correspondences* 6:2 (2018), 109–115.
Rowland, Ingrid D., *Giordano Bruno: Philosopher / Heretic*, Farrar, Strauss & Giroux: New York 2008.
Roy-Di Piazza, Vincent, "Enslaved by African Angels: Swedenborg on African Superiority, Evangelization, and Slavery," *Intellectual History Review* 34:2 (2023), 1–31.
Rudbøg, Tim, "'The Judges of Normality are Everywhere': Has Esotericism and the Ideas of H.P. Blavatsky ever been Normal?," in: Hedenborg White & Rudbøg, *Esotericism and Deviance*, 83–104.
Rudbøg, Tim & Erik Reenberg Sand (eds.), *Imagining the East: The Early Theosophical Society*, Oxford University Press: Oxford 2020.
Rummel, Erika, *The Case against Johannes Reuchlin: Religious and Social Controversy in Sixteenth-Century Germany*, University of Toronto Press: Toronto / Buffalo / London 2002.
Said, Edward W., *Orientalism*, Penguin: London 2003.
Saif, Liana, *The Arabic Influences on Early Modern Occult Philosophy*, Palgrave MacMillan: Houndmills / New York 2015.
Saif, Liana, "From *Ġāyat al-ḥakīm* to *Šams al-maʿārif*: Ways of Knowing and Paths of Power in Medieval Islam," *Arabica* 64 (2017), 297–345.
Saif, Liana, "What is Islamic Esotericism?," *Correspondences* 7:1 (2019), 1–59.
Saif, Liana, "A Preliminary Study of the Pseudo-Aristotelian Hermetica: Texts, Context, and Doctrines," *Al-ʿUṣūr al-Wusṭā* 29 (2021), 20–80.
Saif, Liana & Francesca Leoni, "Introduction," in: Saif, Leoni, Melvin-Koushki & Yahya, *Islamicate Occult Sciences*, 1–40.
Saif, Liana, Francesca Leoni, Matthew Melvin-Koushki & Farouk Yahua (eds.), *Islamicate Occult Sciences in Theory and Practice*, Brill: Leiden / Boston 2021.
Salinger, J.D., "Teddy," in: *Nine Stories*, Signet Books: New York 1954, 122–144.
Sawicki, Diethard, *Leben mit den Toten: Geisterglauben und die Entstehung des Spiritismus in Deutschland 1770-1900*, Ferdinand Schöningh: Paderborn / Munich / Vienna / Zürich 2002.
Schäfer, Peter, *The Hidden and Manifest God: Some Major Themes in Early Jewish Mysticism*, State University of New York Press: Albany 1992.
Schäfer, Peter, "'Adversus cabbalam' oder: Heinrich Graetz und die jüdische Mystik," in: Peter Schäfer & Irina Wandrey (eds.), *Reuchlin und seine Erben: Forscher, Denker, Ideologen und Spinner*, Jan Thorbecke: Ostfildern 2005, 189–210.
Schäfer, Peter, *The Origins of Jewish Mysticism*, Mohr Siebeck: Tübingen 2009.
Schilbrack, Kevin, "A Metaphysics for the Study of Religion: A Critical Reading of Russell McCutcheon," *Critical Research on Religion* 8:1 (2020), 87–100.
Schimmel, Annemarie, *Mystical Dimensions of Islam*, The University of North Carolina Press: Chapel Hill 1975.
Schmidt, Leigh Eric, "The Making of Modern 'Mysticism'," *Journal of the American Academy of Religion* 71:2 (2003), 273–302.
Scholem, Gershom, *Major Trends in Jewish Mysticism*, Schocken: New York 1946.

Scholem, Gershom, *On the Kabbalah and its Symbolism*, Schocken: New York 1969.
Scholem, Gershom, *Sabbatai Ṣevi: The Mystical Messiah 1626-1676*, Routledge & Kegan Paul: London 1973.
Scholem, Gershom, *Kabbalah*, Keter Publishing House: Jerusalem 1974.
Scholem, Gershom, "A Birthday Letter from Gershom Scholem to Zalman Schocken," in: David Biale, *Gershom Scholem: Kabbalah and Counter-History*, Harvard University Press: Cambridge, MA / London 1979, 215–216.
Scholem, Gershom, *On the Mystical Shape of the Godhead: Basic Concepts in the Kabbalah*, Schocken: New York 1997.
Scholem, Gershom, *Alchemy and kabbalah*, Spring Publications: Putnam 2006.
Schuler, Robert M., *Alchemical Poetry, 1575-1700: From Previously Unpublished Manuscripts*, Routledge: London / New York 2014.
Schuon, Frithjof, *The Transcendent Unity of Religions*, Quest Books: Wheaton / Chennais (Madras) 1984.
Schwab, Raymond, *The Oriental Renaissance: Europe's Rediscovery of India and the East 1680-1880*, Columbia University Press: New York 1984.
Scott, Walter, *Hermetica: The Ancient Greek and Latin Writings which contain Religious or Philosophic Teachings ascribed to Hermes Trismegistus*, vols. 1–2, Shambhala: Boston 1993 / 1985.
Secret, François, *Les Kabbalistes Chrétiens de la Renaissance*, new ed., Archè / Arma Artis: Milan / Neuilly-sur-Seine 1985.
Sedgwick, Mark, *Western Sufism: From the Abbasids to the New Age*, Oxford University Press: Oxford 2017.
Sedgwick, Mark, "Islamic and Western Esotericism," *Correspondences* 7:1 (2019), 277–299.
Sedgwick, Mark, *Traditionalism: The Radical Project for Restoring Sacred Order*, Pelican: London 2023.
Sedgwick, Mark (ed.), *Key Thinkers of the Radical Right: Behind the New Threat to Liberal Democracy*, Oxford University Press: Oxford 2019.
Sellars, Simon, "Hakim Bey: Repopulating the Temporary Autonomous Zone," *Journal for the Study of Radicalism* 4:2 (2010), 83–108.
Seng, Helmut (ed.), *Platonismus und Esoterik in byzantinischem Mittelalter und italienischer Renaissance*, Winter: Heidelberg 2013.
Sepielli, Andrew, "Quietism and Counter-Normativity," *Ergo* 7:16 (2021), 457–479.
Shantz, Colleen, *Paul in Ecstasy: The Neurobiology of the Apostle's Life and Thought*, Cambridge University Press: Cambridge 2009.
Sharpe, Eric J., *Comparative Religion: A History*, Duckworth: London 1986.
Shaw, Gregory, *Hellenic Tantra: The Theurgic Platonism of Iamblichus*, Angelico Press: New York 2024.
Shukman, Henry, *One Blade of Grass: A Zen Memoir*, Hodder & Stoughton: London 2021.
Shupe, Anson, "Deprogramming Violence: The Logic, Perpetration, and Outcomes of Coercive Intervention," in: Lewis, *Violence and New Religious Movements*, 397–412.
Siniossoglou, Niketas, *Radical Platonism in Byzantium: Illumination and Utopia in Gemistos Plethon*, Cambridge University Press: Cambridge 2011.
Slobodian, Quinn, *Globalists: The End of Empire and the Birth of Neoliberalism*, Harvard University Press: Cambridge, MA / London 2018.

Smith, Jonathan Z., *To Take Place: Toward Theory in Ritual*, The University of Chicago Press: Chicago & London 1987.

Smith, Jonathan Z., *Drudgery Divine: On the Comparison of Early Christianities and the Religions of Late Antiquity*, The University of Chicago Press: Chicago / London 1990.

Solnit, Rebecca, *Hope in the Dark: Untold Histories, Wild Possibilities*, Nation Books: New York 2006.

[South, Mary Anne a.k.a. Mrs. Atwood], *A Suggestive Inquiry into the Hermetic Mystery; with a Dissertation on the More Celebrated of the Alchemical Philosophers, being an Attempt towards the Recovery of the Ancient Experiment of Nature* (1850), William Tait: Belfast 1918.

Spector, Sheila A., *Francis Mercury van Helmont's* Sketch of Christian Kabbalism, Brill: Leiden / Boston 2012.

Spencer, Herbert, *Social Statics: Or, the Conditions Essential to Human Happiness Specified, and the First of Them Developed*, John Chapman: London 1851.

Sprague de Camp, L., *Lost Continents: The Atlantis Theme in History, Science, and Literature*, Dover: New York 1954.

Staal, Frits, *Exploring Mysticism: A Methodological Essay*, University of California Press: Berkeley / Los Angeles 1975.

Staudenmaier, Peter, *Between Occultism and Nazism: Anthroposophy and the Politics of Race in the Fascist Era*, Brill: Leiden / Boston 2014.

Stausberg, Michael, *Faszination Zarathushtra: Zoroaster und die Europäische Religionsgeschichte der Frühen Neuzeit*, 2 vols., Walter de Gruyter: Berlin / New York 1998.

Steger, Manfred B. & Ravi K. Roy, *Neoliberalism: A Very Short Introduction*, Oxford University Press: Oxford 2010.

Steiner, George, *Martin Heidegger* (1978), The University of Chicago Press: Chicago / London 1989.

Steiner, Rudolf, *Schriften: Kritische Ausgabe* (Christian Clement, ed.), 16 vols., frommann-holzboog: Stuttgart-Bad Cannstatt 2022–2024.

Stengel, Friedemann, *Aufklärung bis zum Himmel: Emanuel Swedenborg im Kontext der Theologie und Philosophie des 18. Jahrhunderts*, Mohr Siebeck: Tübingen 2011.

Stephens, Walter, *Demon Lovers: Witchcraft, Sex, and the Crisis of Belief*, The University of Chicago Press: Chicago / London 2002.

Stevenson, David, *The Origins of Freemasonry: Scotland's Century 1590-1710*, Cambridge University Press: Cambridge 1988.

Stockhausen, Karlheinz, *Texte zur Musik*, vols. 4 & 6, DuMont: Cologne 1989/1998.

Stocking, George W., "On the Limits of 'Presentism' and 'Historicism' in the Historiography of the Behavioral Sciences," in: Stocking, *Race, Culture, and Evolution*, 1–12.

Stocking, George W., *Race, Culture, and Evolution: Essays in the History of Anthropology*, The University of Chicago Press: Chicago / London 1982.

Stocking, George W., *Victorian Anthropology*, The Free Press: New York / Toronto 1987.

Stolzenberg, Jürgen, "Esoterik in der Musik der Moderne: Alexander N. Skrjabin," in: Neugebauer-Wölk, Geffarth & Meumann, *Aufklärung und Esoterik*, 553–581.

Stottmeister, Jan, *Der George-Kreis und die Theosophie, mit einem Exkurs zum Swastika-Zeichen bei Helena Blavatsky, Alfred Schuler und Stefan George*, Wallstein Verlag: Göttingen 2014.

Stoyanov, Yuri, *The Other God: Dualist Religions from Antiquity to the Cathar Heresy*, Yale University Press: New Haven / London 2000.

Streib, Heinz & Ralph W. Hood, "'Spirituality' as Privatized Experience-Oriented Religion: Empirical and Conceptual Perspectives," *Implicit Religion* 14 (2011), 433–453.

Strieber, Whitley & Jeffrey J. Kripal, *The Super Natural: Why the Unexplained Is Real*, TarcherPerigee: New York 2016.

Strube, Julian, *Sozialismus, Katholizismus und Okkultismus im Frankreich des 19. Jahrhunderts: Die Genealogie der Schriften von Eliphas Lévi*, De Gruyter: Berlin / Boston 2016.

Strube, Julian, "Socialist Religion and the Emergence of Occultism: A Genealogical Approach to Socialism and Secularization in 19th-Century France," *Religion* 46:3 (2016), 359–388.

Strube, Julian, Review of Eric Kurlander, *Hitler's Monsters, Correspondences* 5 (2017), 130–139.

Strube, Julian, "Doesn't Occultism lead straight to Fascism?," in: Hanegraaff, Forshaw & Pasi, *Hermes Explains*, 225–231.

Strube, Julian, "The Emergence of 'Esoteric' as a Comparative Category: Towards a Decentered Historiography," *Implicit Religion* 24:3–4 (2021), 353–383.

Strube, Julian, "Theosophy, Race, and the Study of Esotericism," *Journal of the American Academy of Religion* 89:4 (2021), 1180–1189.

Strube, Julian, "Towards the Study of Esotericism without the 'Western': Esotericism from the Perspective of a Global Religious History," in: Asprem & Strube, *New Approaches*, 45–66.

Strube, Julian, *Global Tantra: Religion, Science, and Nationalism in Colonial Modernity*, Oxford University Press: Oxford 2022.

Strube, Julian, "Religious Comparativism, Esotericism, and the Global Occult: A Methodological Outline," *Interdisciplinary Journal for Religion and Transformation in Contemporary Society* (2023), 1–24 (pre-print).

Strube, Julian, "Esotericism between Europe and East Asia: How the 'Esoteric Distinction' became a Structure in Cross-Cultural Interpretation," *Numen* 71 (2024), 9–28 (pre-print).

Stuckrad, Kocku von, *Das Ringen um die Astrologie: Jüdische und christliche Beiträge zum antiken Zeitverständnis*, Walter de Gruyter: Berlin / New York 2000.

Stuckrad, Kocku von, *Western Esotericism: A Brief History of Secret Knowledge*, Equinox: London / Oakville 2005.

Stuckrad, Kocku von, *Locations of Knowledge in Medieval and Early Modern Europe*, Brill: Leiden / Boston 2010.

Stuckrad, Kocku von, "Discursive Study of Religion: Approaches, Definitions, Implications," *Method & Theory in the Study of Religion* 25 (2013), 5–25.

Stuckrad, Kocku von, *A Cultural History of the Soul: Europe and North America from 1870 to the Present*, Columbia University Press: New York 2022.

Suhrawardī, *The Philosophy of Illumination: A New Critical Edition of the Text of Ḥikmat al-ishrāq* (John Walbridge & Hossein Ziai, translation & commentary), Brigham Young University Press: Provo 1999.

Surette, Leon, *The Birth of Modernism: Ezra Pound, T.S. Eliot, W.B. Yeats, and the Occult*, McGill-Queen's University Press: Montreal & Kingston / London / Buffalo 1993.

Sutcliffe, Steven J., *Children of the New Age: A History of Spiritual Practices*, Routledge: London / New York 2003.

Sutcliffe, Steven J., "The Origins of 'New Age' Religion between the Two World Wars," in: Daren Kemp & James R. Lewis (eds.), *Handbook of New Age*, Brill: Leiden / Boston 2007, 51–75.

Swartz, Michael D., *Scholastic Magic: Ritual and Revelation in Early Jewish Mysticism*, Princeton University Press: Princeton 1996.

Sylvan, Robin, *Trance Formation: The Spiritual and Religious Dimensions of Global Rave Culture*, Routledge: London / New York 2005.

Szőnyi, György E., *John Dee's Occultism: Magical Exaltation through Powerful Signs*, State University of New York Press: Albany 2004.

Taguieff, Pierre-André, *La foire aux Illuminés: Ésotérisme, théorie du complot, extrémisme*, Mille et Une Nuits: n.p. 2005.

Taguieff, Pierre-André, *Hitler, les Protocoles des Sages de Sion et* Mein Kampf, Presses Universitaires de France: Paris 2020.

Tart, Charles T. (eds.), *Altered States of Consciousness*, Anchor Books / Doubleday & Co.: Garden City / New York 1969.

Taussig, Michael, *Shamanism, Colonialism, and the Wild Man: A Study in Terror and Healing*, The University of Chicago Press: Chicago / London 1987.

Taves, Ann, *Fits, Trances & Visions: Experiencing Religion and Explaining Experience from Wesley to James*, Princeton University Press: Princeton 1999.

Teeuwen, Mariken, "Music II: Middle Ages," in: Hanegraaff, *Dictionary*, 810–812.

Temme, Willi, *Krise der Leiblichkeit: Die Sozietät der Mutter Eva (Buttlarsche Rotte) und der radikale Pietismus um 1700*, Vandenhoeck & Ruprecht: Göttingen 1998.

Thalmann, Marianne, *Der Trivialroman des 18. Jahrhunderts und der romantische Roman: Ein Beitrag zur Entwicklungsgeschichte der Geheimbundmystik* (1923), repr. Kraus: Nendeln / Liechtenstein 1967.

Thorndike, Lynn, *A History of Magic and Experimental Science*, 8 vols., Columbia University Press: New York 1923–1958.

Thorndike, Lynn, "The True Place of Astrology in the History of Science," *Isis* 46:3 (1955), 273–278.

Tillett, Gregory, *The Elder Brother: A Biography of Charles Webster Leadbeater*, Routledge & Kegan Paul: London / Boston / Melbourne / Henley 1982.

Tilton, Hereward, *The Quest for the Phoenix: Spiritual Alchemy and Rosicrucianism in the Work of Count Michael Maier (1569-1622)*, De Gruyter: Berlin / New York 2003.

Tiryakian, Edward A., "Toward the Sociology of Esoteric Culture," in: Tiryakian, *On the Margin*, 257–280.

Tiryakian, Edward A. (ed.), *On the Margin of the Visible: Sociology, the Esoteric, and the Occult*, John Wiley & Sons: New York / London / Sydney / Toronto 1974.

Toews, John E., "Intellectual History after the Linguistic Turn: The Autonomy of Meaning and the Irreducibility of Experience," *The American Historical Review* 92:4 (1987), 879–907.

Tomlinson, Gary, *Music in Renaissance Magic: Towards a Historiography of Others*, The University of Chicago Press: Chicago / London 1993.

Tooze, Adam, "Welcome to the World of the Polycrisis," *Financial Times*, October 28, 2022.

Toth, Ladislaus, "Gnostic Church," in: Hanegraaff, *Dictionary*, 400–403.

Travaglia, Pinella, *Magic, Causality and Intentionality: The Doctrine of Rays in al-Kindi*, Sismel: Florence 1999.

Treitel, Corinna, *A Science for the Soul: Occultism and the Genesis of the German Modern*, The Johns Hopkins University Press: Baltimore / London 2004.

Trompf, Garry W. (ed.), *The Gnostic World*, Routledge: London / New York 2019.

Truzzi, Marcello, "Definition and Dimensions of the Occult: Towards a Sociological Perspective," in: Tiryakian, *On the Margin*, 243–255.

Tuchman, Maurice (ed.), *The Spiritual in Art: Abstract Painting 1890-1985*, Los Angeles County Museum of Art: Los Angeles 1986.

Turner, James, *Philology: The Forgotten Origins of the Modern Humanities*, Princeton University Press: Princeton / Oxford 2014.

Ulrich, Thomas, *Stockhausens Zyklus Licht: Ein Opernführer*, Böhlau: Vienna / Cologne / Weimar 2017.

Urban, Hugh B., "The Torment of Secrecy: Ethical and Epistemological Problems in the Study of Esoteric Traditions," *History of Religions* 37:3 (1998), 209–248.

Urban, Hugh B., *Tantra: Sex, Secrecy, Politics, and Power in the Study of Religion*, University of California Press: Berkeley / Los Angeles / London 2003.

Urban, Hugh B., *Magia Sexualis: Sex, Magic, and Liberation in Modern Western Esotericism*, University of New York Press: Berkeley / Los Angeles / London 2006.

Urban, Hugh B., *The Secrets of the Kingdom: Religion and Concealment in the Bush Administration*, Rowman & Littlefield: Lanham 2007.

Urban, Hugh B., *The Church of Scientology: A History of a New Religion*, Princeton University Press: Princeton / Oxford 2011.

Urban, Hugh B., *Secrecy: Silence, Power, and Religion*, The University of Chicago Press: Chicago / London 2021.

Ustinova, Yulia, *Caves and the Ancient Greek Mind: Descending Underground in the Search for Ultimate Truth*, Oxford University Press: Oxford 2009.

Ustinova, Yulia, *Divine Mania: Alterations of Consciousness in Ancient Greece*, Routledge: London / New York 2017.

Vernière, P., "Un aspect de l'irrationnel au XVIIIe siècle: La démonologie et son exploitation littéraire," in: Harold E. Pagliaro (ed.), *Irrationalism in the Eighteenth Century*, The Press of Case Western Reserve University: Cleveland / London 1972, 289–302.

Versluis, Arthur, *American Transcendentalism and Asian Religions*, Oxford University Press: New York / Oxford 1993.

Viatte, Auguste, *Les sources occultes du Romantisme: Illuminisme, Théosophie 1770-1820* (1927), 2 vols., Honoré Champion: Paris 1979.

Vickers, Brian, "On the Function of Analogy in the Occult," in: Ingrid Merkel & Allen G. Debus (eds.), *Hermeticism and the Renaissance: Intellectual History and the Occult in Early Modern Europe*, Folger Books: Washington / London / Toronto 1988, 265–292.

Vigenère, Blaise de, *Traicté des Chiffres, ou secretes manieres d'escrire*, Abel L'angelier: Paris 1586.

Villars, Nicolas Pierre Henri Montfaucon de, *Comte de Gabalis, ou entretiens sur les sciences secrètes* (1670), Pierre de Coup: Amsterdam 1715; critical edition by Didier Kahn, Champion: Paris 2010.

Voltaire, François de, *Dictionnaire philosophique, comprenant les 118 articles parus sous ce titre du vivant de Voltaire avec leurs suppléments parus dans les Questions sur l'Encyclopédie*, Garnier: Paris 1967.

Voltaire, François de, *Treatise on Tolerance and other Writings* (Simon Harvey, ed.), Cambridge University Press: Cambridge 2000.

Voss, Julia, *Hilma af Klint: A Biography*, The University of Chicago Press: Chicago / London 2022.

Waite, Arthur Edward, *The Unknown Philosopher: The Life of Louis Claude de Saint-Martin and the Substance of his Transcendental Doctrine*, Rudolf Steiner Publications: New York 1970.

Walbridge, John, *The Leaven of the Ancients: Suhrawardī and the Heritage of the Greeks*, State University of New York Press: Albany 2000.

Walbridge, John, *The Wisdom of the Mystic East: Suhrawardī and Platonic Orientalism*, State University of New York Press: Albany 2001.

Walbridge, John & Hossein Ziai (ed. & translation), *Suhrawardī: The Philosophy of Illumination*, Brigham Young University Press: Provo 1999.

Walker, D.P., *Music, Spirit and Language in the Renaissance* (Penelope Gouk, ed.), Variorum: London 1985.

Walker, D.P., *Spiritual and Demonic Magic from Ficino to Campanella* (1958), Pennsylvania State University Press: University Park 2000.

Wallace, David Foster, *This is Water: Some Thoughts Delivered at a Significant Occasion, about Living a Compassionate Life*, Little, Brown & Company: New York / Boston / London 2009.

Ward, Charlotte & David Voas, "The Emergence of Conspirituality," *Journal of Contemporary Religion* 26:1 (2011), 103–121.

Washington, Peter, *Madame Blavatsky's Baboon: A History of the Mystics, Mediums, and Misfits who brought Spiritualism to America*, Schocken : New York 1993.

Wasserstrom, Steven M., *Religion after Religion: Gershom Scholem, Mircea Eliade, and Henry Corbin at Eranos*, Princeton University Press: Princeton 1999.

Watts, Fraser, "Morphic Fields and Extended Mind: An Examination of the Theoretical Concepts of Rupert Sheldrake," *Journal of Consciousness Studies* 18:11–12 (2011), 203–224.

Watts, Galen & Sharday Mosurinjohn, "Can Critical Religion Play by Its Own Rules? Why There Must Be More Ways to Be 'Critical' in the Study of Religion," *Journal of the American Academy of Religion* 90 (2022), 317–334.

Webb, James, *The Occult Underground*, Open Court: La Salle Ill. 1974.

Webb, James, *The Harmonious Circle: The Lives and Work of G.I. Gurdjieff, P.D. Ouspensky, and Their Followers*, Thames & Hudson: London 1980.

Weber, Max, *Wissenschaft als Beruf 1917/1919, Politik als Beruf 1919* (Studienausgabe der Max Weber-Gesamtausgabe Band I/17; Wolfgang J. Mommsen & Wolfgang Schluchter, eds.), J.C.B. Mohr (Paul Siebeck): Tübingen 1994.

Webster, Charles, *Paracelsus: Medicine, Magic and Mission at the End of Time*, Yale University Press: New Haven / London 2008.

Weeks, Andrew, *Boehme: An Intellectual Biography of the Seventeenth-Century Philosopher and Mystic*, State University of New York Press: Albany 1991.

Weeks, Andrew, *Paracelsus: Speculative Theory and the Crisis of the Early Reformation*, State University of New York Press: Albany 1997.

Weeks, Andrew, *Valentin Weigel (1533-1588): German Religious Dissenter, Speculative Theorist, and Advocate of Tolerance*, State University of New York Press: Albany 2000.

Weigel, Valentin, *Selected Spiritual Writings* (Andrew Weeks, translation), Paulist Press: New York / Mahwah 2003.

Weil-Parot, Nicolas, "Astral Magic and Intellectual Changes (Twelfth-Fifteenth Centuries): 'Astrological Images' and the Concept of 'Adressative' Magic," in: Jan N. Bremmer & Jan R. Veenstra (eds.), *The Metamorphosis of Magic from Late Antiquity to the Early Modern Period*, Peeters: Louvain / Paris / Dudley 2002, 167–187.

Weiss, T., *Sefer Yeṣirah and Its Contexts: Other Jewish Voices*, University of Pennsylvania Press: Philadelphia 2018.

Westbrook, Donald A., *Among the Scientologists: History, Theology, and Praxis*, Oxford University Press: New York 2019.

Westfall, Richard S., *Never at Rest: A Biography of Isaac Newton*, Cambridge University Press: Cambridge 1980.

Whitsel, Bradley C., *The Church Universal and Triumphant: Elizabeth Clare Prophet's Apocalyptic Movement*, Syracuse University Press: New York 2003.

Williams, Leonard, "Hakim Bey and Ontological Anarchism," *Journal for the Study of Radicalism* 4:2 (2010), 109–137.

Williams, Michael Allen, *Rethinking "Gnosticism": An Argument for Dismantling a Dubious Category*, Princeton University Press: Princeton 1996.

Wilson, Adrian & T.G. Ashplant, "Whig History and Present-Centred History," *The Historical Journal* 31:1 (1988), 1–16.

Winter, Alison, *Mesmerized: Powers of Mind in Victorian Britain*, University of Chicago Press: Chicago / London 1998.

Wolfson, Elliot R., *Through a Speculum That Shines: Vision and Imagination in Medieval Jewish Mysticism*, Princeton University Press: Princeton 1994.

Wolfson, Elliot R., *Abraham Abulafia: Kabbalist and Prophet. Hermeneutics, Theosophy and Theurgy*, Cherub Press: Jerusalem / Los Angeles 2000.

Wolfson, Elliot R., *Language, Eros, Being: Kabbalistic Hermeneutics and Poetic Imagination*, Fordham University Press: New York 2005.

Wolfson, Elliot R., *Open Secret: Postmessianic Messianism and the Mystical Revision of Menaḥem Mendel Schneerson*, Columbia University Press: New York 2009.

Wolfson, Elliot R. (ed.), *Rending the Veil: Concealment and Secrecy in the History of Religions*, Seven Bridges Press: New York / London 1999.

Woolley, Benjamin, *The Queen's Conjuror: The Science and Magic of Dr. John Dee, Adviser to Queen Elizabeth I*, Henry Holt and Company: New York 2001.

Wuidar, Laurence (ed.), *Music and Esotericism*, Brill: Leiden / Boston 2010.

Wynter, Sylvia, "Unsetting the Coloniality of Being / Power / Truth / Freedom: Towards the Human, After Man, Its Overrepresentation. An Argument," *The New Centennial Review* 3:3 (2003), 257–337.

Yates, Frances A., *Giordano Bruno and the Hermetic Tradition*, Routledge and Kegan Paul / The University of Chicago Press: London / Chicago 1964.

Yates, Frances A., *The Art of Memory*, The University of Chicago Press: Chicago / London 1966.

Yates, Frances A., *The Rosicrucian Enlightenment*, Routledge & Kegan Paul: London 1972.

Zander, Helmut, *Geschichte der Seelenwanderung in Europa: Alternative Religiöse Traditionen von der Antike bis Heute*, Primus Verlag: Darmstadt 1999.

Zander, Helmut, *Anthroposophie in Deutschland: Theosophische Weltanschauung und gesellschaftliche Praxis 1884-1945*, two vols., Vandenhoeck & Ruprecht: Göttingen 2007.

Zarakol, Ayse, *Before the West: The Rise and Fall of Eastern World Orders*, Cambridge University Press: Cambridge 2022.

Zeller, Benjamin E., "The Euphemization of Violence: The Case of Heaven's Gate," in: Lewis, *Violence*, 173–189.

Zimmermann, Rolf Christian, *Das Weltbild des jungen Goethe: Studien zur Hermetischen Tradition des deutschen 18. Jahrhunderts*, 2 vols., Wilhelm Fink: Munich 1969/1979.

Zinser, Hartmut, *Esoterik: Eine Einführung*, Wilhelm Fink: Munich 2009.

Znamenski, Andrei A., *The Beauty of the Primitive: Shamanism and the Western Imagination*, Oxford University Press: New York 2007.

Zuber, Mike A., *Spiritual Alchemy: From Jacob Boehme to Mary Anne Atwood*, Oxford University Press: Oxford 2021.

Zuboff, Shoshana, *The Age of Surveillance Capitalism: The Fight for a Human Future at the New Frontier of Power*, Profile Books: New York 2018.

Index of Names

Index of Subjects